Tom Chaffin

❖ ❖ ❖ ❖ ❖ ❖ ❖ ❖ ❖ ❖ ❖ ❖ ❖ ❖

Fatal Glory

NARCISO LÓPEZ AND
THE FIRST CLANDESTINE
U.S. WAR AGAINST CUBA

❖ ❖ ❖ ❖ ❖ ❖ ❖ ❖ ❖ ❖ ❖ ❖ ❖ ❖

 Louisiana State University Press

Baton Rouge

Louisiana Paperback Edition, 2003
12 11 10 09 08 07 06 05 04 03
5 4 3 2 1

LIBRARY OF CONGRESS CATALOGING-IN-PUBLICATION DATA

Chaffin, Tom.
 Fatal glory : Narciso López and the first clandestine U.S. War against Cuba / Tom Chaffin
   p. cm.
 Includes bibliographical references (p.   ) and index.
 ISBN 0-8139-1673-9 (cloth); ISBN 0-8071-2919-4 (pbk.)
   1. Cuba—History—1810–1899. 2. López, Narciso, 1797–1851—Relations with Americans.
 3. Filibusters—Cuba—History—19th century. 4. United States—Relations—Cuba. 5. Cuba—
 Relations—United States.   I. Title
 F1783.C44   1996
 972.9105—dc20   96-12978
                                                                     CIP

Frontispiece: Narciso López. From *United States Magazine and Democratic Review* 31 (1852): 209

To Meta

"No character is so fully developed
among our people as restlessness."
—New Orleans *Delta*, June 15, 1850

Contents

Illustrations

Preface

One splendid Sunday afternoon not long ago, I found myself trudging through chest-deep waters off the northwestern coast of Cuba—arms raised, with camera, pen, and notepad in hand. As I negotiated a path along a long, thin sandbar, my eyes remained fixed on a postage-stamp island about two hundred yards offshore; a small obelisk rose from its center. Leading the watery hike were three local children, along for the assignment as soon as they heard why I had come to El Morrillo, a quiet fishing village in the sparsely populated rural province of Pinar del Río, west of Havana. I was in Cuba concluding research for this book, in El Morrillo to see where, a century and a half earlier, a military adventurer named Narciso López came ashore with a clandestine army of hireling soldiers from the United States. When most North Americans think of *yanqui* invasions of Cuba, they think solely of the Bay of Pigs and 1961. Among Cubans, however, memories of invasions from the United States reach back to the middle of the nineteenth century and to a handsome former Spanish army general who led a series of privately financed military expeditions to Cuba.

Cuba's current government officially proscribes López. Indeed, many Cubans regard him as a traitor. His professed intention of making Cuba part of the United States hardly squared with the nationalism of the *fidelistas*. Even so, many islanders still venerate him. López, after all, did lead the first military challenge to Spain's dominion over the island. In Havana, I already had visited Cuba's National Archives and the José Martí National Library. But I also wanted to visit the places where López had landed. I wanted to polish descriptions of scenes in my book manuscript—and something else too: I wanted the sort of glancing intimacy with my subject where mere facts give way to sheer mood, to poetic atmosphere. I longed, however fleetingly, to sample the gestalt of nineteenth-century Cuba.

I longed for ghosts.

Traveling with several Cuban friends, I had visited Cárdenas, the first landing site, the day before. There we found several landmarks associated with López. But no ghosts. The docks where the soldiers had landed were long gone, cleared away for a grimly modern industrial center. Whole ridges in the city had been carted away. Cárdenas, which lies east of Havana, looked and felt nothing like the crisp black-and-white engravings in the various nineteenth-century journals that had chronicled López's exploits. Cárdenas is, after all, a medium-sized city—home to one of Cuba's largest rum factories—and a busy port with other things to think about than Narciso López. Even the local statue of him had been taken down soon after the 1959 revolution.

So, the next afternoon it came as a wholly welcome surprise when, upon arriving at El Morrillo, we met villagers who were knowledgeable about López and eager to talk with proprietary affection about him. And when we met the three children who mentioned the offshore obelisk and offered to take me there, I didn't hesitate: I had worn my bathing suit underneath my jeans that day. I stripped and followed them into the sea.

As the warm tropical waters rose around me, I thought of all the places I had been following López's paper trail over the past few years—from New York to California, from Boston to Havana, so many archives and libraries. Not to mention all the hours spent poring over microfilmed newspapers in the basement of Emory University's Robert W. Woodruff Library. But in all those years, this was the first time that my work as a historian had called me into the water. Here, on Cuba's northwestern coast, the long paper trail had run out into the sea.

I had stumbled upon López one afternoon back in the late 1980s while paging through some mid-nineteenth-century issues of *Harper's Monthly* I had purchased in a used book store earlier that day. For months at a time, for several years running, one individual dominated *Harper's* news section. Whoever López was, *Harper's* editors seem to have had no affection for him. He appealed, they sniffed, to "that class of our people whose opinions of the morality and legality of any action, depend upon its success or failure." ("Monthly Review of Current Events," *Harper's Monthly* 3 [Oct. 1851]: 693). But those same editors also seemed unable to cease writing about López. Over the next few months, I found a handful of articles on López in academic journals, along with glancing references in more general histories of the pre–Civil War years.

As mere curiosity evolved into a commitment to write a history of López's campaign, I began burrowing into newspapers and magazines of the period.

Between the *Harper's* magazines and the warm waters of El Morrillo, as I researched this work, it has been my good fortune to have had the help of numerous talented people. Dan Carter, a gifted historian and writer and one of the most generous souls I have ever known, has been a constant source of advice, encouragement, and good cheer—and I will always be grateful. Thanks also to Jeanne Drewsen, Craig Brown, David Johnson, Mark Cave, and Dick Holway of the University Press of Virginia, who has been a steadfast supporter of this book. Michael Bellesiles, Jim Roark, and Susan Socolow of Emory University's Department of History faculty shared their expertise, providing invaluable suggestions and bonhomie. My appreciation also to other friends at Emory—including Jerrold Brantley, Lloyd Busch, Scott Congata, Ruth Dickens, Andy Doyle, Ernie Freeberg, Steve Goodson, Nick Proctor, Amy Scott, Jackie Stanke, Margaret Storey, and Greg Wills. My friends Steve Johnson and Steve Oney provided sustaining encouragement and comradery throughout my work on this book. Another dear friend, Lyle York, casting caution to the wind, read the entire manuscript and gave me the benefit of her, as always, astute editorial suggestions; and editor extraordinaire Jeanette Hopkins provided clear-eyed direction for the final revision.

I'm also appreciative for the unfailingly courteous assistance that over the past few years I have received from everyone in the reference, interlibrary loan, and Special Collections departments of Emory University's Robert W. Woodruff Library. Special thanks to Marie Nitschke of the reference department for her tenacity and prodigious knowledge of the library's holdings and to Marie Hansen and Karen Lull of the interlibrary loan department for tracking down scores of often obscure newspapers, pamphlets, and government documents. My research and travels were supported by an Andrew W. Mellon Dissertation Fellowship in Southern Studies and by travel grants from Emory's Department of History and the Graduate School of Arts and Sciences, for which I am also grateful.

From this project's inception Jerry Poyo has shared his knowledge of nineteenth-century Cuba and U.S. Cuban exile communities and provided helpful suggestions and encouragement. My knowledge of the subject was also deepened by comments and suggestions from James Crouthamel, Robert Johannsen, Bob May, James McPherson, Lou Pérez, and Russell Weigley. Professor McPherson read the entire manuscript, revealing, in the process, a jeweler's eye for spotting factual errors. I am also indebted to Bob May and Tony de la Cova for kindly sharing their own considerable expertise on Cuban filibustering. Tony's recent dissertation on Ambrosio Gonzales led me to several important primary sources that broadened my knowledge of López's conspiracy, especially his activities in Georgia.

Many archivists and librarians have assisted this project, and I am grateful to the staffs of the the Archivo Nacional de Cuba, in Havana; the Bancroft Library of the University of California, Berkeley; the Biblioteca Nacional "José Martí," in Havana; the Filson Club of Louisville, Kentucky; the Georgia Historical Society; the Georgia Department of Archives and History; the Hill Memorial Library at Louisiana State University; the Historic New Orleans Collection; the Historical Society of Pennsylvania; the Houghton Library of Harvard University; the Library of Congress; the Howard-Tilton Memorial Library of Tulane University; the Latin American Collection of the George A. Smathers Library at the University of Florida; the Margaret I. King Library of the University of Kentucky; the Louisiana Division of the New Orleans Public Library; the Louisiana State Museum; Monmouth Plantation in Natchez, Mississippi; the Manuscripts and Archives Division of the New York Public Library; the Mississippi State Department of Archives and History; the National Archives, in Washington, D.C.; and the National Archives, Southwestern Region, in Fort Worth; the New-York Historical Society; the William R. Perkins Library of Duke University; the Museo "Oscar Maria de Rojas," of Cárdenas, Cuba; the South Carolinana Library at the University of South Carolina; the Southern Historical Collection at the University of North Carolina, Chapel Hill; the Department of Special Collections of the Robert W. Woodruff Library at Emory University; the South Carolina Historical Society; and the Tennessee State Library and Archives.

Portions of my essay "'Sons of Washington': Narciso López, Filibustering, and U.S. Nationalism, 1848–1851," are reprinted by permission from the *Journal of the Early Republic* 15 (1995): 79–108, Copyright © 1995 Society for Historians of the Early American Republic.

Cuba itself was the most personally rewarding discovery of this entire enterprise. During my time there, I was deeply touched by the generosity, material and otherwise, shown by Cubans to me amid the "special period" that they—with amazing grace, good humor, and courage—are now enduring; I hope it, and the blockade, end soon. I am especially grateful to Gladys García of the Instituto de Historia de Cuba for sharing her knowledge of and passion for Cuban history—and for opening Havana's Archivo Nacional and the Biblioteca Nacional "José Martí" to me. Juanito Ortega opened the rest of his beloved island to me, shared tales of his years with Fidel, and showed me how to make a proper daiquiri. Juanito, along with Gustavo Paz and Scott Conguta, also helped in the translations of Spanish texts.

Thanks as well to my parents, Jimmy and Martha Chaffin, for their continuing love and for nurturing my early interest in history. Finally, deep gratitude to my wife, Meta Larsson, for her love, support, and editorial assistance—and for putting up with all the Sinatra albums that set such a swingin' pace for the hours of writing (and, while I'm at it, thanks to Ol' Blue Eyes, too). I also thank Meta for tolerating the clutter of papers, books, and Diet Coke cans that for the past few years have rendered our apartment a clerical Bermuda Triangle—deeply affronting her eminently sensible Swedish sense of order.

The island off El Morrillo that we eventually climbed onto that afternoon—just a rocky speck in the surrounding flat sea—was no bigger in area than the average suburban backyard. The obelisk that rose from it was only about four feet high. It had once been about a foot or so higher, before the elements—or someone—knocked off its top. At its base was an inscription: "General Narciso López landed here on August 12, 1851 with the heroic project of liberating Cuba." The monument was erected in 1951, eight years before the Revolution, by cadets from the Cuban naval academy.

By the time we got back to the beach, word of the foreign historian and his quest had gotten out, and about twenty more villagers were waiting for us.

"Now," said one of the children as we reached the water's edge, "do you want to see Narciso's ship?"

"Well . . . uh . . . sure."

We—it seemed like the entire village—walked a little farther down the beach. As we rounded a bend on the edge of a mangrove swamp, several children who had run ahead of the rest of us suddenly stopped. They were pointing to a murky outline in the ankle-deep water. "*Pampero, Pampero*," they shouted, savoring the expression on my face as I heard them call the name of López's ship.

Actually, the object of all the attention was more like a small boat—about twenty feet in length, perhaps five feet across. But there was clearly some sort of wooden vessel buried in the sand. And, so far as I could tell, this spot seemed as good a guess as any as to where López might have come ashore. I had brought along a sketch of the site published in *Harper's* a few months after the invasion. The cove—and the village—seemed to have changed little in the intervening years.

The villagers watched as I walked around the buried vessel. One even handed me a worm-eaten piece of the wreck to keep as a souvenir. But by the time I had taken a few photos, my curiosity about the relic was fading before an onrush of recalled facts. When several townspeople asked me what I thought, I could not think of a serviceable dodge. I am no archaeologist, but I had picked up a few facts in all those archives.

"Well, there's clearly some sort of boat buried here," I said. "But it couldn't be the *Pampero*."

As I proceeded to explain why it could not be the *Pampero*, my hosts looked crestfallen, and I suddenly felt like the poster boy for *yanqui imperialismo*. This historian to whom these villagers had shown so much hospitality had, in effect, concluded his visit by trying to steal a beloved trophy of their collective memory.

After a few moments a young man in his early twenties softly but deliberately spoke up. "Well," he said, "you people in the United States might want to believe that the *Pampero* returned to the United States. But we know it's right here."

I started to say something else. But then I thought better of it.

"Maybe so," I said.

Ghosts, I suppose, are sometimes worth a little willful amnesia.

Chronology

1847

January   New York journalists and Manifest Destiny advocates John
          O'Sullivan and Moses Beach meet in Havana with members
          of the Club de la Habana, a cabal of Cuba's wealthiest
          planters and industrialists, and formulate a proposal to pre-
          sent to President James K. Polk: if the United States will pur-
          chase Cuba from Spain, the club will reimburse the U.S. trea-
          sury up to $100 million.

January–July O'Sullivan lobbies Secretary of State James Buchanan to ac-
          cept the Club de la Habana's offer, but the Polk administra-
          tion shows no immediate interest. Although an expansionist
          Democrat, Polk is determined to end the Mexican War be-
          fore taking on any new foreign initiatives.

1848

May 10   O'Sullivan and Senator Stephen Douglas meet with Presi-
          dent Polk and press for Cuba's purchase. Polk is nonrespon-
          sive.

May 18   Polk receives a letter from the U.S. consul in Havana, Robert
          Campbell, alerting him to rumors of a planned insurrection
          by Creoles, whites born in Cuba, against the island's Spanish
          government. The conspirators hope to recruit U.S. army
          troops returning from Mexico to make a detour and invade
          Cuba. Campbell informs Polk that if victorious, the rebels
          will make "immediate application . . . for annexation" of
          Cuba to the United States.

May 30   Polk broaches the idea of Cuba's purchase with his cabinet,
          proposing terms almost identical to those suggested by
          O'Sullivan, but takes no action.

June 9   A telegram reaches Polk reporting that Mexico's Congress has approved the Guadalupe Hidalgo peace treaty, which concludes the Mexican War. That same day, he asks Secretary of State Buchanan to order U.S. Minister to Spain Romulus Saunders to offer Spain up to $100 million for Cuba. Fearful that involvement of U.S. citizens in the rumored Cuban revolt could jeopardize purchase negotiations, Polk orders letters sent to General William O. Butler in Mexico and Consul Campbell in Cuba, asking both to keep U.S. citizens out of any revolt in Cuba. To curry favor with Spain, Polk orders copies of the letters sent to Madrid.

June 23   Polk meets with Senator Jefferson Davis and three anti-Spanish Cubans to discuss the planned revolt. They ask Polk to order U.S. troops at Key West and other points on the Gulf to "watch over & protect . . . the interests of American citizens in Cuba." Polk responds with what he calls in his diary "a general evasive reply."

July 23   Spanish officials in Cuba, learning of the conspiracy, summon its leader, Narciso López, to appear before them. Instead, he flees to the United States, arriving in Bristol, Rhode Island, on July 23. Determined to end Spain's rule over Cuba, López divides his time between New York and Washington, enlisting Cuban exiles and U.S. political and military figures in an expeditionary army organized to invade Cuba.

August 15   In Madrid, U.S. Minister Saunders meets with Spain's Minister of Foreign Affairs Pedro J. Pidal, who rejects any U.S. purchase of Cuba.

1849

March 5   President Zachary Taylor, a Whig opposed to Cuba's purchase, is inaugurated.

Late July   As the López conspiracy widens, intelligence reports of activities in New Orleans, New York, and other coastal cities reach Washington. Secretary of State John Clayton initiates a round-robin of correspondence among port officers, U.S. attorneys, and other federal officials, asking them to report any suspicious activities. As more intelligence arrives, the U.S. Navy's Home Squadron is dispatched on July 31 to the Gulf of Mexico to thwart a gathering of López's troops on Round Island, off the coast of Mississippi.

August 11 Taylor issues a proclamation warning U.S. citizens against joining filibusters—clandestine armies bent on conquest in nations with which the United States is at peace.

August 13 Spain's minister to the United States, Angel Cálderon de la Barca, writes Secretary of State Clayton to report that expeditions are being organized in New Orleans and "other points" and asks Clayton to uphold the terms of the U.S.-Spanish friendship treaty by disrupting the conspiracy.

August 15 Ending widespread press speculation about the rumored expedition's destination, the New York *Herald* reports that it is "bent on revolutionizing the island of Cuba. That is their object—their sole object."

September 7 In New York harbor federal agents seize three ships outfitted for war by the conspirators.

October 11 Concluding a U.S. naval blockade of Round Island, the last 65 soldiers, of what had been a gathering of 600 men, accept the navy's offer of a free ride to the mainland. During the same period federal agents seize a steamship in New Orleans being readied for service in the expedition.

December 5 In a widely published public notice, the López conspiracy announces the formation of the Junta Promovedora de los Intereses políticos de Cuba. Based in Washington, the new organization openly solicits recruits for an invasion of Cuba.

December 21 López's associate Ambrosio Gonzales, while attending a reception at the White House meets General John Henderson, an attorney and former U.S. senator, who suggests that the conspirators will find more support if they leave Washington and relocate in New Orleans. A few days later three young men from Kentucky call on Gonzales, make similar claims about widespread support for Cuban filibustering in Kentucky, and offer to raise a Kentucky regiment.

1850

February–April López arrives in New Orleans on about April 1, after traveling through the Ohio and Mississippi river valleys to enlist supporters. Bonds sold in New Orleans raise up to $50,000 to fund an expedition. By mid-April, as López enlists soldiers in Louisiana and Mississippi, recruits from the Ohio River valley are arriving in New Orleans.

April 25 The bark *Georgiana*, carrying 225 filibusters, departs New Orleans.

May 2 The brig *Susan Loud*, carrying about 150 filibusters, departs New Orleans.

May 7 The steamer *Creole*, carrying about 130 filibusters, departs New Orleans.

May 18 After troop transfers at sea and on Contoy Island, off the Yucatán coast, all of the filibusters are aboard the *Creole*, which, just before midnight, sails within sight of Cárdenas, Cuba.

May 19 By daybreak, after battling with Spanish troops through the night, the filibusters control Cárdenas. Later that afternoon, after hearing reports of advancing Spanish reinforcements, the filibusters reboard the *Creole* and, under a hail of Spanish musket fire, take to sea.

May 21 The *Creole* reaches Key West, where the filibusters abandon their ship and, within the next few days, formally disband.

May 25 López arrives by mail steamer in Savannah and, that same day, is arrested by federal authorities. That evening, a judge orders López released for lack of evidence, and enthusiastic crowds celebrate the government's setback. López leaves Savannah on a westbound train the next day.

June 7 López arrives in New Orleans, is immediately arrested, but remains free on bail. By now a national celebrity, he is cheered wherever he goes.

June 21 After two weeks of court hearings, López and fifteen coconspirators are indicted in New Orleans for violations of the U.S. Neutrality Act of 1818.

July 9 Zachary Taylor dies, and Millard Fillmore, also a Whig, becomes president.

September 9–20 Congress passes the various bills that constitute the Compromise of 1850, increasing sectional tensions between free and slave states.

1851

March 7 After the third mistrial of John Henderson on Neutrality Act charges, U.S. Attorney Logan Hunton abandons his prosecution of López's conspiracy. López and his associates, meanwhile, are traveling frequently, organizing another expedition. The next one will have two wings—one along the Atlantic coast, centered in New York and Savannah; another along the Gulf coast.

April 24–26   Acting on new intelligence, President Fillmore issues an antifilibuster proclamation. Federal agents seize three filibuster ships in New York harbor, prompting conspirators mustered in Georgia, Florida, and along the Gulf coast to disband.

July   Reports of widespread republican revolts across Cuba appear in newspapers, prompting López to rush preparations for a new expedition.

August 4–6   López and his army, on August 4, leave New Orleans aboard the steamer *Pampero*, which, hours later, stops below the city for two days of repairs. To relieve overcrowding, about one hundred men are left behind. The army, now composed of about four hundred filibusters, reaches the Gulf on August 6.

August 10   López, upon discovering that the *Pampero* has mechanical problems and lacks an adequate supply of coal, concludes that the expedition must abandon plans to sail around the Florida peninsula, to a point near Jacksonville, to load more soldiers and weapons. During a stopover at Key West that evening, however, hopes are buoyed by "glowing reports" of insurrections already underway in Cuba.

August 12   Just before dawn the filibusters complete their landing at El Morrillo, on Cuba's northwestern coast. One regiment of about 280 men, under López, marches ten miles inland to the highland village of Las Pozas. Another regiment of about 120 men, under William L. Crittenden, remains behind to guard supplies.

August 13   Just after daybreak both filibuster regiments are attacked by the Spanish army—López's at Las Pozas, Crittenden's at the village of Tabla de Agua, about five miles between El Morrillo and Las Pozas. While both respond with credible counterattacks, the Spanish are able to drive a permanent wedge between the two filibuster divisions.

August 14   Crittenden's men, in hopes of escaping Cuba, take to the sea in four small boats but are captured two days later. That same day, August 16, they are taken to Havana, where, hours later, all fifty-one remaining members of the regiment face a firing squad.

September 1 After a general rout of his army in Cuba's highlands, López is captured and, on September 1, garroted in Havana. In the days ahead 135 filibusters from his regiment are sent to a Spanish prison on Ceuta, off Africa's northern coast. Anti-Spanish riots erupt in New Orleans. The Ceuta prisoners are released in 1852 after the U.S. government agrees to pay Spain $25,000 for damage done during the riots to Spain's New Orleans consulate and to property belonging to Spanish nationals.

Fatal Glory

Narciso López and the First
Clandestine U.S. War against Cuba

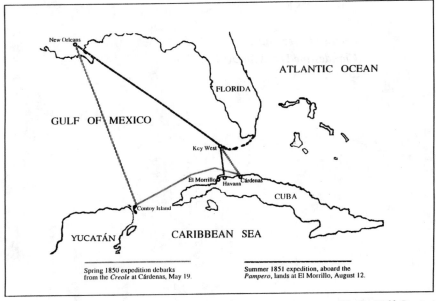

Spring 1850 expedition debarks
from the *Creole* at Cárdenas, May 19.

Summer 1851 expedition, aboard the
Pampero, lands at El Morrillo, August 12.

Narciso López filibuster's Cuban landings, 1850–51

Nicolas Wolfe Proctor

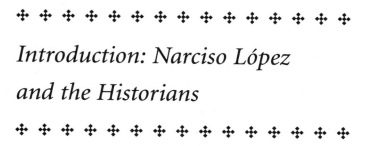

Introduction: Narciso López
and the Historians

"The fashionable word for the members of the late Expedition to Cuba, is *filibuster*–the Anglicised *filibustero* of the Spaniards. Terms, bestowed in reproach, are often accepted as compliments by those to whom they are applied. So it is with the gallant young men who formed the late Expedition to Cuba. . . .Thus, therefore, the word 'Filibuster' has acquired a significance and popularity, which is likely to give it considerable run. It has entirely superseded the word 'Liberator.'" —New Orleans *Delta*, June 23, 1850

"Fired by the contagious enthusiasm that seems spreading all over the land."—New York *Herald*, August 28, 1851, describing a crowd of five thousand demonstrating for Narciso López at Jersey City, New Jersey

Has any individual in U.S. history been so famous in his day, and now so forgotten, as Narciso López? Born in Venezuela in 1797, the son of a wealthy planter, López as a young man rose to high political and military posts in Spain and its colony of Cuba. By 1849, however, after a series of political and personal reversals, he had become the leader of a "filibuster," a clandestine army that he organized in the United States to invade Cuba and end Spain's dominion over the island.

Between 1849 and 1851 López's errands into vainglory—what the popular press, capturing their spirit of reckless adventurism and waste, quickly dubbed his "buffalo hunt"—openly defied two U.S. presidents, Zachary Taylor and Millard Fillmore. To thwart López, the federal government eventually used diplomacy, public proclamations, criminal indictments, even the U.S. Navy. López's private war, federal prosecutors argued, was illegal. But with massive publicity, it was seldom covert. In memoirs and letters of the 1850s, Narciso López emerges as a sort of Zelig of his day, seemingly turning up everywhere— in Jefferson Davis's Washington residence, western trains, stagecoaches, steamships, parades, the U.S. Capitol, federal courtrooms, New York salons. While expansionist zealots in the United States lionized López as a republican hero, critics saw only lawlessness, hypocrisy, and greed. But celebrated or vilified, López's name became a fixture of a mid-nineteenth-century popular culture enthralled with tales of expansionist derring-do. Yet he was soon forgotten. By the next century, when López's campaign was recalled at all by U.S. historians, it tended to be remembered as a curtain-raiser to the Civil War—as a creation of southern planters and southern nationalists.

To what degree are such characterizations accurate? Yes, crowds did cheer López's name in the South. But before we fit him out for a suit of Confederate gray, let us note that many other southerners, especially planters, kept a safe distance. Louisiana sugar growers feared having to compete with Cuban sugar imports suddenly shorn of federal tariffs. Other southern slaveholders feared the precedent that would be set by U.S. interference in the domestic affairs of Spanish Cuba. British abolitionists, after all, based their international campaign against slavery on an assumed right to interfere in the domestic affairs of foreign nations.

In fact, López's U.S. supporters included northerners and southerners, mercantilists and agriculturists—almost all of whom ceaselessly declaimed their allegiance to the United States and the spread of its republican values. Since López's death in 1851, however, those nationalist credentials have been lost. Although López and his coconspirators clearly stated their desire to win Cuba for the United States, U.S. historians usually depict them as surrogates of southern nationalism.

Why? In large part the revisionism bears witness to the old saw that the victors write the history. Indeed, in the United States the sorry, star-crossed tale of López and the motley armies he led to Cuba has been largely told by his domestic U.S. opponents. And those opponents—the victors—have skewed the story. For, in the end, López's story turns less on Unionism versus southern nationalism and more on two competing U.S. nationalisms. López drew on a U.S. nationalism steeped in a Jeffersonian and Jacksonian republicanism that tolerated both slavery and expansionism; his enemies, by contrast, represented a newer, emerging U.S. nationalism arising from free-soilism, a doctrine defined by its opposition to the spread—and, by 1863, the very existence—of slavery.

A little more than a decade after the buffalo hunt, in a war fought very much along sectional lines, the newer nationalism would permanently vanquish the older. Even so, López's campaign was no more about the Civil War than the Boston Tea Party was about U.S. independence. By rendering López's story a political passion play of northern Unionism triumphant over southern secessionism, his enemies—and later historians—have estranged his tale from its proper setting. Their telling of his story and the story itself, however, reveal much about the shaping of U.S. nationalism—and nationalisms—in the mid-nineteenth century.

Who were López's enemies in the United States? On an immediate level, two presidents—the Whigs Zachary Taylor and Millard Fillmore—were his most prominent adversaries. On a broader ideological level, however, much of the animosity directed toward López—both Whig and Democratic—came from another source: the emerging, if still fragmented, constituency of free-soilism that had been politically galvanized by the Wilmot Proviso of 1846. Introduced repeatedly after the Mexican War but never passed, the proposed congressional measure sought to ban the introduction of slavery into any U.S. territories acquired during the conflict; few Free-Soilers sought a total abolition of slavery.

By 1866, however, Lincoln's Emancipation Proclamation and the Thirteenth Amendment to the Constitution had expanded free-soilism's platform to embrace the outright abolition of all slavery in the United States. That platform became the foundation for a newly dominant U.S. nationalism: embraced by the Republican party, it set the stage for the nation's postbellum politics. Many issues would vex the United States in the years after the Civil War, but slavery was no longer one of them.

Of course, even during the 1850s the politics of some Free-Soilers went beyond just opposing slavery's spread. For them, the institution was a manifest evil that warranted an outright ban. Given their deep philosophical opposition to slavery, then, the contempt of figures such as Horace Greeley for López is understandable. The conspirator and his stalwarts called themselves soldiers of liberty and republicanism, yet they had no intention of extending liberties to Cuba's 436,000 enslaved blacks.[1] Understandably, Greeley's antislavery New York *Tribune* viewed López's claims to republicanism as a humbug, declaring: "The 'revolutions' in Europe which The Tribune has favored all looked to the Enfranchisement and Elevation of the Laboring Class—the Cultivators of the Soil—as their chief end. The 'revolution' in Cuba proposes to leave the cultivators of *her* soil in the position of beasts or chattels, subject to be flogged, starved, sold or tortured as the caprice or fancied interest of the landlord caste shall dictate."[2]

Ratified by the Union's Civil War victory, Greeley's estimation of López has emerged predominant; viewed from the front porch of the Appomattox courthouse, López's buffalo hunt has often seemed a force whose U.S. support came exclusively from southern agricultural slaveholding interests. Indeed, some historians have even found in López's ill-funded, ill-planned campaign a snakebit dress rehearsal for southern nationalism, southern secessionism, Confederate militarism—and, finally, Fort Sumter.

For all that, the earliest sustained scholarly study of López, Robert Granville Caldwell's *The Lopez Expeditions to Cuba, 1848–1851*, published in 1915, gave scant attention to López's place in U.S. domestic politics. Focusing largely on diplomatic matters, Caldwell examined how López's filibuster shaped relations among Spain, the United States, and Great Britain. To the extent that he examined U.S. domestic politics and López's personal motivations, Caldwell rendered his subject a reactive hero, a man driven to revolution by the excesses of an arrogant, mercantilist Spanish regime. No particular formal ideology drove Caldwell's López; he was simply an ambitious man, embittered by political and economic reversals, and willing to do whatever was necessary to restore his lost prestige and wealth.[3]

The traditional view of López emerged more clearly—but with a twist—in Cuban historian Hermino Portell Vilá's *Narciso López y su época*. His three-volume study, published between 1930 and 1958, asserted that López's main support in the United States came from slaveholding southerners. But Portell Vilá also argued that López's alignment with southern planters was but a temporary expediency. To Portell Vilá, López was first, foremost, and consistently a Cuban patriot—a republican devoted to the creation of an independent Cuban republic. By Portell Vilá's lights López was a shrewd leader who re-

vealed his political genius in two conspicuous feats: his molding of Cuban annexationists into a single force and his use of annexationists in both Cuba and
the United States to support the cause of an independent Cuba.[4]

What would become the traditionalist view of López emerged more force-
fully in less specialized studies of antebellum U.S. and southern history. In
1936, for example, Samuel Flagg Bemis viewed López's campaign as arising
"from the ambitions of the Southern imperialists to acquire Cuba as another
slave state in the Union." Bemis dismissed López himself as "the tool of the
slavery expansionists in the United States." Similarly, Allan Nevins in 1947,
while acknowledging the "various Northerners" who assisted them, nonetheless viewed López and his comrades as agents of southern "agricultural imperialism." John Hope Franklin in 1956 saw the campaign as driven by the
South's unique "martial spirit," a spirit distinct from U.S. Manifest Destiny.
"This spirit," Franklin wrote, "forced an enthusiastic participation in every expansionist scheme, and supported sectional programs of expansion when
there were none on the national agenda." Along those same lines Frederick
Merk in 1963 identified López and Cuban annexation of the 1850s with a
"Caribbeanized Manifest Destiny"—a thrust more "prosaic," sectional, and
southern than the more national and "poetic" (ostensibly imbued with lofty
principle) Manifest Destiny of the previous decade.[5]

Eugene Genovese in 1965 viewed Cuban filibustering as a defensive action by
southern planters ever aware that they shouldered the burden of defending a
"distinct social system." Southern planters sought Cuba, Genovese argued, for
both commercial and geopolitical reasons. Animating the latter motive was a
fear that Spain might be pressured by France and England into dismantling the
island's slave labor system. "Many far-sighted Southerners understood the danger of permitting the isolation of Southern slavery. They desired Cuba in order
to secure political control of the Caribbean, as well as for economic reasons."[6]

In 1979 John McCardell found both "sectional destiny" and "southern nationalism" behind U.S. expansionism in the Caribbean. According to Mc-
Cardell, after Texas statehood in 1845 and the Compromise of 1850, Manifest
Destiny became a strictly southern affair, a force for "sectional destiny": "The
growth of Southern nationalism in the United States after 1850 operated at
cross-purposes with Northern definitions of American nationalism." A year
later, in 1980, Charles H. Brown offered a similar view of the filibusters' motives: their campaign's professed intentions of ridding Cuba of "Spanish

despotism" and establishing democratic government were "in part camoufl-
age to divert attention from the slave-economy character"—the southern
character—of the movement.[7]

Of course, reasonable, if circumstantial, evidence exists for such arguments: numerous prominent southerners did support López. Some—such as
Calhoun, Georgia governor George W. Towns, Florida's U.S. Senator David
Yulee, and Mississippi governor John Quitman—were planters. And in the
cases of Calhoun, Towns, and Quitman, it is reasonable to assume that had
they lived until 1861, all three would have supported the Confederacy. Indeed,
some of López's southern supporters—such as U.S. senators Jefferson Davis of
Mississippi and Stephen Mallory of Florida—did live long enough to hold
high-level posts in that government.[8] At least two young officers in López's
army, Theodore O'Hara of Kentucky and Chatham Roberdeau Wheat of
Louisiana, both later served in the Confederate army.[9]

Upon closer scrutiny, however, the notion that southern nationalists and
planters—and southern geopolitical concerns—dominated López's conspiracy
falters. For in the end the tangle of U.S. business and political forces that sustained López—and filibustering in general—remained too complex, too sprawling, too national in scope for any narrow, sectional campaign. As William O.
Scroggs noted in his 1916 study of William Walker, filibustering "seemed to enlist
the sympathies in nearly equal degree of California pioneers, Texas plainsmen,
political exiles from Europe, Southern slavery advocates, and Northern devotees
of manifest destiny." Indeed, as Scroggs observed, William Walker, though a native of Tennessee, cut his teeth on Democratic politics in the California party's
antislavery, Free-Soil faction. Joseph Allen Stout, in his 1973 study of filibustering,
took a similarly broad view of the phenomenon. Filibustering, Stout wrote, "was
spawned by the frontier and nourished by the spirit of expansionist adventurism
which permeated all facets of American society during the 1850s."[10]

Indeed, at least since the end of World War II, a revisionist view of López—
and filibustering in general—has been quietly gathering force. While acknowledging López's popularity in the South, this revisionism also recognizes that
his support straddled many economic and geographic lines; López enjoyed
support on both sides of the Mason-Dixon Line and from both agricultural
and mercantile, rural and urban quarters.[11]

As early as 1948 Basil Rauch identified New York as "the second center of the
Cuban movement" and noted the North-South economic and political ties that

undergirded filibustering. "The movement to annex Cuba," he wrote, "expressed the economic community of interests between northern business and southern slavery." In 1960 R. W. Van Alstyne found "Northern, Southern, and Middle Western interests united" during the 1850s "in a common desire for Cuba." William H. Goetzmann six years later offered a similarly expansive vision of López's base of support: "American interest in the island covered a surprisingly comprehensive range of public and private concern in all regions of the country." Underscoring that diversity, in 1994 William W. Freehling pointed out that even in the South of the 1850s, support for the U.S. annexation of Cuba and for filibustering was far from unanimous. While New Orleans's "up-to-date capitalists" favored annexation, South Carolina's "not-very-capitalistic planters often became antiexpansionists." Freehling also argued that New Orleans's profilibuster capitalists—far from being southern nationalists—viewed the Union and its powers as absolutely essential to the conquest of Cuba.[12]

Robert E. May in 1973 argued that filibustering only became an agent of southern "sectionalism" after the 1854 Kansas-Nebraska Act. Up to that point, according to May, López and other filibusters represented a Manifest Destiny national in scope. Later, in a 1991 article, May called for historians to move beyond strictly sectional and diplomatic considerations to appreciate the full breadth of support for filibustering across the entire United States. Historians, May argued, have been too quick to confuse geographical circumstances with political origins: "Since most filibusters left Gulf Coast or California ports, or crossed the boundary of Texas and Mexico, there has . . . been a tendency in historical scholarship to explain the filibusters as products of the southern martial spirit, the geopolitics of slavery expansionism, and the lawlessness and labor surplus of post–gold rush California. What has been obscured is filibustering's place in American social history, both North and South."[13]

Neither does the López campaign's association with slavery and slaveholders disqualify its U.S. nationalist credentials or consign it to regional status. As López recruited soldiers in both the North and the South, so the business interests in both regions that funded his campaign enjoyed commercial links to Cuban slavery. Northerners even owned plantations on the island. Moreover, as Edmund S. Morgan has argued, slavery had long been a staple—even a sine qua non—of U.S. republicanism.[14] The rhetoric of such apologists for southern slavery as George Fitzhugh may have grown shrill by midcentury. The institution's defenders would come to seem desperate. But that does not negate the fact that slavery's pedigree extended to the dawn of the U.S. republic. Like their southern counterparts, northern López supporters expressed no compassion for the island's enslaved black majority. To the extent that any altruism at all burdened their public expressions, sympathies focused on the travails of Cuba's Creoles, whites born on the island.

To unravel the ties that bound the López campaign, we must return to what the filibusters and their supporters themselves tell us about who they were. And what they say in unison—by their deeds, and their public and private words—is that they were republicans and patriots of the United States. And if through their adventures in Cuba, they enriched themselves in the process, was not that too in the best laissez-faire traditions of Jefferson and Jackson? Or, as the patron saint of all filibusters, Aaron Burr, once observed, politics should yield "fun and honor & profit."[15]

However clandestine, Narciso López's tropical wing of Manifest Destiny carried a banner of U.S. nationalism and republicanism that had fluttered in 1800 over the election of Thomas Jefferson to the White House and in 1828 over the birth of Jacksonian democracy. A republican nationalism, it embraced universal white-male suffrage, popular sovereignty, laissez-faire individualism (for whites), slavery, and territorial expansion. Contemporary controversies surrounding López's campaign, then, turned less on the question, raised by historians, of southern versus U.S. nationalism and more on two competing versions of antebellum U.S. nationalism—one moribund, the other ascendant.

Among the many journalists who lent their support to López, none figured more prominently than New York City's John O'Sullivan. The editor of the *United States Magazine and Democratic Review*, O'Sullivan ranked as one of the premier advocates of nineteenth century U.S. expansionism; he even coined the term *Manifest Destiny*.

For students of the transformation of U.S. nationalism during the mid-nineteenth century, O'Sullivan offers a vivid object lesson in the perils of zealotry. For in the arc of O'Sullivan's career we glimpse the demise of one strain of U.S. nationalism, the ascent of another. As a Democratic party gadfly of the antebellum years, O'Sullivan consistently championed a venerable Jeffersonian-Jacksonian nationalism that united the party's southern and northern stalwarts; in the process he became a consistent defender of both slavery and expansionism. By 1861, however, with the South having temporarily departed the Union, a new U.S. nationalism held sway, one descended from the free-soilism of the 1850s. To O'Sullivan that new nationalism represented nothing less than a betrayal of the nation's founding doctrines. The brooding journalist left the United States and spent the war years in England as a self-appointed propagandist for the Confederacy.

From his self-exile in London in 1863, O'Sullivan made clear to Jefferson Davis his reasons for supporting the Confederacy. "Where else am I," he wrote, "to find now any thing left of all that constituted the reasons for my Americanism or patriotism?"[16] As O'Sullivan understood, the urge that by 1861 had ripened into southern nationalism was at its desperate heart an attempt to save, by extreme means, the precepts of an older U.S. nationalism, which sanctioned both slavery and territorial aggrandizement.

By 1863, of course, Davis's and O'Sullivan's cause could no longer claim U.S. credentials; with the South in active military rebellion against the central government, a line had been crossed into undeniable sedition. Ten years earlier, however, the cause championed by Davis, O'Sullivan, and López remained very much in the American grain—a vital expression of a venerable U.S. nationalism. One historian's nationalism is another's sectionalism: David Potter once cautioned historians against treating the period from 1830 to 1860 as nothing more than a prelude to the Civil War. One might add that the division of all antebellum figures into Unionist or secessionist camps misunderstands those years.[17] As the failure of the secessionist platform at the 1850 Nashville convention on territorial rights demonstrated, southern nationalism hardly enjoyed universal support across the region early in that decade.[18] Nor, in most instances, did it enjoy any visible support among López and his supporters.

Was, then, López's campaign for or against slavery? To the extent that the filibuster had no plans to emancipate Cuba's slaves, it must be regarded as proslavery. For the most part, however, López and his supporters sought to avoid the issue. Historians have tended to evaluate López against the backdrop of 1840s Manifest Destiny, a wave of expansionism that by 1850 had become hopelessly burdened with charges of sectionalism and alleged links to the "Slave Power." Generationally and politically, however, the López filibuster perhaps belonged more properly to another, later, wave of U.S. expansionism, the short-lived "Young America" movement of the 1850s. Indeed, López's aide John O'Sullivan, along with such Cuban annexationists of that day as Stephen Douglas and George Law, were among Young America's key agitators.[19] A loose faction of politicians, journalists, and businessmen within the Democratic party, Young America sought to unite all sections of the nation through an aggressive, romantic nationalism; they called for free trade, a subsidized merchant marine, U.S. acquisition of Cuba, and active support for European republicans. In the process the movement sought to elude charges of sectionalism—as well as divisive arguments among its own ranks—by avoiding discussions of slavery. As López propaganda thus tended to collapse into conspicuous silence on the issue of slavery, so Stephen Douglas, while promoting his candidacy for the 1852 Democratic presidential nomination, would urge the party to "come together upon the basis of *entire silence on the slavery question*."[20]

Like López, Young America couched its expansionism in a republican rhetoric inspired by the European revolts of 1848; as a practical matter, then, it sought to continue Manifest Destiny but under a new name. Thus, again like López, Young America merely poured the old wine of Jefferson and Jackson—a broad, nationally based republicanism of slavery and territorial aggrandizement—into a new bottle.

Beyond doctrinal concerns, the view of López and his conspiracy as a warm-up for secession discounts a more tangible matter that even his enemies understood: López's antislavery foes, Democrats and Whigs alike, could count votes. They readily understood that the campaign's danger lay not in secessionism but in its precise opposite. The filibusters were annexationists, intent on enlarging the Union; they were, in Andrew Jackson's words, about the business of "extending the area of freedom."[21]

The danger posed by the filibusters, then, lay not in what they might take away from the United States but in what they might bring in: an island divided to create two or more new slave states.[22] The addition of new slave states would allow the South to regain its numerical parity in the U.S. Senate, an advantage hopelessly lost in the population-based House. A restoration of the South's parity in the Senate would, in turn, renew Union membership as a tenable, long-term proposition for the region's slaveholders. Indeed, reflecting on events three decades later, López's adjutant general, Ambrosio Gonzales, speculated that had the filibuster been successful, "the Union would have been strengthened and our civil war would have been averted." A curious concern for a movement allegedly bent on "sectional destiny" and "southern nationalism."[23]

1   A Marriage of Convenience

Havana, January 1847

The brooding Aldama family palace, with its dark columned recesses, made a fitting scene for the plotting of a political scheme dedicated to the preservation of private wealth. The four-story marble edifice, with its Romanesque arches, wrought-iron balconies, hand-painted tiles, and lavish interior patios stood as a monument to both the beneficence and the curse of Cuban slavery. Certainly it attested to the riches that slavery had brought to Havana's Aldama family. Its patriarch, Domingo de Aldama, was one of Cuba's largest planters and owned a major share of the Havana Railway Company. The parlor furniture alone for his home had cost $30,000. When family members ventured outside, they traveled by coach with liveried servants and outriders. But the palace also augured bloody racial apocalypse. During its construction in October 1841, forty slaves had revolted and fought an intense battle with Spanish troops. Afterwards, Miguel de Aldama, son of Domingo, grew worried about the survival of Cuban slavery under Spain and several years later helped found the Club de la Habana, a cabal of Creoles, whites born in Cuba, dedicated to vanquishing Spain's control over Cuba and binding the island to the United States of America.[1]

Miguel de Aldama typified those wealthy Creoles of Cuba who, fearing slave revolts, had become annexationists, advocates of the island's acquisition by the United States. Fears that Spain—which seemed weaker with each passing year—might eventually yield to pressures from British abolitionists and

free the island's slaves nourished a growing conviction that only membership in the republican union to the north could rescue the island from a rising tide of social, economic, and political troubles. Such fears increased dramatically in 1843 when rumors of a massive slave uprising planned for
Christmas Day swept the island. Whether or not the revolt, alleged to have
been encouraged by the British abolitionist David Turnbull, was ever more
than a rumor, reaction to it was swift and brutal. Captain General Leopold
O'Donnell, the island's chief colonial official, had been appointed to his post
that autumn to end a rash of slave revolts that had already darkened the
decade. In the weeks after Christmas, all of those accused of involvement in
the alleged conspiracy were strapped to a ladder (*escalera*), beaten, then executed.[2]

In the wake of what became known as La Escalera conspiracy, more and
more of Cuba's wealthy Creoles became annexationists. Creole pride might
have preferred outright independence, but fears of inadvertently igniting a
slave revolt were stronger. The United States seemed the best alternative to
royalist Spain: an option that promised relative autonomy, a likely end to the
slave trade, but immediate protection of Cuban slavery—and all without massive social upheaval.[3]

While reciprocal calls from the United States for Cuba's annexation had
been raised since at least 1806, the two movements usually operated without
coordination and, not infrequently, at cross purposes. By the mid-1840s, however, a marriage of the two Cuban annexationist movements—one in the
United States, the other in Cuba—had become inevitable. Only the time and
place of the ceremony, and the officiating minister remained in doubt. When
the political wedding finally did take place, at the Aldama palace in January
1847, however, it was two marriages of the more traditional sort that prompted
the union.

Since at least 1837, when he and his brother-in-law Samuel Langtree founded
the *United States Magazine and Democratic Review*, New York journalist and
Democratic party man-about-town John O'Sullivan had been one of the nation's most strident advocates of U.S. territorial expansion. And after Langtree's
death in 1842 and O'Sullivan's sister's remarriage three years later to a Cuban
planter, O'Sullivan became obsessed with U.S. annexation of Cuba.[4]

Mary O'Sullivan's new husband was Cristóbal Madan, a wealthy planter,
merchant, and shipowner. Madan traveled frequently between the United

States and Cuba, enjoyed extensive associations in both, and, as a leader of the Club de la Habana, stood at the forefront of Cuba's pro–U.S. annexation movement. He also represented the club within its proannexation U.S. counterpart in New York City, the Consejo Cubano, an umbrella organization representing several Cuban activist organizations.[5]

In 1846 it was thirty-three-year-old John O'Sullivan's turn to step to the altar. On October 21 he married Susan Rodgers, daughter of a prominent New York physician. Two weeks later the couple left on an extended honeymoon to Cuba. During that sojourn, in January 1847, O'Sullivan accompanied his brother-in-law Madan to a meeting of the Club de la Habana. There he met twenty-six-year-old Miguel de Aldama and other members of the club, whose roster included prosperous Cubans such as Madan, José Antonio Echevarría, José Louis Alfonso, and the count of Pozos Dulces. John S. Thrasher, the club's sole member from the United States, edited *El Faro Industrial*, a widely read pro–U.S. annexation business newspaper.[6]

At the Aldama palace, O'Sullivan also met another Yankee visitor to Cuba, also a journalist. Forty-seven-year-old Moses Yale Beach was the editor and publisher of the New York *Sun*, among that city's popular papers second only to James Gordon Bennett's *Herald* in circulation. Like O'Sullivan, Beach was an expansionist. A Democrat, he was passing through Cuba en route to Mexico on a secret—eventually remunerated—mission for President James K. Polk. In November 1846 Beach had offered to serve Polk as a freelance peace emissary to end the Mexican War, a conflict that the *Sun* had rabidly supported and which served as a font of sensational, circulation-boosting stories for the paper. Polk was preparing to open a second front in the war with a landing at Vera Cruz, on Mexico's Gulf coast, but accepted Beach's offer in hopes of attaining a truce through talks with prominent Mexicans weary of the conflict. Beach, for his part, had sought the assignment as he prepared for an extended business trip to Mexico. Besides exploring ways to improve the *Sun*'s coverage of the Mexican War, he hoped to acquire transit rights for either a canal or a railroad across the Isthmus of Tehuantepec.[7]

Accompanying Beach to Cuba were his twenty-six-year-old daughter Drusilla and Jane McManus Storms, a thirty-nine-year-old journalist who wrote for the *Sun* under the name Cora Montgomery and acted as Beach's translator. Like Beach, Storms was an expansionist zealot with a long history of political intrigues. During the 1830s, while still in her mid-twenties, she even had a scandalous affair with the elder statesman of U.S. political intrigue, Aaron Burr, by then an octogenarian.[8]

An auspicious moment thus dawned for the Club de la Habana's conspirators as they assembled at the Aldama palace in January 1847. Calls from Cuban planters for annexation by the United States had been made many times only to be rebuffed by timid presidents. The current occupant of the White House, however, seemed cut from a bolder cloth; President Polk's recent military occupation of Texas, New Mexico, and California proved that. Moreover, as a slaveholder himself, Polk seemed a kindred spirit to the Cuban planters. Equally important, the Club de la Habana's coconspirators now included two prominent U.S. citizens, and both Beach and O'Sullivan had ties to Polk and the Democratic party.

Of the two North American visitors, however, O'Sullivan had the longest and deepest ties to the Democrats and would prove to possess the most durable commitment to U.S. acquisition of Cuba. Over the next few years, as all the others, Cubans and North Americans, who had gathered at the Aldama palace fell away from the movement, O'Sullivan would remain the true believer. His ties to Washington's political establishment stretched back to student days at Columbia College during the 1830s when as a fervent member of the New York Democratic party's radical Loco Foco wing, he caught the attention of an admiring President Martin Van Buren. The intervening years only deepened O'Sullivan's party devotion. Most recently, he had been director of publications for Polk's 1844 presidential campaign. During the campaign he and Samuel Tilden, another young party activist, had edited a short-lived party organ, the New York *Morning News*, which—along with the *Campaign*, a four-page partisan newspaper also edited by O'Sullivan—gave editorial direction to Democratic papers around the country and helped Polk eke out a victory against the Whigs' Henry Clay and the Liberty party's James G. Birney.[9]

At the January 1847 meeting, the Club de La Habana's members and their Yankee visitors agreed that Cuba should be annexed by the United States but differed over tactics. By the session's end it was understood that upon his return to the United States, Beach would begin an editorial campaign in the *Sun* and print a Spanish-English newspaper devoted to the cause. O'Sullivan, who opposed such public advocacy, would lobby the Polk administration discreetly on behalf of an audacious club proposal: if the president would purchase

Cuba from Spain, the Club de la Habana would reimburse the U.S. treasury up to $100 million.[10]

Long before John O'Sullivan interrupted his Caribbean honeymoon to talk business at the Aldama palace, Cuba enjoyed an almost mythical status in the annals of U.S. imperial ambition. Just 100 miles south of the Florida Keys, the crescent-shaped island rolled 800 miles from east to west, over 44,000 square miles, an area about the size of England. The largest island of the West Indies—indeed, larger in area than all the others combined—Cuba ranged from 160 miles at its widest to 25 miles, near Havana, at its narrowest. While mountains dominated much of the interior, rising to 5,000 feet in the east, gentle plains and lowlands covered most of the island. Pristine beaches pocketed with natural deepwater harbors hemmed its coastline.[11]

Cuba boasted rich bounties of timber, minerals, coffee, tobacco, and sugar and teemed with wildflowers, more than thirty species of palm trees, waterfalls, spectacular caverns, and sublime rock formations. For foreigners it seemed almost otherworldly in its beauty, at once tropical and brimming with Old World charm. Many North American visitors believed that Cuba's benign spell could cure dropsy, consumption, and other diseases.

Despite misgivings about crowded, unsanitary conditions and the blight of slavery, visitors also were enthralled by Cuba's urban life. By the mid-nineteenth century Havana, Matanzas, Cárdenas, and other cities possessed a picturesque elegance that enchanted sojourners from the United States and Europe. Beyond their vibrant commerce, street life, and colorful festivals, larger cities claimed impressive universities, professional organizations, and a lively procession of arts. Havana's Tacón Theater, opened in 1838, could seat six thousand. On a sojourn from her native England, social reformer Amelia M. Murray found herself completely unprepared for Havana's Moorish architecture, exotic street scenes, and tropical flora, "all this, added to unknown tongues, and a splendid southern sky, mystified me, and made me feel dreamy, as I had never felt before." "No city in America has such an avenue as the Paseo de Tacón," wrote Richard Henry Dana, Jr., after a carriage ride on one of Havana's elegant boulevards.[12]

Christopher Columbus had claimed Cuba for Spain in 1492. By the early sixteenth century, the island was serving as the administrative center for Madrid's entire New World empire and a staging base for expeditions to the

Central and South American mainland. However, as settlements in Mexico and Peru became more self-sustaining, producing their own food and other commodities, Cuba's significance faded—a trend quickened by the discovery of silver in the mainland colonies during the 1540s and 1550s.

Ironically, the same mainland triumphs that rendered Cuba a backwater soon drew privateers commissioned by Spain's European rivals to the West Indies—and gave the island a new strategic importance. In Cuba, after all, Spain possessed an island that commanded the entire region: it straddled the Florida straits to the north, the Windward Passage to the east, the Yucatán Channel to its west and stood like a sentry over both the Caribbean and the Gulf of Mexico. To safeguard homebound ships laden with silver and to halt increasingly frequent attacks on Cuban ports, Madrid after 1563 began gathering its ships at Havana into *flotas*, convoys of merchant vessels that twice each year sailed back to Spain under the protection of Spanish warships. Vera Cruz, Spain's closest other major port in the region, had no natural harbor, and ships calling there were forced to anchor offshore, beyond the protection of the port's cannons. Havana, with its natural deepwater harbor inside an easily defended inlet, thus became the central Spanish port in the New World. It also became the home port for a fleet of Spanish warships that soon harassed European ships in the region. To protect both the *flotas* and Cuba itself, Spain established a permanent military garrison in Havana and constructed three forts— La Fuerza, El Morro, and La Punta.[13]

With its enhanced commercial and military importance, Havana boomed, eroding the monopoly on trade with Spain formerly enjoyed by the Spanish Main ports of Vera Cruz, Cartagena, and Portobelo. Spanish ships at Havana had to be refitted and resupplied, a long and costly process. The wait, often weeks or months, for the arrival of other vessels in the *flota* only extended the delay. Outbound passengers and sailors, many with pockets full of mainland silver, became a captive clientele for Havana. Lodging and dining enterprises prospered, so did businesses and artisans who attended the ships—carpenters, shipwrights, caulkers, mechanics, sailmakers, and lumber millers. By the 1620s entire ships were being built in Havana. The maritime and military activity in turn created new domestic demands, with carpenters and stonemasons needed to meet the housing needs of the city's growing population and its new businesses, garrisons, and forts. And as Havana thrived, so too did the surrounding countryside; to supply the port, nearby farmers and timbermen produced foodstuffs, livestock, and lumber.[14]

As Cuba boomed, North Americans recognized the island's value as both a source of semitropical staples and a lucrative market for manufactured goods. Though the island's Spanish overseers generally tried to monopolize its trade, North American merchants received a tantalizing glimpse of the lucrative Cuban market as early as 1762, when British forces seized Havana during the Seven Years War. Though the occupation lasted only ten months, it achieved far-reaching effects; after having languished as a colony of Madrid under a Bourbon mercantilist regimen for most its life, Havana suddenly became a thriving open port. As trade flowed in from Britain and its North American colonies, Cuban traders prospered, and the local populace could buy textiles, staple goods, and other consumer items at prices uninflated by Spain's government monopolies.[15]

Successive Spanish regimes attempted to restrict Cuban–North American commerce, but by the middle of the nineteenth century, Madrid's calls for an end to the trade increasingly fell on deaf ears in Cuba. The United States by then was Cuba's biggest customer for its biggest crop, for Louisiana's planters were supplying less than one-third of the U.S. domestic demand for sugar. And Cuba consistently placed third or fourth among U.S. trading partners. Reinforcing those bonds, U.S. businessmen and planters seemed to understand the needs of Cuban planters. The island's sugar industry, after all, depended on the preservation of slavery, and the United States—although it had ended its legal international slave trade—showed no signs of ending slave labor on its own soil. In fact, to many the United States seemed "the patron and champion of Negro slavery all over the world," as one British abolitionist put it.[16]

As Yankees during the early nineteenth century reciprocated the amity, Cuba became a popular destination for North American tourists; a string of boardinghouses operated by, and largely serving, visitors from the United States hugged the island's north coast. By 1846 more than a thousand U.S. expatriates were living in Cuba. North Americans established merchant houses, banks, and trade companies in Havana, Cienfuegos, Matanzas, Cárdenas, and other cities. They also owned or held interests in many of Cuba's iron and copper mines, as well as its sugar plantations and refineries. By the mid-nineteenth century, steam engines purchased from U.S. suppliers boosted production at many mills. During the 1830s U.S. engineers (with British capital) built Cuba's—and Latin America's—first rail line, a fifty-one-mile connection between Havana and Güines; U.S. firms subsequently provided both tracks and locomotives for Cuba's growing rail system. In 1844 Havana's streets were lit with gas by a New Orleans capitalist; in 1849 a U.S. citizen obtained the island's telegraph concession.[17]

Even as U.S.-Cuba trade ebbed and flowed, policy makers in Washington nursed a parallel political desire for an outright acquisition of the island. Presidents who eventually balked at acting to secure Cuba agreed that it would inevitably be drawn into the United States, believing that sheer proximity and shared interests eventually would put the island under Washington's dominion. As early as 1805 President Thomas Jefferson contemplated a military seizure of Cuba; fear of British reaction restrained Jefferson, but interest in the island hardly disappeared. Presidents James Madison and James Monroe also actively considered its acquisition.[18]

Like so many U.S. territorial ambitions of those years, those early pinings for Cuba were balanced by stark geopolitical considerations—particularly a recognition of the young republic's limited military powers. An awareness of Britain's stake in the region was especially inhibiting. England possessed a valuable West Indian planter empire and time after time had aggressively demonstrated its resolve to remain a presence in the Caribbean. After seizing Jamaica in 1655, England captured Nevis, Antigua, and Monserrat. By 1803 it also controlled Dominica, Saint Lucia, Saint Vincent, Tobago, Grenada, and Trinidad. Britain thus viewed Spanish Cuba as a southern barrier to any U.S. expansionism that might threaten its own West Indian empire. As a consequence, policy planners in Washington assumed that any overt challenge to Spain's control of the island would entail a disastrous war with England and its superior navy. Thus, they reasoned, any U.S. activism against Cuba would have to wait for another day and better military odds.[19]

Washington took a different view of its interests in Spain's Central and South American colonies. In Spain's mainland New World empire, U.S. policy had focused on trade, not annexation. During the mainland Latin American revolutions that flared between 1809 and 1826, official U.S. neutrality had masked a private preference for antiroyalist forces. From Simón Bolívar to

Camilo Torres, the mainland liberators seemed much like the United States' own founding fathers; like George Washington, Thomas Jefferson, James Madison, and company, most were liberal, slaveholding whites who had led limited revolutions. Once victorious, they created regimes that welcomed free trade with the United States. With the conspicuous exception of Mexico's Father Hidalgo, most mainland liberators were aristocrats who had only grudgingly embraced independence.

The independence movements elevated Creoles, whites of Iberian heritage born in the New World, at the expense of royalist *peninsulares,* whites born in Spain and Portugal. Fundamental social structures, however, remained intact; aristocrats remained aristocrats, the poor stayed poor, slaves stayed slaves—and relationships with foreigners prospered. Few leaders in Washington, however, believed any season of revolution in the West Indies would conclude so benignly. Cuba especially was viewed in both Washington and London as possessing no sizable class of ambitious Creoles with which to replace the *peninsulares'* political leadership. Beyond that, the island's huge and growing concentration of slaves seemed to promise that any revolution there would be as much social as political. That prospect triggered blood-chilling memories of the brutal slave revolt of the 1790s against planters in the French island colony of Saint Domingue, on Hispaniola, which in 1804 had led to the founding of the Republic of Haiti. British and U.S. leaders assumed that a Cuban insurrection would quickly entail similar class and race warfare and, as in Haiti, disrupt sugar production. Politicians in London and Washington thus agreed that Cuba's colonial government and social system should be maintained.[20]

Anxieties about Cuba underlay President Monroe's December 1823 address to Congress. Reflecting the views of Secretary of State John Quincy Adams, the oration—later celebrated as the Monroe Doctrine—opposed European colonization. Less recalled is the fact that the speech accepted existing European colonialism in the Americas.[21] Adams, aware of Cuba's strategic importance, believed that the "laws ... of political gravitation" would eventually fasten the island to the United States. In the meantime, he favored cautious support of Spain's continued domination of the island as a hedge against British and French designs. The Monroe administration's "no-transfer policy" was adopted as it rebuffed a group of Cuban Creole planters seeking support for an anti-Spanish revolt. Despite Secretary of War John C. Calhoun's endorsement of the rebels, caution prevailed in both Monroe's and subsequent administrations.[22]

By the mid-1840s, however, Washington's no-transfer policy toward Cuba was fading before an ever-quickening national appetite for territorial expansion. New titles to Louisiana, Oregon, California, Texas, and New Mexico had concluded the old U.S. rivalry in North America with Great Britain. Two other old U.S rivals, France and Spain, were ghosts of their former glory. Cuba and Puerto Rico now comprised Spain's entire empire in the Americas, and France's New World empire consisted of remote French Guiana and a handful of tiny islands—one off Canada's eastern coast, the others scattered through the Lesser Antilles.

With the 1845 annexation of Texas, the United States won a virtual world monopoly over the production of high-grade cotton, which, coupled with England's industrial reliance on cotton, seemed to promise a powerful new advantage: U.S. exporters could dictate cotton prices to British customers, and Washington could threaten a cotton embargo to preempt British military aggression. Arkansas senator Ambrose Sevier in 1844 thought that the U.S. cotton monopoly would "tend more successfully to insure our peace and security than a standing army."[23]

Possessing Oregon and California, the United States was now a Pacific power with a vested interest in preserving access to its western realm. Since the overland route to the Pacific was long, costly, and dangerous, traders generally preferred crossing Central America or the Panamanian isthmus. To preserve access to those routes, the United States needed to maintain its freedom of movement in the Gulf of Mexico. With Spain fading, Washington began to view Britain as its main Gulf rival. As early as 1839 troubling U.S. memories of earlier overtures by Britain toward the independent Republic of Texas were stirred afresh when the United Provinces of Central America, a short-lived union of Central American states, collapsed, and rumors spread of heightened British ambitions in the Gulf of Mexico. In 1847 Britain backed up its claim to an eight-hundred-mile-long "protectorate" along Central America's Mosquito Coast by seizing the port of San Juan. In Washington the port, renamed Greytown, seemed an obvious eastern terminus for a canal across the Panamanian isthmus—with the recent discovery of gold in California a sensitive matter to the U.S. government. British occupation of the Mosquito Coast could forestall construction of a U.S. canal across the isthmus. And if the British built their own canal and operated it as a monopoly enforced by an aggressive British navy, it could disrupt U.S. access to California.[24]

Increased activities by English abolitionists in the West Indies also troubled Washington. England had emancipated the slaves in its own West Indian colonies in 1833. Even earlier, in 1807, Britain had ended its own slave trade, and by 1815 Sweden, Denmark, France, and the United States had followed suit. In 1817 Spain, weakened by European wars, had signed a treaty with England wherein Madrid promised to withdraw from the slave trade by 1820. London provided the Spanish treasury £400,000 sterling to compensate for lost revenues. Despite that treaty and another, in 1835, Cuba's rising demand for slaves, coupled with official corruption and lax enforcement of the ban, kept the trade open; between 1820 and 1840 almost 290,000 slaves arrived in Cuba.[25]

Many planters, commercial agents, and diplomats in the United States and the West Indies viewed British abolitionism as a front for England's own imperial ambitions. They feared that the end of slavery in Cuba would destroy the island's sugar industry, to the advantage of British West Indies planters. A free Cuba dominated by blacks would then join Haiti to form an independent "Negro Archipelago"—at once blocking U.S. expansion into the Caribbean and threatening slavery in the southern United States. As one Cuban Creole activist recalled, the French Revolution of 1848, which liberated slaves on Martinique and the rest of the French Antilles, opened "the eyes of the more indolent and supine of the Cuban planters to the dangers which beset them on all sides from the abolition policy of England and France."[26]

Washington's no-transfer policy was devised to preserve Cuba's social stability, and slavery was seen as the key to that stability; a continuation of Spanish rule over the island had been presumed to be slavery's best hope. But now it seemed that Spain might accept abolition as the price for continued dominion over Cuba. Beyond that, the limits to Washington's power that the no-transfer policy had implicitly acknowledged in 1819 no longer existed by the 1840s. To U.S. leaders suddenly sodden with the heady wine of territorial aggrandizement, the nation, now more than ever before, possessed both the need and the means to finally place Cuba under the Stars and Stripes. To many in Washington, the no-transfer policy now seemed but an anachronistic obstacle to a long-standing territorial ambition.

Washington, January–July 1847

John O'Sullivan had barely unpacked his bags after returning from Cuba in January 1847 when he began lobbying the Polk administration for a U.S. purchase of Cuba. That same month he suggested to President Polk's secretary of state, James Buchanan, that the administration should dispatch a "confidential agent" to Madrid to "sound" the Spanish government on the idea. Six months later—in a lengthy July 6 memo—O'Sullivan again pressed his argument on Buchanan. In making his case, O'Sullivan kept in mind that any effort to acquire more slave territory for the United States would ignite domestic political controversy. For three years critics of slavery had argued against its extension to any more U.S. soil. O'Sullivan thus stressed to Buchanan that Cuba offered opportunities for all regions of the United States; the island's annexation, he promised, "would be no less popular at the commercial north and East & the grain-growing West, than at the South." He pointed out that since slavery already existed in Cuba, U.S. annexation of the island would entail no extension of the practice. Moreover, the acquisition of slaveholding Cuba would hurry U.S. acquisition of free Canada. The political balance between free and slave states would thus be restored—but in a vastly enlarged republic. Combined with U.S. acquisition of a right of transit across Mexico's Tehuantepec isthmus—another Polk ambition—acquiring Cuba would be a fitting culmination of the president's continentalism. History would "stamp the term of the administration which should affect it, as one of the great epoches, not only of our country, but of the commercial history of the world." O'Sullivan also stressed Spain's growing political weakness and rumored British and French interests in Cuba. In deference to those dangers, he wrote, negotiations must be "above all, *secret and rapid.*"[27]

Unfortunately for O'Sullivan, Moses Yale Beach chose that same month to begin his own very public campaign in the New York *Sun* for Cuba's annexation. On July 19 and 22 two Cuban travel sketches by Jane McManus Storms (signed "Cora") presented sympathetic portraits of the island, its peoples, and the industrial progress of Cuba's Creoles despite the repressive Spanish regime. A July 23 editorial by Beach, "Cuba under the Flag of the United States," mentioning no names, outlined the Club de la Habana's proposal and recalled his recent meeting with the wealthy Cubans who had assured him that the island's residents were ready to join the United States. He had agreed to place their case before his readers as soon as the Mexican War ended. And since that war coming to an end, "The moment has arrived to place [Cuba] in our hands and under our flag. Cuba is in the market for sale, and we are authorized by parties eminently able to fulfil what they propose, to say that if the United States will offer the Spanish government one hundred millions of dollars Cuba is ours, and that with one week's notice, the whole amount will be raised and paid over by the inhabitants of the island."[28]

O'Sullivan for his part was embarrassed by the public airing of a cause that, he had just stressed to Buchanan, required absolute secrecy. On July 31 O'Sullivan—attempting to distance himself from the blowhard Beach—sent the secretary of state a copy of the *Sun*'s "foolish" article. An accompanying letter dismissed Beach's disclosure of having attended the Havana meeting as "a lie . . . calculated to do mischief." O'Sullivan again urged Buchanan and Polk to begin negotiations with Spain.[29]

Beach, meanwhile, continued to argue for annexation in the *Sun*. Six months later, on January 1, 1848, *La Verdad*, a bimonthly Spanish-English newspaper devoted to Cuban annexation joined the chorus. With an initial funding of $10,000 from Cuban sources, the newspaper was produced on the *Sun*'s printing press and operated from editorial offices just across Nassau Street from the *Sun*'s own headquarters.[30]

Washington, May 10, 1848

Neither O'Sullivan's private pleadings nor Beach's public editorials prompted President Polk to act on Cuba. The president was preoccupied with reaching a formal end to the Mexican War. Not until May 10, 1848—two months after the U.S. Senate ratified the Guadalupe Hidalgo peace treaty, as Polk awaited its approval by Mexico's Congress—did Cuba's day in Washington finally seem to arrive. On that day U.S. Senator Lewis Cass urged Cuba's acquisition in the Congress, and at the White House President Polk heard O'Sullivan spell out the Club de la Habana's terms for a U.S. purchase of the island.

It had been almost two years since Senator David Yulee of Florida introduced a resolution calling on Polk to begin talks with Madrid for the island's purchase—a resolution promptly withdrawn only five days later at the insistence of Yulee's "friends." What concerned them was Texas and Oregon: until

Polk resolved the domestic political debates over those two territorial acquisitions, congressional Democrats preferred to delay action on Cuba.[31]

Now with the Oregon issue settled and the Mexican War all but officially over, Democratic party expansionists sensed ripe opportunities. Cass's proposal that the Senate consider Cuba's purchase came on May 10 amid debates over a bill calling for a temporary U.S. occupation of the Yucatán peninsula. Then an independent republic, Yucatán had been neutral during the Mexican War. For months, however, reports of atrocities by Indians against Creoles there had stirred Washington's interest. In April, Yucatán officials even offered the United States dominion over the peninsula in exchange for military intervention. The offer intrigued Polk, and on April 28, while making no specific recommendations, he asked Congress to consider the matter.

In his May 10 Senate speech, Cass supported U.S. intervention in the Yucatán to block what he saw as Britain's intention to use it as a naval coaling station. Taking a longer view of U.S. interests in the region, Cass argued that intervention in the Yucatán, coupled with a prompt purchase of Cuba, should belong to a larger U.S. policy of revitalizing the Monroe Doctrine and asserting Yankee control over the entire Gulf of Mexico. Britain, he said, had preempted Napoleon's ambition "to convert the Mediterranean into a French lake." Likewise, Washington must prevent British domination over waters of the Western Hemisphere. "The Gulf of Mexico, sir, must be practically an American lake. . . . It should be a cardinal principle in our policy, never to be lost sight of, that the command of the Gulf of Mexico must never pass into foreign hands."[32]

At the White House that same day, O'Sullivan pressed his own case for Cuba on President Polk. For this effort the journalist left behind Secretary of State Buchanan, by then O'Sullivan's strongest ally within the Polk administration. Perhaps aware that Polk viewed his secretary of state with growing distrust as a result of Buchanan's rumored presidential ambitions, O'Sullivan took along a new ally: the junior U.S. senator from Illinois, Stephen Douglas.[33]

O'Sullivan's enlistment of Douglas attested to Cuba's growing allure within the highest echelons of U.S. politics and business. More to the point, Douglas linked the eastern and western wings of an increasingly powerful U.S. lobby for annexation. Illinois's "Little Giant," then thirty-five years old, would never become a public firebrand for Cuban annexation, and he kept a safe distance from conspiracies directed toward that cause. But Douglas was a loyal servant to the railroad and steamboat interests that often bankrolled his political ambitions. And support for Cuba's annexation from those industries ranged from lobbying to discreet support for clandestine military operations. Douglas's relationship with George Law was particularly instructive. A New York banker and ship and railroad magnate, "Live Oak" Law ran the United States Mail Steamship Company, which held the U. S. mail delivery monopoly in the Gulf of Mexico. By carrying the mail, the line supplemented its usual private commercial revenues with $290,000 in annual federal subsidies. Not coincidentally, Law also contributed generously to Stephen Douglas's political career. Though Douglas was a westerner and Law an easterner, both wanted more U.S. trade with Cuba. Law reveled in his swaggering public image, and over the years his steamship company's reputation as a conduit for clandestine military propaganda, intelligence, and weapons made it a frequent target of Spanish harassment. In 1854 Law would give financial support to an ultimately aborted campaign against Cuba organized by former Mississippi governor John Quitman.[34]

Indeed, to all of the steamboat lines that increasingly plied the Gulf of Mexico after the discovery of California gold, the prospect of a Cuba joined to the United States enjoyed vast appeal. For U.S. traders, control of the island promised freer movement of ships, longer passenger and cargo lists, and a U.S.-Cuba trade shorn of duties. That last possibility proved especially enticing because many of the lines also owned mercantile houses in New York, New Orleans, and Havana that brokered everything from consignment deals to loans and marine insurance. Mississippi Valley farmers and railroad interests also had reasons for favoring U.S. annexation of the island. Stephen Douglas, in particular, knew that western farmers could increase wheat sales to a Cuba not charging Spanish duties. He likewise assumed that much of that wheat would travel to the Gulf of Mexico via one of his pet projects, the Illinois Central Railroad. In 1850 Douglas would help the rail line to get a federal land grant. The relationship shared by Douglas and George Law, after all, turned on a tidy quid pro quo. Law's "steamboat lobby" in Congress supported Douglas's various rail projects. Douglas in turn provided loyal congressional support for Law's steamship line. The cooperation between the two would become so close that when Douglas sought the presidency in 1852, he quickly became known as "the Steamboat Candidate."[35]

Not all of Douglas's links to boats and trains, however, ran through George Law. The senator also enjoyed connections to the Pacific Mail

Steamship Company, holder of the West Coast U.S. mail monopoly. Douglas supporters J. W. Alsop and G. W. Ludlow—financial backers of the Illinois Central Railroad—were directors of the Pacific Mail Steamship Company. And when the Pacific line's president, William H. Aspinwall, in December 1848 sought a monopoly on government shipments on a proposed Panama railway, Douglas delivered the request to the Senate.[36]

Stephen Douglas and John O'Sullivan thus made a knowledgeable team as they sat in Polk's office on May 10, 1848, and spoke of the benefits of a Cuba under U.S. sovereignty. On this particular afternoon, however, their combined expertise worked no magic. The president listened intently; he was polite and seemed genuinely interested. Then, without expressing an opinion, he sent the two on their way. For the Club de la Habana, the vagueness of the ostensibly bold President Polk made for an anticlimactic denouement to such a long-awaited hearing. But if O'Sullivan that day left the White House crestfallen, he also had misunderstood both Polk and the history of U.S. expansionism.[37]

For all his signature boldness in imposing his country's dominion over new geographical realms, James K. Polk, then fifty-two—a short, slender man with intense gray eyes, thinning swept-back hair, and a perpetual scowl—was a practical politician whose career, as a lawyer, a Tennessee congressman and governor, and finally as president, had been built on hardheaded decisions. He deferred to a skeptical bent nurtured during his youth in Mecklenburg County, North Carolina, where his world view was shaped by a Deist grandfather and a less than devout father.[38] Though an expansionist, the hard-boiled Polk never succumbed to the poetry of Manifest Destiny. His expansionist policies owed as much to prosaic economic concerns as to any sort of romantic nationalism—the same sort of concerns that prompted his slashing of import tariffs in 1846. Tariff reductions and geographical expansion stimulated agricultural exports, boosted the national economy, and blunted the possibility of another panic such as the one that had staggered the nation's economy from 1837 to 1844. Fears of another such slump shadowed Polk throughout his presidency.[39]

While the winds of Manifest Destiny buffeted Polk's ambitions, his territorial attainments owed equally to an older—often bisectional, even bipartisan—tradition of U.S. expansionism. Democrats certainly loom larger than Whigs in the Republic's pantheon of expansionists. But peer beyond the blusterous rhetoric of Jefferson, Monroe, Jackson, and Polk; while Democratic presidents often led in articulating the nation's pre–Civil War territorial ambitions, those projects had support politically broader, and goals more limited in area, than is commonly recognized. Jefferson as a young philosophe, for instance, advocated westward expansion to blunt the influences of cities and factories and thereby preserve the nation's agrarian character. And, as president, Jefferson occasionally embroidered public pronouncements with such flourishes.[40] But what clinched his 1803 Louisiana Purchase was a more hardheaded consideration—a wariness, shared by Federalists, of French ambitions in the Mississippi Valley. A doubling of the nation's geographical size would offer everyone, even Federalists, fresh economic opportunities, and in the end the Senate's Federalists joined their Republican counterparts in approving Jefferson's deal. When President Polk went to war with Mexico in 1846, congressional Whigs objected that the president had overstepped his legitimate powers. Abraham Lincoln, as a young freshman congressman, joined his Whig colleagues in challenging the legality of the war. But he and most of his Whig congressional colleagues, despite voicing frequent opposition to the conflict, regularly supported bills for war expenditures.[41]

Just as Democrats, when the need arose, could abandon pipe dreams of agrarian Edens, so Whigs could put aside legal and philosophical qualms to ponder their own tangible needs. To many Whigs the Mexican War seemed unconstitutional, and they voted funds for it simply because U.S. soldiers had already been put in harm's way. But the war also promised to accomplish specific ends sought by specific Whigs. Daniel Webster, for instance, sharply opposed President Polk's war, but that same war promised to realize a prize long sought by Webster and New England maritime interests: U.S. control of San Francisco and other Pacific ports.[42]

Popular mythology portrays the nation's "Westward Course of Empire" from the Atlantic to the Pacific moving much as a carpet might be unrolled across a room. The course of settlement sometimes moved westward, but at other times it rolled from south to north, into the lower Mississippi Valley. Pioneers from Tennessee migrated south and west to fill Texas; and in California most settlers moved eastward, arriving by boat and then moving inland. Another assumption—that continental expansion issued from a sustained national resolve—also fades before closer scrutiny. Although Polk, for instance, was elected president in 1844 on a promise to annex Texas and Oregon, his elevation to the White House came about with a minority of the popular vote. Many issues shaped the 1844 election, but to the extent that it may be read as a referendum on expansionism, a majority of the electorate voted no. Among voters, specific expansionist goals generally held more allure than visions of open-ended conquest. In the face of often bitter opposition, President Polk, aware of that truism, eventually found requisite support for the annexation of Texas and Oregon. Both regions, after all, had been settled by U.S. citizens. By contrast, when the expansionist press in 1847 called for U.S. acquisition of the entirety of Mexico—for "All Mexico"—Polk realized that such a move would face substantial domestic opposition. With its racially darker population, Mexico seemed an undesirable conquest for many in the United States, and the president never seriously pursued it.[43]

The popularity of particular projects also frequently varied from region to region. Southern cotton interests, for instance, yearned for Texas but had little use for Oregon or the Yucatán. In the months before the Buchanan-Pakenham treaty of 1846 that resolved competing British and American claims on Oregon, southern cotton planters worried that agitation for "All Oregon" might lead to a war with Britain, their main export customer. Similarly, in 1848, when the U.S. Senate considered Yucatán's annexation, John C. Calhoun opposed the initiative because, he said, the Mexican peninsula had no strategic value, and the land itself was "worthless," largely devoid of streams and "rock and barren throughout the greater part." The Yucatán, in other words, would not sustain planter agriculture. Northern Whigs, on the other hand, cared little for Texas, but New England's maritime and fur-trading interests, Whigs included, were overjoyed at the prospects of U.S. title to the Pacific ports of California and Oregon.[44]

In securing Texas, California, and Oregon, President Polk adroitly balanced sectional preferences. He acquired Oregon only after annexing Texas. Tactical discretion, the president reasoned early on, dictated that the two issues be addressed separately.[45] Each annexation project had specific geopolitical and economic purposes and tapped discrete political constituencies. The goal of "All-Mexico," by Polk's lights, served no tangible purpose and inspired no significant constituency of voters. He rejected it. Unlike the messianic expansionism of Manifest Destiny's adherents, Polk's territorial projects tended to be specific, limited, and bounded by realpolitik.

In February 1848 Polk grudgingly acknowledged that the Guadalupe Hidalgo peace treaty delivered by negotiator Nicholas P. Trist embodied such realpolitik. Mexico abandoned all claims on Texas north of the Rio Grande, plus the territories of New Mexico and California. In acquiring Mexico's northern frontier, the United States agreed to pay $15 million and to assume all claims by U.S. citizens against Mexico up to $3.25 million. Those terms, after all, delivered on what Polk had asked Trist to bring back when he dispatched him to Mexico City the previous April. Even so, General Winfield Scott's triumphant capture of Mexico City that September and the Mexican government's recalcitrance in coming to the negotiating table tempted Polk to hold out for more. It was, however, only a fleeting temptation. Rebuking Secretary of State Buchanan's urging to demand more Mexican territory, Polk accepted Trist's treaty. To do otherwise, he confided to his diary, risked too much:

> If I were to reject a Treaty made upon my own terms, as authorized in April last, with the unanimous approbation of the Cabinet, the probability is that Congress would not grant either men or money to prosecute the war. Should this be the result, the army now in Mexico would be constantly wasting and diminishing in numbers, and I might at last be compelled to withdraw them, and thus lose two new Provinces of New Mexico & Upper California. . . . Should the opponents of my administration succeed in carrying the next Presidential election, the great probability is that the country would lose all the advantages secured by this Treaty.[46]

The president, after all, was a working politician, not a newspaper editor afire with the poetry of Manifest Destiny.

In theory and practice Manifest Destiny often proved less a workable doctrine, more a messianic—and rhetorical—devotion to unfettered U.S. territorial expansionism, to what the New York *Tribune* once called "movement, no matter in what direction."[47] Practically a matter of religious faith to its adherents, Manifest Destiny drew upon various doctrines of natural rights, republicanism, Protestant messianism, "geographical predestination," and racial Anglo-Saxon racialism—all with a generous infusion of adventurism and pecuniary self-interest.[48] But if Manifest Destiny was a faith of the 1840s, its adherents had reason to embrace it as a revealed religion. In the course of a single decade, the United States added Texas, Oregon, New Mexico and California to its bounty. A republic begun seven decades earlier as a scraggly seaboard domain of thirteen tenuously connected former British colonies had, by 1849, pushed beyond the Appalachians to reach the Pacific and become an empire of classical proportions, with each new attainment inspiring calls for greater conquests. As Walt Whitman, capturing the spirit of the age, would rhapsodize in "Song of the Open Road," "from any fruition of success, no matter what, shall / come forth something to make a greater struggle necessary."[49]

The expansiveness had reached its zenith in the fall of 1847, with General Scott's capture of Mexico City and the subsequent cry in the popular press for "All Mexico." Typical of such cries, the Philadelphia *Public Ledger* inveighed, "We must not only invade and invest the country to occupy every city . . . but we must establish over every inch of ground so occupied an energetic and enlightened government. We must make the Mexicans feel, not only that, our power is invincible over them, but that, their own interests require our rule."[50]

When less excitable souls, many of them Whigs, questioned the wisdom of devouring the vast sovereign republic to the south, the *Public Ledger* likened such quibbling to arguing with a force of nature. "No more territory!" the paper bristled. "Do they expect to confine the indomitable Anglo-Saxon by artificial boundaries? Do they believe that he will stand still under their resolutions? Let Mr. Webster go back to Plymouth, and Mr. Clay to Daniel Boone. And then let them return through the progress since made, and ask themselves where the race shall stop. No more territory! As well might he say to the Ohio, 'no more flowing.'"[51]

In the end, President Polk rejected such calls and settled for less expansive, though hardly modest, spoils. In turning a deaf ear to the All-Mexico campaign, the president not only chose to end a war whose domestic support he feared might soon collapse. He also weighed the burdens such a conquest would entail: the U.S. military—and Treasury—suddenly would have become responsible for the occupation and maintenance of the civil affairs of a vast country that even before the war, was deeply mired in social, economic, and political woes.

Yes, John O'Sullivan and Stephen Douglas claimed a vast knowledge of U.S. and Cuban politics. But what they did not know as they met with James K. Polk on May 10, 1848, was that the president had already decided to pursue Cuba. As Polk later recalled the meeting in his diary, "I heard their views, but deemed it prudent to express no opinion on the subject. Mr. O'Sullivan read to me and left with me a paper embodying his views in favour of the measure. Though I expressed no opinion to them I am decidedly in favour of purchasing Cuba & making it one of the States of [the] Union."[52] Before taking action, however, the president had decided that all questions about U.S. intentions in the Yucatán must be resolved. Just as three years earlier Polk had been reluctant to deal with Oregon until Texas seemed resolved, so now he wanted the Yucatán issue squared away before taking action on Cuba.

Washington, May 18, 1848

On May 17, 1848—one week after President Polk met with O'Sullivan and Douglas—any possibility of annexing Yucatán vanished when news arrived that a truce had been negotiated in its civil war. With a nominal peace on the peninsula, justification no longer existed for U.S. intervention. Shortly thereafter, rumors of a planned insurrection in Cuba reached Washington in a May 18 letter to Secretary of State Buchanan from General Robert Campbell, the U.S. consul in Havana. The diplomat wrote of growing antagonism by Cuban Creoles toward Spain and increased talk of outright rebellion. "Notwithstanding the want of many of the requisites to ensure success, there appears every probability that the Island will soon be in a state of civil war." The rebels, advised Campbell, hoped to raise sufficient money to entice soldiers from U.S Army regiments now departing Mexico for home to make a detour to Cuba. "If Revolution is attempted, and succeeds, immediate application would be made to the United States for annexation as the most intelligent of the Creoles have an abiding conviction of their utter incapacity for self government, a conviction which must be felt by any one who has had opportunities of studying or even observing their character."[53]

The hesitation of Cuba's Creoles to lobby for complete independence in fact arose from a fearful awareness that their prosperity had become hostage to a dark trinity of sugar, slavery, and Spanish colonialism—a predicament that made it difficult to ponder outright autonomy.

Though Cuban sugar had been produced since the sixteenth century, its early cultivation on the island was small-scale and devoted to domestic sales, not export. During the early years of Spanish settlement in the New World, Portugal's sugar plantations in the Canary Islands and other east Atlantic colonies, and Brazil had more than met Europe's demand for sugar. Most crops in Cuba were grown on small farms, not plantations, and tobacco, leather, meat, and dyewoods—not sugar—were the principal products.

Though Cuba sprawled across 44,000 square miles, a land area roughly equal to all of the other West Indian islands combined, as late as the 1770s it still produced less than 5 percent of the region's sugar.[54]

Only a few decades later, however, Cuba was well on its way to becoming a realm of baronial plantations devoted largely to a single export crop—sugar. The disruption of Haiti's coffee and sugar plantations during the slave revolts of the 1790s opened substantial foreign markets for Cuba's planters. Nurtured by new funds from outside investors, expanding crop production, rising sugar prices, and soaring land values, Cuba also began to upgrade its transportation system, hastening the spread of sugar cultivation deeper into the island's interior. Old roads were improved, new ones built, and in 1834 construction began on railroads. The boom also speeded a shift from water and ox-driven sugar milling to the new steam-powered machines. The average Cuban sugar mill's production jumped from 72 tons in 1830 to 120 in 1841, and annual sugar exports from 35,238 tons in 1805 to 294,952 in 1850. By the mid-nineteenth century Cuba had become the world's largest sugar producer. The island's planters were now dependent on a cash crop whose cultivation and refining were highly labor-intensive. As planters imported more and more slaves, between 1827 and 1841 Cuba's slave population increased by 41 percent to 436,000. In 1762 the average sugar plantation occupied 320 acres and worked six to eight slaves; three decades later it sprawled over 700 acres and worked almost one hundred slaves.[55]

The rising prosperity of Cuba's Creoles—and their growing clamor for more political and economic freedom—increased anxieties among Spanish officials already worried about the steady dismantling of their once vast New World empire. By the mid-nineteenth century, Spain's hopes for an empire on the North American mainland—hopes which had been buoyed by Spain's aid to the United States during its War of Independence were long doomed. With the Pinckney treaty of 1795, Spain accepted a severe readjustment of its Florida boundaries and gave the United States most of its remaining North American claims east of the Mississippi River. In 1800 the Treaty of San Ildefonso, imposed by Napoleon Bonaparte, returned the sprawling Louisiana territory to France. The 1819 Adams-Onís treaty ceded the rest of Florida to the United States. By the 1830s Spain had embraced a defensive colonial policy against both real and imagined threats from England, the United States, Mexico, and Colombia and recommitted itself to blocking free trade between the United States and Cuba.[56]

Cuban planters for their part felt increasingly haunted by the West Indies' history of slave revolts—the Haitian uprising, as well as Cuba's own tradition of rebellions. Scattered uprisings had occurred every few years since at least the 1820s. Between 1825 and 1850 the province of Matanzas alone witnessed at least 399 instances of slave violence. In 1841 new census figures reinforced Creole fears; for the first time in Cuban history, slaves outnumbered whites on the island. Cuba's total population of just over one million included 418,000 whites and 436,000 slaves, and 153,000 free people of color.[57]

The island's ascendant Creole merchants and planters thus found themselves caught on the twin horns of a volatile slave system and a repressive colonial regime. Some began to call for restrictions on the slave trade, entreaties Madrid generally declined. By the government's logic, if the planters secretly yearned for political independence but fears of a slave revolt kept them cowed, why reduce those fears? In 1836 Washington's minister in Madrid, Cornelius Van Ness, recalled the words of a Spanish minister: "He believes that the fear of the negroes is worth an army of 100,000 men, and that it will prevent the whites from making any revolutionary attempts." Fifteen years later a Yankee merchant residing in Matanzas told Secretary of State Daniel Webster of a similar conversation in which Cuba's governor general boasted that "he had positive orders from the Queens Government, that if a Revolution should break out, & look serious, he should proclaim the Slaves all free, & put arms in their hands. This proceeds on the idea, that when freed, the slaves would defend the Island against all attacks, & all attempts, from the United States." Webster's reaction to the threat: "I have heard of this before."[58]

In 1840 President John Tyler dispatched special envoy Alexander Hill Everett to Cuba to investigate rumored ties between Tyler's consul in Havana, Nicholas Trist, and the island's contraband slave trade. While in Cuba, Everett used the the opportunity to try to stir up anti-Spanish activism among Cuba's planters. He need not have bothered. Secret revolutionary clubs had existed in Cuba since the century's dawn. In 1810 and 1823 Spain brutally suppressed Masonic conspiracies fermented in Cuba by Creole liberals. Liberal hopes were raised again in 1826 by rumors of an anti-Spanish expedition to Cuba and Puerto Rico by Mexican and Colombian forces. The invasion's planners hoped, by seizing the two islands, to remove the region's final specter of Spanish colonialism—and eliminate both as possible staging areas for counterrevolutions. Cuba, especially, in the years after the early Latin American revolutions had become an antirepublican fortress as Spanish soldiers and royalist fugitives from the mainland fled to the island. That military concentration, coupled with Spain's refusal to abandon its dream of reconquest of the mainland, led the new republics to view Cuba as a potential danger to their continued survival. U.S. opposition and disputes between Mexico and Colombia canceled the planned 1826 anti-Spanish expedition to Cuba. Three years later, confirming the mainland republicans' worst fears, Spanish forces from Cuba made a naval landing, albeit quickly repulsed, at Tampico, on Mexico's Gulf coast.[59]

During the 1830s Creole political unrest deepened during the first of Spain's two Carlist civil wars. Besides sinking Spain into domestic political turmoil, the conflict muddled lines of authority between Madrid and the colonies. To shore up royal authority over Cuba, Madrid dispatched a succession of unpopular captains general to Cuba, who in the end only exacerbated tensions between Creoles and *peninsulares* and between Cuba and Madrid. The island's exclusion from Spain's Cortes from 1834 to 1837 further deepened Creole resentments. Ascendant in economic influence but barred from the government, the Creoles felt increasingly alienated from Spain and the *peninsulares,* who dominated Cuba's colonial regime. Under the sway of free-trade philosophy, liberal formal education in the United States and Europe, and simple self-interest, they increasingly saw their long-range interests as tied less to Spain, more to the United States.[60]

In 1837 such sentiments crystallized in a widely read essay by Creole historian and polemicist José Antonio Saco, who had fled to New York City three years earlier after his arrest for advocating an end to Cuba's slave trade. Growing Creole unhappiness with Spain's administration of Cuba had swelled exile communities in New York, New Orleans, and the ports of Florida. Saco's essay, "Parallels between Cuba and Some English Colonies," compared Cuba's relations with Spain unfavorably to those between Canada and England, and proposed: "If Cuba, degraded by circumstances, should have to throw herself into foreign arms, in none could she fall with more honor or glory than in those of the great North American Confederation. In them she would find peace and consolation, strength and protection, justice and liberty." By 1849 a visitor to Cuba would report to Secretary of State John Clayton that "the young men educated in the U.S. come back, if not already republicans & annexationists, ready to become such in a few weeks after reaching home—as soon as they have time to draw a comparison between the conditions of Cuba and the United States."[61]

Washington, May–June 1848

As President Polk pondered the rumored conspiracy in Cuba over the spring of 1848, domestic U.S. politics also kept his attention directed toward the island. In May the Democratic party's national convention in Baltimore made Lewis Cass, already publicly identified with Cuban annexation, its presidential nominee. With Cass's nomination, Polk reasoned, whatever damage the Democrats might suffer in the coming election by a premature public endorsement of Cuban annexation was already done; the antislavery forces that might be offended by a move toward Cuba were already bolting the party for Martin Van Buren's third-party candidacy.[62]

Denied both All Mexico and Yucatán, Polk—eager to pluck a final laurel for his dwindling term of office—finally, on May 30, broached the subject of Cuba with his cabinet. The president demanded no "immediate decision," but "I intimated my strong conviction that the effort should be made without delay to purchase the Island." Treasury Secretary Robert Walker, who had crafted the Democrats' 1844 expansionist platform, led the ensuing discussion. With Polk's assent, Walker proposed purchase terms almost identical to those which had been suggested by O'Sullivan and Beach. Secretary of State Buchanan, fearing damage to Cass's candidacy, expressed reservations.[63]

On June 2, however, Cass—undercutting Buchanan's criticism—assured Polk that immediate action on Cuba would not damage his presidential candidacy. A week later, on June 9, a telegram arrived with news that the Mexican Congress had approved the Guadalupe Hidalgo treaty. With the Mexican War now officially over, Polk's final source of hesitation had been removed, and that same day he asked Buchanan, who now supported the overture, to draw up negotiating instructions for Romulus Saunders, the U.S. minister to Spain.[64]

Three weeks later, on June 23, Polk learned still more about the planned uprising in Cuba when Senator Jefferson Davis of Mississippi and three members of the Consejo Cubano—José Aniceto Iznaga, Gaspar Cisneros Betancourt, and Alonse Betancourt—called at the White House. After Polk met briefly and privately with Davis, the two were joined by Assistant Postmaster

William J. Brown and the three Cuban visitors for a longer meeting.[65] As Polk later recalled, "They spoke of the desire of the Cubans to throw off the Spanish Yoke and to become annexed to the U.S. They did not ask the interference of this Government, but suggested that a party of the troops of the U.S. might be stationed at the Key West and at other convenient points on the Gulf coast to watch over & protect, if necessary, the interests of American citizens in Cuba." In response, Polk recalled, "I gave them no answer but a general evasive reply to the effect that I would consider of the information they had given me."[66]

Davis and his three Cuban friends were unaware that the president—a full two weeks earlier—had already taken decisive actions to scuttle the revolt in Cuba. On June 9, the day Polk had decided to attempt a purchase of Cuba, he already knew enough about the conspiracy at that day's cabinet meeting to worry that it might poison negotiations with Spain. Thus, he ordered letters dispatched to Major General William O. Butler in Mexico and Consul Campbell in Cuba. Butler was instructed to uphold his country's treaty obligations with Spain and to prevent any U.S. soldiers from coming to Cuba. Campbell was ordered to discourage any participation by U.S nationals in such a revolt and to "preserve the national faith with Spain." Treasury Secretary Walker then suggested sending Madrid copies of the letters to Butler and Campbell. The rationale, Polk later wrote, "was that the best mode of approaching Spain with the view to purchase Cuba would-be to do so in a manner to satisfy them of our friendly disposition, and that we did not intend to take part in any revolution by which the Spanish authority would be overthrown."[67]

Matanzas, Cuba, July 6, 1848

For Cuba's would be rebels, the letters from Washington to Madrid of June 1848, warning Spanish officials of the conspiracy, proved a curtain-raiser to equally damaging disclosures inside Cuba. In early July, conspirator José María Sánchez Iznaga told his mother of the planned uprising; alarmed for her son's safety, she relayed the information to her husband who, on the advice of his attorney, passed it along to Spanish government officials on July 4. Iznaga and another conspirator, José Gregorio Díaz, were arrested, and on July 6 Narciso López, the leader of the conspiracy, was ordered to appear before the governor of the province of Cienfuegos.

Thus alerted that his conspiracy had been betrayed, López went by mule and train to Cárdenas and from there by boat to Matanzas, on the island's northern coast, where he boarded the *Neptune*, a U.S. brig bound for Rhode Island. He arrived in Bristol on July 23 and from there went to New York City, where he began seeking allies to assist in an armed expedition to Cuba. Spanish officials later sentenced López to death in absentia.[68]

A slight, handsome man with a mustache, Narciso López had dark eyes whose intensity was matched by the fervor of his political ambitions. Forty-eight years old, he was a gifted horseman with an illustrious past as a cavalry leader in the Spanish army. López had been still in his teens when he embarked upon a life of military adventure. He was born in Venezuela, on October 29, 1797, the son of a prosperous landowner.[69] His first taste of combat came during the war of national independence sparked in Venezuela by Simón Bolívar in 1813. When the war destroyed the family's plantation the next year, the elder López moved the family to Caracas and became a merchant. That same year, 1814, father and son were in the town of Valencia, conducting business at a branch of the family's store, when word arrived that Bolívar had been defeated at the battle of La Puerta. As the townspeople of Valencia, a rebel stronghold, prepared to surrender to expected royalist troops, Bolívar sent word asking them to prepare to defend the town's garrison; he and his army, he promised, would soon arrive to resume the fight. Bolívar, however, never arrived, fleeing instead with his army into neighboring New Granada; it would be three years before they returned to secure Venezuela's independence. In Valencia, meanwhile, fierce local resistance kept royalist forces at bay for three weeks, but without Bolívar's promised support, the effort was doomed. Valencia fell, and the entering Spanish army massacred at least eighty-seven townsmen, including the elder López.

Though only fifteen years old, Narciso had picked up a rifle during the fighting and somehow emerged as "leader de facto" of the town's resistance. When Spanish troops finally captured the town, the boy barely escaped his father's fate. "After hiding about for some time . . . he determined to seek safety in the only situation in which it was to be found, by enlistment as a soldier in the army." Narciso had no love for the Spanish or for Bolívar. Like others in Valencia, he believed they had been betrayed by Bolívar, sacrificed so that Bolívar could make his escape to safety. As an early López biographer recalled, "No inhabitant of Valencia . . . would have hesitated to shoot Bolivar. . . . Spain was then moreover under the republican Constitution of 1812, so that, in the civil war at that period, the cause of liberty did not appear to be solely on the Patriot side."[70]

After Bolívar defeated the Royalist forces in Venezuela in 1823, López, by then a colonel in the Spanish army, left for Cuba with the garrison. There, that same year, he married Dolores Frías y Jacott, sister of the count of Pozos Dulces, a prominent U.S.-educated Creole planter, an agitator for liberal reform, and a member of the Club de la Habana. López too threw himself into Liberal reform efforts. Still later that year, when Spain's Ferdinand VII suppressed the Constitution of 1812, in protest López ended his active military duty.[71]

In 1827 the couple moved to Spain, where six years later another political crisis mustered López back into armed conflict. As word spread of King Ferdinand's death, Spain's Liberals, weary of the king's absolutism, seized the moment to urge a restoration of the 1812 Constitution. The ensuing insurrection began in 1833 with Liberals confiscating weapons from the absolutist Volunteer militia. In time, the Liberals, joined by the Spanish army, began demanding that the king's infant daughter Maria Isabel be named Spain's new monarch. Their campaign for Maria challenged the absolutist Don Carlos, Ferdinand's younger brother. To enlist support for young Isabel, Queen Maria Christina, acting as regent, agreed to support a restoration of the banned 1812 constitution. Soon after Ferdinand's death, however, Christina—more court intriguer than Liberal—was driven into exile, and the Cortes named the Liberal Baldomero Espartero as the new regent.

The rivalry between supporters of Isabel and Carlos soon widened into the first of Spain's two Carlist civil wars. Although Isabel's supporters won the war in 1839, Creole hopes for greater democracy were quickly frustrated. Under governments headed by Espartero and then Isabel, absolutist cliques continued to dominate Spain. As for López, his role in the war had quickly expanded: he became first aide-de-camp to Commander in Chief General Gerónimo Valdés, commanded a cavalry of three-thousand men, and served as chief commander of the National Guard militia. By the war's end López enjoyed high stature in both the political and military life of Spain; a general in the Spanish army, he also represented the city of Seville in the Cortes.

López's enhanced public stature, his increasingly long absences, extramarital dalliances, and frequent gambling nourished a growing indifference to his wife and young son, Narciso López y Frías. A contemporary critic later charged that "the gambling table reduced him to the low shift of borrowing money from every body of his acquaintance who would make him a loan." Since husband and wife were Roman Catholic, divorce was impossible, but in 1836 the couple formally separated.[72]

López returned to Cuba four years later after his former commander, Gerónimo Valdés, became the island's new captain general. Under Valdés, López held successive government posts: governor of the province of Trinidad de Cuba, commander in chief of the Central Department (one of the three military districts into which the island was divided), and finally, president of the Executive Military Commission. His responsibilities in that post included the suppression of political dissent.

In 1843 Spain's nominally Liberal regent Espartero and Captain General Valdés both fell from power, taking with them López's government entrée. He launched what would become a series of unsuccessful business ventures, including a bakery in Havana and a sugar mill near Cienfuegos. He also tried running his brother-in-law's coffee plantation near Vuelta—Abajo, south of Havana. As business failures accumulated, so too did López's disenchantment with Madrid's administration of Cuba. By the late 1840s he was contemplating revolution. On May 1848, López's ally José María Sánchez Iznaga wrote to his uncle, José Aniceto Iznaga, then in exile in New York, succinctly framing López's vision for Cuba's future. "Once [we have] installed the Provisional Government and our independence [is] acknowledge[d] by the Great American Republic our next step will be to ask [for] the annexation."[73]

As a cover for his conspiracy, López purchased an abandoned iron mine near Cienfuegos, on the island's southern coast. There he made a special effort to endear himself to the local *guajiros*, peasant Creole horsemen, in whom he saw the raw materials for an indigenous Cuban cavalry, "a mounted force inferior to none in the world." He also traveled often—ostensibly on business—to other parts of the island, seeking confederates for his uprising. In June 1848, while attending a concert in Havana, López met the novelist Cirilo Villaverde and several members of the Club de la Habana. For López the encounter was fortuitous; he was in Havana to investigate rumors of a plan by the Club de la Habana to recruit a U.S. Army general to lead an armed invasion of Cuba. The next day, at the Aldama palace, the club's members—aware of López's own plans for insurrection—confirmed that they were seeking a U.S. general to lead an expedition to Cuba. The following day Manuel Muñoz Castro, a close friend and Venezuela's local consul, introduced López to U.S. Consul Campbell. The North American diplomat confirmed to López the seriousness of the Club de la Habana's plans, but he also made it clear that the United States could not assist an anti-Spanish revolt. President Polk, Campbell assured López, remained committed to strict neutrality in any such conflict.[74]

Before returning to Cienfuegos, López agreed to a request by the Club de la Habana that he delay his own revolt—scheduled for June 24—for two weeks, in order to give the club time to hear from William Jenkins Worth, the U.S. Army general whom they hoped would agree to lead an expedition to Cuba. The club preferred that López begin his own revolt only after Worth had landed in Cuba with his invasion force. Worth and his troops had left Mexico City on June 12 and were marching toward Vera Cruz, where they were to sail for the United States. The Havana Club's agent, Rafael de Castro, had been instructed to catch up with Worth and offer him $3 million to recruit an army of five thousand soldiers from his returning troops and lead them to Cuba.[75]

For all their talk of sedition, the men of the Club de la Habana did not embrace revolution easily. As men of great wealth, they instinctively feared armed rebellions: who, after all, could guarantee that their own riches would not be consumed in the fires of an uprising? In the end, however, they had decided to make their offer to Worth if only to eclipse López, whom they viewed as erratic and perhaps likely to ignite a wholesale slave uprising.

Not that Worth himself was entirely predictable; though a disciplined officer, he too could be temperamental and vain. His courage under fire won him much of the credit for General Zachary Taylor's victory at the battle of Monterey, but subsequent public acclaim nourished an exaggerated sense of self-importance. Worth even hinted that he might run for the presidency, bluster that won him the wrath of his jealous superior, General Winfield Scott. At a meeting in Jalapa, Mexico, Worth accepted the Club de la Habana's offer, agreeing to begin operations as soon as he resigned his commission in the U.S. Army.[76]

As López, in late June 1848, waited in Cienfuegos for instructions from the Club de la Habana, his conspiracy was already fatally compromised. Even before Consul Campbell met López, the diplomat, in his May 18 letter to Buchanan, already had alerted the administration to the planned revolt, and Buchanan had passed Campbell's letter along to Polk. So too, John O'Sullivan, in private conversations with Polk on June 2 and 3, revealed details of the planned insurgency in Cuba. If O'Sullivan was looking for Polk's endorsement, the president once again disappointed him: "I at once said to Mr. O'Sullivan that if Cuba was ever obtained by the U.S. it must be by amicable purchase, and that as President of the U.S. I could give no countenance to such a step, and could not wink at such a movement."[77]

Madrid, August 15, 1848

Romulus Saunders, President Polk's fifty-seven-year-old man in Madrid, spoke no Spanish. Making matters worse, when conducting official business he often relied on diplomats of other nations for translations. A native with Polk of North Carolina, Saunders had held various state government posts and served three terms in the U.S. Congress, winning him along the way a reputation for an often petty partisanship. "There is not a more cankered or venomous reptile in the country," John Quincy Adams once said of him. Saunders had been appointed to the Madrid post in February 1846. His main qualification for the job: he had maneuvered a procedural vote at the 1844 Democratic convention that allowed Polk to clinch that year's presidential nomination.[78]

In his June 17 dispatch outlining U.S. purchase terms for Cuba, Secretary of State Buchanan instructed Saunders to offer Pedro J. Pidal, Spain's minister of foreign affairs, up to $100 million for the island. Letters should be avoided; the offer should be broached during a personal meeting in which Saunders should stress that Washington had no desire to repudiate its long-standing no-transfer policy toward Cuba. In fact, the United States would be happy to see Spain retain the island. The president was concerned about growing signs that even with Washington's backing, Spain's grip on the island might soon falter. Once those reassurances had been tendered, wrote Buchanan, "you may then touch delicately upon the danger that Spain may lose Cuba by a revolution in the Island, or that it may be wrested from her by Great Britain." Amid recent signs of heightened British aggression in Central America, Buchanan urged Saunders to "delicately" suggest that Spain's best course might be to sell the island to the United States.[79]

Odds for a successful meeting, the Polk administration hoped, also had been lengthened by the Spanish government's appreciation of the recent letters from Washington warning Madrid of Narciso López's planned insurrection. Saunders reported that in a July meeting with minister of war General

Ramón María Narváez, "he expressed himself, as thankful for the information, as entirely satisfied with the conduct of our Government and requested me to express, *muchas gracias,* many thanks to the President for his course in the business."[80]

If in his instructions Buchanan had stressed the carrot, Saunders, when he finally met with Pidal, on August 15, clearly preferred the stick. Saunders already had decided that merely to "touch delicately" upon growing dangers to Cuba was not enough. For him to close the sale, Madrid must believe that if Cuba's security became imperiled, Spain could not, as in the past, depend on Washington's help. During the meeting Saunders described Cuba's growing vulnerability and speculated that in the event of war between Spain and Britain, the United States might find it difficult to balance its no-transfer policy against the costs of war with England; "that whilst self-preservation and the interest of her commerce, might prevent her [the United States] from remaining passive, in the event of any pressing danger, she would greatly prefer a direct purchase of Cuba, to involving herself in a war with England on that account." In one moment Saunders—disobeying Buchanan's explicit orders—had taken a decisive step away from the traditional U.S. guarantee of Cuba's security and reversed two decades of State Department policy. Pidal considered the veiled threat an insult and curtly ended the meeting before Saunders could name his government's price.[81]

In Cuba other incidents were further complicating U.S.-Spanish relations. José María Sánchez Iznaga, one of the two coconspirators arrested before López's escape from Cuba, had taken on U.S. citizenship during an earlier trip abroad as a shield against arrest by Spanish officials, a ruse popular among Cuban intriguers of that day. Aware of Iznaga's U.S. citizenship, Consul Campbell, upon learning of the arrest, lodged a protest with Captain General Federico Roncali. The diplomat warned that the United States had already fought a war—the War of 1812—over just that sort of interference with its nationals. Iznaga soon escaped and fled to the United States, but Roncali and other Spanish officials remained miffed by the barely veiled threat of war.

Campbell soon became embroiled with the captain general over the imprisonment of another proannexation partisan, William H. Bush, a steward on the American bark *Childe Harold* and, when the need arose, a conduit between conspirators in the United States and Cuba. In October, Bush was arrested and held incommunicado after officials in Havana caught him delivering copies of Moses Yale Beach's banned pro-annexation paper *La Verdad.* Bush was soon released, but the damage to U.S.-Spanish relations was done. When Saunders and Spain's foreign minister, Pidal, finally met that August in Madrid, the atmosphere was already hopelessly poisoned. Saunders's high-handed diplomacy and Campbell's erratic behavior had jinxed any chance of a deal. When an account of the Madrid meeting appeared in October in the New York *Herald,* the episode became a public embarrassment for Polk and a cautionary tale for the incoming Taylor administration. Several months later, when Ambrosio Gonzales, a Club de la Habana emissary, met with Zachary Taylor just before his inauguration, the president-elect would make it clear that the Cuban insurrectionists could expect no support from the new administration.[82]

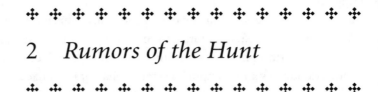

2 Rumors of the Hunt

Washington, July 1848

After arriving in the United States, in July 1848, Narciso López organized the Junta Cubano, a nucleus of conspirators in New York dedicated to launching an armed expedition against Cuba. Assisting the new effort were two lieutenants from the Cienfuegos conspiracy—José María Sánchez Iznaga and the novelist Cirilo Villaverde. By shifting his operations to the United States, López became a filibuster. By the 1880s that term would refer to those who engage in, or the act itself, of using long-winded speeches to obstruct legislative processes. In its original usage, however, the word descended from the Dutch *Vrijbuiter*, itself a corruption of the English word freebooter. During the seventeenth century the term referred to English buccaneers, maritime pirates who roamed the Caribbean in search of Spanish quarry. By the 1840s it more often applied to irregular armies of U.S. adventurers and the individuals who joined them. Mixing political and pecuniary motives, filibusters sought territorial conquests and other booty through involvement in foreign conflicts in which the United States was a neutral; almost without exception, filibusters sailed and marched toward Latin America. Hailed for their colorful, derring-do swagger, during the mid-nineteenth century filibusters such as López, William Walker, Henry A. Crabb, and Joseph Morehead became fixtures of the nation's popular press and the public imagination.[1]

López spent his first months in the United States moving between Washington and New York, gathering a diverse array of supporters, including

Cuban émigrés and U.S. politicians and military men, officers and enlisted men. Over the next three years, he would display neither the mastery of details nor the grand vision required of a great military leader. López would remain more cunning than thoughtful. But with his dignified military bearing, he would provide his conspiracy a sturdy heroic persona to rally around. Moreover, he revealed himself to be a genius at promotion—eventually drawing into his conspiracy Cubans, Europeans, North Americans (northerners and southerners), mercantilists, soldiers, and planters. As the rest of the United States seemed ready to split along fault lines of region, ideology, and economics, López assembled an organization that often seemed breathtaking in its ability to transcend potential discord.

En Route: Cuba to Washington, August 1848

In August 1848 the Club de la Habana, still hoping to instigate an anti-Spanish invasion of Cuba, dispatched Ambrosio Gonzales, then twenty-nine years old, to the United States to make another entreaty to William Jenkins Worth, the U.S. Army general who, on orders from President Polk, had backed out of the earlier Club de la Habana conspiracy.

Unable to obtain a passport, Gonzales on August 5 stowed away aboard the steamer *Crescent City* and reached New Orleans five days later. Seven days later he caught up with Worth at Newport, Rhode Island, on leave from his military duties and ensconced at the Ocean House hotel. Over the next few days Gonzales spelled out the club's offer. With $3 million it would supply, Worth was to raise an army of five thousand U.S. Army veterans of the Mexican War and lead it to Cuba. On the island Worth's army would be joined by a "patriotic movement" led by Narciso López. For Worth, the offer's appeal was enhanced by his personal financial problems: he had just discovered that during his long absence from the United States, his house in Watervliet, New York, had been sold for taxes.[2]

Gonzales then accompanied Worth to Hudson, New York, where, on August 23, citizens of the general's birthplace feted him with a rousing courthouse banquet. They then traveled to the U.S. Military Academy at West Point, where Worth had once taught and where he introduced Gonzales to the school's commandant of cadets and other officers. In Washington, Worth expanded Gonzales's circle of U.S. acquaintances still further to include Treasury

Secretary Robert J. Walker, Navy Secretary John Mason, and other government officials.[3]

Worth, meanwhile, had dispatched an aide, Colonel Henry Bohlen, a prominent Philadelphia merchant and consul for Holland, to Cuba to check on the Club de la Habana's offer. Bohlen returned with maps of Cuban cities and military fortifications and confirmation that the club seemed to have the "willingness and ability" to make good on its offer. But before Worth could act, President Polk in the fall of 1848 named him commander of the new U.S. military departments of Texas and New Mexico. He died of cholera on May 7, 1849, only four months after assuming his new post. Four years later José María Sánchez Iznaga would claim that the Havana club had withdrawn its offer in early 1849, unable to raise the promised $3 million.[4]

Washington, Spring 1849

By the spring of 1849 Ambrosio Gonzales, after failing to recruit General Worth for the Club de la Habana, joined López as adjutant general in the Junta Cubano. As others associated with the Club de la Habana drifted toward López, the club eventually promised him $60,000 to help fund a new expedition. He in return agreed to try to find a U.S. citizen to lead it. The new conspiracy received another boost when Cubans in New York City contributed another $23,000.[5]

López's search for political allies among U.S. citizens, however, was facing difficulties, especially in Washington. Even politicians who favored Cuba's annexation often balked at supporting a military expedition against the island. John C. Calhoun, for instance, had opposed U.S. annexation of Yucatán, but Cuba to him was a wholly different matter: strategically located, it offered myriad harbors and verdant lowlands ideal for cotton cultivation, and it already had a well-entrenched slave system. Gonzales later claimed that in the spring of 1849 López and Calhoun met at least three times in Washington and that the South Carolinian was the first "gentleman" to visit López there; "he even carried his civility to the extent of making a second call before his first had been returned." At one meeting Calhoun brought along four Senate colleagues to hear out López—Henry Foote and Jefferson Davis of Mississippi, Stephen Douglas of Illinois, and Daniel S. Dickinson of New York. According to Gonzales, Calhoun once remarked to him "that two or more Southern States could be carved out of it [Cuba]" and added that "you have my best wishes, but whatever the result, *as the pear, when ripe, falls by the law of gravity into the lap of the husbandman, so will Cuba eventually drop into the lap of the Union.*" "The South," Calhoun told López, "ought to flock down there in 'open boats' the moment they hear the tocsin." In the months ahead Calhoun's name provided added cachet as López sought to enlist others in his campaign. But—all the expansive rhetoric notwithstanding—more public support from the senator never came.[6]

A similarly discouraging vignette played out one summer day of the late 1840s when Varina Davis walked into the drawing room of her Washington home to find her husband, Mississippi senator Jefferson Davis, in quiet conversation with two men whom she had never seen before. "I found there a light-haired man sitting very still beside one whose glowing eyes and silvery hair made points of light in the room." The man with the glowing eyes and silvery hair was López. The other was apparently Gonzales, who, since López spoke no English, often acted as his interpreter.[7] As Mrs. Davis later recalled in her memoirs, "Supposing them to have come on business with my husband, I moved away to the extreme end of the room and when Mr. Davis came in they talked in whispers for some time, and eventually Mr. Davis rose, evidently declining some offer, saying, 'I deem it inconsistent with my duty; you must excuse me.'" Mrs. Davis learned that the two "had invited Mr. Davis to take charge of an expedition to liberate Cuba, and had offered to deposit $100,000 for me, before their departure, with another $100,0000 assured when successful, or a very fine coffee plantation. Of course I was terrified, and grateful to know that the service had been declined."[8]

When López approached Senator Davis in July 1848, the Mississippian was still basking in national acclaim for heroic service in General Zachary Taylor's army during the battle of Buena Vista. Davis's first conversations with proannexation Cuban insurgents had taken place during the Mexican War. And after the war, on June 23, 1848, Davis and his three Cuban friends had met with President Polk to encourage Uncle Sam's goodwill toward López's planned uprising at Cienfuegos.[9]

Although Davis declined López's offer, as he showed his two visitors to the door he offered a suggestion: "The only man I could indicate to you just now is one in whom I have implicit confidence: Robert E. Lee." As a captain in the

Army Corps of Engineers during the Mexican War, Lee was admired for his bold reconnaissance work behind enemy lines. After the war he was restationed at Baltimore.[10]

Lee was intrigued by the offer and traveled to Washington to meet with López. As Jefferson Davis later remembered, "They were anxious to secure his services, and offered him every temptation that ambition could desire, and pecuniary emoluments far beyond any which he could hope other wise to acquire." A "few days" after López's meeting with her husband, Varina Davis recalled, "I was in the drawing-room when an officer came in, that I thought the handsomest person I have ever seen—his manner, too, was the impersonation of kindness. Mr. Davis came in at once, and the handsome stranger and he had a long conversation. Major Lee had been offered the same place, and did not think it consistent with his duty to the U.S. government to accept it."[11]

In the end Calhoun, Davis, and much of the rest of Washington offered López little but discreet words of encouragement. By the late 1840s growing domestic divisions over slavery forestalled more public support for the sort of foreign adventures that had shaped the nation's political life over the past two decades. López would have to appeal to another, less official and more popular, theater of U.S. support—and to another city.

New York, Spring 1849

"New-York is not wanting in capital," boasted E. Porter Belden's popular guidebook of the boomtown where López, frustrated by Washington, was increasingly focusing his efforts by the spring of 1849. With new cargoes and immigrants arriving daily, at midcentury the population of Walt Whitman's "mast-hemmed" Manhattan stood at a half million and counting. Though thousands of the immigrants who arrived in the city each year moved on to America's interior, many others stayed. The city's population had doubled in two decades, and by midcentury roughly half of Manhattan's residents were foreign born. New York installed its first municipal water system only seven years before López's arrival. By midcentury, however, it boasted at least thirty-seven banks, forty-three insurance companies, forty-six foreign consuls, and twelve daily newspapers. A matrix of rail, telegraph, and steamship lines projected the city's powers far beyond the waters of the Hudson River.[12]

The combined forces of immigration and commerce awarded New York a wide economic influence over the rest of the nation that began with its splendid harbor at which ships from both hemispheres called. With the completion of the Erie Canal in 1825, linking New York to the West, and the arrival of the first regularly scheduled transatlantic steamship line three years later, New York became the center of a new international commerce that stretched from the Mississippi River valley to Europe. The arrival of more and more ships transformed New York's harbor into an emporium of world commerce second only to London in annual cargo tonnage. The far-flung investments that followed that trade projected New York's influence still farther. "The capital of New-York is not confined to her own limits," Belden's guidebook boasted, "It is to be found invested in works of internal improvement, as well as traversing the whole world."[13]

In New York, López found no congressional halls to prowl. He did find a city with long-standing ties—public and clandestine, political and economic—to Latin America. Washington's interest in foreign adventures waned with each new round of congressional debate over slavery. But New York City retained a healthy appetite for foreign enterprises. Its large Cuban exile community and a steady stream of immigrants and political exiles furnished an obvious reservoir of potential recruits, and its considerable trade with the Caribbean offered still more possibilities. As early as 1634, when the Dutch West India Company acquired the island of Curaçao as a bootleg trading post, New York's ships had ventured into the Caribbean. During the eighteenth and nineteenth centuries, whether under the British or U.S. flag, New York had numbered among the beneficiaries of those brief episodes when Spain permitted free trade between North America and Cuba.[14]

After West Indian emancipation, in 1833, disrupted exports from Jamaica and other British colonies, Cuba had become New York's principal supplier of sugar. Drawing the island still closer, during the 1840s New York merchants established countinghouses in Havana, Matanzas, and other ports. New York also was home base for George Law's United States Mail Steamship Company and other steamer lines that called on Cuba, many of which had established their own countinghouses on the island.[15]

As New York financiers had won control over much of the South's cotton trade soon after national independence by advancing capital to cash-strapped growers, so they now wielded influence over Cuba's sugar planters. Drake

Brothers and Company, for instance, owned by Law's steamship company, ranked as one of Havana's largest commercial houses. Drake Brothers, along with other northern countinghouses, was drawn still further into the island's economic life by its involvement with Cuba's slave trade.[16]

By the 1850s New Yorkers and other northerners would even own direct interests in Cuban plantations. "I find quite a number of planters from the United States residing here, and they nearly all hail from the Northern States," observed the South Carolina travel writer George W. Williams. New York's Drake Brothers owned Saratoga, one of the island's most lucrative sugar plantations. Such direct ties encouraged sympathies for Cuban annexation among New Yorkers. In still other cases, ties to the cotton South produced the same result: New Yorkers with vested interests in the South's cotton industry acquired the same fears held by southern planters of what the end of Cuban slavery would portend for the South's agricultural empire.[17]

The city's ties to filibustering extended back to at least 1806, when New York provided a ship, financial backing, and one hundred volunteers for Francisco Miranda's ill-fated expedition to Venezuela. Seeking to liberate his native land from Spanish domination, Miranda had claimed, falsely, that he enjoyed the support of President Thomas Jefferson. During the nineteenth century's early decades, privateers from New York who had robbed British ships during the War of 1812 upon the return of peace simply turned their spyglasses toward Spanish ships. Further vexing Spain, New York shipyards constructed ships for Latin American rebels.[18]

Even after national revolutions across Latin America had stripped Spain of most of its overseas empire, New Yorkers continued their pursuits in the region. Since 1830, after all, New Yorkers had been enthusiastic speculators in Mexican land grants in Texas. And in 1846, when war erupted between the United States and Mexico, the city burned with patriotic fervor, furnishing both volunteers and supplies for the war effort. Perhaps equally important, New York's jingoistic penny press—led by the nation's two largest newspapers, the New York *Herald* and the New York *Sun*—fanned the flames of war hysteria with a ceaseless sirocco of Manifest Destiny rhetoric.[19]

In New York City, López also found his most important U.S. ally, the journalist John L. O'Sullivan, with his personal and business ties to Cuba and his long-standing commitment to expansionism. While López could have stepped from the pages of a romantic novel, O'Sullivan carried all the aplomb of an ink-stained scrivener: the New York lawyer, editor, Manifest Destiny propagandist, and Democratic party activist was of slight build and pale complexion. A bushy mustache and thick glasses framed his long narrow face with its high forehead. Henry Thoreau, whose first published work appeared in O'Sullivan's *United States Magazine*, found the editor "a rather puny looking man." Henry Wadsworth Longfellow, who met him in the late 1830s, saw a "young man, with weak eyes, and great spectacles" who was also, Longfellow added, "a humbug."[20]

Still, O'Sullivan had a quiet intensity that snagged attention. As even Thoreau admitted, "His soft, melodic voice, which attracted the attention of the listener, compensated for his unprepossessing appearance." Physical demeanor aside, if any man was born for filibustering, it was John L. O'Sullivan. His father, John Thomas O'Sullivan, a lifelong merchant seaman, had sailed on Francisco Miranda's filibuster to Venezuela. The son was born in 1813 in Gibraltar harbor aboard a British brig under a war-burnished sky. On the day of the future journalist's birth, the father, an Irish-born naturalized U.S. citizen, was serving as U.S. consul to the Barbary states, when a kind-hearted British admiral had taken him and his pregnant wife, Mary, aboard to escape an outbreak of the plague.[21]

Captain O'Sullivan drowned at sea in 1824, trying to save passengers on a sinking ship. Three years later Mary O'Sullivan and her children moved from London to Washington. After becoming a strident Loco Foco Democrat during his 1830s student days at Columbia College, O'Sullivan and his brother-in-law Samuel Langtree in 1835 purchased the *Metropolitan*, a struggling semiweekly literary and political paper in Washington. Two years later they folded the *Metropolitan* and founded the *United States Magazine and Democratic Review*, which would win O'Sullivan his national reputation as a writer and Democratic party gadfly. Even before Martin Van Buren won the presidency in 1836, Langtree and O'Sullivan had been planning a monthly magazine devoted to Democratic party politics and literature. The Whigs by then could claim several such journals, but the Democracy lacked a showcase for its own most important writers and thinkers. With Van Buren's election, O'Sullivan and Langtree hoped that federal patronage, printing contracts, would come their way. Within months of beginning their new venture, they had secured promises of contributions from an impressive roster of writers associated with the party—including Thoreau, Walt Whitman, John Greenleaf Whittier, William Cullen Bryant, and O'Sullivan's close friend Nathaniel Hawthorne.

Expectations of financial assistance, however, went unfulfilled in the wake of the panic of 1837. Even President Van Buren showed little interest in the magazine, though it was often called a Van Buren organ. The president's favored editor remained Francis Blair of the Washington *Globe*, and Blair, jealous of O'Sullivan, saw to it that the two young journalists were denied federal printing jobs. O'Sullivan would spend much of the rest of his life as a seeker of federal patronage. Expected posts from presidents Van Buren and Polk never came. And when the long-awaited patronage finally did arrive—President Franklin Pierce would make O'Sullivan minister to Portugal—he lost the post four years later when James Buchanan moved into the White House.

It was during the summer of 1845 that O'Sullivan coined the term *Manifest Destiny*. At the time President Polk, awaiting the Republic of Texas's acceptance of his annexation offer, also was bracing for an expected war with Mexico. Amid rumors of British and French intrigues in Texas, O'Sullivan, in an editorial in the *United States Magazine*, urged Whigs and Democrats to unite to oppose foreign powers that exemplified "a spirit of hostile interference against us, for the avowed object of thwarting our policy and hampering our power, limiting our greatness and checking the fulfillment of our manifest destiny to overspread the continent allotted by Providence for the free development of our yearly multiplying millions."[22] He repeated the phrase in a December 1845 editorial in the New York *Morning News*, the paper, backed by wealthy New York Democrats, that O'Sullivan and fellow radical Samuel Tilden had founded a year earlier to promote Polk's presidential candidacy and to heal party rifts in time for the general election.

What validated the president's expansionist military policy, O'Sullivan wrote, was "the right of our manifest destiny to overspread and to possess the whole of the continent which Providence has given us for the development of the great experiment of liberty and federative self-government entrusted to us." Days later, the term began appearing in congressional debates and, picked up by journalists, entered the nation's political vocabulary. O'Sullivan left the *Morning News* in May 1846, and the paper soon failed. That same month he also sold his interest in the *United States Magazine*, though he would continue to write for the magazine.[23]

Narciso López and John O'Sullivan apparently became partners soon after López's arrival in New York. To López—apparently unaware that O'Sullivan had given President Polk advance details of the ultimately aborted Cienfuegos uprising of 1848—the famous editor, with his many contacts and expansionist credentials, must have seemed the ideal coconspirator.[24]

But was there an incongruity between O'Sullivan's earlier politics and this cause so devoted to expansionism and to the preservation of elite wealth built on slavery? O'Sullivan had begun his political life as a member of the Loco Focos, a radical insurgency within New York City's Democratic party devoted to Jacksonian laissez-faire economics and the rights of a broadly, if vaguely, defined entity they called "labor." Loco Focos opposed soft money, state funding of canals, and state licensing of banks. Though their name persisted as a Whig pejorative for Democrats well into the century, the Loco Focos withered away during the panic of 1837, and a new radical wing of the state party—after 1846 known as Barnburners—took up their causes. O'Sullivan had cast his lot with the Barnburners by 1848, when López arrived in the United States. The Barnburners' very name linked them to Wilmot Proviso zealotry. Underscoring their insistence on ideology over party unity, it came from the legend of a New York Dutch farmer who, to rid his barn of rats, burned the structure to the ground. Consistent with such pro–Wilmot Proviso zeal, O'Sullivan's own New York *Morning News*, though it supported the Mexican War, called on President Polk to ban the introduction of slave labor into any new territories won in the conflict.[25]

Even O'Sullivan was mindful of the appearance of contradiction between his Barnburner politics and his devotion to López's cause. In August 1847, anticipating Cuba's acquisition, O'Sullivan pointedly assured Secretary of State Buchanan that "we Barnburners will be as much pleased at it as the Southerners themselves." The journalist, of course, had personal links to slavery, elite wealth, and Cuba. His family in Washington had owned household servants, and his sister Mary had married the Cuban planter Cristóbal Madan. O'Sullivan himself believed that blacks were mentally inferior.[26]

The devotion of New York's radical Democrats to the plight of urban laborers was never as unwavering as their rhetoric suggested. Though the Loco Focos, for instance, adopted the rhetoric of New York City's Workingmen's party of the late 1820s, they were not a working-class movement. The Loco Focos supported the rights of "labor" but defined the term in its broadest Jacksonian usage to include all of the "producing classes": mechanics, farmers, small entrepreneurs, laborers, craftsmen, and even planters. They rarely supported strikes, and their membership included few members of organized labor. Like the Barnburners, whose ranks included some of New York's wealthiest men, the Loco Focos were opposed not so much to wealth as to monopolistic practices that stood in the way of their own attainment of riches. In 1836 the Loco Focos' "patriarch" Moses Jacques readily accepted the presidency of an insurance company.[27]

The orthodoxy that Barnburners brought to their laissez-faire positions on state involvement in banking and canals was never duplicated on issues of slavery and national expansion. As the Mexican War agitated long-running debates over slavery in the United States, some Barnburners, such as William Cullen Bryant, did protest that the conflict served only "the slave power" and raised moral questions about U.S. involvement in the conflict. But other radicals—such as O'Sullivan, New York senator John Dix, and Manhattan rabble-rouser Mike Walsh—welcomed the war and its promises of territorial conquests. Expansionist enterprises, after all, had enjoyed the support of New York radicals since at least 1835 when—to the dismay of abolitionists—Alexander Ming, Jr., John Windt, and other prominent Loco Focos joined local bankers, merchants, and western land speculators in supporting the Texas independence movement.[28]

Neither the Loco Focos nor any Barnburner faction embraced abolitionism. Party radicals of the 1840s were generally hostile to it. Indeed, the Loco Focos had broken with New York *Post* journalist William Leggett, their political mentor, over abolitionism. After Leggett, in 1835, condemned President Jackson for antiabolitionist positions, Barnburner leader John Van Buren, son of Martin Van Buren, was among those in Albany who rallied to the president's support.[29]

The Barnburners focused on opposing slavery's spread into new areas—for many a tactical compromise based on the idea, common to that age, that slavery, with its ever-present need for new, fertile lands, had to be constantly expanding to survive. Thus, if the institution could be hemmed in at its existing borders, it would, to use David Wilmot's phrase, "wear itself out." For other—perhaps most—Barnburners, however, support for the congressional resolution that even Wilmot called the "White Man's Proviso" turned less on moral qualms than on their desire to preserve opportunities for free white laborers. As Wilmot put it in an 1847 speech, "In God's name, as we love our country and our race, let us stop in this mad career of human slavery. The negro race already occupies enough of this fair continent." Similarly, in 1848 John Van

Buren, opposing slavery's extension, asserted, "You cannot induce the white labouring man to work beside a black slave."[30]

Loco Foco and Barnburner celebrations of the virtues of free yeoman labor rarely extended to free black labor. Even many New York Democratic radicals who morally questioned slavery viewed debates over it as a distraction from the business of improving the lot of whites. O'Sullivan, for instance, throughout his career urged, according to his biographer, "moderation in debate" when discussing slavery and generally avoided the subject. Where slavery already existed, New York's radical Democrats accepted it as a sad fact of life, an inheritance which southerners had no choice but to maintain. In that spirit of tolerance, Loco Focos and their ideological descendants, in order to secure national influence, established working alliances with party brethren in slaveholding states.[31]

Beyond doctrinal matters, many of López's Barnburner supporters had profitable ties to both slavery and Cuba—among them O'Sullivan, steamship magnate George Law, and former New York City mayor William Havemeyer, a wealthy sugar merchant. Perhaps patrician Whig and New York diarist George Templeton Strong best caught the opportunism of the day: assaying López's supporters, he ventured that many seemed primarily motivated by a simple "lust after other people's productive coffee estates." Radical Democrat Mike Walsh, a prominent politician, gang leader, and journalist of the thirties and forties—a Barnburner when they were up, a Hunker when the Barnburners were down—admitted, "When I look upon some of the mercenary, grasping and unprincipled knaves who call themselves barnburners, I begin to fear that I may lose my identify as the radical leader, and become transformed through the legerdemain of these spurious pretenders into a regular hunker. The fact of the business is, there is not a particle of difference between the leaders of either faction."[32]

Among the prominent New York City politicians who supported López was Captain Isaiah Rynders, commander of a Hudson River sloop during his youth, street brawler, Barnburner orator, and gang leader. A contemporary recalled Rynders as "lithe, dark, handsome," of "sinewy form, with a prominent nose, and piercing black eyes—a knowing smile, and a sharp look together. He was cool and enterprising in his manners, and fluent and audacious in his speech. He had the reputation of being a member of the sporting fraternity."[33] In an era when gangs, headed by colorful bosses, played a vital role in New

York City politics, none achieved more renown than Rynders's own Empire Club, a position paid due respect by the party's more elite leaders.[34] In January 1850, for instance, after local authorities charged Rynders with instigating the Astor Place riots, his attorney was none other than Barnburner leader "Prince" John Van Buren. Later, when federal charges were brought against López's allies in New York, Van Buren, ever the loyal Barnburner, once again stepped in as a defense counsel.[35]

In 1844 Rynders and O'Sullivan served as lieutenants in James K. Polk's New York presidential campaign. On the day before the election, Rynders, "mounted on a white charger," and his Empire Club gang, "one thousand strong," accompanied by fireworks and "twenty bands," led twenty thousand other New Yorkers on a torchlight procession through Manhattan's streets.[36]

In lower Manhattan, where foreign-born workers formed a majority of the electorate in most neighborhoods, each boss ruled a ward, and together the bosses controlled citywide elections. The appeal of individual ward bosses rested on personality, pugilistic talent, and ability to deliver patronage. In exchange for support at the polls or, perhaps, help with breaking up an opponent's meeting, bosses rewarded their minions with appointments to anything from a tax assessor's post to a job sweeping streets. As political boss of lower Manhattan's Sixth Ward, Isaiah Rynders presided over a crowded district teeming with single, white, young males of foreign birth—as it happened, exactly the sort who flocked to López in late 1849. That September, describing a filibuster recruiting meeting in Manhattan, the New York *Tribune* reported that "there was a great want of stability about the proceedings, most of the persons present being boys, who amused themselves playing about, making noises, &c."[37]

Newspaper accounts of the 1849 conspiracy abound in references to the youth, working-class status, and foreign origins of New York recruits to López's army. Any list, if one ever existed, of the individual New Yorkers who joined López that year is long lost. However, a list of prisoners sentenced to hard labor by the Spanish from another López army, organized two years later, offers a revealing glimpse into the demographics of filibustering. Of the 142 men on the list, their ages range from 16 to 40, with an average age of 24.6.[38]

One also assumes that most of López's single, white, young male enlistees were restless and enjoyed a good fight. In the summer of 1851, Tom Bryan, a twenty-one-year-old Tennesseean, would sign up with López hoping to compensate for all the adventures he had missed by not fighting in the Mexican War. Finding his way to New Orleans, Bryan checked into a hotel, bought a newspaper and sat down to read it. The *Picayune* and the *Delta*, he recalled, both brimmed with stories of "the great revolution in Cuba." "It set me on fire," he later wrote. "The only thing I was affraid of was that I would not get there in time to see any of the funn." Richardson Hardy, another volunteer, would recall of his experiences with López in 1850 that young boys and men "flocked to the standard. They cared not where it was to be planted, so [long as] it should be the emblem of a noble cause, and those who flung it to the breeze peril all in its defense."[39]

The New York *Tribune* described López's enlistees of late 1849 as "young men of that class who are usually most ready for any adventure that promises movement, no matter in what direction, or for what purpose." Similarly, the New York *Herald* would describe an 1851 pro-Lopez rally in Jersey City, as composed "chiefly of the hard fisted working class, fired with the contagious enthusiasm that seems spreading all over the land." López's August 1849 offer to his New York enlistees of "$1,000 and 'plenty of plunder' " was in a sense, then, just another cut of Democratic patronage—a bit riskier than sweeping streets, perhaps. But with promises of far more "funn" and a far thicker slice of pork.[40]

Harrisburg, Pennsylvania, August 11, 1849

The throngs struggled to grasp Zachary Taylor's hand as his clanking open barouche, drawn by "four splendid horses," rolled through downtown Harrisburg, Pennsylvania, from the train stop at the foot of Vine Street. Even with his long, world-weary, chiseled face and unruly tangle of gray hair, the sixty-four-year-old president—garlanded for the occasion with a wreath of flowers around his neck—seemed a man on top of the world. Accompanied by a martial band and other carriages bearing local dignitaries, the president was greeted by "cheer upon cheer" as his entourage snaked through the mile-long parade route. Church bells rang, necks craned from every window, cannon salutes roared. Amid the din, cries of "*Old* Zack!" "Buena Vista!" and "Give 'em Grape!" could be clearly heard, testimony to Taylor's other renown as the chief U.S. Army general in the recently concluded Mexican War. When Taylor finally mounted the speaker's platform in front of Coverly's Hotel, the entire square facing the building teemed with noisy admirers.[41]

It was shortly past three o'clock on August 11, 1849, on the new president's first trip out of Washington since taking office six months earlier, and Taylor meant to flatter his hosts. "The object of my visit to Pennsylvania is in no way connected with politics," he assured the crowd. "I have long desired to become somewhat familiar with the resources of this great commonwealth. Her agricultural and manufacturing improvements have always been to me objects of the highest interest." But even casual observers of the day's politics knew that the president had other reasons for touring Pennsylvania. With support in his native South slipping away, Taylor had embarked on a rail tour of the North to preserve the goodwill he still enjoyed in Pennsylvania and other mid-Atlantic states.

Many voters had come to suspect that the job of president was too big for Zachary Taylor. The country was one million square miles larger than it had been when his predecessor James K. Polk took office four years earlier. The annexation of Texas and Oregon, coupled with the conquest of California and New Mexico, territorial spoils of the recent Mexican War, had increased the nation's total area by a third and given it a new Atlantic-to-Pacific breadth. As commanding general of the U.S. Army of the Occupation in the Mexican War, Taylor had played a hero's role in that expansion, and subsequent popular acclaim had catapulted him to the presidency. A grand irony, however, attended that succession. As President Taylor soon discovered, the federal government's control over those new and vast western provinces existed mainly on paper. He often spoke of such lofty principles as the primacy of federal law and Washington's exercise of sovereignty over the nation. But, excluding post office employees, the central government's entire executive branch at midcentury numbered only 4,322 officials.[42]

While the federal government continued its increasingly irritable debate with the southern states over the limits of the central government's authority, in much of the Republic's new western realm Uncle Sam lacked even debating partners. In some parts, Mexican town governments continued to operate. In isolated cases, gold miners in California and Mormon settlers in the Salt Lake basin had adopted some degree of self-governance. But aside from those far-flung exceptions, no civilian government existed in California and vast New Mexico, which sprawled across areas now occupied by the modern states of Nevada, Arizona, Utah, and parts of New Mexico, Wyoming, and Colorado. With the exception of Texas's state government and Oregon's new civilian territorial government, most of the Far West lacked any functioning day-to-day government.

The federal government's claim of military authority over largely unsurveyed and unexplored California and New Mexico, uncrossed by telegraph or rail lines, resonated as an empty boast. Even the system of Franciscan missions that had once provided a semblance of organized society for whites in Spanish North America had all but disappeared after the founding of the Mexican republic in 1822. In California and New Mexico, as in Texas, Mexico's new government had secularized the missions, in an effort to wean them from the state-supported Franciscans and to make missions self-supporting, with salaries for priests and other expenses defrayed by tithes from local parishioners. In practice, however, the missions simply became targets for rampant anticlericalism and greedy politicians and fell into ruin.[43]

In parts of the West, ad hoc cabals claimed "squatter's sovereignty" over local affairs. Indians dominated other sections, and a dispersed mix of gold prospectors, thieves, adventurers, pioneers, and self-fashioned sagebrush potentates, holders of vast Spanish and Mexican land grants, filled in the rest. Taylor had the army at his disposal. But who could govern by military fiat a republic dispersed over three million square miles? Vast distances of mountains, deserts, and plains yawned between the Atlantic seaboard and faraway Pacific ports, overwhelming the army's capabilities.

Only to a limited degree could Taylor even call on his own Whig party to enforce his will. The annexation of the Republic of Texas in 1845 and the subsequent Mexican War had reawakened national and intraparty debates over slavery, and since August 1846 "Conscience Whigs" of the North had pounded a steady drumbeat for congressional passage of the Wilmot Proviso banning the introduction of slavery into any recently won lands. The measure had passed the House several times but never the Senate. Even so, its constant resurrection underscored the growing divisions that bedeviled the Republic, with "Cotton Whigs" of both the North and South opposing it as needless "agitation" and a slap at southern veterans of the Mexican War.

Thus, it was a badly fractured Whig party that had delivered Taylor's victory in the presidential race the previous November. What produced his triumph was less Whig unity than the fact that even greater troubles bedeviled the Democrats and their standard-bearer, Michigan's U.S. Senator Lewis Cass—vexations compounded by the third-party Free-Soil ticket candidacy of former Democratic president Martin Van Buren. General Taylor won the race even though he remained a novice and untalented politician throughout the campaign. Though a war hero of popular acclaim, he had no stable ideological or regional constituency to call upon. The fractious Whig party, seeking unity by avoiding troublesome issues, had nominated Taylor in 1848 precisely because his political views were largely unknown. The subsequent race did little to diminish the mystery; surrogates spoke for Taylor during most of the campaign. After one gaffe, an aide advised him to keep silent before any further inquiries about his beliefs.[44]

Disdainful of the spoils system, President Taylor was slow to uncork the traditional tonic of party unity, federal patronage. And even when the Taylor patronage finally did pour, it was hardly the elixir of old. Earlier, more politically able presidents such as Andrew Jackson and James Polk had used patronage to punish enemies, reward allies, and generally preserve party order and discipline. By 1849, however, growing divisions among the Whigs had weakened the potion. When Taylor, under the sway of northern advisers like publisher Thurlow Weed, did get around to dispensing the patronage—to Conscience Whigs—it deepened, rather than healed, party wounds.[45]

Whigs often had been reluctant partners in the continental expansion promoted by Democrats in the 1840s, but now the task of enforcing Washington's control over the vast empire had fallen to a Whig. It was a thankless job, compounded by the growing debates over slavery. President Polk had resolved at least one territorial conundrum for Taylor. Treaty negotiations with Britain in 1846 had ended the two nations' "joint occupation" of the vast Oregon territory. The treaty gave the United States sole title to the territory south of the forty-ninth parallel, to what later became the states of Oregon, Washington, Idaho, and part of Montana. Settlers in the new territory soon organized a provisional government that banned the introduction of slavery, thereby delaying for two years Washington's acceptance of Oregon's territorial status. Polk, in 1848, reasoning that the territory lay north of the old 36° 30' line of 1820 dividing free and slave states, signed legislation allowing Oregonians to organize a government without slavery.

The more difficult territorial questions, however, remained for Taylor to solve. In Texas, already a state when he took the oath of office, slavery was long entrenched, and no movement emerged to challenge it. California and New Mexico, however, with no civilian territorial or state governments, remained under military rule, while the federal and state governments—and western émigrés—quarreled over whether slavery would be allowed in either. Although black slavery did not exist in either place—and many southerners were convinced that for reasons of topography and climate, it never could— the South's planters still pressed for the legal right to introduce the practice. National acknowledgment of that right, Calhoun and other planter politicians argued, would preserve the sanctity of the South's own "peculiar institution."

Growing sentiment for the Wilmot Proviso, meanwhile, favored containing slavery within its existing southeastern and Texas boundaries. But even those boundaries lay in dispute: the state government of slaveholding Texas argued that its borders extended deep into New Mexico, westward and northward to the source of the Rio Grande—a claim that took in the bustling trading town of Santa Fe. Polk had tacitly accepted the Texas claim, but Taylor challenged it as a defiance of federal authority. There was even talk of a military confrontation between Washington and the state of Texas.[46]

By the summer of 1849 the new president knew that he faced widespread disaffection. Many northern Whigs saw his professed nonpartisanship as a sour aloofness, and among party members from his native South, there was fuming over his stand on Texas's claims in New Mexico. There was also anger, vented in recent Whig defeats in southern congressional elections, over the predominantly northern composition of the Taylor cabinet. Only Secretary of War George W. Crawford and Navy Secretary William B. Preston could claim southern origins. And in the cabinet only Secretary Crawford seemed favorably disposed toward slavery. Moreover, as the Jackson *Mississippian* mourned, neither of the two occupied a post abundant with civilian offices to dispense: "These are the weeping willows—the solitary monuments in the Cabinet—mournful in their solitude—of the existence of our Southern States! What is *their* influence!"[47]

Powerful southern planters of both parties complained about the president's increasingly obvious preference for the early admission of New Mexico and California as free states. Taylor had decided that he and the Congress could avoid endless bickering by allowing each territory to hold a constitutional convention to decide whether or not to allow slavery—and Taylor had no doubt that each would elect to ban it: "The States will be admitted—free and Whig," he secretly assured an ally in the spring of 1849.[48]

Even so, by August the combined miseries of Washington's political and meteorological heat had taken their toll on the president. Taylor, said a visitor, looked "put down considerable." A tour of the northern states—increasingly viewed as his main political base—seemed a good idea, despite the deadly cholera epidemic sweeping much of the nation that summer. And so on August 9, two days before he reached Harrisburg, the president had abandoned Washington for a tour of Pennsylvania, New York, and New England.[49]

On August 11, after his speech in Harrisburg, President Taylor repaired to Coverly's Hotel and spent the early evening greeting well-wishers. But despite his best efforts, the old man's spirits soon flagged, and he retired early. When his chronic diarrhea struck the next morning, he delayed his scheduled departure. The next day, August 13, still visibly weak, the president finally left for his next stop, Carlisle, Pennsylvania. Clearly, the tour had become a burden. "The president is quite-unwell," reported the New York *Tribune*. "The fatigue which he is compelled to undergo in shaking hands, standing for a long time, getting in and out of carriages and cars, added to the constant excitement of the thousands of questions that are put to him concerning almost every imaginable thing in the moral, political and physical world, is enough surely to wear him down."

Among those in Harrisburg who saw and heard Taylor talk of the various sectional issues plaguing the nation, most were unaware of an entirely new problem facing him. On the day he arrived, the president, without fanfare, had issued a proclamation. "There is reason to believe," it read, "that an armed expedition is about to be fitted out in the United States, with an intention to invade the Island of Cuba, or some of the provinces of Mexico." The document warned that participation in such an enterprise—what popular venacular called a "buffalo hunt"—violated the U.S. Neutrality Act of 1818, as well as treaty obligations to Spain, and cautioned that those who joined it should not "expect the interference of this government, in any form, in their behalf, no matter to what extremities they may be reduced in consequence of their conduct."[50]

Days later, as Taylor's proclamation appeared in newspapers, supporters praised it as evidence of his ironclad devotion to the rule of law. The New York *Herald* assured the nation, "The proclamation of the President against the buffalo hunt, believed to be organizing for a descent upon Cuba, with a view to the seizure of the island, is another proof of the fixed determination of the administration rigidly to stand to its treaty obligations."[51]

To detractors, however, the Harrisburg proclamation offered but the latest opportunity for public ridicule of a president widely viewed as a mere figurehead for more powerful northern politicians. The Cincinnati *Enquirer*, noting the place and timing of the proclamation and the fact that it also bore the signature of Secretary of State John Clayton, charged that it sought to deceive a gullible public into believing that Taylor actually ran his administration. "It was a weak invention—a shallow trick. The proclamation was prepared at Washington with the understanding that it was to be transmitted to Washington after the General had got on his travels." The Detroit *Free Press*—mocking neoclassical attributes ascribed to the president by his admirers—even suggested that Taylor had been the butt of a practical joke by local tormentors. "That was a cruel hoax that those Pennsylvania Dutchmen played off on the 'Second Washington' in this 'Heroic Age,'" the *Free Press* crowed.[52]

No doubt many readers reacted with puzzlement to the warning and its imprecision ("Cuba, or some of the provinces of Mexico"), while others barely noticed it. Newspapers of the day teemed with rumors of such conspiracies. Over the past few months alone, newspapers had published rumors of expeditions by U.S. filibuster armies to Canada, Ireland, Cuba, New Mexico, and Mexico.[53]

On August 11, the day that Taylor issued his proclamation, the New York *Herald* had tantalized its readers with a report on a "secret expedition" allegedly being assembled in New Orleans and coastal cities of the North, principally New York. A *Herald* correspondent in New Orleans reported that the New York army represented only one tentacle of a much larger effort "fitting out at New Orleans" and bound for the far northern tier of Mexico's states. "Now, the object of this expedition is to carry out the formation of the Republic of the Sierra Madre, to separate that territory from the Mexican republic, proclaim its independence, and maintain it by force." A bold mission, perhaps; but then again, as the correspondent noted, "it was in this way that the separation and independence of Texas was brought about." In New Orleans alone, the correspondent claimed, more than fifteen hundred men had already "announced their readiness to embark on this expedition, and the number is increasing every day." Fifteen or twenty thousand muskets had been shipped to New Orleans from New York and other eastern cities. Commenting on its correspondent's report, the *Herald* speculated that the expedition might yet satisfy all of the appetites for wealth, adventure, and land left unsated by the Guadalupe Hidalgo treaty a year and a half earlier: "It is highly probable that the restless spirits left in this republic by the Mexican war, and who were unable to reach California, may bestir themselves with such activity as to be able to get up this expedition."[54]

Over the next few weeks, the *Herald*—and soon other popular papers— began reporting that in lower Manhattan a shadowy group was meeting every other night at Lafayette Hall, a Broadway theater. The men constituted some sort of expeditionary army bent on conquests in southern climes, but their precise destination remained unclear—perhaps Mexico, or Cuba, or even New Mexico, now under U.S. title. The vagueness of the stories only made them more intriguing.

After Taylor's proclamation, press accounts of the expedition became more specific: three hundred mercenaries, soon to be joined by others from New Orleans, had gathered on tiny Round Island, a windswept crescent of sand off Mississippi's Gulf coast, ostensibly on their way "to protect the mines of California." But that, the newspapers claimed, was just a cover designed to forestall federal interference in a vast conspiracy with "highly respectable men at the head of it, several of them officers of the United States Army." Recruiters, the papers asserted, were busy casting the conspiracy's nets well beyond Manhattan to Philadelphia, New Jersey, and other locales; "agents are out in all directions enlisting men," reported the *Herald*. The recruiters, however, said little about final destinations. At one Lafayette Hall meeting, a "respectable looking young man" asked for more details and was told, "If you mean really to join, we shall be happy to give you all [the] information that 'we' can—but otherwise [we] don't like to answer persons inquiring through an idle curiosity." Even after the young man declared he was "in earnest," the recruiter offered only more vagueness. "We want men to have a gun and use it—ours is no child's play—we may land at Brazos or New Orleans and go overland [whither not stated]—you must be prepared for every emergency." Recruiters promised volunteers $7 per month, plus two bounties—$300 after four months, $1,000 after one year. "Beside this you shall receive subsistence and clothes; all you are required to bring is a blanket and a gun."[55]

For weeks the *Tribune* and other New York papers remained vague about the conspiracy's goal. Finally, on August 15, the *Herald*—owned and edited by the brash Scotsman James Gordon Bennett—asserted that since news of the president's proclamation had "spread like wildfire throughout the city, and formed the all-absorbing topic of conversation, inquiry and conjecture," it was time to lift all remaining veils. The "language of this proclamation is very loose and indefinite," observed the *Herald*. "Ours is more precise, and we shall now proceed to lay it before the public." The expedition, the paper avowed, was bent on "revolutionizing the island of Cuba. That is their object—their sole object. The movement has been long contemplated, and originates not in this country, but in Cuba itself. It has been set on foot by a number of the most influential and wealthy planters in that island." Two weeks later the *Herald* added that the expedition's U.S. leaders were "in constant communication with Havana merchants, who somehow or other, happen to be here just now. Some of these gentlemen have been at the meetings; and may easily be distinguished by their complexion, dress, and moustache. All of these men seem earnest and serious. You will seldom see them smile."[56]

That summer, as word of the conspiracy began reaching the White House, Secretary of State Clayton on July 31 wrote Malcolm M. Mearis, a departmental "special agent," and asked him to visit "Baltimore, Philadelphia and New York and perhaps Boston" to investigate reports of an armed expedition being organized "for some foreign destination." Widening his search, Clayton over the next few weeks generated a round-robin of correspondence among federal officials in those cities, asking marshals, special agents, U.S. attorneys, and customs agents to report anything suspicious. He also dispatched two more special agents to travel the country and scour the conspiracy's likely haunts.[57]

That same day the administration dispatched the U.S. Navy—the Home Squadron, based in the Gulf of Mexico—against the filibusters gathering on Round Island, off Mississippi's coast. Navy Secretary William Preston reported to the squadron's commodore, Foxhall A. Parker, that some six hundred men, apparently recruited in New Orleans, had been landed on the island. Federal officials expected another eight hundred from New Orleans would soon arrive; and "corresponding numbers," Preston believed, had been enlisted in Boston, New York, and Baltimore. Another navy commander described the men on Round Island as "unquestionably a band of reckless adventurers. Four-fifths of the privates, I am happy to state, are foreigners—Irish and Dutch, chiefly."[58]

At least for now, Preston assured Parker, the Round Islanders were un-armed. Their leader was a flamboyant Louisianan, Colonel George W. White, a veteran of the Mexican War and, more recently, of Yucatán's civil war. White had led a group of volunteers from the United States to join whites loyal to Yu-catán, then an independent state, fighting Indian insurgents. According to a deposition later taken from one of the Round Island filibusters, White had lured his recruits with promises of "*plunder, drink, women* and *tobacco.*"

Publicly, White claimed that his troops were emigrants to California awaiting a passing steamer. Navy Secretary Preston, however—still convinced that the men on Round Island constituted an army awaiting arms and reinforcements—believed that the entire Gulf wing of the filibuster was plan-ning a rendezvous on nearby Cat Island. He believed that the hireling soldiers would undergo military drills on Cat Island before sailing for Cuba sometime between August 20 and 25 aboard a steamship, the *Fanny*, then berthed at New Orleans. Preston ordered Commodore Parker to spare no efforts in blocking the *Fanny*'s departure or, if that was not possible, interdicting its passage to Cuba. "Should you, on reaching Cat Island and its vicinity, ascertain that a hostile movement is on foot and has proceeded against the Island of Cuba, you will repair with the force under your command to that island, and use all proper means in your power by preventing their landing, so as to avert and prevent the violation of our obligations of amity and peace with Spain."[59]

On August 7 Logan Hunton, the U.S. attorney in New Orleans and a trusted Taylor loyalist, wrote the secretary of state to inform him that the conspirators had cells in Boston, New York, Baltimore, and New Orleans. They planned to rendezvous off Mississippi's coast, with their numbers likely to reach into the thousands. Their destination was definitely Cuba. An August 13 letter to Clay-ton from Angel Calderón de la Barca, Spain's minister in Washington, warned of a conspiracy in New Orleans "and at other points of this Union" that planned "to strike a sudden blow at the Island of Cuba." The diplomat asked the administration to take "prompt and adequate measures" against the ef-fort.[60]

Round Island, Mississippi, August 18, 1849

On August 18, when the U.S. Navy's sloop-of-war *Albany* sailed within sight of Round Island, V. M. Randolph, the ship's commander, was hoping to disperse the men gathered on the island with a few cannon blasts. But when wide shoals kept him ten miles from the island, far outside cannon range, he decided to summon other ships, form a blockade, and wait for hunger—or boredom—to disperse them.

By August 28 the navy steamer *Water Witch* had joined the *Albany*, and two other navy steamers, the *Zachary Taylor* and the *Walker*, were due. As they watched Round Island, the crews of the U.S. ships also kept a nervous lookout for the *Fanny* and the *Maria Burt*, two steamers, rumored to be under the conspiracy's command and being outfitted in New Orleans to sail for Round Island. To navy chief Preston, Randolph wrote, "Our present force is too small to keep the men on the island from being received on board, particularly should the two steamers come provided with arms, which is expected." He implored Preston to charter the *Creole*, a commercial "fast steamer" based in New Orleans, and dispatch it—armed and crewed by the U.S. Navy—toward Round Island. On that same day—seventeen days after Taylor's proclamation from Pennsylvania—Randolph sent the Round Islanders a broadside. "The very *mystery*," it read, "which marks the movements and actions of your officers, and the blind ignorance of the men as to the destination of the enterprise, clearly show that the objects and purpose of those at the head of your affairs are known to be *unlawful*, and that *plunder* is the inducement held out to all who embark in this reckless expedition." Later that day the *Flirt*, a U.S. Navy schooner, joined the blockade, but with a draft shallow enough to tempt its captain to sail in close range, it promptly grounded on Round Island's lee.[61]

Randolph's proclamation produced no immediate defectors, but no reinforcements joined the Round Islanders either. As more U.S. Navy ships arrived, sailors from the navy's schooner, the *Flirt*—now free of the sandbar—made routine visits to the island. Filibuster officers, meanwhile, drilled their ragtag volunteers in companies and battalions. Boredom, a searing Gulf sun, restlessness, and material privations, however, bedeviled the islanders; at least one filibuster died in a brawl. Conditions became so bad that to avoid starvation they were reduced to accepting food from the U.S. Navy. On September 5 ninety filibusters, accepting an offer from Randolph, boarded the *Zachary Taylor* for free transportation to New Orleans.

Though President Taylor left day-to-day diplomatic affairs to Secretary of State Clayton, ad hoc armies of U.S. citizens were another matter. Although he embraced the Whigs' concept of a limited presidency—as a candidate he had pledged to let Congress set the nation's direction and to veto only bills he deemed unconstitutional—Taylor was also an experienced military man who believed in a cast-iron chain of command. And in foreign policy matters he believed that chain began at the White House. To Taylor, foreign policy and military matters constitutionally remained the president's exclusive domain, not to be intruded upon by Congress, or states, or private citizens.

Recent Democratic presidents Andrew Jackson and James K. Polk, by contrast, had often tolerated filibusters. Jackson hardly flinched in 1836 when U.S. volunteers, defying his nominal ban on such activity, streamed into Texas to join the fledgling republic's fight for independence against Mexico. After U.S. filibusters rushed to join the Yucatán civil war of the late 1840s, Polk even considered lending official support. Still later, President Franklin Pierce, another Democrat, would give tacit if fickle support for filibustering against Cuba.[62]

Taylor condemned such freelance initiatives. He made it clear early in his administration that he had no patience with Texas's land claims in New Mexico. In July 1849, when Texas's state government threatened to challenge federal authority in New Mexico, he vowed to personally lead a military charge against the threatened rebellion and, if necessary, to execute its leaders, "with less reluctance than I hanged spies and deserters in Mexico!"[63]

In foreign policy Taylor underscored his insistence upon presidential authority with a steely devotion to the Neutrality Act of 1818, the sequel to an April 1793 proclamation by President Washington. As a maritime war erupted that year between France and Great Britain, Washington's fiat had enjoined U.S. citizens from private acts that might compromise official U.S. neutrality. The Neutrality Act of 1794 that followed and revisions in 1797 and 1818 strengthened the president's hand in rooting out filibusters. The 1818 revision enjoined U.S. citizens from joining the independence movements then raging across mainland Latin America, thus extending existing bans against participating in wars between nations to foreign civil conflicts and internal rebellions. It gave the president the power to arrest and punish filibusters before they got under way. Customs agents, suspecting illegal activities, could seize private ships before they sailed. Owners of private armed ships were required to post bond guaranteeing adherence to the law and assurance that the vessel would not be sold to any warring party. Finally, it forbade organizing or assisting any "military expedition or enterprise" against any nation or territory with which the United States was at peace. Punishment was set at up to $3,000 in fines and three years in prison.[64]

In a September 1848 letter to soon-to-be secretary of state John Clayton, presidential candidate Taylor cited the law while condemning a rumored filibuster expedition to northern Mexico. On March 19, 1849, after Taylor had assumed the presidency, Navy Secretary William Ballard Preston cited it as he terminated the conversion of the steamer *United States* into a war vessel for North German Confederation rebels, a project that Polk had tacitly approved. Later that same summer Taylor again stressed the demands of official U.S. neutrality as he challenged the Cuban expedition. The president, Secretary of State Clayton informed agent Malcolm Mearis, equated the disruption of the expedition with "the maintenance of our neutral relations with foreign countries, and the safety of our foreign intercourse."[65]

Timing was everything in enforcing the Neutrality Act. A premature arrest—before a suspect could "begin, or set on foot"—risked acquittal. But delaying arrest chanced allowing the expedition to proceed. A successful prosecution demanded discretion and precise timing. Clayton thus instructed Special Agent Mearis, "You will conduct this investigation with the utmost secrecy and make reports to this Department from time to time as the facts connected with the expedition may be developed."[66]

New York, September 8, 1849

On September 8, as President Taylor, continuing his northern tour, arrived in New York City, good news greeted him. Over breakfast J. Prescott Hall, the U.S. attorney in New York City, told him that the day before, federal officials had seized three expedition steamers: the *New Orleans* and the propeller ship *Florida*, at berths at the foot of lower Manhattan's Grand Street; and the *Sea Gull*, at a Staten Island quarantine station. Aboard the *Sea Gull* government agents found 130 boxes containing 1,000 muskets, swords, and "powder and provisions in plenty." The *New Orleans* had been refitted to seat "800 to 900 passengers."[67]

In the South, meanwhile, Uncle Sam's duel with the Round islanders slouched toward an equally bathetic end. By September 14, as more filibusters accepted the U.S. Navy's offer of free transportation back to the mainland, only 350 of the original 600 remained on Round Island. By October 7 there were 120. Four days later, the final sixty-five filibusters boarded the U.S. Navy steamer *Vixen*. In New Orleans federal agents seized the *Fanny*, the steamer for which the filibusters on Round Island had been waiting in vain.[68]

None of the conspirators were prosecuted; only one was arrested, and he was quickly released. The administration was eager to wash its hands of the entire episode. On September 7, the day before he informed President Taylor of the ship seizures in New York, Secretary of State Clayton had sent a telegram to U.S. Attorney Hall: "No vindictive proceedings are desirable in my judgement, after the enterprise is broken up."[69]

President Taylor and his secretary of state had correctly identified Cuba as the filibusters' destination. But if, upon seizing a few ships, they assumed too quickly that the conspiracy lay "broken up," their overconfidence was understandable. After all, the movement in the United States to annex Cuba had lingered for many years, flaring occasionally, but to no effect. So why shouldn't a simple show of federal muscle suffice to vanquish this latest outbreak? Yes, many questions remained unanswered, but the administration decided it could live with such mysteries, and the president continued his northern tour.

López and O'Sullivan, meanwhile, were left to ponder the perils of their growing reliance on newspapers to promote their cause. Through much of 1849, while López remained in New York, O'Sullivan, as the campaign's business and propaganda manager, had traveled the country calling on his far-flung Democratic party contacts to bolster the conspiracy. Drawing on his experiences as a publicity manager for Polk's presidential campaign, O'Sullivan also began talking to journalists.

In the end O'Sullivan talked too much—too much for a Democratic conspirator operating in a country whose ports were controlled by federal officials who answered to a Whig president and whose hotels and bars often teemed with Spanish spies. About those spies, the *Herald* had fumed: "Is there no law under which these pimps and secret agents of Spanish tyranny can be put out of the way of doing mischief? Do they not come under the vagrant act?" The same *Herald*, however, also chose to boost its circulation—to the peril of the filibusters—with coy hints about a "mysterious" expedition soon to depart Manhattan. By August's end President Taylor and his aides had only to pick up a newspaper to learn all they needed to know about the conspiracy. Such disclosures, recalled Richardson Hardy in his filibuster memoirs, were a bitter lesson in the double-edged sword of publicity: "The next time they would be more prudent than to let such a 'Bagwind' as Bennett, of the Herald, into the secrets; who, by his continual allusions to the subject, mysterious hints, and flaming articles in favor of Cuban Independence, brought the patriotic operations to public notice, and challenged the vigilance of the Government officers." By mid-autumn of 1849, though, the conspiracy had fallen out of the newspapers, the nation had refocused its attention on the debate over slavery in the West—and thoughts of Cuban filibusters had faded like some vaguely recalled late summer storm.[70]

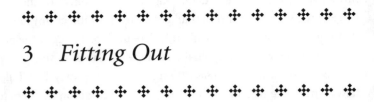

3   Fitting Out

November–December 1849

During the fall of 1849, newspapers friendly to Zachary Taylor praised his use of federal muscle to block what they regarded as a piratical expedition against a sovereign nation. The New York *Herald* gloated that the "foolish attempt at revolution in that island" had been a disaster "because the poor Cubans entrusted their cause to a set of speculators, knaves and cheats." The Whiggish New Orleans *Commercial Bulletin* declared, "Gen. TAYLOR has acted precisely as the emergency required, with a degree of precaution and decision demanded by the occasion, and which meets with the approval of all right minded people."[1]

Antiadministration publications, however, found only arrogance in Taylor's actions. John O'Sullivan's *United States Magazine and Democratic Review* condemned the navy's "inglorious service of the blockade of our own shores." The use of the military, the New Orleans *Delta* charged, abused federal powers and directly assaulted the "sovereignty" of Mississippi. "Men living in the State of Mississippi have been denied the right of free passage within its limits—have had their property seized and appropriated by strangers to the laws of the State."[2]

Another ongoing controversy involving Cuba only sharpened resentments. On July 5 Juan Garcia Rey, a Cuban living in New Orleans, had been discovered to be missing from his rooms by his landlord. Newspapers reported that he had been forcibly returned to Cuba by Spanish officials. Rey had been a jailer in Havana, who, so said Spanish authorities, the previous March had allowed two prisoners, Cirilo Villaverde and Vicente Fernández—the two men arrested for assisting López's foiled uprising of July 1848 inside Cuba—to flee to the United States.

By August, as the nation followed the confusing stalemate on Round Island, the expansionist press was demanding Rey's release and federal prosecution of Carlos España, Spain's consul in New Orleans. By the end of August, freed by diplomatic pressure from Washington, Rey had returned to New Orleans. A federal grand jury in New Orleans, meanwhile, declined to indict Consul España, and the local U.S. attorney dropped the case. The prolonged legal maneuvering, however, stirred anti-Spanish sentiment throughout the nation. In the South especially, wounded feelings about violated rights of "sovereignty" meshed with the increasingly legalistic cast of southern arguments against President Taylor's efforts to prevent the spread of slavery into the West.

By December the quest to invade Cuba was showing new signs of life, with Cristóbal Madan and his colleagues in the Club de la Habana and in New York's Consejo Cubano deciding that any new expeditionary army to Cuba must be larger, better funded, and led by an officer recruited from the U.S. Army. Narciso López, they decided, was unsuitable for the command.[3]

In late 1849 Madan traveled to the West and began negotiations with Colonel John Williams, a U.S. Army officer. The Consejo eventually promised to provide Williams with $8 million to raise a force of four thousand soldiers, and he agreed to lead the expedition. On November 14, the day after Madan returned to New York, the Consejo Cubano approved the deal, and he began seeking loans from U.S. banks. New York banker Matthew Morgan agreed to provide $400,000, and Madan promised that it would be repaid by Cuba's new government after the invasion.[4]

Madan and his friends, meanwhile, had remained in contact with López after the collapse of the 1849 conspiracy and had belatedly sent along the second half of the $60,000 that they had promised to assist it. But they kept López in the dark about their dealings with Colonel Williams and refused to turn over to him the weapons and the two ships they had acquired for the aborted August 1849 expedition. Though the federal government, after seizing the ships, had returned them, the Consejo Cubano by the end of 1849 would sell both of them.[5]

López's simmering anger with the Consejo reached a boil when he learned of the deal with Colonel Williams. At a November 17 meeting with Madan, Ambrosio Gonzales, representing López, expressed López's displeasure at

Williams's appointment and suggested a compromise: let the bankers who would fund any new conspiracy decide who should lead it.

Madan refused the offer and, as John O'Sullivan later recalled, "insisted on the General's [López's] abondoment of his own arrangements and the adoption of his." Colonel Williams, Madan insisted, must be "placed at the head, and the enterprise . . . conducted in his way." Underscoring their determination to move without López if necessary, Madan and his associates on November 22 formed a new organization, the Consejo de Organización y Gobierno Cubano. Although López refused to join the new organization, he retained hopes for a compromise. By December 3, however, he was complaining to fellow Cuban exile Juan Manuel Macías of having "consumed too much time in futile efforts to conciliate the cooperation of some of our friends." Thus, "I have decided to appoint a public junta to cooperate with me . . . to promote Cuba's political interest, to be immediately made public as the center in charge of the movement and organization."[6]

Two days later, López issued a soon, widely published statement establishing the Junta Promovedora de los Intereses políticos de Cuba. The statement, distributed to at least sixteen newspapers around the country, appeared above the names of Gonzales, Macías, Cirilo Villaverde, and José María Sánchez Iznaga. "The undersigned beg leave to avail themselves," it began, "that, by appointment from General Don Narciso Lopez, well known in the United States, as well as Cuba, as the head of the late projected revolution for the liberation of that Island from the oppressions and degradation of its present condition, they have accepted and undertaken, in concert with General Lopez, the duties and responsibilities of a 'patriotic junta for the promotion of the political interests of Cuba.'"

While denying any intention of "infringing on the laws of this country," the notice nonetheless openly solicited soldiers for a new expeditionary army and invited correspondence from "the thousands of noble spirits who, in all sections of this Union, sigh to behold the slavery and sufferings of Cuba, and long to contribute any aid honorably and legitimately in their power, for her relief." The junta "will shortly establish itself at the city of Washington, to which city may be addressed directly to General Lopez (post paid,) all correspondence of its friends, box 51, post office."[7]

The spectacle of a clandestine organization issuing public solicitations for recruits underscored Narciso López's desperate personal situation. By December 1849 his financial fortune in Cuba was a distant memory, and a death sentence hung over him. But such public brazenness also highlighted the often paradoxical politics of filibustering and nineteenth-century republicanism. The clandestine nature of López's mission practically dictated that his army would embrace many trappings of the various republican "brotherhoods" that had arisen in post-Napoleonic Europe. López and his followers shared with their European counterparts an assumption that the common people in whose name they toiled would never, on their own, initiate a war of liberation but would join the fight once it began. Since each operated beyond the pale of the law, the filibusters also shared with Europe's secret societies a concern for secrecy and a passion for rituals. López and his cohorts at the Club de la Habana, for instance, had adopted secret code names: López was "El Capo," Gonzales was "D. German." The U.S. journalist John Thrasher was, of course, "El Yankee."[8]

After Napoleon's defeat in 1815 and the rise across Europe of absolutist regimes dedicated to preventing any further outbreaks of revolution, a generation of republican activists had turned toward plotting in secret nationalist cells. In their closed meetings outlaw groups like Italy's Carbonari and Russia's Decembrists reveled in various republican rituals and symbols.

López's filibusters shared that affinity for ritual. López, after all, knew Europe's republican milieu well from his days in Spain as a Liberal opponent of royalist absolutism. The organization that he had cobbled together in Cienfuegos, Cuba, for his eventually aborted uprising of 1848 was modeled on such secret republican societies. A vivid testimony to López's debt to European republicanism, the coat of arms he eventually adopted for his U.S. filibuster featured the *bonnet rouge* or *bonnet de la liberté*, the red liberty cap popularized by French revolutionaries a half century earlier.[9]

It was in the degree of their commitment to secrecy that the filibusters parted company from European republicans. Europe's republican brotherhoods borrowed many of their official symbols and hierarchies from Masonic societies, and knowledge of such matters remained confined to members, thus tightening their bonds. Operating in societies dominated by a harsh absolutism, groups like the Decembrists remained small and politically isolated from any larger body politic. Their survival truly did depend upon a commitment to secrecy.[10]

Narciso López's army, by contrast, operated in a relatively open milieu. López's public announcement in December 1849, soliciting soldiers for a new expedition to Cuba, had typified this public approach to conspiracy. Like demonstrations, parades, street gangs, and political pamphleteering, López's filibuster belonged to a very public tradition of U.S. protest that dated from the nation's days as a colony of Great Britain. Acting in that tradition, López broadcast the official symbols of his army far and wide. The filibusters used their flag and coat of arms to nourish internal cohesion, a sense of belonging, within the conspiracy. But such symbols, disseminated openly and widely, also were employed to deliberately attract public attention: López and his comrades routinely talked to journalists. They wrote newspaper stories, issued public proclamations, organized public rallies, and sold bonds boldly festooned with the conspiracy's coat of arms. In May 1850 supporter Laurent Sigur, editor of the New Orleans *Delta*, would mark the filibusters' ostensibly secret departure from New Orleans for Cuba with front-page engravings of both López and the "flag of the Cuban patriots."[11]

Beyond that, López's conspiracy covered too much ground and involved too many people to remain a secret. His sprawling conspiracy reached from soldiers in the expeditionary army to politicians, journalists, businessmen, and the larger body politic that attended rallies and purchased bonds. As outlaws, the filibusters had a genuine need for secrecy. But the public nature of their enterprise rendered their commitment to discretion more nominal than genuine, more coy than serious.

López's manifestos and speeches became regular features of the nation's newspapers. Translated from the Spanish and widely published in papers both for and against the filibuster, these cliché-ridden descents into republican rhetoric became so routine that by 1850 the Philadelphia *Public Ledger* would complain, "If Lopez fights as bad as he writes, there is not much chance of his becoming a 'liberator' very soon." Typical of such dispatches, his "Address to the American People," published in May 1850 in the New Orleans *Delta*, attacked the morality of Spain's governance of Cuba: "In an age when the despotisms of the Old World are fast crumbling to the ground, in spite of the myriads of bayonets by which they are vainly propped, it cannot be that one of the most oppressive and corrupt of them all should continue, any longer, to maintain an unnatural dominion over a land almost in sight of your free and happy shores."[12] Time after time, however, López and his followers learned that such propaganda, however necessary to raise troops, funds, and political support, inevitably compromised their ability to keep secrets.

In December 1849 López, who was still in New York, dispatched Ambrosio Gonzales to Washington to begin organizing their new Junta Promovedora de los Intereses políticos de Cuba. Like López, dapper mustachioed Adjutant General Gonzales was handsome. Indeed, in later years he was often confused with the dashing Confederate general Pierre Beauregard—coincidentally an old classmate from student days in New York City; Gonzales later served under Beauregard as a colonel during the Civil War. Unlike López, however, who was often limited by his dependence upon interpreters, Gonzales was thoroughly conversant in English, hence his frequent role as López's interpreter. South Carolina diarist Mary Chesnut would later recall that Gonzales had "a fine voice," "sings divinely," and was a master raconteur. She also would recall Gonzales's own recounting of his service with López: "His way of telling it all was modest and so interesting that the evening slipped away very pleasantly. Cubans must be very nice if Señor Gonzales is a sample."[13]

Gonzales was born in Matanzas in 1818. Typical of the sons of prominent Cuban families of that day, he had received four years of education in the United States before returning to Cuba and earning a law degree at the University of Havana. By the late 1840s, then in his early thirties, Gonzales was a strident annexationist. In 1849 he became a U.S. citizen.[14]

Tightening the ties to his adopted country, Gonzales's associations soon stretched from Jefferson Davis to former Texas republic president Mirabeau Lamar to James K. Polk. Gonzales's introduction to the president, in December 1848, through Massachusetts congressman Caleb Cushing, took place within four months of his arrival from Cuba. Gonzales also had ties that antedated his arrival in the United States. During the same month in which he met Polk, Gonzales wrote to his old friend Nicholas Trist, the former U.S. consul in Havana, to ask for letters of introductions to Washington's political elite. To South Carolina congressman Isaac E. Holmes, Trist immediately wrote, "I very cordially recommend him as a gentleman of high intelligence and one in whose honourable principles & generous sentiments I have great confidence." A few weeks later journalist and political intriguer Jane McManus Storms sent a similar entreaty to New York's Senator Daniel Dickinson. "I would request," she wrote, "for Mr. Gonzales your introduction to the most liberal of our northern members who desire to hear of Cuba." In the same letter Storms, who had accompanied New York *Sun* publisher Moses Yale Beach on his trip through Cuba in January 1847, praised Gonzales as "a gentleman of Cuba and a republican patriot in theory as well as action." Dickinson and Holmes's fellow South Carolinian John C. Calhoun were among the five congressmen with whom López met in 1849 in the U.S. Capitol.[15]

In December 1849 a new set of recruits, ushered into the conspiracy by Ambrosio Gonzales, breathed fresh life into the filibuster. On December 21, while attending a reception at the White House, Gonzales met John Henderson, a prominent New Orleans lawyer, Mexican War veteran, and former U.S. senator from Mississippi. Henderson described himself to Gonzales as "a friend of Cuba" and said, "if ever he thought of moving in behalf of Cuba, to come to New Orleans and see him."[16]

"Some days after," as Gonzales later recalled, three "young gentlemen from Kentucky, hearing in Washington of his being a representative of Cuba, called." All three—Colonel Theodore O'Hara, thirty-one years old; Colonel John T. Pickett, twenty-six; and Thomas T. Hawkins, thirty—had expansionist credentials. O'Hara and Hawkins had served in the Mexican War as officers in Kentucky's volunteer regiment.[17] Pickett had no war service, having dropped out of West Point in 1841 to become the U.S. consul on Turk Island, in the West Indies. That post and extensive travels throughout the Caribbean, however, made him a zealot for U.S. annexation of Cuba. After he returned to the United States, he joined López's thwarted conspiracy of 1849.[18]

The three young men told Gonzales that if he and López would accompany them back to Kentucky and provide proper "authority," they would "raise at their own expense" and bring to New Orleans a regiment of Kentuckians, "as fine material as could be found anywhere" and all ready to go to Cuba.[19]

En Route: Washington to New Orleans, January–March 1850

López moved to Washington in January 1850. Beyond raising funds and U.S. recruits, he also hoped through his new Junta Promovedora de los Intereses políticos de Cuba to direct the revolutionary energies supposedly simmering inside Cuba. In a January letter López claimed to have two agents in Vuelta de Abajo, south of Havana, who had recruited "over two thousand armed, organized men who are impatient to begin the struggle." In Havana, López added, "there is a true organization and even some secret weapons drills. I know of one person who has more than two hundred men chosen and others who are involved in similar activities." A recent conversation with a prominent U.S. congressman, López claimed, furnished even more proof of the new winds blowing across Cuba. "Senator Houston from Texas has recently met someone whom he did not want to name, who had recently come from Cuba, who told him that the people were extremely impatient to begin the revolution and were convinced that the landing of a popular chief with four or five hundred men would be enough."[20]

Needless to say, López knew who was best qualified to be that "popular chief," and by February 1850 he had reached a final break with Cristóbal Madan and the Club de la Habana. For John O'Sullivan the rift created a painful dilemma, forcing him to choose between his brother-in-law Madan and his new political ally López. O'Sullivan's eventual decision to remain with López marked the end of his friendship with Madan.[21]

In February, along with Gonzales and the conspiracy's newfound Kentucky allies, O'Hara, Pickett, and Hawkins, López left for the South, convinced that their best hopes lay in New Orleans. They traveled across the Alleghenies by stage to Pittsburgh, then sailed down the Ohio River to Louisville. As O'Hara, Pickett, and Hawkins stayed behind to organize their promised regiment in the Ohio River valley, López and Gonzales, after meeting with supporters in Kentucky, resumed their journey, sailing down the Ohio and Mississippi rivers to New Orleans, stopping along the way to talk with supporters in Tennessee and Mississippi.[22]

The Mississippi Delta, April 1–10, 1850

On about April 1 Gonzales and López arrived in New Orleans, where Gonzales was reunited with General John Henderson, the lawyer he had met the previous December at the White House reception. Henderson in turn introduced López and Gonzales to other Cuban annexation supporters, including

Laurent Sigur, editor of the New Orleans *Delta*, Justice John Cotesworth Pinckney Smith of the Mississippi Supreme Court, and General John Quitman, governor of Mississippi.[23]

John Quitman enjoyed a good Cuban cigar, but most of what Mississippi's fifty-one-year-old, bushy-haired, mustachioed governor knew about the Cuban annexation movement came from his old friend and state legislature colleague Henderson. Moreover, by the spring of 1850, Quitman, who had become governor the previous January, was already courting another movement fraught with political peril—southern secessionism. The previous fall Quitman had taken time out from his gubernatorial campaign to attend the Southern State Convention, in Jackson. Called to underscore planter opposition to President Taylor's Free-Soil tendencies, the convention eventually balked at calling for outright secession. Even so, for Quitman's critics the meeting had produced enough veiled threats of such action to brand him a secessionist.[24]

The son of a Lutheran minister in Rhinebeck, New York, Quitman had migrated to Mississippi when he was twenty-two years old. He married the daughter of a prominent planter, acquired a plantation, and soon had successful careers in law, politics, and the military. He also became a zealous defender of slavery and the states' rights doctrines of John Calhoun. But what most appealed to Narciso López was Quitman's war record. When war broke out in Texas in 1836, Quitman had assembled a regiment of Mississippians and headed west. The brigade arrived too late to see any action, two days after the battle of San Jacinto, which concluded the Texas republic's war of independence. Even so, Quitman's zealotry won praise from both Texans and Mississippians. Sam Houston, the Texas's republic's first president, even offered to make him second-in-command of the Texas army, an offer he declined. A decade later, Quitman's prowess during the Mexican War earned him the rank of brevet brigadier general. He was a hero at the battle of Monterey, participated in the naval landing at Vera Cruz, and led a brigade in the storming of Chapultepec Castle, outside Mexico City. Aware of Quitman's military record, López thus had high hopes as he arrived in the Mississippi capital in the spring of 1850. Jefferson Davis's and Robert E. Lee's polite but firm rejections had frustrated López's earlier efforts to recruit a U.S. citizen to command an expedition to Cuba. In Quitman, however, López finally seemed to have found the right U.S. military hero.[25]

López met with Quitman in Jackson at the governor's mansion, a graceful two-storied, yellow-brick building fronted by a portico of Corinthian columns. As Gonzales translated, López, conversing with the governor in one of the front parlors, opened with flattering talk of Quitman's service in the Mexican War. He then spoke of Cuba, showing Quitman letters from allies in the United States. López stressed that "the people were ripe for revolution, and he came in their name to solicit the auxiliaries that the citizens of the great republic should not refuse to their oppressed neighbors." He then offered Quitman $1 million—to be drawn against Cuba's land and property—to lead a force of four thousand soldiers to the island. While López in silence paced the room "like a sentinel on guard," Quitman "long and anxiously" pondered the offer. "My spirit often reverts to the free air of the camp," the governor wrote to a friend after the meeting. "I am by nature a soldier. No other life charms me." Yet he declined López's offer, agreeing instead—with stipulations—to lead a second assault. López and his army hoped to leave for Cuba on May 1. If that landing proved successful and other Cubans rallied to the cause, Quitman would arrive with his own army of volunteers sometime between June 1 and 15. He also agreed to raise money for the campaign.[26]

In August 1849 John O'Sullivan had urged John C. Calhoun to move from private to public support for López. "If I," he wrote, "a 'New York Free Soiler' am so deeply interested in behalf of this movement, what ought not to be the enthusiasm of Southern gentlemen?" Like his friend John Henderson, who had grown up in New Jersey, Quitman was a native of the North and a youthful convert to the slaveholder ideology. Quitman's contemporary critics often charged that his well-publicized zealotry on such issues as slavery, secession, and filibustering was overcompensation for not having been born in the South.[27]

Regardless of the merits of such charges, as a planter supporting López, Quitman was hardly typical. As a group southern planters tended to shy from López. Debates about slavery's place in the West notwithstanding, the 1850s were good years for planters, with steadily rising sugar and cotton prices. Many planters for good reason thus cherished the status quo. In the spring of 1850, for instance, as diplomatic relations between Washington and Madrid worsened, the Democratic Richmond *Enquirer* warned that though any war was undesirable, war between the United States and Spain would be especially dangerous because it could provoke "the interposition of Great Britain," a ruinous prospect for the South's cotton exports.[28]

Many nationally prominent Democrats favored U.S. acquisition of Cuba—including President Polk, his secretary of state, James Buchanan, and his treasury secretary, Robert J. Walker, as well as U.S. senators David Yulee of Florida, Lewis Cass of Michigan, and Stephen Douglas of Illinois. And a few well-known Democrats, at one time or another, intimated their support for López—including Georgia governor George W. Towns and U.S. senators John C. Calhoun of South Carolina, Jefferson Davis of Mississippi, and Stephen Mallory of Florida.[29] But none of those Democrats provided any ringing public endorsement of the expeditions to Cuban, and no state Democratic party organization openly endorsed López. Indeed, the most prominent public officials publicly linked with López were a trio of Mississippians: Governor Quitman, state supreme court justice John Cotesworth Pinckney Smith, and former U.S. senator John Henderson. And none of those three enjoyed national or even strong regional constituencies.[30] Sensitive to other political considerations in their public statements—and to the implications of endorsing violations of federal laws—most Democrats sympathetic to the filibuster merely challenged the legality of Whig presidential actions against it.[31]

The ambivalence expressed by Calhoun toward López's cause—favoring Cuba's annexation but believing the political price too high—reflected a misgiving common among southern planters. Many like-minded newspapers of the region even opposed López.[32] Washington's *Southern Press*, an organ of congressional southern radicals, saw only mischief in López's scheming. Manifest Destiny zealots, after all, preferred their places of conquest to contain at least one ostensibly abused but morally worthy class, if only to give their invasions a moral patina. To the *Southern Press* Cuba's Creoles, López's nominal beneficiaries, hardly seemed a suffering people: "Cuba is governed by a military despotism, and is subject to enormous taxations for its support. Yet, the white population of Cuba is probably the most wealthy and prosperous of all that live under European government. It demonstrates the immense vigor of slave institutions."[33]

Other southerners declined to support the filibuster precisely because they believed Cuba's Creoles were oppressed. In an 1851 letter to López, former Texas republic president Mirabeau Lamar would reject a request for support, even though he favored Cuba's annexation and thought the island's Creoles "have very powerful motives for starting a revolution." "Why they have not done it ere now?" he asked, and then answered his own question. "It is because the Cubans lack one thing—to wit—spirit. They do not have that noble disinterestedness, that loftiness of spirit and that manly courage which always characterizes real patriots and without which no people can acquire liberty nor be worthy of it either."[34]

The conservative New Orleans *Crescent* considered Cuba's annexation a worthy goal but, echoing Calhoun, thought that support for López would weaken the united southern front needed for more pressing sectional debates. "If we wish to keep an eternal agitation of the slavery question between the North and the South, then let us conquer Cuba after the Spaniards shall have emancipated the negroes and declared the island to be, in the cant of the times, 'free soil.'"[35]

The *Crescent* neglected another reason why its readership might shy from López: the cultivation of sugar, Louisiana's main crop, required federal tariffs to protect it from Cuban imports. López's supporters, by contrast, tended to oppose all manner of governmental interference, whether it be the Neutrality Act or protective tariffs; they preferred both their politics and business laissez-faire. For Louisiana's planters, not surprisingly, biases against federal protections for native crops approached the heretical; a Cuba joined to the United States, with its own sugar exports suddenly unburdened of U.S. tariffs, could ruin Louisiana's sugar planters. Indeed, the Philadelphia *Public Ledger*, which opposed López, would surmise in 1851 that a Cuba joined to the United States would be disastrous, politically and economically, for both sugar and cotton planters. The Philadelphia paper quoted a recent editorial from the Richmond *Whig*, a journal, according to the *Ledger*, "representative of what may be regarded as the sound, moderate old-fashioned portion of the Slave states":[36]

Let us suppose Cuba annexed, and then let us contemplate the consequences. Every sugar plantation in Louisiana and Texas would be abandoned, and the chief source of wealth to those two States would be *dried*. These sugar planters must then emigrate with their negroes, to Cuba, or fall back upon cotton. . . . If [present duties] . . . be removed from Cuban sugar, as it would be by annexation, our sugar planters must fall back upon cotton. What will South Carolina, Georgia, Mississippi and Alabama say to *that*? With the new competition from the new cotton lands of Louisiana and Texas, they will wish Cuba set *farther*. And with full foresight of all this, even the seceders oppose its annexation.[37]

In the long run, predicted the *Public Ledger*, echoing a widespread fear among southern planters, even Virginia and Maryland planters "would gladly emigrate to Cuba, or sell their slaves to others bound that way. This would *clear out* these two States, render them *free* States, and leave their Southern neighbors as *border* states." As the *Ledger* in an 1849 editorial had asserted, while it assumed that southerners numbered among López's supporters, it also had no doubt that the conspiracy's "chiefs" were northern investors, "a knot of fradulent bankrupts." López's key U.S. allies, the paper suggested, were speculators like those who had made millions through "Texanization," the purchase of secondhand Mexican land grants of dubious legality, ultimately—and profitably—redeemed by America's acquisition of Texas.[38]

In words and deeds López and his followers, as self-styled republicans, consciously emulated other "liberators" who had warred against monarchical abuses. And more than a few southerners, most of whom were Democrats, found López's particular brand of republicanism—with its unquestioning tolerance of expansionism and slavery—enticing and joined their northern brethren in hailing any revolt against monarchy. Republicanism, after all, with its detestation of monarchs and its exaltation of individual liberties and representative government, had been the ideological mainspring of the United States' own founding. Passed on to the North American colonists by radical British Whigs of the eighteenth century, the ideology claimed an honored past that stretched back to Lord Cromwell's Protectorate and to the late Roman Empire and classical Greece. Yet by 1850, some southerners, especially planters, found republicanism a troubling doctrine full of dangerous precedents for a slaveholding society.

López and his filibusters drew their republicanism from three main historical sources: the U.S. War of Independence, the Mexican War, and the European uprisings of the late 1840s. Of course, by the time he organized his filibuster, whatever contemporary controversies that had attended the republican heroes of the U.S. War of Independence and the Mexican War had given way to a marbled veneration; Concord's and Buena Vista's heroes rested snugly in the muffled pantheon of U.S. patriots. The third source of López's republicanism—Europe's feckless republican heroes of the late 1840s—enjoyed no such settled acclaim. Indeed, republicanism's struggle in Europe remained far from over.

López's followers could read of ongoing events in Europe and proudly assume that they rode the same wave of republican liberation. By contrast, southern planters—Democrats included—could read of the same events and shiver with fear. By necessity, European republican revolutionaries and U.S. filibusters both operated beyond the pale of the law. It was that relationship between filibustering and the law which troubled many southern planters. By 1850 much of the South's defense of slavery had come down to a defense of laws—the sanctity of the Fugitive Slave Act, the sanctity of the civil statutes that sanctioned slavery's very existence. Filibustering violated federal laws, most immediately the Neutrality Act of 1818 and the 1797 friendship pact between Spain and the United States, which as a treaty enjoyed the status of a federal civil law. Whence the filibusters' sanction to violate such laws? Like European republicans, filibusters appealed to morality over law. Just as republicans like Louis Kossuth believed their causes transcended the ancient writs of medieval Europe, so López and his followers dismissed what supporter Laurent Sigur once called the "bugbear of treaty stipulations."[39]

In the end many planters—including otherwise expansionist Democrats—shied from López for the same reason they distanced themselves from Kossuth and other heroes of the failed European uprisings. Nominal López supporter Jefferson Davis, for instance, on the eve of the Civil War would insist that sculptor Thomas Crawford remove the liberty cap from the bronze female figure of Freedom just placed atop the U.S. Capitol. To mollify Davis, Crawford substituted a helmet topped by plumage resembling an Indian headdress.[40]

The reaction of many southern Senate Democrats to the European uprisings typified the predicament of the region's planters. As defenders of a slaveholding society, southern Democrats were in no hurry to endorse diplomatic interference in the domestic affairs of another country. Were not, after all, similar appeals to morality over law at the core of Britain's international abolition movement? More specifically, were not such moral arguments behind Britain's recently stepped-up efforts to persuade Spain to abolish Cuban slavery?—a prospect that terrified planters of the southern United States.[41]

Thus, when Ohio's William Allen in March 1848 introduced a House-Senate joint resolution praising the creation of the new French republic—the same government that had recently abolished slavery in its West Indies colonies—John C. Calhoun sought to avoid an embarrassing vote by trying to table the motion. The endorsement eventually passed unanimously, with Calhoun and fellow southern opponents tactfully abstaining. Southern discomforts with European republicanism received a more public airing in early 1850, when Michigan's U.S. Senator Lewis Cass urged a suspension of diplomatic relations with Vienna to punish Austria for its role in crushing Kossuth's rebellion. On January 31, when Virginia's R. M. T. Hunter rose to tell his colleagues just why he opposed such an action, he might as well have been talking about English abolitionism: "It assumes the right of one Government to interfere in the domestic affairs of another—a right which would be dangerous, in the last degree, to the peace and liberties of mankind."[42]

Echoing that sentiment, when López and his followers asked for U.S. support in another foreign theater, the Southern Press had a ready rejoinder. While favoring a legal U.S. purchase of Cuba from Spain, "with the internal affairs of Cuba, however, we have nothing to do. And we regret and oppose any interference with them by any of our people." Such actions would violate legally binding obligations to Spain, "and we of the South, we should think, have seen and felt enough of the mischief of violated compacts and impertinent interferences, to abstain from them ourselves."[43]

If so many southern planters—for so many different reasons—remained skeptical of López, where did his support in the region originate? The Philadelphia Public Ledger noted that the filibuster had friends among many New Orleans papers. But it wondered when it would hear from the planters who controlled much of the rest of Louisiana. "Their organs," the paper noted archly, "are not in New Orleans."[44]

Hydrologically, New Orleans was a risky proposition. Yellow fever–haunted, mosquito-harassed, the city occupied a flat, low-lying swath of delta along the lower Mississippi River's north bank. A system of dikes protected the city from the surrounding rivers, swamps, and lakes that marked its boundaries. Mark Twain recalled seeing the city from a boat at "high-river stage": "the water is up to the top of the inclosing levee-rim, the flat country behind it lies low—representing the bottom of a dish—and as the boat swims along, high on the flood, one looks down upon the houses and into the upper windows. There is nothing but that frail breastwork of earth between the people and destruction."[45]

Commercially, however, New Orleans occupied a blessed position: 107 miles from the Gulf of Mexico, the city sat at the southern end of a vast riparian plain fanning out over thousands of square miles—northwesterly to the foot of the Rockies, northeasterly to the Alleghenies. During the early nineteenth century, as white settlers from the forested East pushed into the valley, filling it with new farms, New Orleans became the port through which they sold their products to the world. By the 1820s, like the spout of a giant funnel, New Orleans had become the principal emporium for the entire Mississippi Valley.

The New Orleans, then, to which López came in the spring of 1850 was a busy polyglot city of 120,000, a locale renowned for both boisterous frontier energy and Old World sophistication—teeming with gambling, drinking, prostitution, and violence. "Should a stranger jostle an American by accident, he runs extreme risk of being shot or stabbed," warned one European visitor. But New Orleans also claimed some of America's best hotels, cuisine, theaters, and opera. Jaded New Orleanians even gave Swedish singer Jenny Lind a "cold" reception during her otherwise triumphant 1850–51 tour of America. As one of her agents recalled the local audience, they were "not disposed altogether blind to receive and adopt the verdict of New York respecting Jenny's excellence. They were there to hear her with their own ears."[46]

Beyond the brick warehouses and the tangle of sails, masts, ropes, and boats that silhouetted New Orleans's riverfront, the city claimed some of the nation's most dazzling architecture. Since the 1820s, local merchant princes had busied themselves erecting opulent Greek Revival–style banks, hotels, and shops in the city's main business district. The edifices stood as ostentatious monuments to the city's prosperity.

With a resident population abounding in North Americans, French, Cubans, Spanish, Germans, black slaves, and freemen, New Orleans claimed an often baffling political and social life. Of the city's 120,000 people, 17,000 had migrated from other states, and 51,000, about one-fourth of the total, came from other countries. Residents could choose among English-, French-, and Spanish-language newspapers. Even on maps, the city seemed a crazy quilt of competing identities, a puzzle of rival radial and angular street plans, none drawn to any true compass direction. Overlaid, crunched together, petering out as they reached the Mississippi River and other watery boundaries, the street plans seemed to war with each other and with the city's odd snake-like shape. As Anglos, in the wake of the 1803 Louisiana Purchase, poured into New Orleans, the city's politics had become dominated by a ceaseless rivalry between its North American and Latin populations. By 1837 that rivalry had grown so heated that New Orleanians divided their city into three separate municipalities: French and Spanish residents occupied the First Municipality, later known as the French Quarter. To the west, beyond Canal Street, lay the Second Municipality, inhabited by North Americans and Irish immigrants. East of the First Municipality, past Esplanade Avenue, lay the Third Municipality, dominated by Germans, Spanish, French, and free blacks. New Orleans's 1850 population included 10,000 free blacks, many descended from refugees of the Haitian slave uprisings of a half century earlier. Black slaves numbered 18,000.[47]

Though New Orleans's three governments shared a common mayor, by 1850 the Second Municipality dominated the city's economic life. The thriving American Quarter rose from what had been Faubourg St. Marie, a sparsely settled waterfront suburb. As émigrés from the United States poured into the Second Municipality, the blocky one- and two-story stucco buildings of the First Municipality, with their pastel tints and iron-filigreed balconies, faded into relics of another day. Business activity shifted to the Second Municipality, and the old French Quarter seemed more and more a mere spectator at a lavish banquet, a sad victim of neglect and excessive rents set by absentee landlords.

It was in the Second Municipality that the city's new merchant princes erected their Greek Revival showcases. For ambitious North Americans, New Orleans was at once a southern and a western city. As a trade entrepôt in the heart of the Mississippi Delta, the city reaped brokerage and docking fees from the South's cotton and sugar empire; and as a Gulf port New Orleans kept an eye on both the West and the West Indies.

New Orleans had long been entwined, politically and financially, with expansionist activities. Just outside the city in January 1815, only two years after Louisiana gained statehood, General Andrew Jackson and a force of five thousand volunteers had vanquished a British expeditionary force—a victory that culminated the War of 1812 and consolidated U.S. claims on the entire Mississippi Valley. Still later, New Orleans investors speculated in lands in Texas and other western enclaves. And in 1826 and 1846 volunteer soldiers from New Orleans had flocked to the War of Texas Independence and the Mexican War. In the latter conflict, the New Orleans press had led the nation in cheering U.S. expansion into Mexico.[48]

Beyond its links to legal wars, New Orleans claimed extensive ties to filibustering in both its piratical and political incarnations. By the early nineteenth century, the city had become the principal market for plunder seized by Jean Lafitte and other buccaneers of the Gulf of Mexico. And, by the 1820s, as filibustering settled into its political phase, New Orleans proved an equally commodious setting for Aaron Burr, James Wilkinson, Davy Crockett, William Travis, and other territorial adventurers. Operating from New Orleans, some—such as Wilkinson and Burr—dreamed of carving new republics from Louisiana and other western realms already under the Stars and Stripes. Others, such as Crockett and Bowie, dreamed of creating new nations from western territories then claimed by Mexico and Spain.[49]

López, too, found New Orleans true to its filibustering tradition. Much of the same local press that had touted Yankee acquisition of all of Mexico soon fell eagerly behind the conspiracy to invade Cuba. The New Orleans *Picayune,* the *Delta,* and the *Bee* boosted López's campaign with scores of favorable stories and bold headlines. Laurent Sigur, editor of the *Delta,* even allowed López to move into his home, on Customhouse (now Iberville) Street in the First Municipality, during his stay in New Orleans.

Even Bank's Arcade, the building in which López established his office, attested to New Orleans's filibustering past, having already served as headquarters for Texas filibusters such as Crockett, Bowie, and Travis. The three-story Greek Revival building at the intersection of Magazine and Gravier streets in the Second Municipality occupied half a city block and contained offices, sleeping rooms, shops, billiard rooms, restaurants, auction rooms, a large ground-floor bar, and—at its center—a three-storied, glass-roofed courtyard capable of holding five thousand people. Ambitious men bent on territorial conquests in the unsettled West conspired in offices on the Arcade's second and third floors, recruited "openly over clinking glass in the bar-room," and held public rallies in the Arcade's spacious courtyard.[50]

To complement the volunteers expected from Kentucky, López authorized Mexican War veterans Colonel Chatham Roberdeau Wheat of Louisiana and Colonel W. J. Bunch of Mississippi to raise regiments from their own states, using the standard promises of U.S. Army pay and cash bounties. To convey soldiers to Cuba, John Henderson paid $16,000 for the *Creole,* the same "fast steamer" that U.S. Navy commander V. M. Randolph had requested, to no avail, during his standoff a year earlier with the Round Island filibusters. The filibusters also acquired two sailing ships, the *Georgiana* and the *Susan Loud*. *Delta* editor Sigur, meanwhile, used his Democratic party contacts to secretly obtain a cache of arms and ammunition from Louisiana's state arsenal.[51]

By 1850 López could no longer expect financial support from Madan and his friends in the Club de la Habana, and Madan still refused to turn over the ships, weapons, and ammunition that had been acquired for the aborted expedition of 1849. But in New Orleans anxieties about raising funds soon faded, as López found no shortage of speculators willing to purchase bonds issued by the conspiracy. Bonds, after all, enjoyed a venerable republican history. They had been sold to support the recent Italian and Hungarian uprisings, and, as Gonzales would later recall, the United States' own birth had been attended by speculative papers, "a certain fund raised by certain rebels, called continental money."[52]

More importantly for the conspirators in New Orleans, bonds were sold in 1836 to finance the Texas revolution. Though any investment dependent upon the triumph of a revolution was risky, such bonds could yield substantial profits. Most Texas bonds, for instance, had sold at a discount—some for as low as five cents on the dollar—and those who bought López's bonds no doubt recalled that after what had been the Republic of Texas joined the United States, Washington had redeemed those papers at full face value.[53]

López and his lieutenants had been selling bonds since at least the previous January, when they were based in Washington. That month Secretary of State Clayton had informed the U.S. attorney in New Orleans that "the Minister of Spain residing in [Washington] . . . has again invoked the attention of the Executive, to probable designs against the Island of Cuba by persons in the United States, of whom and of whose schemes he has received intelligence through channels which he conceives to be worthy of credit. Besides the organization of juntas & their secret introduction into Cuba of papers inciting the inhabitants to revolt, they are said to have issued bonds payable on the rents of the Island in order to raise money for the purpose of recruiting men."[54]

The bonds were pledged against the "public lands and property of Cuba." Festooned with the expedition's coat of arms (a shield flanked on one side by an American flag, on the other by the filibuster's own "lone star" banner), they promised nothing less than a dawning of democracy over Cuban soil, with a provisional regime under López to be followed quickly by a freely elected government—and all with 6 percent interest. Over the spring of 1850, bonds with a face value of $2 million were sold in New Orleans, most sold at ten cents on the dollar. Between $40,000 to $50,000 in cash was raised through bond sales. Of that, $17,400 came from one man alone—John Henderson.[55]

Among those who invested and fought in filibuster armies, prospects for personal gain did not dim their claimed idealism. Mid-nineteenth-century republicanism found no contradiction between patriotic military service and personal advancement. As President Polk in his December 1848 address to Congress had explained, "In battle, each private man, as well as every officer, fights not only for his country, but for glory and distinction among his fellow-citizens when he shall return to civil life." While Polk's apologia defended the political careers launched by Mexican War veterans after their return from war, López's filibusters simply gave the president's argument a more pecuniary application. Indeed, as George W. White had recruited his 1849 Round Island filibusters with promises of "*plunder, drink, women* and *tobacco*," so, in a published memoir of his own filibustering experiences, the Louisiana regiment's J. C. Davis recalled joining López in 1851 "to propagate republican principles, disseminate republican doctrines, cultivate republican feelings, and multiply republican governments." Only a few sentences later, however, Davis cited quite another motivation: "Because it was whispered about certain places that there was *gold* as well as *glory* in Cuba." Lest that admission create any confusion, Davis quickly added, "Now, I do not believe that any gentleman engaged in the expedition was influenced in the least by mercenary motives, yet I feel compelled to acknowledge that the reflection of such a termination to our laudable undertaking was by no means disagreeable."[56]

"True, the temptations of ambition and gold were strong," recalled Richardson Hardy, a member of the 1850 Kentucky regiment, in his published memoir. "But never would these men go forth as they do with no higher or holier designs than personal aggrandizement. How much such motives may have weighed in any heart, is a question which, as in everything else where justice, truth, charity and religion are concerned, every man must answer to his own conscience."[57]

The willingness of speculators in New Orleans to invest in such a long-shot enterprise as Narciso López's conspiracy might have suggested to some that the city enjoyed robust economic health. More thoughtful observers, however, knew better. New Orleans in the spring of 1850 suffered growing economic woes. The city's trade with Europe was increasingly imperiled by competition from Atlantic ports, and many local merchants had begun to look to other markets for their livelihood. Some were even willing to gamble on an invasion of Cuba.

New Orleans had weathered the panic of 1837 and its local bank failures well enough. By the decade's end port revenues were even climbing. Echoing the city's recovered optimism, an 1845 guidebook had only cheery words about New Orleans's place in the world: "The facilities which this metropolis affords for reaching any accessible portion of the world, particularly all sections of the union, are not excelled."[58] But for all the outward signs of prosperity, New Orleans's future in many ways had grown as hollow as the cast-iron pilasters that fronted so many of the Second Municipality's gleaming Greek Revival buildings. What the guidebook declined to note was that New Orleans's "not excelled" links to the world by the mid-nineteenth century consisted mainly of the preferred channels of another day. The steamboats that had graced New Orleans's port since its 1820s heyday were quickly becoming passé. By 1850 another era had taken hold—one in which canals and railroads, not palatial riverboats, dominated U.S. commercial transportation. The southern and midwestern goods that had once crowded the city's docks were increasingly going to other ports. Even as new Greek Revival palaces rose from New Orleans's loamy soil, the Erie Canal, completed in 1825, and followed by other canals and railroads were quietly encroaching upon the city's port business. During the 1847–48 business year, 3,177 seagoing vessels docked at New Orleans. By 1850–51 that figure had dropped to 2,019, a 36 percent decline.[59]

Unlike New York's maritime industry, which projected its powers to the world's farthest reaches, New Orleans's influence tended to stop at the river's edge. As New York expanded its dominion through railroads, steamship companies, and far-flung mercantile houses, New Orleans for the most part remained simply a place where ships loaded and unloaded cargoes. Though steamships regularly called at New Orleans, not one line of ocean vessels was locally controlled or owned. Unlike New York's traders, merchants in New Orleans claimed no direct powers to regulate oceanic shipping rates or schedules to their advantage. Further undercutting local economic autonomy, an estimated seven-eighths of New Orleans's mercantile houses were subsidiaries of firms on the eastern seaboard; deals negotiated in New Orleans to ship Louisiana cotton to England were apt to be closed in offices in New York, Boston, or Philadelphia.[60]

By midcentury, then, the city faced a chronic shortage of capital. During the 1840s New Orleans traders enjoyed unchallenged domination of midwestern farm production and the regional cotton trade. By 1850 those same traders had less than $10.5 million at their disposal. Their New York counterparts, by comparison, boasted resources exceeding $48 million. The capital shortage limited New Orleans's ability to provide competitive port facilities and docking fees. Private local banks were strapped for funds to lend. And by reinforcing Louisiana's traditional conservatism toward funding public works, the capital shortage hampered the construction of the state's own interstate canals and railroads, the very agents that might have reversed New Orleans's decline. Underscoring the city's diminished prestige, the state legislature voted in 1845 to move Louisiana's capital from New Orleans to Baton Rouge.[61]

By 1850 New Orleans mercantilists viewed stronger commercial ties to Latin America and the Pacific West as the city's best hope. From that vantage, after all, not all of the recent news was bad: yes, port revenues were down, but the city's merchants also now sat astride a much enlarged sphere of potential commerce, in the West Indies and on the West Coast. The conclusion of the Mexican War, which had increased the nation's size by a third, promised new western markets. And tales of gold from California suggested new prospects.

News of gold's discovery in California had reached the East in August 1848, and by the spring of 1850 thousands of men dreaming of quick riches were leaving New Orleans each week for the Sierra Nevada.[62] What caught the attention of the city's mercantilists, however, were the new trading opportunities created by the boom. Mining would nourish settlements in the West, and what established U.S. port on the Atlantic or Gulf of Mexico was better situated than New Orleans to supply all those new towns and cities?

Louisiana's links to the West, the New Orleans *Delta* pointed out, would also be increased by the completion of a trans-Panamanian isthmus railroad and the recent creation of federally subsidized U.S. commercial steamer lines, one in the Gulf of Mexico and another in the Pacific. Those new links to the West, the *Delta* predicted, presented the city a chance to regain economic momentum lost over the previous decade. "The Pacific is about to pour her cornucopia into America. It behooves our merchants, whose intelligence, public spirit and enterprise are unsurpassed in the nation, to exert themselves to secure a full share of the enriching harvest to the Emporium of the Southwest."[63]

California also increased New Orleans's enthusiasm for Latin American trade. More U.S. ships in the Gulf of Mexico meant more calls at Latin American ports. Anticipating that trade, by 1850 many New Orleans merchants and politicians had joined with other southern maritime interests in common cause with Mississippi Valley grain interests. As the Charleston *Courier* noted in May 1850, "The annexation of Cuba holds out temptations to the commercial, navigating and manufacturing interests of New York and New England that no anti-slavery feeling can withstand." Had the *Courier* gazed farther west, it might have noticed that support for Cuba's annexation extended far beyond New York and New England, deep into the nation's new agricultural heartland in the Mississippi Valley. Across that vast valley farmers and merchants clamored for more markets in which to sell their ever-increasing corn and wheat harvests. They sought more access to foreign markets, lower import tariffs, and in at least one case—Cuba—outright acquisition of more U.S. territory. In the broadest sense, such aggressive free-trade capitalism belonged to the mid-nineteenth century's vast program of U.S. geopolitical expansionism. As the *United States Magazine and Democratic Review* had predicted in 1844, "The energy of unrestricted American enterprise will carry the country to the highest pinnacle of power." By contrast, "The protective system will strangle the infant giant before it can put forth its strength."[64]

By the 1840s the Mississippi Valley's delegation in Washington included some of the nation's most combative advocates of free trade and territorial expansion—including senators Lewis Cass of Michigan, Stephen Douglas of Illinois, Joseph Chalmers of Mississippi, and Representative John Wentworth of Illinois. During the Polk administration, supported by Treasury Secretary Robert J. Walker (formerly a U.S. senator from Mississippi), they won several key free-trade victories. Most notably, in 1846 the administration rescinded a large tariff increase implemented four years earlier; later that same year Britain reciprocated and repealed its Corn Laws, thus opening an important new market for U.S. grain exports.[65]

By 1850, with Zachary Taylor as president, Mississippi Valley expansionists no longer had an advocate in the White House. But they did enjoy a key advantage over their competition: in the East debates over slavery increasingly strained traditional Democratic party alliances between northern merchants and southern agriculturists. Even within their own state parties, Democratic expansionists of the East had to negotiate the shoals of growing party factionalism.

Mississippi Valley farmers, their coastal agents in New Orleans, and their local Democratic political allies, by contrast, occupied a region where neither secessionism nor free-soilism burned with any intensity. Stephen Douglas—though vastly overstating his case—described the valley as one vast peaceable kingdom, at once industrious and insulated from rancorous quarrels over slavery, "one and indivisible from the gulf to the great lakes." "We indulge in no ultraisms,—no sectional strifes—no crusades against the North or the South."[66]

What the Mississippi Valley did indulge in by 1850 was a fixation on California and Cuba. New Orleans merchants and their agricultural business partners were smitten by prospects of massive wheat exports to Cuba. For decades midwestern farmers and New Orleans traders had competed with Spanish merchants for the Cuban market. But with U.S. wheat by midcentury carrying a duty of $10.31 per barrel, compared to the $2.52 charge on Spanish wheat, U.S. traders knew they faced a losing battle. Between 1848 and 1851 wheat from the United States captured only 2.4 percent of the island's market for imported wheat. A Cuba suddenly opened to U.S. grain would give New Orleans merchants and their midwestern business partners an unprecedented opportunity. "The trade between Cuba and the West would be increased ten-fold," the New Orleans *Crescent* predicted. "Just think, when the duty of ten dollars on each barrel of flour is taken off how much greater will be the consumption! The independence of Cuba will be felt on the thrashing floors of Minnesota!"[67]

The sticky matter of Cuban sugar, however, best illustrated the divergence between the interests of Louisiana planters and New Orleans merchants. Louisiana planters had good reasons to fear the arrival on New Orleans's docks of duty-free sugar from a Cuba under the Stars and Stripes. Cuba was both climatically and topographically better suited to sugar cultivation than Louisiana: one acre in Cuba could produce twice as much sugar as one in Louisiana. Moreover, labor costs in Cuba were cheaper. The island, after all, still participated in the international slave trade, and its planters paid far less for slaves than did their U.S. counterparts.

For New Orleans merchants, of course, Cuba loomed as an opportunity. Even as they paid the protective tariffs, New Orleans merchants by 1850 already claimed a growing business in imported Cuban sugar. Between 1848 and 1850 annual sugar imports at New Orleans climbed from 14,775 boxes to

18,843. During the 1850–51 trade season, almost 30,000 boxes arrived in New Orleans.[68] Shorn of protective tariffs imports, Cuban sugar would yield even greater profits. Occasional downturns in Louisiana's sugar production, which by 1850 met less than one-third of U.S. demand, and growing U.S. consumption guaranteed that the U.S. domestic demand for Cuban sugar would grow even stronger.[69]

To charges of economic disloyalty lodged by Louisiana's sugar industry, New Orleans's advocates of Cuban annexation pointed out that the island would provide the United States with a near monopoly on the world's sugar production, thus opening new export markets for the Louisiana product. Annexation, they also argued, would lead to higher production costs on the island, putting Louisiana and Cuban planters on an equal competitive footing. And, if all else failed, they suggested, Louisiana planters unable to compete with the new Cuba could simply transfer their slaves to new sugar plantations there.[70]

In a city like New Orleans, enthusiasm for trade with Cuba inevitably led to talk of a military seizure of the island. Expansionism in general, and filibustering in particular, tended to collapse tidy distinctions between commerce, politics, and war. For maritime merchants in New Orleans and throughout the coastal South, then, Cuban filibustering sounded an irresistible siren. As the *Southern Press* observed, "The contiguity of the South-western States to the theater of action, as well as the intimate relations recently established, and the intercourse which the steamers have made so frequent and easy—all these tend to excite a great interest in the minds of these neighbors to the gem of the Antilles." The Jackson *Mississippian* located future southern prosperity in a similarly nautical vision. A Cuba under U.S. control, it predicted, would form a "nucleus for the extension of Republican liberty over every island in the Gulf, until the whole shall comprise one glorious Ocean Republic!"[71]

For the most part, then, López's constituency in the South came from the same quarters as his northern support: urban mercantile and maritime interests, as opposed to rural planters. In New Orleans in 1851 unlanded investors—including many journalists, lawyers, and merchants—would make up the majority of López's financial backers. Of the 153 members of López support committees organized that year in New Orleans to generate financial support for his army, 84, or 55 percent, owned no real estate.[72] Pro-López editorials in

New Orleans newspapers rarely agonized over the plight of Louisiana's planters. The city's merchants were the papers' concern, and increased maritime trade in the Gulf and Pacific was widely viewed as a means of rescuing their flagging fortunes. The *Delta* doubted that the federal government, "at least for some length of time," would construct canals or rail lines linking New Orleans with California. Memphis, St. Louis, and more northerly western cities seemed more likely to benefit from any such federal largesse.

Filibustering also thrived as a phenomenon of local popular politics. In New Orleans the merest expression of support for filibustering offered tangible rewards for politicians, bartenders, newspaper editors, and anyone else with a vested interest in winning popular acclaim. Though in Louisiana, as elsewhere, party organizations kept an official distance from López, individual Democrats and even some Whigs heartily and publicly embraced his campaign. Few in New Orleans needed reminding of expansionism's hold on the popular imagination, a hold demonstrated by the presidential elections of 1844 and 1848. In 1844 Whig opposition to the annexation of Texas had been a main factor in James K. Polk's victory in Louisiana. In 1848, the Whigs carried the state with Zachary Taylor, a war hero who caused voters to forget the party's past military timidity.

By 1850, with President Taylor opposing López's campaign, Louisiana Democrats suddenly had a new expansionist issue to take before the voters. It was not necessary to explicitly endorse the buffalo hunt. Some Democrats, like U.S. Senator John Slidell and the journalist James D. B. De Bow, highlighted their differences with Taylor merely by endorsing the general concept of Cuban annexation. The politicians who actually supported López, however, included both Democrats and Whigs. In an earlier day the city's Democrats might have had Narciso López all to themselves. But by 1850 local Whigs could ill afford to pass up such a popular cause. As debates over slavery divided their national party and Zachary Taylor grew increasingly identified with causes unpopular in the South, many New Orleans Whigs did what their planter counterparts across the region had refused to do: they publicly endorsed López. Of ninety-nine López supporters in New Orleans in 1851 whose political affiliation could be ascertained, sixty-nine were Democrats, and thirty were Whigs.[73]

Among López's Whig supporters in New Orleans was hardware merchant C. M. Waterman, who in 1851 would become chairman of the Second Municipality's Committee on Internal Improvements. Similarly, I. N. Marks, an importer of Cuban sugar, found López an electorally appealing cause in his campaign to win control of the Second Municipality's Whig machine. At least one locally prominent Whig, J. A. Kelly, would even serve as an officer in López's army and in 1851 accompany him to Cuba. (True to the Whig faith, the following year Kelly became president of the local Winfield Scott presidential campaign organization.) Indeed, New Orleans's most celebrated Whig orator, the congressman and trial lawyer Seargent S. Prentiss would lend his dying breath to a passionate defense of López's cause.[74]

Urban Whigs, after all, often had more in common with urban Democrats than with Whig planters—and had to appeal to the same urban electorate. And since many of those Whigs were, like many of their Democratic counterparts, merchants and mercantilists, they also shared a common stake in an enlarged Gulf and western trade. In New Orleans such muddling of party lines proved fortuitous for Narciso López, allowing his local appeal to transcend party affiliations.

As López and Gonzales, during the early spring of 1850, worked out of Bank's Arcade in New Orleans, the young Kentuckians, Hawkins, Pickett, and O'Hara, traveled about Ohio and Kentucky assembling their promised volunteer army. By all accounts their task was made easier by López's earlier passage through the valley en route to New Orleans. According to one account López had left "the Queen City of Cincinnati, and the adjacent country in Kentucky . . . considerably excited," and no shortage of young clerks, farmers, and Mexican War veterans signed up with the expedition.

The three young Kentucky officers were always careful—at least in public—to claim that they were soliciting young men for labor in California's gold mines. Ostensibly they were bound for Chagres on the Panamanian isthmus; they would cross overland to the Pacific coast and then complete their journey to California's goldfields. The three Kentuckians were mindful that the Neutrality Act forbade any private military expedition begun "or set on foot" from "within" the United States. However, if an expedition at least departed the United States unarmed—as, say, a business venture to California—how could it later be prosecuted under the Neutrality Act? If, as the campaign's organizers planned, arms were supplied only after the expedition had cleared the United States, would not mere geography place them beyond the reach of the Neutrality Act?

It was a thin legalistic conceit—just thin enough for potential recruits to see through. Later that same year filibuster volunteer Richardson Hardy, a young newspaper editor from Cincinnati, would publish his own account of the conspiracy in which he recalled the wink-and-a-nod transparency of the expedition's cover story: "In fact, this company, according to madame Rumor, was going anywhere but to California *proper*; and would engage in anything but the business of grinding gold out of mountain quartz. It might be, as was sneakingly surmised, that there was a little cruise of piracy in the wind!"

Of course, to restless young men of the Ohio Valley—many from farms and eager to get their first look at an ocean—the whispered intimations of military glory made the venture all the more appealing. Throughout the valley, "notwithstanding all these doubts and suspicions, the excitement waxed warmer every day." Young boys and men "flocked to the standard. They cared not where it was to be planted, so [long as] it should be the emblem of a noble cause, and those who flung it to the breeze peril all in its defense." The conspiracy also promised its privates standard U.S. Army pay and a bounty of "$4,000 in money or lands in Cuba." Officers were promised $10,000. All bounties would be paid after one year, or sooner "if the revolution is completed before."[75]

By early April, when volunteers began gathering at pickup points along the Ohio River, the Cuban expedition had become an exciting open secret, "an unusual buzz" shared by the entire valley. To the young Kentucky volunteer Marion Taylor, who kept a diary of the affair, the eve of embarkation provoked an almost religious yearning. "It is dusk, and the bell announces our departure upon the long journey before us," he wrote. "It is joyful news. I must look forward to what is before me. It is the future I have to prepare for—time alone can reveal it."[76]

On April 6 the Cincinnati *Enquirer* greeted its readers with a poignant tale. "Several old farmers from Clermont county and Warren county, in this State, were here yesterday and the day before, on the hunt of sons who had slipped off from home quietly, and who are supposed to be on some secret expedition." After professing to have no certain knowledge about the whereabouts of the missing lads, the *Enquirer* coyly suggested that "Cuba, in our opinion, is destined to change owners."[77]

On page 3 in the same issue, a routine posting in the daily "Steam Boat Register" noted that two days earlier, on April 4, the *Martha Washington* had departed Cincinnati for New Orleans. At 4:00 that afternoon the old steamer, chartered by O'Hara to sail to New Orleans, had quietly eased away from its berth at the foot of Vine Street, with O'Hara, other filibuster officers, and 120 Ohio volunteers aboard. Under the cover of darkness that night, the steamer made stops at Covington and Louisville, Kentucky, where more men boarded. Days later, when the ship reached the wide Mississippi, the numbers of its little army stood at 170.[78]

Over the next few days, as "the steamer plowed her way, under full press of steam, through the turbid waters of the Mississippi," the *Martha Washington's* passengers suffered no shortage of diversions. "There were several good musicians on board, among the company, and at night great hilarity generally prevailed—singing, dancing &c." Even the daily fencing lessons offered by one volunteer were regarded as "a useful method of killing time," more farce than a serious drilling in a deadly martial art. "He would have his class parade on deck two or three times a day, every scholar with a cane, stick, umbrella or some such substitute for the proper weapon, in hand. He would then mount upon the chicken-coop, and proceed—'Draw swords! Guard! Cut one, two, three, four. Give—point!'"

During brief stops at towns along the Mississippi, the crew relished exchanges with the locals they met. With reports of the expedition by then surfacing in newspapers, the townspeople not only knew the crew's destination, they shared their excitement. "At all the principal places in the South where our boat stopped, the people were surprised at the crowd, and many remarks and inquiries were made as to who we were, and what was our destination. When told for *California*, they would put on dubious looks, that almost plainly said—'A nice party for California!'"

The soldiers relished their self-image as gentlemen warriors. Their recruiters, after all, had boasted that they were "as fine material as could be found anywhere." Since western gold miners by the spring of 1850 were often considered to be society's worst elements, the men of the *Martha Washington* delighted in the fact that locals along the river openly scoffed at their claimed destination of California. During a stop at Vicksburg, as onlookers gathered, staring at the crew's "appearance, and deportment," a "very intelligent gentleman, standing on the wharf-boat as we came up, gazed at the crowd [of filibusters] a few minutes, and then exclaimed involuntarily as it were—'Cuba, by G—d! No such men as these go to California to dig. Did you ever see such a body of men! D——d if they ain't all gentlemen! What fire, intelligence and energy glows in every countenance!' "[79]

New Orleans, April 11–24, 1850

At "about 3:00" A.M. on April 11, the *Martha Washington* tied up at Freeport, Louisiana, three miles upriver from New Orleans. "The little burgh was soon in an uproar, every bar-room and coffee-house brilliantly lighted up, and crowded with *Californians*. The landlords scarcely [k]new what to apprehend when they were roused up so early, and saw such a concourse in the streets."

Though tiny Freeport's hotels barely accommodated the filibusters, sleeping space was eventually found for all. Two of the party's senior officers, captains William Hardy and H. H. Robinson, meanwhile, continued on to New Orleans, after putting that city off-limits to the men left behind at Freeport. The order arose from concerns about drawing undue attention to the army—a risk, as it turned out, that was even greater than they had imagined. After meeting with their cohorts in New Orleans, Hardy and Robinson returned to Freeport the next day with distressing news: "Owing to some woeful misunderstanding, we had arrived ten or fifteen days too soon."[80]

Upon arriving in Louisiana, the men aboard the *Martha Washington* were supposed to have been immediately transferred to the bark *Georgiana*. Instead, as Hardy and Robinson learned in New Orleans, local agents had yet to secure either the ships or the arms needed to fit out their expedition. The delay around New Orleans increased the exposure of the growing filibuster army to intervention by federal authorities. The portion of the Kentucky regiment that arrived at Freeport aboard the *Martha Washington* on April 11 numbered 170. Over the next few days, newly arriving Kentucky volunteers aboard two other steamers, the *Saladin* and the *Chancellor*, swelled the regiment to 250.[81]

Hiding an army of 250 men in the middle of a town was no easy task. The delay also entailed additional lodging costs, further burdening the conspiracy's fragile finances. To reduce expenditures, most of the army moved the next day to cheaper lodgings in Lafayette (today's Garden District), a thriving suburb west of the Second Municipality. Captain Hardy and other senior officers, meanwhile, checked into more commodious digs in the Second Municipality, in the St. Charles and Verandah hotels.

Over the next two weeks, the filibusters proved an uneasy occupying force. As the army's lower ranks cooled their heels in Lafayette, resentments grew against the senior officers ensconced in New Orleans. There, it was alleged, those privileged officers "drank Juleps . . . visited the theatres, masked balls, etc. at an expense of $25 or $30 per week." Beyond that, the junior officers back at Lafayette were having trouble keeping their charges out of New Orleans and its bars. "It was no easy task to restrict within the bounds of prudence and propriety nearly two hundred idle young men, in such close proximity to New Orleans."[82]

To pass the time, the filibusters visited cemeteries, auctions, and churches. Boredom, however—as the May section of Marion Taylor's diary makes clear—proved the main constant: "21st, 22d, 23d and 24th—Passed without incident." Even suicide proved an overrated respite; on a group drinking binge at nearby Lake Pontchartrain, one filibuster "got very desperate and said he was fifteen-hundred miles from home and did not have a cent so he would drown himself." Ignoring the pleadings of "an old oyster woman" who begged him not to "commit the desperate act," the young soldier jumped into the lake—only to discover "the water was only two feet deep."[83]

The presence of Spanish spies kept the filibusters ever alert to their mission's illegal nature. Spain, since at least 1830, had possessed an extensive espionage system in the United States devoted to countering Cuba annexationist activities. In New Orleans the spies reported directly to Juan Y. Laborde, Spain's consul in New Orleans. As Richardson Hardy recalled, "The Spanish consul at New Orleans had a completely organized and well trained corps of such minions and wretches, constantly in active service." And Laborde's agents were hardly confined to Louisiana. Writing to Cuba's captain general one year later, Laborde noted that he had recently dispatched spies to Texas, Alabama, and Mississippi. In New Orleans, during the spring of 1850, Spanish spies on occasion would try to elicit information by feigning the role of a sociable sailor, plying the filibusters with drink. "Sometimes one of them would appear among our men as a jolly tar, seemingly half drunk, invite them to drink, and talk with nautical eloquence of life on the ocean."[84]

Not that all informants answered to the Spanish crown. President Taylor, in 1850, got a full account of the filibusters' activities from James Robb, a New Orleans banker who earlier that year had offered to initiate talks with Spain on Taylor's behalf about a U.S. purchase of Cuba. Though the president had declined the offer, Robb remained a Taylor loyalist. In a confidential letter on May 6, he warned that a conspiracy "not only formidable in number, but connections" had been organized to invade Cuba. Robb suggested the dispatch of "a strong 'naval force'" to the area.[85]

The filibusters in Lafayette, meanwhile, grew increasingly frustrated at the continuing delay. One evening, they became so impatient that "a large deputation from the various boarding houses . . . formed a procession of about two hundred, and marched in good order down to the city." The volunteers confronted the senior officers before the St. Charles Hotel's columned portico. Topped by a gleaming white dome, the six-story hotel looked more like a national capitol than a place of public lodging, fixing the city's skyline as dramatically as St. Paul's Cathedral did London's.[86]

Taken by surprise, the officers reminded their insubordinate troops of the political risks their public display entailed. The volunteers returned to Lafayette, but at least one of them—Richardson Hardy—had no regrets about the parade: "It did no harm, for our object and destination was then as well known in New Orleans as it could be. We had been the subject of several newspaper notices, and the Cuba expedition was the bar-room conversation all over the city."[87]

By mid-April newspapers across the country were filled with news of the filibusters. Even as the *Martha Washington* was steaming down the Mississippi, the Baltimore *Sun* had predicted that "the second edition of the Cuban hunt" would soon be leaving from New Orleans. On April 15 the New York *Herald* reported that Spanish officials in Cuba, bracing for an expected expeditionary force from the United States, had assembled a garrison of twenty-five thousand men, "and this number is daily increased by new levies from Spain." Making matters still worse for the filibusters, the Spanish government even funded its own U.S. newspapers. *La Crónica* in New York and *La Patria* in New Orleans produced a steady barrage of antifilibustering disclosures. For this increasingly public "secret expedition," the ante was rising with each passing day.[88]

4 Cárdenas

En Route: New Orleans to Yucatán, April 25–May 1, 1850

On the afternoon of April 25, 1850, Lieutenant Richardson Hardy—the young Ohioan who had traded a career in newspapering for one in filibustering—stopped by a shipping office on Poydras Street, in New Orleans's Second Municipality. There, he picked up a bundle of tickets—225 in all, each with a different name written on it, each bearing the same inscription: "One steerage passage on the bark *Georgiana* to *Chagres*."[1]

Nobody, of course, was going to Chagres, the Panamanian hamlet from which California-bound sojourners crossed the isthmus to the Pacific. The tickets were merely one more prop supporting the filibusters's legal ruse designed to thwart federal prosecutors. If the diversion threw off Spanish spies too, so much the better. Within a few hours, all of the tickets were distributed among the Kentucky regiment back in Lafayette. Each soldier was then instructed to go to Lafayette's dock and board the awaiting bark, the *Georgiana*. The filibusters could bring carpetbags or bundles; no boxes or trunks would be allowed. As afternoon's shadows lengthened, soldiers dragging bags and bundles quickly filled the two-masted square-sterned bark to capacity. A logistical bungle, however, delayed the filibusters' departure; the towboat needed for the *Georgiana*'s ninety-mile river passage to the Gulf of Mexico had yet to arrive.[2]

At nine o'clock P.M., after a four-hour wait, the towboat arrived and was tied to the old bark; someone called out, "All aboard, push her out, Captain," and Rufus Benson, the *Georgiana*'s master, edged the ship away from its mooring. Three cheers rose from a crowd gathered on the dock; and as the departing Kentucky regiment gazed back, three faces stood out among the onlookers—Narciso López, Ambrosio Gonzales, and John Henderson. The three "stood upon the pier, waving adieus long as their eyes could discern the bark. They seemed to be overjoyed at our safe departure, and filled with admiration for all on board."[3]

Downriver, the lights of New Orleans faded, and a solemn quiet settled over the *Georgiana*. "All were much fatigued, feeling more disposed to dream of past joys or future glories, than muse on the present," recalled Richardson Hardy in his published account of the expedition. "A sadness crept over each breast as our bark ploughed her way toward the broad Gulf." Marion Taylor, the young volunteer from Shelbyville, Kentucky, who kept a diary of the journey, slipped into a similar repose. "Many thoughts crowd upon me[.] Success, or perhaps an untimely grave is near—time will tell the story," he wrote. "I drew my blanket and threw it over my shoulders, and laid down upon the deck, with the vault of heaven for a covering and went to sleep."[4]

A blazing sun the next morning, April 26, found the *Georgiana* only a few miles from the Mississippi's mouth when a passing fishing boat hailed it to stop. Benson, the *Georgiana*'s master, had been expecting the boat and asked the towboat's captain to drop anchor and allow it to pull aside. The towboat captain, however, as Hardy recalled, declined the request, "probably well knowing the object of such a junction, and not wishing to be an aider or abettor."

The towboat had been hired to pull the *Georgiana* to the southern terminus of the Mississippi and across the broad but notoriously shallow sandbar whose edge limned the river's mouth. Once the bark was in the Gulf of Mexico, sails would be raised on its two masts, and the filibusters would leave the towboat behind. But as the *Georgiana* and its escort came closer to the Gulf, it became apparent that the winds remained too still for any marine sailing that day. So near the tiny hamlet of Balize, just inside the sandbar, the two boats parted ways; the towboat returned to New Orleans, and the *Georgiana* dropped anchor. Another towboat would have to be summoned to complete the bark's transit to the ocean.[5]

Balize lay at the brackish edge of Pass à l'Outre, fanning out to almost a mile in length, one of the Mississippi Delta's five main channels into the ocean. Though only a few rough-hewn houses on stilts, Balize occupied an auspicious place in marine lore. Indeed, "bound for Balize" was how sailors throughout the world declared themselves New Orleans–bound. Just beyond Balize, incoming ships were met by a "bar pilot." Once the incoming vessel cleared the shallow sand barrier that marked the delta's edge and had cleared Pass à l'Outre, the bar pilot departed, and during a brief call at Balize, a river pilot came aboard to navigate the more than eighty remaining miles to New Orleans.[6]

Amid such bustle, Pass à l'Outre made a conspicuous resting place for a ship on a clandestine mission. "There she lay in the broad stream, literally covered with men—having on board more than her tonnage allowed her to carry. A number of vessels and boats were all around and below her, and everything that was going on could be distinctly seen from the pilots' houses at Balize." Further discomfiting the filibusters, the crowded *Georgiana* had caught the attention of a passing U.S. revenue cutter. "No little anxiety and trepidation was felt among the officers who knew her character, as the cutter came tacking up stream, and sailed completely around us two or three times, within good reconnoitering distance."

Fortunately for the filibusters, the federal revenue cutter disappeared minutes before the pursuing fishing smack caught up with the *Georgiana* and anchored alongside. It carried three men: New Orleans *Delta* editor Laurent Sigur and two Kentucky regiment officers, Major T. T. Hawkins and Lieutenant Albert W. Johnson, and they were escorting the remaining supplies needed for the expedition. After the two ships had been lashed together and were bobbing at anchor in the shallow but swift channel's waters, the work of transferring cargo from the fishing smack to the *Georgiana* began. "Several of the stoutest men went to work, and ten boxes of splendid, recently cleaned United States muskets were soon stowed away in the hold, and about ten thousand ball cartridges in the captain's cabin." The open display of the weapons ended any remaining naïveté about the expedition's true purposes. "Countenances wore a serious aspect. Whoever had been so credulous as to the character of the Expedition could do so no longer." The pretext of being bound for California survived only as fodder for knowing jokes about the ship's true destination.

"What's in those boxes?" asked one filibuster in mock ignorance.

"Oh! a few spades and pickaxes that were forgotten!" another joshed.

They found "regular old brown muskets and shining bayonets" when they opened the box. "Curious looking spades and pickaxes," the first filibuster marveled as he inspected the weapons. "We've shouldered those old fellows before!"

Lieutenant William Hardy and another officer, meanwhile, sat in the *Georgiana*'s main cabin and began compiling a list, requested by López, of the names and origins of all the men on the ship. Since editor Sigur would soon be returning to New Orleans in the fishing smack, still other filibusters dashed off farewell letters to loved ones. "While this was going on, Senator Sigur complacently smoked his *segar*, conversed in a low tone, and smiled as he read the ladies' names on many of the letters handed to him, to put in the post-office on his return to New Orleans. The letters all sealed at last, he got into his boat again . . . pushed out, and the last chance of communication with home was gone."

The more "anxious and fearful" among the expedition's privates soon began to yearn for a more explicit accounting of just exactly what they had joined. When several began pounding on Colonel O'Hara's cabin door with their demand, he decided to address the troops en masse. As Richardson Hardy recalled, "He came out, and briefly said, that the expedition was going to Cuba to engage in a revolution. We were first going to rendezvous on an Island, where in a few days, we would be joined by Gen. Lopez in a steamer with several hundred more men. He spoke of it as a patriotic and glorious enterprize, which he had the utmost confidence would succeed, and redound to the honor and benefit of all who engaged in it." The *Georgiana*'s rendezvous with the Louisiana and Mississippi regiments would be on tiny Mujeres Island, off the Yucatán peninsula. From there, all three regiments would sail together on one ship to Cuba.

O'Hara concluded by suggesting that all "who did not feel disposed to encounter such hazards which of course belonged to such an enterprize" should leave on the towboat expected the next morning to pull the *Georgiana* into the Gulf. By the next day's sunrise, April 27, "*three* or *four*" men had decided to accept O'Hara's offer. But when the towboat came alongside, the would-be returnees were so busy trying to get others to join them that they missed their escape. By the time they realized their folly, the towboat had moved ahead of the *Georgiana* —still bound by cable but fatefully inaccessible.[7]

Upon reaching the Gulf of Mexico later that same morning, the filibusters finally hoisted the *Georgiana*'s sails. As the white canvas draping the ship's two masts billowed in the strong Gulf winds, the bracing salt air revived damped spirits. Even the seasickness that soon attacked most of the filibusters did not—at least initially—dull the ocean's invigorating effects. As Richardson Hardy recalled, "It was lovely weather, and the grandeur of the broad Gulf, as we passed out of the Mississippi's muddy waters into the dark blue waves, far from land, caused much sublime and romantic musing. There was, indeed, something dramatic and poetic in the story of that ship." To his diary Marion Taylor confided a similar exultation. "Our bark ploughed the waters as a thing of life. Often had I read and heard of the grandness of the ocean, but it must be seen to be appreciated."[8]

Their exultation, however, soon faded before the routine of life at sea. Though "a fair wind" and clear skies kept the *Georgiana* on course, life as a filibuster was hardly all martial grandeur. "I became military today," Taylor recalled in his diary; "stood guard over a cask of water in the forenoon, and afternoon the provisions." Seabirds, sailfish, and the occasional passing ship offered welcome distractions but proved no match for chronic seasickness, homesickness, bland rations of pork and beans, hopelessly crowded conditions, and the boredom of endless days under the glaring Gulf sun. "The men began to grow tired enough of the crowded deck and sweltering hold." The regiment's 250 men were stuffed onto a single-decked ship only 102 feet long and 26 feet wide. Many soon settled into debilitating introspection: "Various indeed are the speculations among the men as to the result of this expedition," wrote Taylor. "Many of them are very visionary and idle."[9]

Yucatán, May 2–15, 1850

On the evening of May 2, after five days at sea, spirits rose when the filibusters spotted the Yucatán peninsula. "Columbus himself could hardly have manifested more joy than the pent-up Liberators, at the cry of 'land ho!' that echoed through the Georgiana's sails." But the excitement proved short-lived when the filibusters realized that they had overshot their destination, Mujeres Island, by eighty miles. Three more times in as many days the *Georgiana* came within "a few miles" of the island; but each time stiff winds pushed it away. "The wind was dead ahead, and beating up against it the flat-bottomed, crab-sided old bark would not gain twenty miles in twenty-four hours." On May 6, the *Georgiana*'s officers decided to settle for Contoy Island, yet another cay off the Yucatán peninsula, twelve miles north of Mujeres. But the next morning,

May 7, as the *Georgiana* sailed toward Contoy, "the wind was so high that we could not approach nearer than one mile of the shore, and had to land by means of small boats, and it required most of the day."[10]

Contoy was a half-mile long and a few hundred yards wide. A decade earlier the U.S. explorer John Stephens had found its coast "wild and rugged, indented occasionally by small picturesque bays." Richardson Hardy, too, was struck by its wildness. "Contoy is nothing but rocks and sand, the only specimens of vegetation being immense prickly pears, some bushes, long grass, a few dwarf trees, and numberless *lizards!*" Still, Contoy was dry land, and after two weeks aboard a tossing, crowded ship, the young soldiers were glad to arrive on any shore. They stripped and plunged into the roiling surf—"a most delightful, refreshing and invigorating sport." Afterwards, the soldiers claimed several grass huts they found not far from the shore. But after discovering that the structures were inhabited by swarms of insects, the filibusters established camp on higher ground. At Camp Pelican—after "the immense number of those ugly birds which are continually flying over the Island"—the filibusters set to work improvising tents from tree limbs and bushes. Aside from visiting fishing smacks from Cuba and the United States and the occasional Indian from Yucatán, the filibusters' new home was uninhabited. Contoy had no fresh water, and food was sparse; even so, the volunteers got their first taste of sea grapes and the sweet fruit of the icaco tree. Some also met friendly Indians from the mainland, who offered milk and corn and showed them how to make soap from a local weed.[11]

Beyond the quotidian tasks of survival lay the job of transforming a ragtag collection of young volunteers into a cohesive army. Just before leaving the *Georgiana*, senior officers had appointed commanders for six companies, each to include about thirty-five men. Once the officers were appointed, privates selected the company each wanted to join. To reinforce the army's nascent organization, the landing at Contoy had proceeded by individual companies. Over the next few days, officers attempted to step up the military regimen. "After the first comfortable night's rest since leaving New Orleans, the Liberators were up betimes next morning; companies were paraded, and some of them . . . had quite a creditable drill on the sand, for men who had as yet hardly lost the motion of the ship."[12]

The style and organization of López's troops owed much to European republican organizations such as Italy's Carbonari and Russia's Decembrists. More obviously, however, the filibusters aped the hierarchies, protocols, and rules of a more familiar military model—the U.S. Army. Marion Taylor's diary records a ceremony at sea, in spring 1850, in which "the boys signed an instrument binding themselves to obey the regulations of the army, which were to be in accordance with the regulations of the U.S. army." Charles Wilson, a veteran of the López army that had mustered on Round Island a year earlier, recalled that officers were always addressed by military title. As if to counterbalance rules with rights, López in May 1850 provided his soldiers with what a filibuster from the United States recalled as a "declaration of rights, similar in many respects to our own glorious declaration of Independence."[13]

Filibuster privates were recruited with promises of pay equivalent to that of their U.S. Army counterparts. And if the filibusters lacked all but the most rudimentary of uniforms, so did most of the volunteer "citizen soldiers" who two years earlier returned as republican heroes from the Mexican War. Indeed, López's soldiers, and political filibusters in general, drew much of their self-image from those celebrated volunteer patriots of the Mexican War. The romantic term *adventurers*, so often applied to filibusters, had been used in the Mexican War to describe freelance soldiers who, without authorization, simply showed up and informally joined volunteer units.[14]

The filibusters and their public supporters reveled in comparisons to Mexican War volunteers. Praising native sons who had joined López, the Jackson *Mississippian* compared them to other brave young men of the state who had volunteered for the Texas Independence and Mexican wars. "Their valor on the fields of San Jacinto, of Monterey, and Buena Vista," the paper promised, "will achieve fresh laurels in this new theatre of action." Similarly, Kentucky volunteer Richardson Hardy identified the force driving the filibusters as a "patriotism which once led many of them . . . to the walls of Monterey, to the field of Buena Vista, to the gorges of Contreras, and Churubusco's heights." López himself boasted that he commanded "a legion of choice spirits amply powerful to deal Buena-Vista fashion" with any Spanish opposition. In calling his soldiers to arms, he challenged them to present "to Cuba and the world, a signal example of all the virtues as well as all the valor of the American Citizen-Soldier."[15]

Likening the filibusters to Mexican War volunteers made for flattering propaganda. But valid reasons also propelled the comparisons. "Three-fourths of them have served with distinction in Mexico," declared the New Orleans *Delta,* describing López's 1850 expeditionary force. Richardson Hardy claimed that the Mississippi regiment was composed of "the very flower of the Missis-sippi Volunteers in Mexico." Self-conscious comparisons to Mexican War vol-unteers gained added currency from the filibusters' style and approach to war. On the eve of the Mexican War, just under 7,000 men made up the entire U.S. Army. As the war progressed, the army's ranks approached 110,000. About 74,000 of those belonged to volunteer units—the various independent and state militias mustered by individual states to meet federal recruitment quo-tas. The volunteers, soon dubbed citizen soldiers, changed the way U.S. citi-zens thought about their military. Indeed, the most revered Mexican War vic-tories were those—such as the battles of Monterey and Buena Vista—in which volunteers had proved critical.[16]

The republicanism that drove the U.S. War of Independence had be-queathed to the nation a profound distrust of standing armies. Before the Mexican War, most U.S. citizens felt at best ambivalent about their men in uniform, most of whom were career professionals. Even the full-time warriors of the Continental army, who secured the nation's independence from Britain, failed to win deep popular affection; they were widely viewed as an expensive, potentially corrupting institution likely to nourish the sort of abuses of power associated with British rule. The necessity of the Continental army was only grudgingly accepted after volunteer units proved inadequate in defeating the British.[17] Career militarists, after all, were unlikely to stir deep affection among the citizenry of a republic founded in rebellion against what the Dec-laration of Independence called "absolute Tyranny."

Citizen soldiers were different, and the qualities that set them apart from regular soldiers were those they shared with filibusters. Both Mexican War volunteers and López's filibusters bristled with a U.S. republicanism that sanc-tioned expansionism, slavery, and, implicitly, a deep attachment to individual states—a bond at least equal to that felt for the entire nation. Both Mexican War volunteers and filibusters celebrated a pride of local place, and rivalries among states were never far during assessments of battlefield heroism. To an officer seeking counsel on how to motivate soldiers in tough situations, Gen-eral Zachary Taylor had advised, "Call upon their State pride . . . they will not resist that." Similar rivalries animated the soldiers of López's spring 1850 expe-dition. As the Mississippians claimed to represent "the flower" of their state's heroic stock, so the Kentucky regiment reveled in its self-image as "all gentle-men!": "What fire, intelligence and energy glows in every countenance!"

Richardson Hardy contrasted the "world-renowned characteur" of the military heroism of his Kentucky regiment with the "degraded characteur" of the Louisiana regiment. Compared with the Mississippi and Louisiana battalions, Hardy claimed, the Kentucky regiment richly deserved its status as the "van guard of the Liberating Army."[18]

The U.S. public also warmed to its Mexican War volunteers because, unlike standing armies, citizen soldiers declined to make a career of war. Volunteers came to their avocation (so they claimed) reluctantly; they served a limited period of time (most for one year or the war's duration) in the service of a worthy but limited objective (avenging U.S. honor in Mexico). Soldiers in López's army claimed a similar selflessness: the Kentucky regiment's Captain William Hardy, a veteran of "the bloody charges on Buena Vista," was said to be a "democrat in politics, with sentiments and impulses ever ready to be enlisted in the cause of popular rights and elevation, whether to be contended for on the 'stump,' or with weapons to tyrants and oppressors more eloquent than words." Writing home, one López filibuster recalled earlier volunteer service in the Mexican War: "I lost an arm in defending her [the United States'] rights and the National honor—I regret the loss of the arm, but glory in the cause in which it was lost." As for his remaining arm, "I have another left, that I am now going to peril for the liberation of the Cubans."[19]

During the filibusters' first night on Contoy, May 7, they burned three signal fires in case the steamer carrying López and the Louisiana regiment passed by en route to Mujeres. The *Creole*, López's ship, failed to appear. Instead, the soldiers awoke the next morning to find themselves "surrounded" by Spanish ships—three skiffs, each anchored on a different side of the island. Later in the day, a delegation of filibusters boarded one of the ships and discovered the Spaniards were merely fisherman. Before returning to Camp Pelican, the scouts even shared a repast of wine and fruit with their visitors.

Though a false alarm, the incident had underscored the little army's perilous position. Biding their time at Contoy, miles from where they were supposed to meet López, the filibusters made an easy target for any Spanish warships that might happen by, or who were alerted to their presence by any other passing mariners. The signal fires in the night increased that vulnerability. The *Georgiana*, still laden with most of their provisions, lay at anchor with only "eight or ten" defenders. Making matters worse, several filibusters had become ill after drinking the island's brackish water.

At Camp Pelican any sense of esprit de corps warred with a growing malaise. Were they heroic liberators or just desperate castaways? And why were they marking time on this hot, barren stretch of sand and prickly pear? As frustrations mounted, Colonel O'Hara hired a sailor from one of the Spanish skiffs to pilot the *Georgiana* to Mujeres. They left Contoy on May 8, but Mujeres again proved elusive; for three days, the bark tried but failed to reach the island.

By May 11 the *Georgiana* again lay anchored off Contoy. With high winds now keeping the soldiers hostage to the elements aboard their own ship, "impatience and discontent began to breed mutiny." One group of schemers plotted to seize a stash of weapons aboard the ship, confine the *Georgiana's* officers to their cabins, and force the vessel's return to New Orleans. Senior officers, however, were aware of the plot. That evening, as the plotters prepared to execute their revolt, Captain H. H. Robinson, "just at the critical moment appeared before the mutineers, informed them in a determined tone, that all the ammunition was in the cabin, and sooner than they should succeed in their cowardly design, he would blow them, ship and all, 'sky high.'" The mutineers "were terrified and never again thought of attempting to carry things by force."

Even Captain Benson, the expedition's hireling commander, tried his hand at mutiny, putting out the word that if a majority of the filibusters signed a petition demanding a return to New Orleans, he would gladly comply; though nothing came of the plot, "fifty or sixty" signatures were quickly gathered. Still another insurrection percolated among a group of discontented senior officers. Among those, Major William Hardy informed Colonel O'Hara that he would be leaving the expedition unless O'Hara appeared before the entire regiment with a coherent explanation of his plans.[20]

The loose, even fluid, command structure of López's filibuster—with its easy tolerance of insubordination—no doubt would have affronted many professional officers. But such martial laxity remained endemic to the unique republican tradition that both created and sustained filibustering. As good republicans, volunteers and filibusters—unlike professional armies—shared a qualified tolerance of democracy within their ranks. The acceptance of such democracy began in the very composition of those ranks: as soldiers in Mexican War volunteer units ranged from polished professional men to unlettered frontiersmen, so the composition of López's army ranged from the Kentucky regiment's "gentlemen" to the Louisiana regiment's "degraded men."[21]

Further enhancing the democratic spirit, Mexican War volunteers—to the horror of regular army officers—elected their commanders, a practice duplicated in López's army up to the level of company commander. Even company membership was a matter of choice. After the Kentucky regiment elected its company commanders, privates were then "directed to make choice of the companies which they prefered to join." In the same spirit the Louisiana regiment, after "a drink all round," divided itself into ten companies, then selected officers for each unit. The new officers, in turn, were instructed to "draw lots for rank." In size Mexican War volunteer companies differed from their filibuster counterparts. Under a law of 1792, U.S. Army volunteer companies generally contained about sixty-five privates. Each company in López's 1850 expedition, by contrast, numbered only about thirty-five privates. Perennial optimists, the filibusters expected to bring the companies "to their full strength with Cubans that would join them on their arrival in Cuba."[22]

Both U.S. volunteer units and López's army were liberal in dispensing promotions, a tendency compounded during the Mexican War by the awarding of honorary brevet ranks. Similarly, memoirs of López's expedition abound in references to promotions; beyond advancements awarded within the expeditionary army to Cuba, filibuster officers were "offered *high rank* in the future permanent Army of the Republic." Upon Cuba's annexation by the United States, such rankings presumably could be converted to U.S. Army commissions.[23]

In such an egalitarian milieu, the U.S. Army volunteer unit officer and his filibuster counterpart each balanced two ethos—one military, another democratic. In word, deed, and deportment, each had to demonstrate martial authority and an implicit awareness of that authority's limits. Of the two officers, however, the filibuster commander faced the more delicate balancing act. O'Hara, for instance, managed to thwart potential mutineers with his threat to blow the *Georgiana* "sky high." But he did not shoot them, as an officer wielding the authority of a sovereign state likely would have done: among Mexican War volunteer units of the U.S. Army, mutineers and deserters were routinely executed in the field.[24]

One key difference did firmly set filibuster commanders apart from those of U.S. Army volunteer units. López's commanders, for all purposes, were stateless. They enjoyed no anointed sanction from any government or from any other awe-inspiring institution. As J. C. Davis recalled, "We . . . sailed under a strange flag, one identified with no government, as yet, on earth." Beyond whatever sense of shared mission filibuster officers could generate through sheer force of will—or rhetoric, rituals, and regalia—the only tangible adhesive binding privates to the army was their promised pay.[25]

Amid the crush of a filibuster officer's duties, that burden could be easily forgotten. As the Kentucky regiment's Richardson Hardy complained of O'Hara and "most of his staff," they "seemed poorly to appreciate their position, and their conduct in many respects evinced a sadly deficient knowledge of human nature." What especially grated was the officers' "supercilious dignity and high-toned authority." As Hardy put it, "*their* commission was nothing more than the acquiescence and support of those men, yet they for a long while acted as if it bore the signet of a nation. They heard that discontent was threatened, but merely made use of some scornful expression or abusive allusion, and kept their 'awful state,' without *deigning* to make an effort for pacification."

López's conspiracy had its own flag and coat of arms. It issued bonds and routinely published documents brimming with official-sounding legalese. To instill esprit de corps, a filibuster commander could drill his troops and deliver speeches linking them to other republican ventures. They were, López and his officers constantly told them, spiritual heirs to the heroes of the U.S. Independence and the Mexican wars. For obvious reasons, foreigners who had assisted the Continental army, such as Lafayette and Pulaski, were especially prized. For all that, the filibuster army remained a strictly ad hoc proposition whose day-to-day survival rested on dubious credentials. López's commanders claimed no "signet of a nation." A filibuster officer confronting insubordination could make no threats of turning over an offender to "proper" authorities. If, on the other hand, the officer executed the offending insubordinate, he risked sparking mutiny. One Kentucky regiment lieutenant, for example, was merely "reduced to the ranks" after being hauled before a filibuster "Court Martial" on "charges of disrespect to his superior officer." But even that meager punishment, Richardson Hardy noted, "smacked of rigorous discipline, rather new to the Kentuckians."

Even the expedition's commander-in-chief faced the consequences of such lax discipline. On May 7, the *Creole*'s first night out from New Orleans, a mutiny erupted that was eventually "quelled by speeches from General Lopez, and others." López also had to guarantee the early payment of promised bounties and the filibusters' prompt return to the United States once the revolution was "accomplished."[26]

If, by contrast, a filibuster officer simply accepted a certain amount of insubordination as the price of keeping the peace, he could safely depend on a fast unraveling of his remaining authority. Colonel Chatham Roberdeau Wheat, commander of the fractious Louisiana regiment, learned that lesson well in May 1850 after he backed down in an argument over money with a group of filibuster privates. A veteran of the Seminole Indian wars who had joined López's army, F. C. M. Boggess later published a memoir of his military exploits in which he recalled how he and two other volunteers each paid $10 for "the privileges" of an officer's cabin aboard the *Susan Loud,* the ship on which the Louisiana company sailed from New Orleans. Upon being told by Wheat that their privileges did not include dining in the cabin, the three demanded the return of their money. When Wheat refused and the privates persisted in their demand, the dispute widened within the regiment into "an open rupture . . . and a resort to arms."

Wheat eventually yielded and returned the money. As Boggess gleefully recounted the incident, the complaint of the ejected diners "was just and they were in the majority and Colonel Wheat was in the minority." The reversal, however, won Wheat no favor among his troops; in the wake of the capitulation, according to Boggess, "Colonel Wheat lost his popularity for all times to come." In the end, the beleaguered filibuster officer's only real chance of preserving his authority lay in preempting problems before they festered into mutiny.[27]

As complaints mounted among the restless troops confined by stormy weather aboard the *Georgiana* off Contoy Island, Lieutenant Colonel O'Hara on May 11 decided to make a speech. After supper he gathered them together and announced that if they were not joined by General López and the expedition's other regiments within eight days, the *Georgiana* would return to New Orleans. "Unanimous enthusiasm" greeted O'Hara's blunt promise, and—at least for the moment—the old martial republicanism revived; three cheers rose for López, another three for "*annexation.*" "Then followed a regular mass meeting—speakers were called out, and nearly a dozen of the officers made glowing speeches, full of war, glory, heroism, independence, 'Lone Stars,' fame and immortality!"[28]

The next day, May 12, as the mutineers "sneaked off ashamed of themselves," steadier warriors stoked the fires of martial ardor. "An oath was that day drawn up for every true Liberator to sign, pledging himself to obey the orders of his officers, to submit to the rules and Articles of War of the U.S. Army, with true allegiance and support to the Republican Government of Cuba, at present represented in the person of General Narciso Lopez." All but about eighteen of the army of 150 signed the document. Those who declined would not be allowed to continue to Cuba. "Thus by a very little exertion and *condescension* was harmony and spirit restored to the battalion."[29]

On May 2, as the *Georgiana*, fighting Gulf winds, was making its first failed attempt to land on Mujeres, J. C. Davis of New Orleans walked down to the docks of the city's Second Municipality. Reaching the river front at 4:00 P.M., he climbed to the top of the planked levee. There, amid the jumble of ships, gangplanks, ropes, boxes and bales, Davis finally spotted a brig called the *Susan Loud.* Boarding the ship, Davis observed that its deck was already crowded with men. "Every one seemed occupied in stowing away certain significant-looking demijohns, baskets (square ones of course), boxes, junk bottles, Bowie-knives, etc., etc."[30]

The 150–filibuster-strong Louisiana regiment that sailed that night of May 2 aboard the *Susan Loud* had been recruited by Colonel Chatham Roberdeau Wheat, a young New Orleans lawyer. A round-faced man with thick black hair and protruding brows, the twenty-four-year-old Wheat already enjoyed "a flattering reputation as a cavalry officer" for his service under General John Quitman in the Mexican War. The son of an Episcopal minister, Wheat by age twelve had acquired a taste for martial adventure after reading the English romantic novelist Jane Porter's *Thaddeus of Warsaw*, a fictional depiction of the Polish patriot Kosciusko. After his turn with López, Wheat would fight in William Walker's filibuster in Nicaragua and, still later, in the Confederate army.[31]

As a regimental leader in López's army, Wheat attracted some credible officers to his side. But his Louisiana regiment lacked the panache of the *Georgiana*'s Kentucky battalion. The Kentucky regiment had been assembled over a period of months by recruiters who had promised "as fine material as could be found anywhere." Wheat's regiment, by contrast, was mustered in only a few weeks. And while the "gentlemen" of the Kentucky regiment were drawn from the broad expanse of the Ohio River valley, the Louisiana regiment was recruited from one city—most of its members from a single bar. Although the opulent Bank's Arcade bar warranted its reputation as one of the nation's most stylish saloons, it was hardly an auspicious venue for the recruitment of distinguished military gentlemen. Richardson Hardy even suggested that "many of the worthless characters and blackguard rowdies" of the Louisiana regiment had originally "applied for and been refused admission into the Kentucky Battalion." Indeed, true to their barroom propensities, once aboard the *Susan Loud*, many in the Louisiana regiment killed idle time in long games of poker with dubious stakes. As Wheat observed, "During the card playing, I noticed that the boys not only betted very freely with the money they had before them, but they also bet in prospective, large amounts in . . . Cuban bonds."[32]

After supper on May 6, with the *Susan Loud* safely beyond U.S. territorial limits, Wheat assembled his Louisianans on the ship's deck for a formal speech. Addressing the men as "FELLOW CITIZENS," he began by invoking the legal conceit that their destination was Panama and eventually California. But though obliging port officials in New Orleans had cleared them for Chagres, he added, perhaps they might prefer a less distant port. "Capt. Pendleton informs me that it is a matter of perfect indifference with him whether we proceed to Chagres or not, since he has been paid the charter for his vessel to that place; hence, if we stop short of our destination, he cannot be injured."

The filibusters, as a chorus, assented to going to Cuba, and Wheat waved a folded sheet of paper before them. "I hold in my hand," he said, "a paper delivered to me by one of Gen'l Lopez's aids, the seal of which he told me to break when in Lat. 26° N. and 87° W., which point we have now reached." He opened the paper and began to read General López's instructions. They were to remain in the area until the next day, May 7. After nightfall that same day, López would depart New Orleans aboard the *Creole*, the filibusters' third ship. The *Susan Loud*, meanwhile, would reverse course and sail on a straight line toward Balize. The two ships should rendezvous on the eighth somewhere roughly midway between Louisiana and the Yucatán peninsula.

"I have addressed you as FELLOW CITIZENS," Wheat continued, "because it is perhaps the last time I shall ever address you as Citizens of the United States.

Long ere the sun has sunk beneath the world of waters which now surround us, we shall perhaps have consummated an act that will throw us beyond the protection of the *stars* and the *stripes* under whose auspices we have sailed thus far. *This act* is simply organizing our little band into a skeleton Regiment for the purpose of landing on and wrenching Cuba from the grasp of bigoted and besotted Spain. *The* moment we organize, *that* moment we pass beyond the protection of our own government, we have no longer any right to sail under her flag. . . . I shall therefore henceforth address you as SOLDIERS of the LIBERATING ARMY OF CUBA."

Thoroughly warmed to his subject, Wheat then spoke of the transforming powers of republicanism, a force, he assured them, that had even imparted a new morality to the act of war; "It has well been said, that we live in an age of *progress*, and no circumstance, perhaps, is more indicative of the onward march of the time, than this *expedition!* When civilization was in its infancy, nation made war upon nation for conquest and booty, more recently, they have gone to war for principle, such was the case in the American revolution." During that conflict, he reminded them, the marquis de Lafayette, a French-man, had come to the aid of the patriots "after they themselves had taken up arms." Today's patriotism, he added, commands even more sacrifice. "Every patriot's duty . . . now consists, not so much in going to the rescue of an op-pressed people . . . as in striking the first blow for them, which we propose to do for the Cubans."[33]

As Wheat concluded, the "Free Flag of Cuba" rose for the first time on the *Susan Loud*'s masthead. As a colony of Spain, of course, the island had no offi-cial flag. This banner, designed for the filibuster by José Teurbe Tolón, a Con-sejo Cubano member and editor at *La Verdad*, evoked the "Lone Star" flag of Texas; its left side bore a white star on a blue triangular field; four broad blue and white horizontal stripes ran across its right side. As the banner was "thrown to the breeze," Wheat shouted to the cheering filibusters: "Liberators! Behold your flag!"[34]

Over the next two weeks, when Moses Yale Beach of the New York *Sun* and Laurent Sigur of the New Orleans *Delta* hoisted the same banner over their re-spective offices, New Yorkers and New Orleanians also had their first look at the filibuster flag. Such public bravado, which naturally drew the ire of Spain's minister in Washington, marked a long-awaited moment for López and his supporters. On the evening of May 7, López, Ambrosio Gonzales, and the 130 members of the Mississippi regiment finally slipped away from New Orleans aboard the *Creole*, the old steamer that former Mississippi senator John Henderson had purchased for $16,000 with funds from the bond sales. The regiment aboard the *Creole*—reputed to include "the flower of Mississippi chivalry"—had been organized by Lieutenant Colonel W. J. Bunch and had received a "glowing" review from Gonzales.[35]

Three days later, on May 10, at about 1:00 P.M., the rowdies of the Louisiana regiment aboard the *Susan Loud* had just finished toasting their ship's captain with "about 4 gallons of the best old whiskey" when they spotted a plume of smoke curling against the horizon. They were sailing on the line on which they were supposed to meet the *Creole*, but who could be sure that the smoke was not rising from a Spanish brig? Or perhaps a U.S. Navy warship? President Taylor, after all, had already dispatched two warships to sail along Cuba's coast in search of López's ships. And three other U.S. warships had been ordered to put in calls at various Cuban ports. All five ships carried instructions to do whatever necessary to prevent a filibuster landing.[36]

The suspense ended just before dark when the vessel sailed close enough for the filibusters on the *Susan Loud* to spot a red flag flapping in the breeze; it was the *Creole*. As planned, the *Susan Loud* answered the *Creole*'s signal with its own white flag, and soon both ships were waving the Lone Star banner of Free Cuba. Within minutes the *Creole* sailed alongside the *Susan Loud*, "greeted by three as hearty cheers as stout men and old liquor could command."

López and Gonzales met with the Louisiana regiment's officers aboard the *Susan Loud*, then returned to the *Creole* for the night. The army spent most of the next day, May 11, transferring the Louisiana regiment and its provisions to the *Creole*. Even the *Susan Loud*'s master mariner, Simeon Pendleton, was—in J. C. Davis's words—"induced" to come over to the *Creole*. According to Davis, although the Boston trader Pendleton was a latecomer to the conspiracy, he was as interested in the main chance as anyone else aboard the *Creole*. "The Captain being a pretty shrewd yankee had an eye to the trade between the *new* Republic [of Cuba] and the United States, which of course will be ten-fold what it is at present, within twelve months from the time it becomes a free State."[37]

By other accounts, however, Pendleton's induction into the filibuster's life was more of an impressment. In a government deposition later that year, Pendleton—in an assertion that concurs with Richardson Hardy's account of the incident—claimed to have been "forcibly detained" aboard the *Creole* and to have been ignorant of the entire conspiracy. Until his impressment, he said, he had believed that the *Susan Loud* really was transporting California émigrés to *Chagres*. And why was López so eager to gain Pendleton's assistance? According to Davis, shortly after the rendezvous of the two ships, López learned that "Captain Pendleton was well acquainted with all the principal harbors in Cuba, having traded to the island for many years."[38]

After all of the filibusters, on May 11, had boarded the *Creole* to sail for Mujeres, the *Susan Loud's* mate, Thomas Hale, assured Pendleton that he would return the chartered ship to its home port of Boston. The *Creole* and the *Susan Loud* parted ways at 4:00 P.M. that afternoon. Two days later, the *Creole's* master, Armstrong Irvine Lewis, spotted the Yucatán coast but soon realized that a storm the previous evening had taken them about thirty miles off-course. The next morning, the fourteenth, as the *Creole*, still fighting a stiff breeze, tacked toward Mujeres, its crew spotted a sail just off Contoy. At 8:00 A.M., after the *Creole* had sailed closer to the island for a better look, its crew could clearly see the *Georgiana* bobbing at anchor on Contoy's lee.[39]

The Kentucky regiment also was watching the ocean that morning of May 14. As the *Creole* smoked toward Contoy, the filibusters encamped there were gathered on the beach, watching as Colonel O'Hara tried to identity the mysterious ship sailing toward them. "At first, only a moving cloud of smoke could be discerned, but in a few minutes Col. O'Hara, with the spy-glass, made out a steamer of the *Creole* build, heading directly for us. In a short time more, the patriot signal was clearly seen—a white flag, which was also soon flying at the main-mast of the Georgiana. Words can give but faint expression of the feelings which now swelled the hearts of both divisions on this safe and glorious union."[40]

As the *Creole* came within shouting distance, cheering erupted from both regiments—one still at sea, the other on the beach. The Kentucky regiment gave "some of those famous Old Kentuck' yells, which used to terrify the Mexicans so awfully." As the "Free Flag of Cuba" rose over the *Creole*, the ship's master, Captain Lewis, with López at his side, stepped forward with a "speaking trumpet." "General Lopez's compliments to the Kentucky Battalion," Lewis's voice blared over the crashing surf; "the Colonel will please come aboard."

Colonel Theodore O'Hara and Major William Hardy of the Kentucky regiment boarded the *Creole* for a conference of senior officers, during which they decided that the *Creole* would sail to Mujeres Island and bring fresh water back to Contoy. A steamer would have a better chance of beating the winds than any sailing vessel—especially a "flat-bottomed, crab-sided old bark" like the *Georgiana*. Upon its return, the entire army would board the *Creole* and sail directly to Cuba.[41]

The *Creole* prepared for an immediate departure for Mujeres. Before it sailed López distributed a broadside among the filibusters. Topped by the conspiracy's coat of arms, the document—addressed to "Soldiers of the Liberating Expedition of Cuba!"—praised the filibusters as idealistic Americans who "are going to give to Cuba that freedom for which your example has taught her to sigh." After comparing them to such European republicans of the U.S. War of Independence as Lafayette, Pulaski, and Kosciusko, the sheet promised that "our first act on arrival shall be the establishment of a Provisional Constitution, founded on American principles and adapted to the emergencies of the occasion." And if rhetoric alone failed to instill the proper esprit de corps, the Kentucky regiment soon received uniforms. Each soldier got a red flannel shirt, similar to those worn by the European revolutionists of 1848, and "a black cloth cap, with a Lone Star cockade." Pants colors differentiated ranks: captains wore white, lieutenants black, and privates had to content themselves with "various shades and stripes."[42]

By 4:00 P.M. that same afternoon, May 14, the *Creole* lay anchored off Mujeres's western shore. Among the ship's restless crew, some of whom had been at sea for two full weeks, "the officers discovered that all discipline was at an end." Rowboats were dropped into the sea to hasten their movement ashore, but some of the filibusters were so eager to reach dry land that they plunged from the ship's deck and began swimming.[43]

Once all were ashore, the burial of Private John Moore of the Louisiana regiment was among the filibusters' first tasks. Moore, a young printer from Mississippi, had been shot to death the day before by an accidentally fired musket. Only two days earlier Moore, popular for his improvised sing-alongs, had regaled his comrades with his own filibuster version of "Oh! Susanna":

> O, Cuba, Cuba is the land for me,
> I'm bound to *make some money* there!
> And set the Cubans free—

Now, as the Reverend John M. McCann of Paris, Kentucky, the "chaplain of the expedition," offered the eulogy—"officiating according to the ceremonies of the Episcopal Church"—Moore's lifeless body, in a box that days earlier had contained muskets, was consigned to a lonely grave on an island far from his native Mississippi; afterwards, his comrades placed a "rough hewn cross" over the grave.[44]

Still other filibusters busied themselves exploring Mujeres. Even before reaching the shore, the soldiers had discovered that the island was far from uninhabited. There seemed to be about "thirty or forty ranches, and from sixty to one hundred men, women and children, of Spanish descent." All seemed to be refugees, driven to Mujeres by Indians in the "caste war" that, though officially over, still ravaged the Yucatán mainland.[45]

Reconnoitering Mujeres over the next two days, the filibusters delighted in the discovery of an abandoned stone fortress, an "ancient vestige of Spanish dominion." They also relished the island's natural bounties: reptiles ("the largest lizard, that any of us had ever seen, heard or read of . . . about 18 inches long"), "beautiful specimens of the Cactus," and "rare and beautiful tropical flowers." They also delighted in their encounters with "real, genuine Mexicans." "The women were for the most part dressed in a loose flowing gown, with large sleeves, no waist, and fastened around the neck by a drawing string and not drawn over tight at that. The children were dressed after the same fashion, that is, that of them that were dressed at all." The native attire shocked the Christian mores of these southern boys of the Mississippi and Louisiana regiments. But like the volunteer U.S. soldiers in the Mexican War—who often imagined that they had stumbled upon a tropical Eden—the filibusters found a biblical innocence in the islanders' ways. The nude children were, after all, only "honoring . . . the early customs of those unsophisticated people known in all the catechisms as Adam and Eve."

Filibusters shared with Mexican War volunteers a lust for adventures in exotic climes. For thousands of soldiers the Mexican War, their nation's first true foreign war, had provided their first trip out of the country. Because the entire eighteen months of the war included only about a dozen substantial battles, they also had time to indulge in the pleasures of the traveler: soldiers passed time reading (and in some cases writing) books on Mexico, learned to cook Mexican, studied Spanish grammars, and visited and collected souvenirs from archaeological sites. In some cases, they even attended Mexican concerts and theater, as well as religious and funeral services. They also indulged a fascination with

Mexico's topography, flora, and fauna. "I was struck dumb with admiration and amazement," wrote one soldier after gazing upon the sun's first light against a high Mexican mountain. "What a country to dream in!"[46]

Attending the admiration for Mexico's natural bounty and ancient history was the conviction that the modern nation was peopled by a "degraded" race, a society of "dirt, slovenliness, and misery." That perception, then rampant in the U.S. press, helped defeat the All-Mexico movement in 1847. Acquisition of the entirety of Mexico was unfeasible, critics charged, because republican government can survive only among "a virtuous and intelligent people."[47]

Wandering the Gulf of Mexico on their own republican mission, López's soldiers indulged a similar tropical exoticism. From Contoy to Mujeres to Cuba, they displayed an abiding delight in unfamiliar animals and landscapes. The folkways and history of indigenous cultures also captivated, as did historical ruins. Writing in the New Orleans *Delta*, one "Liberator" described Cuba as "this bright Isle, that stretches its floral length beneath the soft and balmy influences of the tropics—begirt, on either side, by the blue waves of ocean, and fanned by its health-diffusing breezes—that Isle, from whose base rises in majestic heights the broad blue mountains, where the songsters of richest plumage pour forth their sweetest notes—the 'land of the orange and vine'— the golden key, even, to our own portals."[48]

Only one flaw marred this blessed island—its greedy *peninsular* overlords: "dwarfish, inane and penury-striken dons, who drain its substance to furnish them means to bluster of their exploded nobility at home." As the Mexican War volunteers had viewed Mexico as a degraded Eden, so the filibusters adopted the view, then popular among U.S. writers, that Cuba was a paradise and the Creoles were a race which had been brought low by Spanish tyranny. As one filibuster complained to his mother, "The people who inhabit this lovely spot are the most degraded, downtrodden dagos on earth."[49]

But if Cubans were so degraded, why bother to liberate them? The "Liberator" had a simple answer: those "downtrodden" souls "have heard of the beauty, justice, liberty and fame of our glorious republic, and desire to have a government like it." Like that of the antigovernment, anticlerical *Puros*, whose deserved liberation had justified Washington's conquest of otherwise degenerate Mexico, so the desire of Cuba's Creoles for republican government raised filibustering to a secure moral summit.[50]

When not exploring Mujeres, the filibusters stayed busy loading fresh water onto the *Creole*, washing clothes and, with Spanish and U.S. coin, purchasing foodstuffs from the islanders—everything from tortillas to chocolate, dried turtle eggs to hens' eggs. Beneath the outward industriousness, however, discontents were eroding the army's cohesion. As word spread that all of the filibusters would soon be boarding the *Creole* for Cuba, fears grew of overcrowding aboard the weathered old ship. Skepticism about the *Creole's* seaworthiness were nourished by a rumor that forty miles at sea on a recent New Orleans-to-Havana trip, it had been forced to return to port "in consequence of a leak, that was near sinking her." Within the Louisiana regiment, the fears ripened into murmurs of desertion and mutiny. When senior officers learned of such talk, Colonel Wheat on May 15 decided to do what Colonel O'Hara of the Kentucky regiment had done—to stare down potential insurrection with a morale-building speech. Gathering the troops together, he began his oration by thanking them for joining the mission and likening their service to "those gallant souls that rushed so nobly to the aid of Mexico, Poland, Hungary, and Texas."[51]

Wheat's oration evoked the usual filibuster themes—patriotism, republicanism, the need for military valor—eventually landing upon the subject of war atrocities. He urged upon the filibusters "the necessity of the most rigid discipline, for in that consists our strength." During the Mexican War abuses of civilians had blemished the claimed selflessness of the nation's citizen soldiers. That the murders, thefts, and rapes usually were linked to volunteers rather than regular army soldiers only darkened the stain. For however flawed their actual record, U.S. soldiers of the Mexican War had taken great pride in what one writer called their "chivalric generosity" toward civilians. As emissaries of an exemplary republicanism, how else could they behave? Similarly, officers in López's army repeatedly urged that, once in Cuba, they should direct no violence against noncombatants. As Wheat warned, "Let it not be said that female virtue has been violated by one of my brave Louisianians—guard strictly too the rights of property."[52]

Wheat concluded with a call to arms: "And now my brave boys, let us under command of our noble chieftain rush to the field of glory, pluck the besotted usurper from her Island pedestal." Three cheers greeted the conclusion of Wheat's address. Afterwards, López gathered all the officers aboard the *Creole* for a short conference. As the army prepared for sleep that night, "all felt that dissension was at an end."[53]

En Route: Yucatán to Cuba, May 16–17, 1850

The next morning, May 16, when a group of officers gathered aboard the *Creole* for another conference, they learned that thirteen privates had disappeared during the night. "At first it was proposed to go after them and bring them on board, but upon more mature deliberation it was thought best to let them remain without molestation, as the rest were better off without them." By 8:00 that morning the *Creole* was steaming away from the island without the deserters. Upon spotting a few of the castoffs, ashore waving the black flag of piracy, López was informed that they planned to steal a Spanish fishing smack anchored in the bay, sail it to Tampico, Mexico, then return to the United States. Rejecting calls that he take musket in hand and draw a bead on the miscreants, López instead ordered the *Creole* to pull alongside the fishing boat. He then told its captain of the renegades' plan. Since no winds stirred the bay that morning, the *Creole* towed the smack away from Mujeres and released it in the Gulf.[54]

The thirteen-mile return trip to Contoy passed quickly, and "great joy" erupted when the *Creole* once again dropped anchor and was lashed to the *Georgiana.* Lieutenant Colonel Pickett of the Kentucky regiment, duly "deputized" by López for the ceremony, formally presented the filibuster flag to his men. Speeches and three cheers followed. As the diarist Marion Taylor recalled, "It was truly an inspiring scene to behold upon the tossing billows of the ocean two vessels upon each of which was seen the flags being presented to troops going to fight for the liberty of the oppressed of Cuba." López, however, soon received sobering news from the Kentucky regiment's Colonel O'Hara: "two small Spanish sail vessels had reconnoitered them the day before and then sailed for Havana." Fearing that Spanish warships might already be headed toward Contoy, López ordered that they depart as soon as possible. Arms and provisions now aboard the *Georgiana* would have to be transferred at sea to the *Creole*—against strong winds, no small task: "A heavy sea was rolling while the vessels were lashed together, and the waves drove them against each other with fearful force."[55]

The Kentucky regiment included a group of men who, though aware of the expedition's true intent when they joined, nonetheless had believed that it really would be stopping at Chagres en route to Cuba. After getting their free ride to Chagres, the men had planned to desert, cross the Panamanian isthmus, and sail for California. Now, with the *Creole* readying to sail for Cuba, they, wanted to return to the United States. López offered them passage to New Orleans aboard the *Georgiana* and that night "ten or twelve" accepted the offer. They, along with others who elected to leave the expedition, gained their freedom the next day, but only after some of them were forced to transfer coal from the *Georgiana* to the *Creole* and suffer a humiliating forced march through the ranks of their "hissing and groaning" former comrades.[56]

By one o'clock on the morning of May 17, both soldiers and cargo had been transferred to the *Creole*. The filibusters were ready to leave for Cuba, but were their numbers sufficient? In all, about 560 filibusters had departed New Orleans over the past three weeks. But 42 had deserted, and another 21 were either "unwell" or part of the ship's commissary. Attrition thus brought the number of "efficient men" to "about 500," still a heavy load for a ship only 166 feet long and 22 feet across.[57]

The *Creole* sailed from Contoy sometime after 1:00 A.M., on the morning of May 17. At sea crowded conditions aboard the old steamer warred against military order. "Guards were regularly detailed to keep the men in their quarters; none but commissioned officers, or those under their direction, were permitted to pass from one part of the ship to another." If nothing else, simple physics required such discipline: during its first two days out of Contoy, the *Creole* faced "a tremendous heavy sea"; unless the weight aboard the overcrowded ship was reasonably balanced—"trim"—the steamer's two giant paddle-wheels "would not half the time touch water."

Privates' quarters were especially unpleasant. "Several companies were almost smothered in the hold, whilst others scorched on the deck, during the heat of the day." Even so, Richardson Hardy recalled, the *Creole's* deck remained the preferred post; during the morning and evening, it was even "really delightful." Companies assigned to the deck had the opportunity to drill "several hours" each day, "and some of them attained a most creditable state of discipline." To bolster fledgling military esprit, López often left his captain's cabin and walked on the main deck, mingling with privates.[58]

During the *Creole*'s first full day out of Contoy, May 17, López gathered the filibusters together and finally unveiled his strategy to the entire army. They would land, he said, at the port of Cárdenas, seventy miles east of Havana. With a population of only three thousand, Cárdenas, López believed, could be taken by surprise without gunfire. There the filibusters would seize a train and travel westward to the larger coastal city of Matanzas. With its population of thirty thousand, Matanzas would serve as the army's recruitment center. About one hundred filibusters, meanwhile, would continue by rail to within nine miles of Havana, where they would blow up a key bridge, eliminating the captain general's option of sending troops to Matanzas by train. López remained convinced that Cuba teemed with latent Creole revolutionaries, insurgents who simply awaited the spark of an outside invading force. In Matanzas he expected to recruit about five thousand men, enough to fill out his existing three regiments and organize three new ones. Building from that nucleus, López expected to reach Havana eight days later with some thirty thousand soldiers.[59]

Aboard the *Creole* on May 17, as the landing at Cárdenas loomed closer, López's bold strategy seemed increasingly at odds with his personal demeanor. "As we neared the Island, the old General began to grow visibly more restless. He usually sat upon his bed, smoking a cigarito and conversing with his Aids, or examining a map of Cuba." When not in his cabin, López "paraded the deck rapidly, spy-glass in hand, eagerly watching and examining the vessels, numbers of which were all the time in sight." Richardson Hardy recalled that each time a ship was spotted, the filibusters heard the same tiresome command. "The order, 'off with your red shirts,' was repeated several times a day."[60]

Cárdenas, Cuba, May 18–19, 1850

On the morning of May 18—which the filibusters assumed would be the day of their landing on Cuban soil—they awoke to a good omen; the Gulf of Mexico's waters, so troubled for the past few days, were suddenly "smooth." Buffeted by a "delicious breeze," "the *Creole* was gliding gracefully and rapidly with her cargo of *War*." That afternoon López ordered a full-dress "grand review" of the Kentucky regiment. The Kentuckians had just begun to strap on swords, polish muskets, and don their red shirts when the familiar order suddenly came across the deck: "Off with your red shirts—down in the hold!" Minutes later some "fifteen to twenty" ships surrounded the *Creole*. All, as it turned out, were commercial vessels. Even so, because the *Creole* was now nearing Cuba, any attention was unwelcome. As López surveyed the other vessels with his spyglass, the *Creole*, like an "artful dodger," steamed carefully through the forest of sails. "It was almost a dead calm—the sail vessels could make little progress, while the steamer running first one way and then another, at last left them all astern."[61]

At dusk, when the *Creole* seemed to have the entire Gulf of Mexico to itself, López finally got his military review. "The battalion was drawn up, forming nearly a circle around the entire deck; General Lopez and staff being at the open space." "As the setting sun threw its last beams upon the Gulf," López stood before the men. His "keen black eyes" fixed each soldier, and as O'Hara translated, López addressed the regiment. He thanked them for their confidence in him, then told them they were "about to strike the *first* blow in a glorious revolution, the success of which would crown all with honor equal to that which clusters around the memories of their revolutionary fathers, with present rewards far greater." Toward that heroic end, he reminded the filibusters, they must show "respect for the property and persons of the people of Cuba. They would meet no enemies but the Spanish army." After stressing military discipline and the necessity of seizing Cárdenas, "He concluded by saying that we were sons of Washington and had come to free a people."[62]

A full moon illuminated the *Creole's* main deck at 10:00 P.M. when the filibusters spotted the lighthouse that stood fifteen miles from Cárdenas, on the western edge of the town's bay. Mostly, however, they saw only the moon and, beyond the ocean's rippled waters, the silhouetted tropical forests and mangrove swamps that limned the bay. From the *Creole's* deck the dark, distant shore seemed a lonesome place, apparently empty of people. Perhaps this was a good place for a midnight landing. The bay was twelve miles long, eighteen miles wide. Unlike the typical Cuban bay—a *bolsa* (pocket) bay—Cárdenas had no easily defended bottleneck opening to the sea; its mouth was broad, wide open. Beyond that, the city—reflecting the influence of the North Americans who had founded it twenty-two years earlier—was built on a grid and, unlike cities of Spanish design, had no walls around it, no fortifications to protect it. Indeed, a full four decades later, a U.S. Army field manual would

describe the area as "entirely without defense": "The coast is so entirely unpro-
tected that the line between Matanzas and Cárdenas has been a favorite resort
for those wishing to land arms and ammunitions for . . . insurgents."[63]

The filibusters savored the moment's tranquillity. "The full moon shone
clear and bright; one could almost read by its light. A fine breeze was blowing off the land, and occasionally vessels would fly past the steamer under
full sail. The Liberators stood motionless and silent; the whispered cry of the
leadman, or the officers giving orders, with now and then the clank of a
sabre as they moved about, was all that broke the dead silence on that
stealthily moving ship for hours." When the Cárdenas Bay lighthouse drifted
into view, the expedition's officers had just finished distributing weapons
and ammunition. Each soldier received sixty rounds of cartridges; privates
got a standard-issue musket, officers a saber and a Jenning's Patent Rifle (capable of firing "leaden cartridge, deadly as grape shot at the rate of fifteen
per minute"). A full two-thirds of the men also received bowie knives and
revolvers."[64]

As the steamer's two paddle wheels churned past the tiny islands clustered
along the opening to the bay, the Kentucky regiment, which would be the first
to land, gathered on the *Creole*'s main deck. By one o'clock A.M., May 19, as
Cárdenas came into view, the moon had vanished, leaving the ship and its
crew sheathed in darkness. "The city lay sleeping in beauty; sweet odors from
its gardens already scented the air,—the Sabbath had just begun!" Cárdenas
sprawled across a low slope that rose from the harbor bay. Though the city, a
sugar-exporting center, had Yankee origins, to filibuster memoirist Richardson Hardy its architecture seemed "a beautiful blending of the antique Moorish with the more modern and fantastical Spanish orders."[65]

At 2:30 A.M., only twenty yards from the Cárdenas pier, the *Creole* grounded
on a sandbar. For thirty minutes the filibusters struggled to move the old
steamer. As they worked, "occasional lights flitting about the wharf conveyed
the fearful intelligence that suspicion was aroused." Finally, the ship's first
mate Collander Fayssoux, with rope in hand, plunged into the bay, swam to
the dock, and tied up the ship. A veteran of the Texas republic's navy, Fayssoux
also had participated in López's aborted 1849 expedition.[66]

The Kentucky regiment immediately debarked, forming into columns of
companies, and was quickly followed by the Mississippi and Louisiana regiments. Each company had its orders, so the filibusters wasted no time. "Two

companies of Kentuckians, under Lieutenant Colonel Pickett, without halting, passed rapidly through the city, following the railroad track, to take possession of the locomotive and cars." The other four Kentucky companies—about 180 men—under O'Hara headed toward Cárdenas's Spanish army garrison, home to about four hundred Spanish army regulars.[67]

To find the garrison, which the filibusters hoped to seize, O'Hara had expected help from a Cuban guide attached to the expedition. But in the rush at the pier, the two had been separated. O'Hara would have to find the soldiers' barracks on his own. Though it was past midnight, Cárdenas's streets were "full of teams and large wagons, under charges of negroes, who had to be driven out of the way." O'Hara seized several "citizens and negroes," demanding directions to the garrison, but the captives "were so terrified they could not speak." Fortunately for O'Hara, however, López, commanding another detachment, soon caught up and led the way.

The garrison sat on the north side of Cárdenas's main public square, a graceful plaza shadowed with royal palm trees. Across the square from the garrison stood the residence of Florencio Ceruti, the town's lieutenant governor. A massive stone church rose along the square's western edge. As O'Hara and four Kentucky regiment companies approached the square, a Spanish sentinel called out, "*Halta! qui vive!*"

"Friends and Lopez," O'Hara answered.

Gunfire shattered the night's silence, and, moments later, O'Hara lay bleeding in the street. As a group of filibusters hung back to tend to O'Hara, the rest of the detachment, now under the command of Major John Hawkins, rushed toward the stone-walled garrison, meeting even more fire; "incessant vollies poured from three immense iron-barred windows."

As the 179 filibusters of the Kentucky regiment returned the fire, they were joined by about 130 men of the Louisiana regiment and another 145 from the Mississippi battalion. Suddenly facing superior numbers, some of the Spanish soldiers retreated into the lieutenant governor's residence across the plaza. After winning control of the wide plaza, a group of filibusters stormed the lieutenant governor's residence. Still others charged the army garrison. With hopes of securing Cárdenas without a fight now dashed, López himself "rushed into the battle with perfect fearlessness; sometimes approaching within a few feet of the Garrison windows, careless of the tremendous firing on both sides, endeavoring to speak to the Spaniards within."[68]

For three hours the warm Cuban night seethed with smoke and gunfire. To young Kentuckian Marion Taylor, the long-awaited taste of war seemed an epiphany: "It was magnificent to hear the grand roaring of musketry and rifles." Richardson Hardy recalled that "some companies stood pouring volley after volley of musketry against the thick garrison walls, against the [Lieutenant] Governor's house, and even the church, of course doing very little damage, but making an awful uproar. Others rapidly traversed the streets in search of foes, whose locality could only be made out in the thick darkness by the flashing of their guns from house tops and windows. So long as the Spaniards kept their concealment, they fought with deadly determination."[69]

The Spanish army's resistance broke with the new sunrise. "About daylight," Richardson Hardy recalled, "the garrison door was battered down, when, before the Liberators had time to rush in, the Spanish soldiers rushed out, threw down their arms, and surrendered." Only a few minutes earlier—as Spanish troops inside the lieutenant governor's house continued firing even after he was taken prisoner—López torched the edifice's first story. "It was soon enveloped in flames; but even after the roof had fallen in, a party of soldiers kept firing from one corner, killing and wounding several men." Only after filibusters entered the burning building through a back entrance and bayoneted several Spanish soldiers to death did the fighting end. By eight o'clock a white flag waved from the lieutenant governor's residence.[70]

The filibusters marked their triumph by raising their flag over the lieutenant governor's charred two-story residence. Their prisoners included Lieutenant Governor Ceruti and "three other of the highest civil and military functionaries," plus "some forty" Spanish soldiers, those who had failed to escape before the garrison's capture. The filibusters estimated their losses at "some six or eight killed, and twelve or fifteen wounded; the Spanish loss was probably about the same." The wounded among the filibusters included some of their key officers: Adjutant General Gonzales, Colonel O'Hara of the Kentucky regiment, and Colonel Wheat of the Louisiana regiment.[71]

López established a temporary headquarters in the Spanish army garrison, then "walked about among the people, talking to them as he distributed his proclamation. He also made a speech to the Spanish soldiers, who had been captured, giving them some of his printed appeals to the Spanish army." The broadsides and speeches, however, produced only isolated displays of support.

Indeed, not one individual in Cárdenas joined the filibusters. Many townspeople even seemed scared of their ostensible liberators. "Where were those 'hosts of friends' who were to have welcomed us?" Richardson Hardy wondered. "The Cubans scarcely dared to speak. They merely walked about, bowing and scraping to the red shirts."[72]

Whatever favor the townspeople felt toward the filibusters was inhibited by their awareness of the paltry size of López's army. The entire filibuster force numbered only "about 500 men," a puny outfit compared to what Cuba's captain general commanded. As Richardson Hardy observed, "The universal remark of the Cubans was that the [filibuster] force was too small; that before the next day five thousand Spanish troops would be upon them, and therefore to join Lopez, or show him the least favor, would only be to ensure their ruin and destruction. With so small a force, and no artillery, it was impossible that he could get possession of Matanzas, between which place and Cardenas he would have to meet several thousand Spanish troops well appointed."[73]

During the night the filibusters had comported themselves with soldierly discipline. Now, in the bright haze of day, military order was collapsing. Over the past three days, aboard the *Creole*, the filibusters had subsisted on "hard crackers, with a very small allowance of water." By that morning "the grand inquiry was for something to eat and drink." Though the filibusters apparently obeyed López's injunction against looting, they still managed to sate their hunger and thirst. The haggard conquerors "walked around the city, eat, drank and slept, as if there were no Spanish army on the Island." Among their other indulgences, the filibusters "drank a great deal of liquor of every description, most of which had a stupifying effect; from which it was afterwards generally believed to have been drugged."[74]

As Cárdenas's plaza had rung with musket fire the previous evening, Lieutenant Colonel William S. Pickett and his sixty men of the Kentucky regiment had been busy seizing the trains needed for the assault on Matanzas. Cárdenas had two train stations—one inside the city; another, the one Pickett captured, "a mile and a half south-west of the town." According to the little army's grand strategy, by securing the town's rail connections they could disrupt official government communications between Cárdenas and Matanzas—and thus, they hoped, preserve the element of surprise on which the expedition's grand strategy depended. In 1850 Cuba's Spanish overseers had yet to construct a telegraph system across the island.[75]

During the night Pickett's soldiers had captured the rail station outside of town and, by sunup, May 19, had several rail cars and three locomotives fired and ready to take the entire army to Matanzas. "The object was accomplished without resistance," Pickett later recalled in an "official" report on the expedition. "The depot was held until late in the afternoon, when I received an order through an aide-de-camp to march my detachment back to the town." López had decided that rather than moving toward Matanzas, the filibusters should reboard the *Creole* and sail to another Cuban port.[76]

In short order the filibusters had secured both Cárdenas and the trains needed to take them to Matanzas. But well before the first shot had been fired, they had lost the element of surprise essential to their plans. Watchmen posted on the city's docks on the night the *Creole* landed had spotted an approaching warship and immediately notified Lieutenant Governor Ceruti. He, in turn, had ordered the rail tracks to Matanzas cut. By dawn, Ceruti also had dispatched two messengers to Matanzas to alert its local Spanish officials of the invasion. John Bagley, the U.S. consul in Matanzas, later wrote that by ten o'-clock the next morning, the entire city knew of the invasion. By nightfall, he added, the city was "armed and ready" for the filibusters.[77]

Hours after securing Cárdenas, on the morning of May 19, López learned that Spanish reinforcements would be arriving later that same day. Fearing a rout, by 2:00 P.M. he had ordered the filibusters to begin reboarding the *Creole*. A hasty retreat from Cárdenas seemed to him their best option; once at sea, they could sail toward Mantua, a remote village just inland from Cuba's far western coast. López knew western Cuba well, and the region, he insisted, teemed with discontented Creoles. He also assumed that most of the captain general's army would be tied up on a fool's errand to Cárdenas. And, finally, Mantua lay closer to New Orleans than did Cárdenas and thus made a convenient destination for John Quitman's expected second wave of invaders—or for any other U.S. reinforcements who might head toward Cuba upon hearing of the filibusters' landing at Cárdenas.[78]

An hour after the filibusters began reboarding the *Creole*, more details about Spanish troop movements arrived. As J. C. Davis recalled, "About 3' o'-clock, Gen. Lopez received a dispatch from Matanzas, saying, that two thousand troops had left there for . . . Cardenas and would be there in the course of the evening." But even as the filibusters reloaded the *Creole*, they caught a terrifying preview of the sort of attack they were leaving to avoid. Earlier that day a Spanish force of "about two hundred Infantry and one hundred Lancers" had entered Cárdenas. The Spaniards seemed "in no hurry to attack," spending most of the day "concealed in yards and houses on the upper side of the Plaza."[79]

Their assault came at dusk, against a group of 175 soldiers from the Kentucky regiment who had remained at Cárdenas as the other filibusters, down at the harbor, loaded the *Creole*. With regimental bravado, Richardson Hardy described the assault: "The Lancers came thundering on in gallant style. But they were soon taught that it would take something more than a brilliant display to conquer American Liberators. No sooner had they come within range, than horses and riders began to bite the dust in bloody confusion." Repeated filibuster attacks eventually drove the Spaniards back. The skirmish, according to Hardy, cost the Kentucky regiment "eight or ten" casualties and some "twenty odd" wounded. Of Spanish losses, "out of a hundred, seventy or eighty lay killed and wounded, their maddened horses dragging and trampling them to death."

At 9:00 P.M. the Kentucky regiment became the final filibuster division to reboard the *Creole*. Minutes later—still under fire from Spanish troops on the pier—the old steamer pulled away. As before, the *Creole* was overloaded. As Hardy recalled, "The [Lieutenant] Governor, and other Spanish officials, with thirty-four soldiers who joined the Liberators, made the vessel more crowded than she was in coming in, the cabin being filled up with wounded men." The ship's new passengers even included seven runaway slaves. "The deck was literally covered with loaded muskets, rifles, pistols, sabres, and bowie-knives, thrown down by the exhausted men, who lay down to sleep in the very jaws of death." Indeed, "within a few minutes" of the ship's departure, the jumble of firearms resulted in the accidental wounding of "several" filibusters.[80]

The extra weight caused the *Creole* to run aground, again, in the shallow bay—a harrowing situation. The filibusters were only five miles from Cárdenas, and more Spanish troops would arrive any minute. As Hardy recalled the ship's predicament, "The tide falling left her there, and now commenced a scene of horror rarely equaled. The whole night was spent in tremendous effort to get her off, the officers well knowing that unless she got off before many hours, all were destined to perish miserably. Many began to regret having left Cardenas, where they might at least have died fighting; but caught by a man-of-war on the sea, they were totally helpless, could only go to the bottom in despair."[81]

To reduce ballast, heavy provisions—including, eventually, arms and ammunition—were cast overboard. When the ship still did not budge, about one hundred men were evacuated in small boats to an island a quarter mile away. With the lighter load and a rising tide, the *Creole* by morning—May 20— floated free of the bar. After picking up the filibusters waiting on the island and releasing the Spanish prisoners in a small boat, each with "a few dollars in silver" given to them by López, the *Creole* finally steamed out of Cárdenas Bay.[82]

At Sea, May 20–21, 1850

López, undaunted, still favored a second landing near Mantua, in Cuba's far west. But hierarchical authority aboard the *Creole* had given way to democratic, if not mob, rule. An hour after clearing the bar, an "excited meeting" of filibuster officers split on the question of a second landing. Some, including Colonel Wheat of the Louisiana regiment and Major Hardy of the Kentucky battalion, favored going to Mantua. Others, including Colonel O'Hara, declared "the proposition to be madness." Unable to reach a consensus, the officers submitted the question to a vote of the entire army.

Richardson Hardy later claimed that "fifteen or twenty" in the Kentucky regiment "expressed themselves willing to go *anywhere* with General Lopez." But among the ranks at large, "there was an almost universal expression of unwillingness" against any second landing. Furious, López announced that he was resigning his command; whether the act was a bluff intended to pressure the filibusters into accepting his will or simply a face-saving gesture, one can only speculate. In tendering his resignation López said that he asked but one favor: "that they would land him in Cuba alone, or with the few who were still willing to follow him." That request also was declined. As Hardy recalled, "On investigation to see whether this could be done, it was found to be simply *impossible*, for want of coal and water. Key West was the only place the vessel *might* reach with her supply of coal, a great portion of it having been consumed while she was aground. After this, no man was in favor of going to Mantua, or rather *trying* to get there."[83]

The *Creole* anchored that night about forty miles west of Key West. The next morning, May 21, a pilot from a local "wrecker," a scavenger of sunken ships, came aboard to guide them into port on that sleepy Florida island. Whatever relief the filibusters felt as they steamed toward Key West vanished, however, "when within about thirty miles of that port, the smoke of another steamer was seen several miles off." Raising his spyglass, López surveyed the ship for several minutes and determined it to be a Spanish man-of-war. It was the *Pizarro*, which had for weeks been roaming the Gulf in search of the filibusters. Fortunately for the filibusters, however, at that particular moment the *Pizarro* seemed to be sailing in an opposite direction, its commander apparently unaware of the *Creole's* presence.[84]

Minutes later, as the paths of the two ships narrowed to within "four or five miles" of one another, the *Pizarro* suddenly "whirled about with astonishing rapidity" and began chasing the *Creole*. The filibusters began throwing extra coal into the *Creole's* furnace. "The Gulf was smooth, the wind in her favor, and under a perilous press of steam, the little *Creole* flew through the water as if she knew what stakes depended on her race." The *Pizarro* "was throwing huge clouds of black smoke from her chimneys, and ploughing the waves with a stately speed, as if confident of achieving a great and memorable service to her Queen."[85]

With the *Creole* now within "eight or ten miles" of Key West, the gap between the two ships had shrunk to "within two miles." The filibusters got their first glimpse of Key West's lighthouse as they burned their last load of coal. "Bacon meat was then substituted, with red shirts, and such other combustibles as could be found, which kept up steam, and still the little steamer darted towards her haven."[86]

The western terminus of a coral-and-limestone archipelago, Key West is four miles long, two miles wide, and lies one hundred miles south of the Florida mainland. Salt mining, fishing, sponge diving, and wrecking—the salvaging of booty from ships sunk on the surrounding reefs—were the main vocations for the island's two thousand residents. The *Pizarro* had visited their port the previous night, and sailors aboard the Spanish ship had told them about López's landing at Cárdenas.[87]

So the islanders were not surprised when, just before 1:00 on the afternoon of May 21, they spotted both the *Creole* and the *Pizarro* steaming toward them. To get a better view, many raced up to the cupolas that capped the pitched roofs of many of the town's sun-bleached wood-frame houses. "As the *Creole* ran into port, many a hat and handkerchief waved in welcome to her worn and weary passengers." A sense of foreboding, however, mingled with the festive atmosphere. All day, rumors had circulated of a possible cannon attack on

Key West by the *Pizarro*. Thus, even as the townspeople cheered the filibusters, "flags ran up on every ship and public building, in anticipation of a bombardment."

The bombardment never came. As the *Creole* steamed into a dock owned by a local merchant, the filibusters raised the Stars and Stripes on the ship's masthead. Spotting the U.S. flag, the *Pizarro*'s captain, though less than a quarter mile behind his quarry, abruptly turned away. A few minutes later the man-of-war dropped anchor in a narrow passage between Key West and Fort Taylor, a brick U.S. army fort on a sandy spit a quarter mile offshore.[88]

The hero's welcome for the filibusters proved short-lived. As F. C. M. Boggess recalled, "Most persons have seen a flock of sheep jump a fence when the leader has gone over. That is the way the *Creole* was unloaded." Richardson Hardy noted that the ship "had scarcely touched the pier, when the men began to jump hastily upon it." After a semblance of order returned, the filibusters, "unshaven . . . sunburnt, and hair uncombed," formed into a long line and marched along the beach for a half mile to a U.S. Army barracks—all the while in full view of the *Pizarro*, still anchored offshore, and its guns. Since "ten or twelve" artillery pieces were assembled on the barracks' grounds, several filibusters discussed "the feasibility of knocking the *Pizarro* to pieces." The "more influential" among the filibusters, however, prevailed on the others to abandon the idea; aware of their vulnerability to arrest by federal authorities, the filibuster's officers were "determined to do nothing in violation of the laws of their country."[89]

Federal agents quickly seized the *Creole*. Though some of the expedition's officers were permitted to retain their sidearms, U.S. Navy agents seized most of the weapons aboard the ship. The seven stowaway slaves aboard the *Creole* were turned over to Spanish officials, who later returned them to Cuba. For the next two days, rumors circulated of an imminent attack on Key West by four hundred Spanish soldiers from Cuba. The filibusters, meanwhile, ensconced at the army barracks, officially disbanded. "It was soon generally understood that each man must take care of himself—the organization was formally dissolved, and officers no longer claimed authority."[90]

Key West, May 23, 1850

Two days later, on the evening of May 23, the *Pizarro* finally sailed away from Key West. Many of the filibusters assumed the Spanish warship's departure was a feint, designed to draw them into international waters aboard the *Isabel*, a Havana-to-Charleston U.S. mail ship scheduled to arrive that night. Though López himself suspected as much, he nonetheless boarded the mail ship and two days later debarked at Savannah. Ambrosio Gonzales remained at Key West for several more weeks, tending the wounds he had suffered at Cárdenas. He convalesced at the Key West home of attorney Stephen Mallory, who later that year would be elected to the U.S. Senate and, a decade later, would serve as secretary of the Confederate navy.[91]

Over the next few weeks, the other filibusters—one by one, often assisted by local residents—also left Key West. Richardson Hardy boarded a U.S. Navy brig, landed at Cedar Key on northern Florida's Gulf coast, and from there boarded a schooner for New Orleans. Marion Taylor sold his double-barreled shotgun to a Key West attorney and used the money to book passage on a New Orleans–bound schooner; in New Orleans a chance encounter with an old friend led to a $10 loan, which Taylor used to book passage on a Mississippi River steamer. He reached his home in Kentucky by the middle of May. The filibusters' relief at returning to their former lives was sharpened by reports from Cuba of five comrades inadvertently left behind at Cárdenas: all five within days had fallen before a Spanish firing squad.[92]

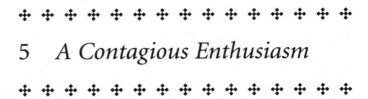

5 A Contagious Enthusiasm

Savannah, Georgia, May 25, 1850

When Savannahians awoke on the morning of May 25, 1850, to discover that Narciso López had arrived during the night, "great excitement" spread among "citizens of all classes" through the city. After the local Spanish consul wired Secretary of State John Clayton, demanding López's detention, he was arrested at 8:30 that evening. The arrest took place in López's quarters in the opulent four-story City Hotel, on the south side of Bay Street, between Whitaker and Bull streets. For his defense López was represented pro bono by two of Savannah's best legal talents, attorneys William B. Gaulden and Robert Milledge Charlton. A former federal judge, U.S. attorney, and U.S. senator, Charlton was also a poet whose verse had appeared in New York's *Knickerbocker* magazine, once edited by John O'Sullivan's brother-in-law Samuel Langtree.[1]

The two lawyers demanded an immediate hearing to determine if the government had evidence, probable cause, to justify the arrest. When the hearing, held that same evening in the Greek Revival Chatham County courthouse on Wright Square, failed to convince federal district court judge J. C. Nicoll that the government possessed such evidence, he ordered López released. The courtroom "rang with the applause of the audience, and could not be suppressed by the officers." "An immense party" of cheering supporters then escorted López back to the City Hotel, where, as a local supporter interpreted, the general spoke from the building's front steps. "The substance of his remarks," the Savannah

Georgian later reported, "were that he had felt the galling influence of the old Spanish rule, that his all had been taken from him in former years, and that now every thing was gone from him but his undying love for his country, which would only yield with his life." When he concluded, "nine cheers" rose "for Lopez and liberty." Still later that evening, at the Our House restaurant, on Bay Street, two blocks east of the City Hotel, a banquet in López's honor brimmed with toasts, speeches, and "full spirit." Summing up the day, the *Georgian* observed that "such an excitement as was witnessed on Saturday night, has seldom, if ever occurred in Savannah. There appeared to be [but one] feeling among our citizens, which was in favor of General Lopez and his cause."

López's arrest and release took less than three hours, a denouement hardly calculated to please President Taylor, Secretary of State Clayton, and others eager to end what they viewed as flagrant disregard—even usurpation—of the central government's authority. The next day, May 26, to the frustration of the local U.S attorney, Henry Williams, López boarded a westbound train. In a telegram to Clayton only hours after López left Savannah, the prosecutor struck a note soon to become a major theme in the federal government's long effort to convict the filibusters on Neutrality Act violations. Even if the judge had granted a two-day delay of the hearing Williams had requested, to give him more time to gather testimony, it probably would have made no difference. Savannah was too distant from the places where López had organized his conspiracy; thus, no local witnesses could be found with firsthand knowledge of the expedition's preparations.

The Savannah *Republican* noted that López made no "imprudent disclosures" during his stay. The general had been social, even loquacious, but also discreet. He knew that the Neutrality Act did not, strictly speaking, forbid fighting in a foreign war in which the United States was not a party. It merely targeted anyone who, from within the United States, would "begin or set on foot, or provide or prepare the means for" an expedition bound for such a conflict. According to U.S. Attorney Williams, López had been careful not to speak about preparations for the Cuban expedition, directing all conversations "exclusively to the acts performed after the landing at Cardenas."[2]

On May 28, two days after López left Savannah, U.S. Attorney Prescott Hall of New York City sent Clayton a similarly discouraging letter, reporting that while he planned to bring some individuals suspected of being in cahoots with López before a grand jury, he had no expectation of convicting—or even indicting—any of them. "I do not believe that any evidence will be produced to justify them in preferring a Bill [of indictment] against any individuals here." The prosecution, Hall admitted, was a pro forma gesture that he hoped would "have a good effect upon the public mind."[3]

Since federal officials believed López was headed for New Orleans by way of Mobile, Alabama, Clayton wired Peter Hamilton, Mobile's U.S. attorney, and ordered him to arrest López if he did pass through.[4]

En Route: Savannah to Mobile, Alabama, May 26–30, 1850

On May 26, 1850, only hours after Narciso López left Savannah, a northern travel writer journeying by train through southern Georgia had grown weary of gazing out on the flat, piney terrain along the Savannah-to-Macon rail route when he noticed "a dark handsome Spaniard" seated in the same car. A fellow passenger quickly assured him that, yes, as the writer had suspected, it was indeed the famous General López.[5]

By the spring of 1850, López enjoyed a personal celebrity rare to his day—the sort of fame that evoked everything from whispers and nudges in train cars to theatrical impersonations, and volatile street demonstrations. In the weeks following López's retreat from Cárdenas, profilibuster demonstrations erupted across the United States, from New York to Savannah, from Baltimore to Cincinnati. Describing a large rally in lower Manhattan that May, even William Cullen Bryant's pro-Whig New York *Evening Post* had to admit that "not, perhaps, since the day when reports of General Taylor's first victories on Rio Grande were received, has more excitement been shown than was displayed yesterday afternoon throughout the city. . . . Every body had the evening paper, or an extra Sun or Tribune in his hand, and every body was speculating as to the probable upshot of the Cuban invasion."[6]

Even as López stole away from Key West aboard the *Isabel*, Laurent Sigur's New Orleans *Delta*, festooned with engravings of López and the "flag of the Cuban patriots," was proclaiming, "THE BLOW IS STRUCK!" and predicting that "the flag of the single star and three stripes will soon wave in triumph over the Queen of the Antilles." A full month later the Baltimore *Sun* was still resorting to almost metaphysical language to describe the public's fascination with the story: "Like a stone in a mill-pond, the dropping of Lopez in Cuba, is likely to send its undulations far and wide throughout the social and political world[.] The splash was in itself of small moment, but the ripples are growing into waves and diffusing a peculiar influence throughout all the channels of national and *natural* feeling."[7]

During the same season, in a play entitled *Invasion of Cuba,* an actor would portray López, "large as life," on the stage of Philadelphia's Chestnut Theatre. Even advertisers were not immune. Almost a full year later, an Ohio dry goods merchant, advertising in the Cincinnati *Enquirer,* still believed that a plug for López might even move a few more shoes out the door: "'CUBA! CUBA!!' The young Americans say we must have Cuba now that the 'war has actually commenced,' and ESHELBY's patrons say that he has the finest stock of boots and shoes in the West, at his store on the north side of Sixth street, nearly opposite the Mayor's office."[8]

Writing three decades later, Ambrosio Gonzales would remain impressed with the strategy that he and General López had concocted for the Cárdenas invasion. Though most of it was never executed, Gonzales still believed that the plan represented a tour de force of military planning. He even claimed that the Italian liberator Giuseppe Garibaldi—"a friend of ours" from shared days of exile in New York City—had copied the strategy for his 1860 landing at Marsala, Sicily.[9]

Few would join Gonzales in arguing that Cárdenas elevated either him or López to any pantheon of military strategists. As a propaganda effort, however, the landing—even in defeat—proved an unmitigated success. As López and the haggard men who had made up his army fanned out from Key West toward the mainland, newspapers and speakers at profilibuster demonstrations around the nation were transforming the failed invaders into glorious heroes of U.S. republicanism.

López's newfound prominence attested to the growing power and independence of the nation's press; it also bore witness to the demise at midcentury of the country's two major political parties and their subservient organs, newspapers editorially disciplined by, and financially reliant upon, partisan political sponsors. López's stellar arc across the U.S. imagination, after all, belonged to an age in which a new generation of newspaper editors was transforming both the nation's journalism and its politics. Bolstered by new printing, papermaking, and news-gathering technologies—and a ready willingness to exploit sensationalism—editors such as Moses Yale Beach, James Gordon Bennett, and Horace Greeley waged an aggressive fight for a new and growing body of readers in U.S. cities.[10]

In that charged firmament López's name by May 1850 had become a lightning rod in an ever-darkening storm of debates shadowing U.S. political life. Hero or scoundrel, he could not be ignored. López personified U.S. expansionism to an age whose newspaper readers, already enthralled by press sagas of imperial adventures in Texas and Mexico, hungered for still more tales of Yankee conquest. So great was that need and so plentiful the heroes that when the contemporary historian Justin Smith wanted an epithet to dismiss the widely trumpeted heroism of Mexican War veteran Charles May, he knew just the term he wanted. May, Smith sniffed, was a "newspaper hero."[11]

If any readers had trouble making the connection, for good or ill, between López's filibusters and the exploits of earlier heroes, editors happily assisted them. The Philadelphia *Public Ledger*, for instance, would scornfully liken López and his financial backers ("whose object is *Texanization*") to eastern speculators in Texas bonds who had reaped millions of dollars after the Mexican War. The *Mississippian*, by contrast, in May 1850, called López's followers "the flower of American chivalry" and suggested that the heroism of the Mississippians in López's army recalled that of other native sons in the Texas Independence and Mexican wars: "Their valor on the fields of San Jacinto, of Monterey, and Buena Vista, will achieve fresh laurels in this new theater of action."[12]

Sympathetic editors—and even those who just wanted to sell newspapers—also rushed to link the swarthy, mustachioed Latin to foreigners who had assisted the United States's own War of Independence. To those who called López and his allies "pirates," the Boston *Daily Times* answered, "They are welcome to make the most of the word, but if they are right then so was General LaFayette a pirate, and so was every other foreigner who joined our fathers in the war of The Revolution while his country was at peace with England." If more recent republican antecedents were required, there were, of course, the European uprisings of 1848. Predicting the triumph of republican virtue over superior Spanish numbers, the Memphis *Daily Appeal* suggested that "the Cubans, animated by the example of the American republicans and impregnated with the revolutionary spirit now struggling in Europe, will be able to cope with a far greater power."[13]

Some journalists, not content with merely writing and editing pro-López stories, actually joined the conspiracy: The list of journalists with direct ties to

López and his allies included, most prominently, O'Sullivan of the *United States Magazine and Democratic Review*, Beach of the New York *Sun*, and Sigur of the New Orleans *Delta*. Still other journalists enlisted in López's army and accompanied him to Cuba. The Kentucky regiment of the 1850 expedition included at least three journalists: Richardson Hardy and John McCann both had been editors at the Cincinnati *Nonpareil*, and Theodore O'Hara had been an editorial writer for the Frankfort *Yeoman* and an editor for the *Democratic Rally*, a Polk campaign organ in Kentucky.[14]

John S. Thrasher, the U.S.-born journalist and Club de la Habana member, who published the proannexationist Cuban business newspaper *El Faro Industrial*, also wrote pro-filibuster dispatches under the pseudonym "Peregrine" for the New Orleans *Picayune*. Thrasher's actual role in the López conspiracy remains shadowy.[15] But according to the U.S. consul in Havana, Allen Ferdinand Owen, Thrasher was "very deeply implicated"; Spanish authorities in Havana would arrest him in October 1851.[16] Even López supporter Stephen Mallory, later U.S. senator and Confederate navy chief, had press ties. From his Key West home, Mallory served as a correspondent for Horace Greeley's New York *Tribune*.[17]

While most López supporters in the press confined their advocacy to their writings, the fact that so many did take a direct role in the conspiracy highlights a fascination with filibustering among those who produced the nation's newspapers. That fascination, in turn, illustrates how much those newspapers had changed in two decades. With the founding of the New York *Sun* in 1833, followed two years later by James Gordon Bennett's New York *Herald*, a proliferation of cheap, popular urban newspapers began to radically reshape both the nation's politics and its journalism. These papers—often called "pennies" after their cheap price—have come to be identified with a host of innovations in U.S. journalism.[18]

Before the new popular papers, most U.S. dailies charged six cents a copy or from six to ten dollars a year in advance for subscriptions, more than a skilled worker's weekly salary. The new popular papers brought single-copy prices down to as low as one cent. Unlike their commercial predecessors—including the so-called mercantile papers—these new popular dailies were also widely sold on the street. With their larger circulations they developed a broad readership among urban workers, the emerging middle class, and urban elites—and introduced a new economy of scale to U.S. journalism. In 1833, for instance, the New York *Courier and Enquirer*, with a claimed circulation of 4,500, stood as the nation's largest newspaper. By 1850 the circulation of Bennett's New York *Herald* exceeded 30,000—a figure he doubled over the next decade. The number of papers also grew; the 1850 census counted 254 dailies, over twice the total in the 1840 census.[19]

The mercantiles had catered to an elite audience of merchants, financiers, and political leaders, and often doubled as political party organs. Typified by the New York *Journal of Commerce*, the mercantiles offered a staid mix of partisan editorials, select financial and political news, and ship schedules. They carried no illustrations, no bold headlines, and reportorial initiative was rare. News consisted mainly of official political pronouncements, market statistics, and stories copied from other papers.

The new popular papers created a different formula for success. Papers like the New York *Sun* and *Herald* were political but nonpartisan, cravenly opinionated but independent of party dogma. Largely, if not completely, unbeholden to either parties or elite subscribers for financial sustenance, they staked their survival on ever larger circulations and increased advertising. Taking advantage of the newly invented cylinder press, the country's newspapers grew in circulation, as well as page size and number of pages. The economy of scale and increased advertising, in turn, awarded these papers a new, financial independence from both political and mercantile patrons. Increased revenues also allowed editors to invest in better news-gathering and publishing technologies. Editors catered to their audiences with a new sensationalism, further boosting circulation and ad revenues. Although financial statistics, editorials, and official government pronouncements continued to be published, writing styles grew sharper, and headlines larger. Illustrations, in the form of wood engravings, become more common. And as circulation wars erupted, both the scope of what constituted news and the aggressiveness with which it was pursued grew. The public's notion of news now suddenly included the private lives of the rich, executions, suicides, murders, sports events; disasters—all told in "spicy" or "saucy" prose, to use two terms the *Herald* applied to itself.[20]

Though the popular papers continued to reprint stories culled from exchanges with other newspapers, now they supplemented those pieces with "intelligence" from telegraph dispatches and from their own local and foreign correspondents. To get a "beat" on the competition, larger papers such as the

New York *Herald* and the New Orleans *Picayune*, copying a practice pioneered by the Charleston *Courier*, sent "news-boats" to meet incoming ships carrying foreign news. The race for fresh news also enlisted the nation's growing system of railroads, telegraph lines, and steam ships. To cover the vast new domestic expanses of the West, then unserved by railroads or telegraphs, some editors organized their own pony expresses, often used in combination with the trains and telegraphs of the East. Press coverage of the Mexican War became a show-case for many of these new practices. As it had during the War for Texas Inde-pendence, New Orleans served as the nation's chief source of news about the conflict in Mexico. In 1847 the city boasted nine dailies. At least four sent re-porters to the war, and their stories were regularly copied by papers across the nation. The *Picayune* even ran speedboats across the Gulf of Mexico to meet ships from Vera Cruz carrying dispatches from field correspondents. The ves-sels were equipped with composing rooms so that stories were already edited and set in type when they reached New Orleans.[21]

The pennies and other popular papers shaped—and were shaped by—the changing politics of the mid-nineteenth century United States. In the process they became an important independent voice in U.S. political life—and a powerful force in promoting Manifest Destiny. Technological innovations alone, after all, did not secure the editorial independence of the nation's press; political changes dovetailed with technological ones.

In 1836, as the rebellion that led to the founding of the Texas republic flared, a slew of western editors readily threw their support behind filibusters by An-glos into the Mexican province. Yet for all their bluster, such editorial strayings remained confined to the Democratic party's less important papers. The Ken-tucky *Gazette* and the New Orleans *Commercial Bulletin*, for instance, chal-lenged President Jackson's opposition to official U.S. involvement in Texas. But the far more powerful national party organ, the Washington *Globe*, toed the administration line. Since the founding of the United States, and well into the early years of the penny press, the nation's dominant newspapers had care-fully cultivated their role as mouthpieces—as organs—for particular political parties or politicians. Editors measured words carefully, lest they offend those who controlled the informal matrix of graft, favoritism, and patronage that linked party and newspaper. Loyal partisan editorial service could be worth anything from a customs house position for the editor to lucrative govern-ment printing contracts. Local postmasterships were especially valued; an editor holding a postmastership enjoyed a free first glance at any other papers moving through the mail system. Moreover, that same editor also had franking privileges that allowed papers to be sent through the U.S. mails at no cost. Of course, at election time, the editor was expected to return the favor and use that same office to disseminate party campaign materials.[22]

The sort of editorial support Old Hickory generally could depend on was founded on his party's ability to pronounce a consistent position, then back it up with a durable party consensus. By the late 1840s, however, such consensus was growing rare among both Democrats and Whigs. As the Mexican War reawakened divisive debates over slavery and sectional balance, what in 1844 had been hairline fractures in the Democratic and Whig establishments by 1848 had become gaping fissures.

The growing coverage of those debates in the nation's newspapers only widened those fissures. National unity among both Whigs and Democrats, after all, had often rested upon the ability of each party to conceal internal debates that might otherwise generate rancor between their northern and southern constituents. Well into the first few decades of the nineteenth century, party leaders had been able to conduct much of their business in private, often orally with no written records. As late as the 1830s, congressmen were still able to "embargo," to postpone the publication of, potentially inflammatory speeches. In most cases, however, politicians simply entered into discreet gentlemen's agreements—understandings that went unreported in the various party organs.

By the 1840s, as a more aggressive, independent, and sizable press highlighted debates within both parties, voters became increasingly aware of growing intraparty differences over slavery, the Mexican cession, and other troublesome matters—exposure which exacerbated those growing tensions. Southern Democrats, for instance, were shocked to learn that more and more leading Democrats of the North were embracing positions at odds with those widely held below the Mason-Dixon Line. Whig unity encountered similar peril. As newspapers reported growing differences between Whigs of the North and South, the party of Alexander Stephens and Abraham Lincoln found a growing number of members calling themselves either "Cotton Whigs" or "Conscience Whigs."[23]

Determined to deliver the Democrats from such factionalism, President Polk in 1845 sought for the party's Washington *Globe* an editor more attuned to the direction he was trying to chart for the party. He replaced editor Francis P. Blair with Polk loyalist Thomas Ritchie and changed the paper's name to the *Union*. The new editor proved a loyal cipher but ultimately disappointed Polk. In the end, Ritchie could not fashion in the *Union* a consensus not found in the party itself and thus failed to set a steady beat for other Democratic papers around the country.[24]

Nor could "Father Ritchie" and other political editors depend on political patronage, which became increasingly uncertain after 1846 when the federal government began awarding printing contracts to the highest bidder—a move toward more governmental efficiency but also a measure of the ailing condition of the two major parties. To survive, even papers once dependent on elite subscriber lists and political patronage embraced the business and journalistic methods of the penny press.[25]

In 1848 the initial push for the Whigs' eventual nominee of that year, Zachary Taylor, came not from party leaders but from a newspaper editor, Thurlow Weed of the Albany *Evening Journal*. A new order seemed to be emerging—newspapers, after all, traditionally followed the lead of parties, not vice versa. On May 4, 1850, the Whigs' Baton Rouge *Gazette* declared that "the only fact that keeps the democrats so closely cemented together in this State is the cordial support given to their local presses by all classes, [for] every democrat belonging to the party, either in office or out of office, feels as strong an interest in the prosperity of his party paper as if he were a stockholder."[26]

Amid the disarray of a crumbling two-party system, newspapers and magazines often seemed to fill a breach. In a sense, then, the dissolution of the Whig and Democratic parties during the 1840s and 1850s ideologically liberated the press. Lacking broad-based political parties to toil for—and emboldened by the innovations of Bennett, Beach, and others—editors and reporters published with fewer inhibitions. As slavery and the debate over its extension muddled traditional lines of party alliance, the nation's political life became increasingly volatile and public. And as the monolithic Whig and Democratic organizations fractured into factions and parties during the 1840s and 1850s, newspapers grew in both numbers and independence.

Boasts of editorial independence became routine. Bennett bragged that his *Herald* soared above "the dirt of party politics." In day-to-day practice, however, such claims rarely survived scrutiny. It did not follow that papers unbeholden to party dogma lacked political conviction or were above political intrigue. Bennett and Greeley, for example, constantly indulged bombastic political prejudices and were inveterate political schemers. Both also attempted, unsuccessfully, to gain public office. Greeley even became the Democratic party's presidential nominee in 1872.[27]

Likewise, the New Orleans *Delta* presented itself as an organ of no party and was thus officially independent. But the paper was in fact deeply involved in both Louisiana and local politics. Beyond the paper's aggressive Democratic editorial stance, its editor, Laurent Sigur, was a Democratic member of the state senate. Lest any reader was unaware of that fact, in March 1850 *editor* Sigur's paper reported that *Senator* Sigur had recently "made a powerful appeal" to the legislature for the state's purchase of slaves to improve New Orleans's levees.[28] There was also, of course, Sigur's alliance with López, a connection that for all practical purposes made the *Delta* a filibuster organ. The *Delta* nonetheless clung to its claim of an Olympian detachment from partisan matters—declaring in the fall of 1849, as New Orleans prepared for municipal elections, that "the *Delta* will not be a silent observer of these events and movement. Standing on the elevated pinnacle of perfect independence, we shall survey these events with the impartial eye of faithful historians."[29]

More than a few skeptics detested the new style. "Some of the presses seem to be edited by infuriated madmen," an editor in Georgia complained. After traveling in the United States in 1851, English reformer Hugh S. Tremenheere condemned what he viewed as the irresponsible behavior of pro-López editors. Who, he asked, could expect "the universal mass" of Americans to take a dispassionate view of the day's news when editors invest such energies in "flattering their vanity, pandering to their passions, and striving to fill them with exaggerated notions of their self-importance?"[30]

Editors such as Bennett, Beach, Weed, and Greeley reveled in their idiosyncrasies and powers. In a letter to another editor, Greeley, of the pro-Whig New York *Tribune*, mulled over his disaffection with his party's 1848 presidential ticket and boasted of how, if he so desired, he could swing his paper behind another candidate and thus "shake down the whole rotten fabric by a bugleblast." With similar bravado, during the Mexican War, after reading Polk's December 1847 speech on the terms required from Mexico to end the conflict, Democrat Beach of the New York *Sun* boasted, "We can almost detect our own thunder reverberating in the Message."[31]

Editors of the era's independent popular newspapers freely expressed and changed their opinions, often from day to day. During the late stages of the Mexican War, for instance, as Washington policy makers debated whether to annex all or just part of their southern neighbor, papers such as the New Orleans *Delta* and the New York *Herald* never could decide what they wanted: they supported "All Mexico" one day and opposed it the next. Three years later Bennett displayed a similar fickleness toward Narciso López. On August 16, 1849, as López's forces were mustering in New York and along the Gulf coast, Bennett praised President Taylor's recent antifilibustering proclamation and the administration's apparent resolve to "rigidly stand to its treaty obligations." The next week, however, the *Herald* called the mercenaries the "active and energetic spirits" of a "glorious enterprise." Three months later Bennett found August's heroes considerably less heroic: "Upon the whole, this movement appears to be a matter a little beyond a joke. In fact, it has become *opera seria.*" By January 1851, after traveling to Cuba and mixing with Havana's high society, Bennett would declare that the once despotic Cuba, by then under a new colonial overlord, seemed poised for a renaissance. "Under the vigorous and enlightened sway of [General Jóse] de la Concha, the new Captain General, a better day for Cuba is come." Concha would prove to be more the despot than the captain general he had replaced.[32]

If any political constant propelled the mid-nineteenth-century popular press, it was a sense of urgency exacerbated by the latest conspiracy theory. Whether opposing slavery or supporting its extension through filibusters, Whig and Democratic editors alike implicitly argued that only bold action could save the Republic. Free-soil advocates such as Greeley railed against López's links to slaveholders. Filibuster supporters, by contrast, saw the invisible hand of British abolitionists and monarchists guiding anti-López forces. The New Orleans Daily *Delta* asserted that Britain's minister in Washington was "prepared to remonstrate against any relaxation" of President Taylor's opposition to filibustering. Similarly, in a pamphlet printed by the *Delta*, López's aide Ambrosio Gonzales dismissed the Whigs' *National Intelligencer*, a particularly strident opponent of filibustering, as "an English hot-house for the exotic weed of monarchy."[33]

The press's newfound authority was not solely vested in editorials. President Polk himself—albeit backhandedly—paid tribute to the new reportorial vigor after the New York *Herald* in April 1847 disclosed special agent Nicholas

Trist's secret peace mission to Mexico. "I have not been more vexed or excited since I have been President than at this occurrence," he confided to his diary. A year later Polk's efforts to purchase Cuba came to naught after the same paper reported Romulus Saunders's secret mission to Madrid.[34]

By the mid-nineteenth century U.S. newspapers had achieved an apparent and unprecedented power in the nation's political life much greater than their circulation figures would suggest. Their ability in 1848 to elevate a politically inept war hero to the White House attested to those powers. So too did their ability in 1850 to raise to hero's status a man dismissed by the Taylor administration as "an obscure and worthless foreigner." Through their preoccupation with Narciso López, U.S. newspapers gave the cause of U.S. annexation of Cuba a prominence in the nation's political life that elected officials, by and large, had declined to provide. For much of the press, support for political expansionism came as naturally as their zeal for finding more readers and advertisers. For such press barons as Bennett and Beach, the quest for stories from ever greater distances, in shorter amounts of time, dovetailed with a missionary zeal to create and spread the technologies needed to secure those beats. Allowed to simmer, the two passions combusted into a fierce expansionism that exploded distinctions among commerce, politics, and militarism. The spirit's heady fumes rise from a Bennett editorial calling for steamers to enhance U.S. control of the Pacific and the Gulf of Mexico: "We want," Bennett wrote, "a steam navy, and a general system of mail steamers, readily convertible into ships of war."[35]

To ambitious newspaper editors intoxicated with visions of larger circulations, Manifest Destiny became a calling capable of overcoming all ideological reservations. During the Mexican War, Brooklyn *Daily Eagle* editor Walt Whitman put aside his reservations about imperialism to celebrate U.S. military prowess: "Let our arms be carried with a spirit which shall teach the world that, while we are not forward for a quarrel, America knows how to crush, as well as how to expand." Even Whig papers found Manifest Destiny difficult to resist; on his 1851 tour of the United States, the Englishman Tremenheere expected Democratic papers to ring with pro-López sentiments. It was the jingoism and inconsistency of their political opponents that surprised him:

> I confess I did not expect to see so many of the Whig papers at that time fall in with
> the same tone. The conduct of some few of them was manly and honourable. They
> resisted from the first the popular impulse towards that unprincipled aggression.

But it was lamentable and of evil augury to read, in other papers of that party, leading articles, the premises of which were for, and the conclusions against that act of piracy; sentences one day condemning the offender, yet defending the offence; another day sentences taking the opposite line, and so written as to be quoted as proofs of consistency should the turn of events render the "cry for Cuba" an available one for the next election. The trimming of some of the Whig papers during several weeks displayed as complete a want of principle as the aggression.[36]

In their quickened quest for more readers and advertising, newspaper editors shunned such potentially troublesome concerns as the morality of slavery, the rights of foreign states, and the rule of law. While politics and party loyalties wandered from day to day, jingoism remained a constant siren. Lured by that call, editors also often disregarded concerns about accuracy, editorial consistency, and sobriety of judgment. For all the emphasis on new technologies and faster reporting, rumors still played a major role in the reporting of the popular papers. In the spring of 1850, for instance, with López in New Orleans organizing his second expedition, it was widely reported that his odds of success had been greatly shortened by a revolt brewing in Cuba itself. In fact, the odds seemed so good that Moses Yale Beach went ahead and reported López's victory:

The New York Sun is in receipt of *the* GLORIOUS NEWS OF THE SUCCESSFUL LANDING OF THE CUBAN PATRIOTS, AND THE COMMENCEMENT OF A GENERAL REVOLUTION FOR FREEDOM THROUGHOUT THE ISLAND OF CUBA!

Liberty has triumphed!
CUBA IS FREE![37]

López had landed at Cárdenas, of course, but he and his army had barely escaped with their lives. In the next day's New York *Herald*, Bennett noted that only a day before the "simpletons" at the *Sun* published their "GLORIOUS NEWS" story, the same paper had reported that López was probably defeated at Cárdenas. Wrote Bennett: "It is more than sickening—it is criminal, to see such stuff palmed upon an intelligent community, in the face of the simple facts recorded in our columns, and received by every journal yesterday, from Cuba. Nothing can save the expedition from utter and overwhelming defeat. The contrivers and supporters of this silly expedition are guilty of piracy and murder, and ought to be punished accordingly."[38]

By March 1851, it would be difficult to tell whether the mercurial Bennett's anger about sensational coverage of López was directed more toward the competition or his own paper. Noting that his indictment included "some of our own correspondence," Bennett charged that "correspondents engaged in New Orleans, Baltimore, New York, and elsewhere, continually color their representations with the most vivid tints drawn from their own imagination, producing in the public mind no clear comprehension of [i]deas, but a blurred and indistinct mass of mist and confusion."[39]

Reporters and editors routinely injected both sensationalism and their own opinions into stories. And as coverage of López made clear, even when editors were trying to get facts straight, reporting still proceeded serendipitously, with notations like, "The Mobile paper publishes some very interesting particulars . . ." and "A startling rumor reached here last night."[40] Though the popular papers published sporadic reports from participants in López's conspiracy, none—even the *Delta*—seems to have had regular correspondents attached to his army. Mostly they reprinted stories from other journals and garnished them with new information, often spurious, gleaned from travelers, sailors, and residents of New Orleans and Cuba.

For coverage of López, U.S. papers were thus forced to rely heavily on stories from the New Orleans *Delta*, the New York *Sun,* and other papers with ties to the filibusters. And those papers, of course, had strong political motivations to skew stories to favor or even protect the filibusters. In the wake of President Taylor's August 1849 proclamation against the conspiracy, for instance, the New Orleans *Delta* professed complete ignorance of any planned invasion of Cuba. "We have not heard a whisper to sanction the idea of a design of this extent is in course of preparation," it declared disingenuously. As for those suspicious men gathered on Round Island and alluded to in Taylor's proclamation, "the limited numbers and resources of the party, however, lead us to suspect that it contemplates nothing more criminal than an armed emigration to Mosquitia—a country which can scarcely be said to be a friendly power, as it is a dreary, uninhabited waste, of indefinite extent, and is ruled over by nobody, and is the rightful property of the first settlers." Two weeks later, editor Sigur, abandoning his see-no-evil farce, defended the filibusters, attacked federal preoccupations with the "bugbear of treaty stipulations," and commenced what became two years of strident editorial proselytizing for López.[41]

A year later, in a fit of editorial pique even further removed from the ostensibly objective journalism of modern newspapers, the *Delta* took the rival New

Orleans *Commercial Bulletin* to task for prematurely publishing details of what became the failed expedition to Cárdenas:

> The success of this Expedition depended in a great measure upon secrecy. The exposure of its objects and arrangements not only put the Spanish Government on their guard, and provoked the interference of our own Executive, but it seriously obstructed all the operations of the friends of the Expedition, and prevented their raising the means which they were in a fair way of realizing before these developments were made. These statements, made by the journal in question with an air of verity and authenticity, served their purpose of exciting doubts and apprehensions, which led to a disappointment in procuring two steamboats for which the Expedition had nearly concluded their negotiations. This was the most serious mishap of the Expedition. Men of the very best character for such an enterprise, were ready to proceed to Cuba, at a moment's warning. They were fully organized and prepared.[42]

Later readers, of course, would have quite different expectations of newspapers. Editors on modern papers work tirelessly to reconcile, if not eliminate, apparent contradictions within their pages. Modern papers like the New York *Times* and the Washington *Post* implicitly vouch for the veracity of whatever appears in their pages. The desired end—a single, monolithic voice of authority. The claimed independence of the nineteenth-century popular press, by contrast, remained far removed from such self-professed objectivity. The tacit promise of the pre–Civil War popular papers to present both—even many— sides of the same story entailed no compulsion to select and edit stories so as to produce a unified voice of authority. Little effort was made to reconcile factual contradictions among their stories. From day to day—even within the same issue—wildly contradictory accounts of the same news event appeared, with little or no effort to reconcile discrepancies.[43] In a sense readers were asked to join the editor in assessing each story's veracity. In May 1850 the Baltimore *Sun* noted that some readers had doubted the paper's report two days earlier of "the descent of Lopez on Cuba." It therefore fully expected some readers not to accept the current issue's account of "the descent of Cuba on Lopez," and "in this dilemma we entreat our readers to do as we do—believe just as much of either as suits their fancy or convenience."[44]

By May 1850 the López story had grown so complex and popular that even editors nominally opposed to the filibuster found it—and him—impossible to resist. After López's release in Savannah, the Savannah *Republican* dutifully condemned his actions as the "illegal enterprises of those who neglect the beaten and honest avenues of industry for the fields of military adventure." But the *Republican*'s editors, who had savored the pleasures of López's company, also breathed a sigh of relief that a want of evidence had prompted his quick release. They were grateful that they had not been called to testify against their charming visitor; for whatever information they might have acquired certainly constituted a confidence among gentlemen. And no one, they observed, truly believed, "that Gen. LOPEZ should be convicted upon the strength of facts disclosed by himself in confidential conversations with others who had sought his society in a friendly manner. Happily the General made no imprudent disclosures; but had he done, we are constrained to say, so far as we are concerned, that under the circumstances, we could not without dishonor have given them in evidence, whatever might have been the penalty of recussancy."[45]

By May 1850 Narciso López's prominence in U.S. popular opinion owed as much to editors who simply wanted to sell more newspapers as to his ability to convince U.S. citizens of the righteousness of his cause.

Narciso López. (From Alexander Jones, *Cuba in 1851*)

Cuban industrialist and planter Miguel de Aldama. (From Willis Fletcher Johnson, *The History of Cuba*)

Ambrosio Gonzales, Cuban Creole activist and adjutant general to López. (Copy print courtesy of the South Carolinian Library, University of South Carolina)

New York *Sun* publisher and U.S. expansionism zealot Moses Yale Beach. (From Frank M. O'Brien, *The Story of the Sun*)

Filibuster officer Theodore O'Hara. (From Anderson S. Quisenberry, *Lopez's Expeditions to Cuba*)

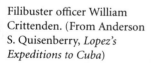

Filibuster officer William Crittenden. (From Anderson S. Quisenberry, *Lopez's Expeditions to Cuba*)

John Quitman, Mississippi governor and López supporter. (Courtesy of Lani and Ronald Riches)

John O'Sullivan, Manifest Destiny advocate, journalist, and López accomplice. (From *Harper's Weekly*)

$ 2,000 N.º 30

Be it Known to all Men,

That I, GENERAL NARCISO LOPEZ, *Chief of the "Patriotic Junta" for the promotion of the political interests of Cuba," established in the United States of North America, and the contemplated head of the Provisional Government and Commander-in-Chief of the revolutionary movement about to be now undertaken through my agency and permissive authority, for the liberation of the people of Cuba from the tyranny and oppression to which they are now subject by the power of Spain, and to be prosecuted by me till superseded by a superior Executive Officer, or such form of Government and authority as the people, by their free will and choice shall prescribe ; do by these presents, to subserve the cause and object aforesaid, make and execute this obligation on behalf of the people of Cuba, by whatever designation of nationality, or form of body politic, they shall hereafter assume, to wit :*

I do by these presents, for and on behalf of the said people of Cuba, and their successors in government for ever, and for value received, promise to pay to

or bearer, in equal annual instalments at one, two, three, four and five years, the sum of

Two ———— thousand dollars, with six per cent. interest from date, payable rateably on each annual instalment, until both principal and interest be fully paid and discharged. And I, the said General Narciso Lopez, in virtue of the authority, and for the promotion of the object aforesaid do by these presents, pledge to the said

or bearer, the public lands and public property of Cuba, of whatever kind, and the fiscal resources of the people and government of Cuba, from whatever source to be derived ; and do further pledge the good faith of the people and government of Cuba, in perpetuity, for the faithful and complete discharge of this obligation.

In testimony whereof, I, the said General Narciso Lopez, do hereto affix my signature and the Seal of the said Provisional Government, which is further witnessed by Ambrosio José Gonzalez and José Maria Sanchez Yznaga, members of said "Patriotic Junta," and

This done and executed in the City of New Orleans, and State of Louisiana, one of the United States of North America, on this 30 day of April, A. D. 1850.

Sanchez Yznaga   *Narciso Lopez*

Ambrosio José Gonzalez

C. P. Smith

GOBIERNO PROVISIONAL

F1784
.P3
x

$2,000

Bond sold to raise money for expeditionary army. (Courtesy of the Bancroft Library, University of California, Berkely)

GENERAL NARCISO LOPEZ,

COMMANDER OF THE LIBERATING ARMY OF CUBA.

In presenting our readers the above wood-cut of the gallant chief at the head of the Cuban revolutionary movement, we feel bound to remark, that owing to the haste with which it has been prepared, it is far from doing justice to his fine features and noble expression. A very good full length lithograph of the General, represented in the act of unfurling the standard of the Cuban Republic, may be seen on the walls of our office.

The May 25, 1850, issue of the New Orleans *Delta* announced the filibusters' departure for Cuba.

Soldiers of the Liberating Expedition of Cuba!

The noble mission on which we have started together, is one which would alone suffice to nerve to heroism the arm of every one holding a place in our ranks, even if you were not already the men of the field of Palo Alto and Cherubusco, or brethren and worthy peers of the men of those immortal victories.

Citizens of the great Republic, you are going to give to Cuba that freedom for which your example has taught her to sigh; to strike from the beautiful limbs of the Queen of the Antilles the chains which have too long degraded her, in subjection to a foreign tyranny which is an outrage upon the age; to do for your Cuban brethren what a LAFAYETTE, a STEUBEN, a KOSCIUSKO and a PULASKI are deathless in history for having aided to do for you; and eventually to add another glorious Star to the banner which already waves, to the admiration of the whole world, over "The land of the Free and the home of the Brave."

The people of Cuba would not need that the first guard of honor around the Flag of her nascent independence should be mainly composed of their future fellow-citizens from the United States, but for the peculiar circumstances which have hitherto given to her tyrants a paralyzing clutch upon the throat of their prostrate victim. Unarmed, unable to effect the first beginning of organization for insurrection, and menaced by Spain's perpetual threat of converting into a worse than San Domingo, the richest and loveliest of Islands beneath the sun: your Cuban brethren have been compelled to wait and long for the hour when a first nucleus for their revolution shall be afforded them by a gallant band of sympathizing friends, like that which I esteem it now the highest honor of my life to lend to this brilliant enterprise. The Flag on which you behold the Tri-color of Liberty, the Triangle of Strength and Order, the Star of the future State, and the Stripes of the three departments of Cuba, once unfurled to the wind on her shores, and guarded by a legion of choice spirits amply powerful to deal Buena-Vista fashion with any force which the detested Spanish Government in Cuba will be able to bring against it; the patriotic people of Cuba will rally in joy and exultation to its support; while you leave behind you untold thousands, eager to tread in your glorious track, under the head of one of the most eminent chief of the unparalelled Mexican campaigns, unless indeed we anticipate them by consummating our splendid task before they have time to follow.

Soldiers of the Liberating Expedition of Cuba! Our first act on arrival shall be the establishment of a Provisional Constitution, founded on American principles and adapted to the emergencies of the occasion. This Constitution you will unite with your brethren of Cuba in swearing to support, in its principles as well as on the Field of Battle. You have all been chosen by your Officers as men individually worthy of so honorable an undertaking. I rely implicitly on your presenting to Cuba and the world, a signal example of all the virtues as well as all the valor of the American Citizen-Soldier; and cannot be deceived in my confidence that by your discipline, good order, moderation in victory, and sacred respect for all private rights, you will put to shame every insolent calumny of your enemies. And when the hour arrives for repose on the laurels which await your grasp, you will all, I trust, establish permanent and happy homes on the bountiful soil of the Island, you go to free, and there long enjoy the gratitude which Cuba will never fail generously to bestow on those to whom she will owe the sacred and immeasurable debt of her LIBERTY.

NARCISO LOPEZ.

A broadside distributed among Narciso López's volunteers in April 1850, after they were at sea, bound for Cuba. (National Archives, SW Region, Fort Worth, Texas)

On September 1, 1851, López, at age fifty-four, was garroted in a plaza just across the harbor from Havana's coastal fortress, El Morro. (From Hermino Portell Vilá, *Narciso López y Su Epoca*)

In September 1852, after Narciso López's death, *Harper's Monthly* published engravings of El Morrillo, where the filibusters had landed, and Las Pozas, where they had battled Spanish soldiers.

The *Illustrated London News* in October 1851 published engravings showing Havana sites where filibuster executions took place. In the center here is Castle Atares.

This view of Havana from the October 1851 *Illustrated London News* shows Morro Castle in the center and, to the right, the Punta, in front of which, facing the harbor, López was executed.

6   A Paper Sovereignty

Mobile, Alabama, May 31, 1850

Narciso López arrived in Mobile, Alabama, on the morning of May 31, 1850. Though the local U.S. attorney, Paul Hamilton, reported that López "immediately left for Pascagoula (on the coast) in a buggy," he did linger long enough to discuss the Cárdenas expedition with some townspeople. Upon learning of those exchanges, the local Spanish consul had alerted Hamilton, who had orders from Secretary of State John Clayton to arrest López.

Hamilton, however, like his counterparts in Savannah and New York, could find no usable witnesses and later that day wrote Clayton that he had been unable to make an arrest. While López had conversed with some townspeople, the consul had heard those remarks secondhand—so the government had no direct testimony to offer. Those who had talked with López told Hamilton that, as in Savannah, the general had been "very guarded in the remarks he made." Hamilton was thus "without any kind of evidence, that would justify . . . detention." Even if the prosecutor had found López, he would have had no choice but to let him pass freely.[1]

New Orleans, June 7, 1850

In New Orleans, where the actual fitting out had taken place, U.S. Attorney Logan Hunton also had orders to arrest López.[2] A week after López's departure from Mobile, however, federal officials had no trace of his whereabouts.

Had López—certainly aware that federal officials in New Orleans would be waiting for him—headed in yet another direction?

On June 7, a week after López left Mobile, New Orleans's U.S. marshal received a succinct, courtly letter from López, written a day earlier at Pass Christian, Mississippi:

> Sir—Having understood that you desire to see me in reference to matters connected to your office, I take the liberty of informing you that for that purpose I shall repair to-morrow to the city, and shall await your orders in the gentlemen's parlor of the St. Charles Hotel, from 4 to 6 o'clock, P.M.
>
> With the highest consideration and respect, I subscribe myself, your obedient servant.
>
> NARCISO LÓPEZ[3]

The two met at the St. Charles, then went to the federal circuit court at Municipal Hall, a two-story Greek Revival building on Lafayette Square. For U.S. Attorney Hunton and his colleagues, López's entrance into the courtroom—under arrest once again—was a moment to savor. Federal officers finally had their man in both the room and the city where they wanted him: *United States v. Narciso López* could now commence.[4]

No doubt some in Washington over the summer of 1850 allowed themselves to believe that with López's arrest in New Orleans, they were close to concluding their long campaign against his intrigues. U.S. Attorney Hunton in New Orleans, however, harbored no such illusions. "I fear the examination will be protracted," the prosecutor, then in his mid-forties, wrote to Secretary of State Clayton on June 7, the day of the arrest. Clayton concurred; three days later he wrote to Hunton, "You will probably be opposed by much of the legal talent of your city—probably also, by much popular feeling, and although I know well that neither the one nor the other deters a Lawyer from the full execution of his duty, yet you ought not be required to stand up against both, unsupported." Hunton was thus authorized by President Taylor to hire an additional lawyer, "who will be paid a reasonable compensation for his services."[5]

Two days later Clayton wired Hunton and reiterated the federal government's determination to convict López. "The honor of the Government requires that no just effort be spared to bring him to trial and punishment. The president instructs me to enjoin upon you as you value the faith and character of your country to spare no pains to execute the law. Do your whole duty."[6]

To assist in the prosecution Hunton hired Judah Benjamin, one of New Orleans's top criminal lawyers (and a decade later the Confederacy's treasury secretary).[7] Once in court, the two lawyers quickly learned that they faced a formidable defense team. López's attorneys—Laurent Sigur, John Henderson, and Seargent S. Prentiss—joined polished legal cunning to an alley fighter's style of attack.[8] López's other supporters—journalists, government accomplices, and street mobs—waged their own fight both in and outside the courtroom, employing everything from rumormongering to sensational newspaper stories and public demonstrations. Attempting to smear federal officials as politically motivated hypocrites, they even floated rumors accusing both Hunton and Clayton of being secret filibuster accomplices. Likewise, Henry Bullard, a federal district judge in New Orleans, was accused of joining a filibuster into Mexico during his youth.[9]

The government's lawyers got their first look at López and his defense team during the two-week-long preliminary hearing in U.S. district court that began on Friday, June 7. The New Orleans *Picayune* described the defendant as "middle size, rather stout, dark complexion, with very black eyes, and black eye brows, high forehead, hair slightly gray, and with gray whiskers under his throat. He was dressed very plain, in blue linen pants, and a black dress coat, dark vest and blue cravat, with no attempt at show, and without anything particularly striking about him to attract attention."[10]

The hearing was called to determine whether the arrest warrant against López—based on an affidavit from Juan Y. Laborde, the local Spanish consul—rested on adequate evidence. In his sworn statement Laborde had alleged that López, in violation of the Neutrality Act, did indeed "begin and set on foot" from within the United States a military expedition against Cuba.[11]

Attempting to quash the warrant, López's attorney John Henderson asserted that to be legal, the document required direct knowledge of a crime. And Laborde's affidavit, said Henderson, supplied no such testimony. "The affidavit merely averred the belief of the Spanish Consul that General Lopez had committed a certain offence, but it did not state that he knew a violation of the law had been committed." After Hunton answered that the affidavit did provide the required probable cause, defense cocounsel S. S. Prentiss retorted that the U.S. attorney was abusing his prosecutorial powers. The affidavit against López, Prentiss argued, rested solely on Laborde's "belief" of what had happened. "It seems to be the opinion of many District Attorneys that all that is necessary in an affidavit is to spread the law on it, just as a body spreads his butter on his bread; and very often it happens, in both cases, there is too much butter for the bread."[12]

New Orleans, June 8, 1850

To get to their ten o'clock court appointment the next morning, June 8, López and his lawyers had to wade through crowds of cheering supporters who had surrounded Municipal Hall, blocking both St. Charles Avenue and Hervia Street. Once inside the courtroom, the defense team learned that because of ill health, the presiding judge, T. H. McCaleb, was withdrawing from the case. The hearing was transferred to the courtroom of U.S. Commissioner Joshua Baldwin, and at the end of the day's session, a band of raucous filibuster supporters crowded into Baldwin's office as López posted bond of $3,000 to guarantee his continued presence in court. In testament to López's local popularity, James Caldwell, recorder of the Second Municipality—the equivalent of mayor—signed the defendant's bond, pledging himself as security should López fail to appear.[13]

New Orleans, June 9–17, 1850

The next day's court session, on June 9, moved beyond questions of procedure to those of facts, many of which were hardly in dispute after all the newspaper stories. Though Hunton easily established that López and his friends had departed the United States, traveled to Cuba, and fought Spanish troops, he still needed to prove specific factual links between López and preparations for the expedition. Once on the stand, however, prosecution witnesses often dissembled or claimed they had forgotten what they had seen and heard. David Adams, harbormaster at Lafayette, for instance, had witnessed the loading of the *Creole* on May 6, but when asked what was loaded, he answered, "I saw nothing but some barrels of pork, marked 'stores.'" When pressed, Adams finally acknowledged he had seen "some persons" boarding the ship. Were any armed? Hunton asked. "I saw a few guns," Adams answered, "ten or twelve, or more; I paid no attention to the number." Laurent Sigur—then in his mid-thirties—when called to the stand as a witness, could not even recall where López was going when he boarded the *Creole*. Asked to name the destination of the "expedition" to which López had so often alluded in the public speeches that Sigur had translated, Sigur responded, "I do not recollect that General Lopez ever told me what particular expedition he referred to on these public occasions."[14] Sigur was both a journalist and a lawyer; like Henderson, he was well aware that he, too, could face criminal charges arising from the expedition. To dodge the prosecutors' inquiries, he cited Fifth Amendment protections against forced self-incrimination. He also said that his role as counsel to López precluded his answering questions. Pioneering a new category of privileged communications in U.S. jurisprudence, Sigur even argued that since López had been a guest in his home, divulgence of any conversation held under his own roof would constitute "a breach of hospitality."

In court, López's attorneys dealt soberly with facts and laws. Other supporters, meanwhile, waged a far more boisterous and explicitly political campaign—packing the courtroom, occasionally prompting warnings from the bench for disruptive behavior. On consecutive afternoons, following the June 7 and 8 court sessions, a noisy crowd followed López to the St. Charles Hotel, where, from the hotel's portico, as Sigur translated, López called for an end to Spain's rule of Cuba. After the next day's session, filibuster supporters, accompanied by a band of musicians, repaired to Sigur's house on Customhouse Street, where López was again residing. After the band serenaded López with, among other songs, "The Star Spangled Banner," he delivered another speech, from the house's balcony. All were then invited inside to toast Cuba's future liberty. By then, López had become a cause célèbre throughout the city; the Orleans House even named a drink for him.[15]

By June 17, with no end to the court hearings in sight, defense attorneys waived the pretrial hearing and asked Commissioner Baldwin to send the case directly to a grand jury. The grand jury convened that same day and began sifting through the government's evidence. Among the more notable disclosures elicited over the preceding two weeks: Sigur, of the *Delta*, and Donatien Augustin, commander of the state militia, had been positively linked to the removal—on May 7, the day the *Creole* departed—of a cache of 104 boxes of gunpowder from Louisiana's state arsenal.[16] On June 21, after four days of deliberations, the grand jury returned indictments for Neutrality Act violations against López and fifteen coconspirators—including Sigur, Henderson, Commander Augustin, John Quitman, John O'Sullivan, John Pickett of the Kentucky regiment, Ambrosio Gonzales, Chatham R. Wheat of the Louisiana regiment, and Judge Cotesworth P. Smith of the Mississippi Supreme Court.[17]

Washington, July 4–9, 1850

Taking a break from his troubles in early July, President Taylor attended Independence Day ceremonies at the unfinished Washington Monument. It was already hot and humid that Thursday morning, July 4, when the president joined his cabinet on a shaded platform at the base of the obelisk. The highlight of the day's ceremonies was to be the interment in the monument of some dust from the tomb of Thaddeus Kosciusko, the Polish nationalist who had fought in the U.S. War of Independence. After an oration by Senator Henry Foote of Mississippi, Taylor left the shaded platform and stood in the blazing sun for several more hours for additional speeches and the deposition of Kosciusko's ashes. He then took a leisurely walk along the Potomac River and returned to the White House, exhausted, at 4:00 P.M., where he consumed large quantities of ice water, chilled milk, and cherries—all of which Washingtonians had been told to avoid that summer lest they contract the Asiatic cholera sweeping much of the country.[18]

The president fell ill that night, attended a few duties the next day, but by evening was showing symptoms like those he had displayed when diarrhea attacked him in Pennsylvania the previous summer. The next day, a doctor was called to the White House. The president, he concluded, was suffering from cholera morbus, not the Asiatic cholera but a milder variety of diarrhea or dysentery. Calomel and opium were prescribed, but Taylor's condition worsened over the next three days. He died at 10:30 P.M. on July 9. He was sixty-five years old.[19]

"You have a Sparta . . . embellish it!" With those words, Daniel Webster during the 1840s had taunted the heady expansionism that then gripped the Democrats.[20] Recalling such taunts, many Democrats in 1848 reveled in the delicious irony that upon Whig Zachary Taylor's election to the presidency that year, the task of governing—of embellishing—that vast Sparta had fallen to those same bashful Whig conquerors.

As president, Taylor had sought no new continental conquests. When he came to office, the United States already spanned the North American continent from east to west. In non-continental matters, then, in foreign affairs, Taylor's aversion to expansion had emerged most clearly. On a day-to-day basis, he gave Secretary of State Clayton, whose conservatism matched that of the president, full charge of the foreign policy portfolio. Secretary of State Clayton reaffirmed the federal government's decades-old no-transfer policy toward Cuba. In yet another instance of the administration's resolve to make no waves in the Gulf, Clayton in April 1850 concluded the Clayton-Bulwer treaty between Washington and London. Britain pledged to acquire no more territory in Central America, and the U.S. and Great Britain agreed not to build a canal across the Panamanian isthmus without each other's consent. Generally, however, the administration had developed no unified foreign policy. Nor had it sought to expand U.S. power beyond its borders. Taylor, after all, had his hands full with the domestic problems still ravaging the enlarged Sparta left to him by James K. Polk.[21]

Indeed, Taylor's long effort to arrest Narciso López occurred amid the much larger struggle between the federal government and southern planters over slavery's future in the lands won in the Mexican War. The domestic debates initiated by the Cárdenas expedition only thickened an already brewing soup of sectional and partisan discord over slavery and states' rights. Beyond that, the episode acutely embarrassed Zachary Taylor; it was his administration, after all, that—antifilibustering rhetoric notwithstanding—had failed to prevent López's departure for Cuba.

Against a rising tide of free-soilism, planter politicians like John C. Calhoun and John Quitman by the winter of 1849 had been urging southern states to leave the Union to preserve their rights to own and trade slaves. In January of that year, a full two months before Taylor entered the White House, Calhoun gathered fourteen colleagues into a southern political caucus to ensure that Congress imposed no bans on slavery within the Mexican cession lands. During his presidency's early months, Taylor tried to sidestep debates over slavery in the West. He was publicly pledged to let Congress govern; as a candidate he had promised to represent no partisan or regional interests and to veto only acts he deemed unconstitutional. True to that spirit, Taylor on December 4, 1849, had recommended that Congress grant statehood to both California and New Mexico whenever each applied. Questions about slavery should be left to each state's constitutional convention; each should select a government "in such form as to them shall seem most likely to effect their safety and happiness."

Under Taylor's plan, then, the western settlers and Congress would bear the brunt of decisions over slavery in the West, and he would avoid the personal political damage that making the decisions himself would certainly bring.[22]

Zachary Taylor suffered the sad distinction of being the first president in U.S. history to govern when his party controlled neither house of Congress. And for all its nominal shrewdness, his strategy, to have been successful, would have required a far more collegial Congress than the one that came to Washington in the fall of 1849, during the waning days of Polk's administration. Deep sectional rivalries riddled both the House and the Senate. While the 34 Democrats who nominally controlled the Senate were hardly inclined to do President-elect Taylor's bidding, the House presented yet another kind of obstacle. No party ruled there: the House was deadlocked with 111 Democrats, 105 Whigs, and 13 Free-Soilers. Compounding Taylor's woes, as president-elect and after he assumed office in March 1849, he generally remained aloof from day-to-day congressional activities; he and his aides assumed no significant role in trying to shape legislative branch decisions.[23]

Not surprisingly, then, when the House of Representatives reconvened in January 1849, attempts to organize the Mexican cession quickly collapsed into bickering, then stalemate. Hopes turned toward the Senate, where Kentucky's Senator Henry Clay was trying to fashion a compromise solution to the congressional deadlock over the western lands. Clay's compromise, presented on January 29, took the form of an omnibus bill carrying several legislative acts: California's admission as a free state, the organization of the rest of the Mexican cession into territories without reference to the slavery issue, a remunerated settlement of Texas's claims on New Mexico, stronger federal legislation to guarantee the return of runaway slaves, an end to the slave trade in the District of Columbia, and a federal guarantee not to otherwise interfere in the interstate slave trade.

Neither Free-Soilers nor Calhounites embraced Clay's compromise. Nor did Taylor. Although a southern slaveholder himself, Taylor was aligned with northern opponents of Clay's proposals, the same people he would seek to flatter later that summer with the tour of northeastern states, which produced his antifilibuster proclamation. Indeed, in December of that year, New York senator William H. Seward had boasted to publisher and fellow Taylor adviser Thurlow Weed that the president "will be put on the North side of the Mason & Dixon line, and he will not flinch from any duty."[24]

By March of the next year, 1850, with Congress still deadlocked, Taylor's powers were sapped still further by a financial scandal within his administration, revelations of a $100,000 legal fee paid from the federal treasury to War Secretary George W. Crawford. A lawyer, Crawford had earned the fee before he joined the administration by representing a client who was suing the federal government. Besides questioning the settlement's size, critics found it unseemly that final approval for the fee's amount had come from Crawford's friend and colleague Attorney General Reverdy Johnson. No criminal charges resulted from the scandal, but Taylor, a man of strict personal probity, was so embarrassed by the affair that by early July 1850 he had decided to replace his entire cabinet.

With President Taylor's death on July 9, 1850, the cabinet's overhaul, the western lands, Narciso López—those and all of the federal government's other problems—now suddenly belonged to Millard Fillmore. The new president was, at fifty, a rotund man with an even rounder face and a shock of thick wavy hair. The son of a poor upstate New York farmer, he had labored in the mechanized textile industry as a young man and educated himself, keeping an open dictionary by his carding machine, learning new words as he fed spools of thread to the contraption. A local Quaker judge was so impressed that he provided the young man with a legal education.[25]

Fillmore became a successful attorney, a New York state legislator, and a four-term member of the U.S. Congress. Like Zachary Taylor, he had been drawn toward the antislavery Conscience wing of the Whigs. But unlike Taylor, who had no real political experience before coming to the presidency, Fillmore had a knack for political compromise. While Taylor the slave-owning southerner had been even prepared to wage war on his native region to enforce federal sovereignty, Fillmore preferred a more conciliatory approach to controversies over the western lands. Early in July 1850 he had warned Taylor that, in the event he as vice-president was called on in the Senate to break a tie, he would vote for Clay's compromise. Upon Taylor's death, of course, the sentiments animating Vice-President Fillmore's threat became President Fillmore's policy. With Taylor no longer there to pressure Whig congressmen to vote against Clay's program, all of its measures—albeit passed separately—were enacted by the end of September.[26]

López, however, remained a problem. Fewer than four weeks after assuming his new post, the new secretary of state, Daniel Webster, received an angry letter from Angel Calderón de la Barca, Spain's U.S. minister, asking why "the pirates" of Cárdenas remained free. The diplomat reminded Webster of the 1795 friendship treaty between Spain and the United States and of how Madrid had remained a neutral during the Mexican War. López's campaign, Calderón de la Barca charged, was "a war de facto, in the midst of official peace." His government thus needed to know "whether the United States are able, legally to suppress, these military expeditions, which are fitting out in their own territory for the purpose of invading the colonies of Spain?—What is the opinion of the American Government in regard to the neutrality stipulated for, in existing treaties, and to what extent they are willing to act, in order to enforce its observance?—In short, it desires to know, whether these violations of treaty obligations can be suppressed on American soil, and those concerned in them punished?"[27]

Viewed from the widest vantage, the debates over the western lands, the Compromise of 1850, and the prosecution of López belonged to a larger Whig struggle to preserve federal authority amid a rising tide of insurgency against the central government. Taylor and Fillmore sought to preserve what Whigs had traditionally viewed as the primacy of the central government in Washington over powers asserted by individual states.

President Polk and his Democratic predecessors on occasion allowed both states and individual citizens to encroach upon diplomatic and other public policy realms that Whigs believed were reserved for the federal government. The Whigs Taylor and Fillmore, by contrast, believed that only one sovereignty, that held and exercised by the central government, properly held dominion over the nation's political life. The Whigs adamantly rejected the state of Texas's claims on the federal territory of New Mexico; Taylor had even threatened to use the U.S. Army if Texas sought to enforce any claims to land west of the Rio Grande. Likewise, both Taylor and Fillmore were willing to use federal military, diplomatic, and judicial force to thwart López. In each instance, they believed, the primacy of federal authority lay challenged. In New Mexico, Taylor and Fillmore sought to preserve the federal government's powers to adjust the boundary of a territory acquired by a treaty between Mexico and the government in Washington. Similarly, in prosecuting López the Whigs sought to preserve—in fact and by example—the federal government's constitutional monopoly on the conduct of U.S. foreign policy and war.

Unfortunately for both Taylor and Fillmore, however, in daily practice Washington's claimed absolute sovereignty usually proved just that—a mere claim on paper, a vast paper sovereignty that withered in execution. The arm of federal law was long, but its grasp was weak; Uncle Sam's day-to-day assertion of authority over the nation's political life was frequently overwhelmed in—often *by*—the vast distances that separated Washington from much of the rest of the country.

New Orleans, October 2, 1850

Over the summer of 1850, with López and his lieutenants finally under federal indictment, presidents Taylor and Fillmore had successively pledged the federal government's resources to helping Logan Hunton, the U.S. attorney in New Orleans, convict the filibusters. As in 1849, support from Washington came through the departments of state and interior. Assistance rendered during Taylor's presidency by Secretary of State Clayton and Interior Secretary Thomas Ewing came during Fillmore's administration from their respective successors, Daniel Webster and Alexander Stuart.

In New Orleans, meanwhile, Hunton continued his own investigation of López through the summer and into the fall of 1850. "It is very certain," he wrote to Webster on October 2, "that the Arms of the State of Louisiana were procured for this lawless adventure through Genl. Augustin, the Commander of the Legion: and I believe it is equally certain that arms of the State of Mississippi were by some means procured for the same purpose." Hunton then confessed that despite the publicity that had attended the expedition to Cuba, he, too, had been fooled by the filibusters about many details. "I desire now, Sir, to say that great secrecy and caution was observed in fitting out this Expedition—it is very certain that I was baffled in my inquiries in relation to it before its departure." Hunton recounted the filibusters' Chagres cover story, how soldiers had been recruited in Cincinnati under the ruse of going to mine California gold, how ships had been cleared for Chagres, how they had taken on arms below New Orleans.[28]

Those details, wrote Hunton, were now "historical fact"; there could be no doubt that "a Military Expedition was thus fitted out in this District to be carried out from hence against the Island of Cuba." But convicting those responsible for that expedition, Hunton wrote, would be difficult, for "the persons who alone can bear testimony to convict the parties accused are themselves offenders against the same law." Fearing prosecution themselves, these witnesses declined to divulge any information that might "constitute a necessary link in the chain of testimony to convict the witness if indicted."

Hunton's one recent glimmer of hope, he told the secretary of state, had come during a recent interview with some of the "Contoy prisoners," the forty-two reluctant filibusters who had been left behind by López on Contoy Island on May 16, 1850. Two days after López left, the young men had been captured by the Spanish when the warships *Pizarro* and *Harberno* anchored at the island. The Spaniards also captured two filibuster ships anchored at Contoy, the *Georgiana* and the *Susan Loud*. The *Georgiana* had been left behind by López to transport the deserters home. However, before it could leave, the *Georgiana* had been inexplicably joined by the *Susan Loud* and its skeleton crew. Because the Contoy prisoners all claimed to have been left behind by López because they opposed filibustering, President Taylor had felt obliged to seek their release from the Spanish, which for most had occurred late that summer.[29]

Upon learning of the Contoy prisoners' release, U.S. Attorney Hunton had requested a meeting with some of them. After his subsequent meeting with the ex-prisoners, Hunton admitted to Webster that most "were not the best witnesses against Lopez, not having been with him" either on the same ship or at Cárdenas. One, however, did show promise: John H. Finch of Cincinnati had claimed that he knew some veterans of the Cárdenas expedition, now back in Ohio, who might yet agree to testify against López. Hunton wondered whether Webster would be willing to dispatch John Goddard to Cincinnati to gather the witnesses?[30]

Goddard, Washington's municipal police chief and, when the need arose, a Department of Interior special agent, had assisted Hunton in New Orleans the previous spring during López's preliminary hearing in U.S. district court. Although the visiting agent failed to produce any witnesses for the state, Hunton nonetheless had been impressed. "I thought him shrewd, sagacious, and discreet," the Louisiana prosecutor informed Webster. "And he is already acquainted with some of the parties engaged in the Expedition." Webster granted Hunton's request, and on November 17 Goddard left Washington for Cincinnati.[31]

In 1850 the federal government had no national intelligence service, no national police force, and, beyond Washington, no well-staffed judiciary. Not until the Civil War would a national intelligence service be organized. Not until 1908, with the creation of the Federal Bureau of Investigation, would there be a national police agency. In gathering evidence against López, then, the federal government relied on the same ad hoc system that it had used to gather intelligence during the Mexican War: it hired temporary special agents on a per mission basis.[32] Working alone, far from Washington, those agents quickly discovered that the nation's hinterlands had no reverence for the federal government and that federal subpoenas alone did not bring reluctant witnesses into court. Working in Cincinnati in November 1850, for instance, Special Agent Goddard was reduced to listening to subpoenaed witnesses demand promises of cash before they would come to New Orleans to testify against López. To Interior Secretary Alexander Stuart, Goddard reported that he had located six witnesses from the Cárdenas expedition: "They all voluntarily agree to go to New Orleans, and testify to all they know provided they get paid the usual mileage and per diem while attending court." Federal officers outside Washington suffered an often staggering isolation. To be sure, much of that isolation arose from growing sectional debates ravaging the Republic; debates over slavery created tensions between state governments and the federal bureaucracy. In the South federal officials dispatched from Washington could not even depend on the loyalty of their own local counterparts. In several instances López's organization received help from sympathetic local federal officials. As a Spanish spy who infiltrated López's organization charged, when it came to filibustering many federal officials of the South "were tainted with the most damnable heresy."[33]

To administer the 2,936,160 square miles that comprised the United States in 1850, excluding those who worked for the post office, the federal government's executive branch had but 4,322 full-time employees—one for every 679 square miles. In day-to-day life, then, Uncle Sam's emissaries were often hard to find. When, for instance, López and his army retreated from Cárdenas to Key West in May 1850, the town's U.S. marshal, W. C. Maloney, fearing a loss of civil control, complained in a May 21 letter to one of his superiors that "the number of men thus thrown into this town and all armed exceed the number of effective male inhabitants. . . . I pray to be excused for the liberty I take in suggesting the propriety of a United States armed force on this Island to enforce if necessary the execution of the laws of the U.S." Two weeks later, Key West's U.S. Attorney William R. Hackley echoed the lament to President Taylor, writing that "I regret much that from want of force we were unable to arrest more of these offenders, but we have done the best we could under the circumstance." Since no telegraph line linked Key West to the mainland, to send a dispatch asking for military reinforcements local federal officials had to await the arrival of the *Isabel,* the mail steamer that called once a week. But even if they could have gotten their request to Washington sooner, what regiment might have come?[34] After peaking at 49,000 soldiers during the Mexican War, the ranks of the U.S. regular army by 1850 had dropped to 11,000, only 2,500 more than its meager size on the eve of the war.[35]

The civilian force arrayed against López was hardly more impressive than the military that he defied. At the top of the pyramid, neither Taylor nor his successor Fillmore was a strong leader. In earlier years strong presidents like Andrew Jackson and James K. Polk had accumulated vast powers. But the heightened executive powers of those administrations were never written into law.[36] They arose, rather, from the unique personal qualities of Jackson and Polk and the political milieu that nurtured their rise. By 1848 nagging intraparty divisions bedeviling both Democrats and Whigs had prompted each to move toward more pliable presidential candidates.

Further diminishing executive authority, cabinet officers of that day tended to be weak, ineffective, and ill-coordinated to work with one another. No single agency assumed full responsibility for directing López's prosecution. What executive branch direction that did emerge came from the departments of state and interior. The State Department's interest in the case during Zachary Taylor's administration had arisen from the president's habit of giving John Clayton almost complete control over diplomatic affairs. President Fillmore took a more active interest in foreign policy than had his predecessor. But, then again, Fillmore's secretary of state, Daniel Webster, had held the same post during the 1840s and thus tended to seize the initiative in formulating his department's policy. Beyond that, as a former senator who had shown little patience with filibusters, Webster had a personal interest in thwarting López that antedated the Fillmore administration.[37]

López also worried the State Department because filibustering poached on its diplomatic prerogatives. As for the department's role in the actual prosecution, that emerged because no other government agency laid clear claim to the task. The Office of the Attorney General in 1850 was still little more than a tiny sinecure for a single lawyer.[38] The Department of Interior's interest in López arose from the general catchall role of its early years. Popularly called the Home Department upon its founding, Interior was created in 1849 at the urging of Polk's treasury secretary, Robert J. Walker, to relieve Walker's own department of a welter of domestic responsibilities, many in the nation's new western domain. Thomas Ewing, Sr., the first interior secretary, thus headed a department whose responsibilities included the census, maintenance of federal buildings, the Mexican boundary survey, agricultural statistics, public lands, Indian affairs, patents, pensions—and, on occasion, intelligence gathering on filibusters. In its first fiscal year, 1850–51, the Department of Interior was expected to meet all of those responsibilities with a budget of $5,403,000, the outlay from which Ewing extracted the $500 that was advanced to John Goddard for his trip from Washington to Cincinnati to New Orleans—and, as it turned out, the federal government's entire expenditure for field intelligence on López during the spring of 1850.[39]

That paltry $500 contrasted starkly with the bluster with which the Taylor administration had begun its campaign to break up the filibuster. Writing to U.S. Attorney Hunton on June 9, 1850, John Clayton had staked the very integrity of the nation's laws upon a successful prosecution of López. "The honor of the Government requires that no just effort be spared to bring him to trial and punishment," Clayton wrote. "The President instructs me to enjoin it upon you as you value the faith and character of your country to spare no pains to execute the law." In a letter to the same prosecutor the next day, Secretary of Interior Ewing added that it would not suffice to convict just López. "It is a matter in which the good faith of the Nation's interest is implicated and it will not do to confine the retribution of justice to an obscure and worthless foreigner and suffer our own citizens who knew the law which they have violated to escape unpunished."[40]

Whig preoccupation with López was only compounded by the brazenness with which filibustering publicly mocked—and symbolically undermined—the party's insistence on the primacy of the central government and federal law in the nation's life. A government already perceived as weak could ill afford to tolerate such public disregard of its claimed authority. Sadly for the Whigs, however, many of their efforts to apprehend López only reinforced the very perception of weakness the government sought to dispel. With López's prosecution, as in so many other instances, Whig efforts to affirm the primacy of federal laws and the central government fell victim to Congress's tightfisted funding of the federal bureaucracy. Despite the vast federal correspondence dedicated to López's apprehension in 1850, in the end only one agent, Goddard, was dispatched into the field to gather testimony against him. From cabinet offices to the far-flung and overworked federal courts, officials of the central government labored under budgets set by a parsimonious Democratic Congress reluctant to fund any program that might diminish the powers of individual states.[41]

When, for instance, the Interior Department was first proposed, in 1849, southern Democratic senators such as South Carolina's Calhoun and Virginia's James M. Mason opposed it, fearing that Congress might be creating a new centralizing department that could weaken powers claimed by individual states. Calhoun and Mason need not have worried. Even if the Interior Department had been adequately funded, its centralizing powers would have been undermined by the long-standing tradition of "dual sovereignty." An idea that reached back to the founding of the American republic, dual sovereignty posited that each individual state enjoyed its own separate sovereignty: the sovereignty of the individual states at once equaled and antedated that claimed by the central federal government. Over the years, both politicians and jurists embraced the concept. Indeed, as late as 1859, in *Ableman v. Booth*, a U.S. Supreme Court decision written by Chief Justice Roger Taney, the court would hold that "the powers of the general government, and that of the State, although both exist and are exercised within the same territorial limits, are yet separate and distinct sovereignties, acting separately and independently of each other, within their respective spheres."[42]

López's federal adversaries, in short, operated in a nation far more politically decentralized than that which would emerge after the Civil War. Most crucially, federal officials in 1850 enjoyed limited leverage when demanding cooperation from state or local governments. As State Department special agent James E. Harvey lamented in 1849, the threads of cooperation joining the federal government with local and state governments were thin indeed. Writing to John Clayton from Philadelphia on August 13, 1849, Harvey reported that he and a local federal marshal planned to "endeavor to organize an efficient corps of investigation between these federal functionaries & such cooperation from the Municipal police, as can be obtained; which I suppose will be limited, since there is no inducement offered for activity or vigilance." Though Harvey hoped that a forthcoming conference among himself, the U.S. marshal, and Philadelphia's mayor might help, "I cannot predict the success of this conference, knowing as I do, how difficult it is to invoke aid from the local authorities without substantial considerations."[43]

Outside of Washington, federal officials worked ever aware that they were vastly outnumbered and that any too conspicuously unpopular federal action could provoke local outcry. In Key West, for instance—as in Savannah, New Orleans, New York, and other locales—many local residents seemed to have genuinely liked the filibusters. "With very few exceptions, the people at Key West were disposed to act cleverly towards the Liberators," Richardson Hardy recalled. "A year earlier, U.S. Navy Commander V. M. Randolph, while supervising his blockade against López's troops on Round Island, noted a similar public affection for the filibusters, among the townspeople of nearby Pascagoula, Mississippi. "These are wretched doings, sir, on our waters," he complained to a superior, "on an island only four miles from a fashionable watering-place, and where there are justices of the peace, a sheriff, and not very far off, a circuit judge,—all afraid to act."[44]

When López on June 7, 1850, finally faced his federal adversaries in New Orleans, he stood in a courtroom inside the Second Municipality's Municipal Hall, a building owned by the local city government—the same government whose chief officer, Recorder James Caldwell, had paid López's bond. Like foreign diplomats, the handful of federal officials posted in New Orleans enjoyed their offices as, quite literally, tenants of the local municipal government.

Typical of the shorthandedness that bedeviled the federal bureaucracy outside Washington, when agent Goddard arrived in New Orleans with his six witnesses from Cincinnati, U.S. Attorney Hunton had no assistant to watch over his visitors—or any place to put them. How could he ask for assistance from officials of the same state government that had provided gunpowder for the filibusters? Instead, Hunton simply asked Special Agent Goddard to "keep charge of the witnesses and prevent any tampering with them." The caution, according to Goddard, was well warranted; "a short time" after arriving in New Orleans with his charges, he discovered "that attempts were making, by the friends of the accused parties to intimidate the witnesses, and prevent their appearing on the stand."[45]

In May 1850 Hunton had explained to John Clayton why extreme caution should attend any arrest of the filibusters in New Orleans. Any too precipitous action, Hunton warned, "would only have served to inflame the public mind, and to have emboldened these adventurers"—an apt warning but sadly incongruous with the absolute powers claimed by Webster and his Whig colleagues back in Washington.[46]

In other instances limits to federal powers turned on more practical considerations. That same month, May 1850, Mobile's U.S. Attorney Paul Hamilton pondered how, if the need arose, he might get an arrest warrant to hold López in Mobile. In a letter to Clayton, Hamilton wrote that the local federal judge was "holding a Court in the Middle District in the State, and we are without a U.S. commissioner." Unable to exercise the powers claimed by the central government he served, Hamilton wondered whether perhaps a state court judge might be willing to issue a warrant.[47]

In 1850 the few lines of organized communication and transportation that bound the nation—the mail system, the telegraph, the steamship—often subverted the very centralization they ostensibly promoted. It was not for nothing that expansionists such as James Gordon Bennett and John O'Sullivan spoke almost romantically about telegraphs and mail steamships. The lack of federal controls over both rendered each vulnerable to manipulation by filibusters. Not until 1861, when President Lincoln seized the nation's civilian telegraph network and rechristened it the U.S. Military Telegraph, would the federal government gain an even nominally secure wire network. It was, after all, the federal government's arrest in Maryland of a Confederate sympathizer for cutting the wires of that system that would spark that year's controversy over Lincoln's suspension of the writ of habeas corpus.[48]

But Confederate sympathizers were hardly the first to tamper with the telegraph system. In November 1850 Special Agent Goddard reassured Interior Secretary Stuart that he would exercise caution in telegraphing intelligence to U.S. Attorney Hunton in New Orleans. "I will," Goddard promised, "telegraph him in such a way that *he* may understand me, and not the telegraph agent, for those agents are not *at all* to be trusted with secrets." In September 1851, venting his own frustrations at López's continued filibustering, President Fillmore would exclaim, "In times like this, the telegraph in the hand of irresponsible and designing men, is a tremendous engine for mischief." That same year, according to a federal informant, López's agents bribed telegraph operators to alert them to any federal communications pertaining to their filibustering.[49]

Steamships, too, undermined federal authority and often assisted filibusters. López on May 23 escaped Key West by sailing to Savannah on the *Isabel*, a mail steamer. Passing through Charleston two weeks later, Special Agent Goddard heard "Captn. Peck," commander of a Savannah-to-Charleston mail steamer, say that he was "favorable" to the filibusters' cause. Only a day earlier the mariner gave six López filibusters free passage from Savannah to Charleston. In an even more chilling example of steamship mischief, on the day López landed at Cárdenas, May 19, 1850, Spain's minister to the U.S., Angel Calderón de la Barca, wrote to John Clayton to complain that four steamers owned by George Law suddenly "were found assembled at Havannah, with remarkable punctuality." Among steamship lines of López's day, George Law's United States Mail Steamship Company proved the greatest irritant to presidents Taylor and Fillmore. His federally subsidized mail ships regularly transported filibuster arms, propaganda, and men.[50]

On board Law's vessels in Havana harbor on May 19, according to Calderón de la Barca, were men "connected with the plan of invasion . . . [who] wore the same red shirt and the same oil-skin cap, which constituted the uniform mode of dress of those who landed at Cardenas." In the wake of the alleged incident, Captain General Federico Roncali denied Law's ships ordinary docking facilities and required them to anchor offshore. The allegation by the ever-suspicious Calderón de la Barca against such a well-known filibuster sympathizer as Law might be easily dismissed as the work of a partisan Spanish imagination—except for the existence of yet another letter. On May 26, 1850, one week after the Cárdenas landing, Lieutenant H. J. Hartstene, commander of the Falcon, one of the targets of Calderón de la Barca's ire, wrote to John Quitman, "If the invaders had only made a descent upon the City [Havana] after their diversion at Cardenas, they would have received assistance from over twelvehundred well armed Americans, on board the Steamers Georgia, Ohio, & Falcon, and carried with ease this most important point."[51]

New Orleans, December–January, 1850

John Henderson matched his devotion to Cuban annexation with his feistiness as a trial lawyer. Appearing in Judge McCaleb's court in early December 1850, he asked to be tried alone and at once. The judge granted Henderson's request. Trials for the other defendants would be postponed until Henderson's case was adjudicated. Confident he had a strong case against Henderson, U. S.

Attorney Hunton welcomed McCaleb's decision. Indeed, Hunton believed, if Henderson could not be convicted, neither could any of the other defendants.[52]

The trial began on January 6, with Henderson representing himself. In the state's opening argument, prosecutor Hunton portrayed the defendant as ubiquitous during preparations for the Cárdenas expedition. "We do not expect to prove that the accused, now on trial, was ever at Cardenas, or went with the expedition," Hunton told the jury, "but we shall show that he, with others, contrived and plotted the expedition—that he gave it aid, countenance, and support; that he purchased the steamer *Creole* for the purpose of conveying men and arms to the island; that he did not take the title for her in his own name, but in that of Wm. H. White, for purposes best known to himself; that he purchased bonds called Cuban bonds, with a view of raising a fund for the expedition. In fine, gentlemen, we shall show, that, though not there in person, the accused was one of the master-spirits—one of the leaders of the enterprise."[53]

Hunton then called his first witness, John Higgins—one of the Cárdenas veterans from Cincinnati—and began his direct examination by eliciting a chronology of the expedition. After Higgins acknowledged he had departed New Orleans on "about the 7th or 8th" of May, Hunton asked, "For what place?"

"Chagres."

"Did you go there?"

"I have never seen it."

"Where did you go?"

"Mugeres Island is the first place we stopped after leaving the Balize."

"Where did you go from Mugeres?"

"To the Island of Contoy."

"Where did you go thence?"

"To the Island of Cuba."

"What vessel did you leave on?"

"On the steamer Creole."

"At what time did you leave New Orleans?"

"In the evening, about eight or nine o'clock. The Creole was lying up at the Bull's Head, Lafayette."

"When you went on the Creole, did you expect to go to Cuba?"

"No, I did not."

"Where did you expect to go?"

"They said it was an expedition."

Henderson objected—it was the word *expedition* that troubled him, he said. The state "had not averred that an expedition had gone from the United States," he said, descending into a lengthy exposition on what he considered ambiguities in the language of both the Neutrality Act and the nine-count indictment that had brought him to court. The fundamental flaw in the government's case, he said, lay in the Neutrality Act's sixth section, the heart of the 1818 statute: "If any person shall within the territory and jurisdiction of the United States, begin or set on foot, or provide or prepare the means for, any military expedition or enterprise, to be carried on from thence against the territory or dominions of any foreign prince or state, or of any colony, district, or people, with whom the United States are at peace, every person so offending shall be deemed guilty of a high misdemeanor, and shall be fined not exceeding three thousand dollars, and imprisoned not more than three years."[54]

Under the indictment, said Henderson, he was charged with "beginning, and setting on foot an expedition." But what precisely did that phrase mean? "How could four men begin a plan simultaneously? The word 'begin' means the first inceptive process, the first conception, and was it possible that four men could concur in the first inception or beginning of a plot? . . . The word 'begin' means to originate, and the same idea could not originate in four brains at the same time."

Henderson also challenged the Neutrality Act's phrase "setting on foot." It lacked legal precision, he said; it had "undergone no legal interpretation. . . . Laws must be made so that they can be comprehended by ordinary understandings, and if there is any obscurity they must be construed in favor of the accused."

Henderson saved his most vigorous challenge for what he regarded as the sixth section's implicit preoccupation with contemplated, rather than actual, events. The statute, he said, did not forbid participating in a military expedition; it spoke, rather, of anyone who would "begin or set on foot, or provide or prepare the means for" such an enterprise. Such preoccupation with contemplated rather than actual events, Henderson argued, rendered the statute hopelessly impotent. "There are laws which punish intent, such as the law against slave-trade, against parties who are fitting out vessels to engage in that unlawful traffic," Henderson told the court. "But here the language of the statute was different; and besides, the policy of the law, which is the preservation of the neutrality of the nation, is not violated, except when the expedition actually sails and carries out the intent of its organization and equipment." The sixth section, Henderson said, addressed only "prospective acts"—"to begin or set on foot on an expedition." To prove such an act, he said, the state must prove intent; but the Neutrality Act did not use the word *intent*. Congress, Henderson argued, had thus created an internal contradiction within its statute: by not demanding proof of intent, the law rendered itself impotent.

Henderson then turned from the Neutrality Act to the language of the indictments. Following the language of the Neutrality Act, he said, the indictments against him and his codefendants accused them of "contributing *means* to begin and set on foot a military expedition, instead of charging them with an *intention* to begin and set on foot a military expedition." Henderson went on:

> Now, men are not "means"—they are responsible agents. Money is not *means* in the language of the statute—it is one of the most ineffectual articles which could possibly have been put on board of the Creole for the conquering of Cuba. Brandy, flags, musical instruments and cigars may be, and usually are, employed in military expeditions, yet they are not to be considered as *means*—the means contemplated by Congress in framing the statute. Now, John Henderson is not charged in the indictments with furnishing the steamer Creole, consequently all evidence on that point is inadmissible. He is only charged with furnishing what may be understood by that most potent, yet legally meaningless of all terms, *means*—to "begin" an expedition, not for already having contributed to, and set on foot, an expedition. The indictment does not charge the matters now attempted to be proved.[55]

Henderson's ponderous assault on the Neutrality Act delayed for three days the resumption of government testimony from Cárdenas veteran John Higgins. Throughout the trial, as prosecutor Hunton focused on evidence, Henderson drew the jury's attention away from the case's facts, toward the law under which he stood indicted. Many of his arguments—delving into arcane matters of law and the origins of the Neutrality Act—might have been more appropriate for a panel of appellate court jurists than for a trial court jury of laymen. Henderson's mix of erudition and rhetorical legerdemain, however, did suffice to confuse, to his advantage, the panel of nonlawyers gathered to decide his fate. On January 20, after it became clear that the jury was hopelessly divided—eight for conviction, four for acquittal—a mistrial was declared.[56]

Jackson, Mississippi, February 3, 1851

On February 3, 1851, two weeks after the jury in Henderson's trial deadlocked, Governor John Quitman tendered his resignation as governor of Mississippi. The act, which surprised few, ended a long stalemate between the fiery governor and the federal government.

Of all the antifilibustering indictments issued in New Orleans in June 1850, the one against Quitman had quickly proved to be the most politically awkward. In the charged atmosphere left by the debates over the Mexican cession, the arrest of any sitting southern governor by a federal official would have made for an unenviable task. The passage of the Compromise of 1850 the following September only compounded the unpleasantness and deepened Quitman's public commitment to southern secession. Indeed, since John Calhoun's death in March 1850 after a long illness, Quitman had largely inherited the South Carolinian's mantle as leader of the decade's southern secessionist movement. Ever ready, then, to find federal malevolence in any and all actions out of Washington, Quitman's supporters eagerly construed the indictment against him as a strike at southern and states' rights.

But while Quitman's indictment stirred devotees of sectional politics, a stalemate soon settled over the actual legal proceedings against him. Indicting a sitting governor, it soon became clear, was one thing; arresting him quite another. Despite letters urging Quitman's arrest from Hunton and Horatio J. Harris, the U.S. attorney in Vicksburg, federal judge Samuel J. Gholson balked at issuing a warrant. He had read too many letters from prominent Mississippians urging him not to order Quitman's arrest.

Quitman declined a suggestion from prosecutor Harris that he go to New Orleans, submit to arrest, then post bail. That way, Harris explained in a September 28 letter to Quitman, all could avoid the inflammatory spectacle of having papers served on Quitman at the governor's mansion. In rejecting Harris's proposal, Quitman said that though he was eager to answer the "baseless charges" lodged against him, the press of gubernatorial duties required his continued presence in Jackson until the end of his term. As the impasse stretched deep into the autumn of 1850, U.S. Attorney Harris felt obliged to explain his predicament to President Fillmore. In a November letter, the prosecutor noted that Judge Gholson had thus far refused to issue a warrant against Quitman. Beyond that, Harris wrote, "various sources" had reported that Quitman had pledged, if necessary, to resist arrest "by force" and "to call out the militia to prevent his removal from the state." To avoid such a confrontation, Harris wrote, several "gentlemen of high public standing in this State" had advised that the governor's arrest be postponed until the conclusion of a special session of the state legislature later that month.

Quitman himself had called the special legislative session to determine how Mississippi, in the wake of the Compromise of 1850, could "assert her sovereignty." On November 30, the day the special session ended, Governor Quitman signed legislation authorizing a special state convention, to be held in November 1851, to consider secession. Once that state convention was concluded, U.S. Attorney Harris suggested, "there can be no reason why the warrant should not be executed; and I feel assured, that the great mass of our people will heartily sanction all such steps, as may be necessary, to vindicate the supremacy of the laws."[57]

By February 1851, Quitman's predicament was perilous. The indictment against him was no casual enterprise; the federal government had invested too much time, effort, and prestige in the case to walk away from it. What, then, were Quitman's options? He could act on his threat to resist any arrest and call out the state militia. But that would only increase the resolve of his federal adversaries. To be effective, Quitman decided, any defiance of federal authority would have to produce a powerful groundswell of popular support among Mississippians. Would there be such support? Or would Quitman's constituents simply dismiss him as an ambitious politician using his office to escape the consequences of lawbreaking?

Answers to such questions inevitably turned on the popularity of secessionism in Mississippi. And just how popular was secessionism? The special state convention on secession, scheduled for November 1851, would provide some answers. But in February 1851, as the Quitman crisis came to a head, that convention was still months away. In the meantime the governor had no way to gauge statewide enthusiasm for secessionism. Narciso López enjoyed demonstrable popularity in Mississippi, but to what extent could his popularity be considered a measure of support for secession? How could Quitman gauge where support for López ended and that for secession began?

López's filibuster—so brazenly steeped in defiance of federal powers—certainly drew moral strength from, and reflected, antifederal passions stirred by southern nationalists. But it was no bellwether of secessionism's popularity. Some of López's contemporary critics—later echoed by historians—accused the filibuster of secessionist impulses. Indeed, as early as August 1849, the New York *Herald*'s New Orleans correspondent—then still believing that the filibuster was Mexico-bound—had speculated that it was run by "the leading southern politicians" and sought the "dissolution of the Union." And, to be sure, some of López's supporters later would be associated with the Confederacy. Over and beyond all such speculations, however, lay one paramount fact: during López's life, neither he nor any of his key lieutenants—with the conspicuous exception of Quitman—advocated southern secession. If nothing else, López's campaign straddled too many lines—between free and slave states, between North and South, between agriculturists and mercantilists—to risk any such advocacy. Though often blown by the winds of sectional agitation, López's conspiracy enjoyed a life independent of debates over the Mexican cession and southern secession.

By February 1851, Quitman—concluding that to resist arrest could damage both his political career and secessionism's future—decided to submit to arrest. To avoid setting a precedent for the arrest of a sitting governor, he resigned his office and then accepted U.S. Attorney Harris's earlier proposal: after leaving office on February 3, he went to New Orleans and surrendered as a private citizen to federal officials.[58]

Quitman's detractors dismissed him as a lawbreaker. To the New Orleans *Picayune* he fell because "the federal administration is in the hands of men who intend to enforce the laws." To his admirers, however, Quitman had packed his bags in Jackson as a mere governor and arrived in New Orleans a political martyr. By leaving office before submitting to arrest, he had spared both his country and his state the divisive spectacle of a trial in federal court of the governor of a "sovereign" state. Declaimed the New Orleans *Delta*, "His allegiance was due to the State of Mississippi and to the laws of the United States. He sought to do his duty to both."[59]

Free after posting bail of $1,000, Quitman became an honored guest among New Orleans's most "elite and most recherché gentlemen." Though careful in conversations to emphasize that he was "entirely innocent" of all pending charges, Quitman also left no doubt that he admired the filibusters. At one "sumptious and elegant" banquet in the St. Louis Hotel, he told an audience of admirers that whatever aid he had given the filibusters was entirely consistent with his past support for republican ventures. Reminding his audience that the idea of the United States annexing Cuba enjoyed a long pedigree extending at least back to President James Monroe, he told them that "it would be strange indeed, if he, who had contributed aid to Texas when she was struggling for her liberty . . . should not have sympathized in that great revolution avowed by Mr. Monroe, of the right of the [United States], rather than of any foreign nations, to control the destiny of the continent."[60]

New Orleans, February 11, 1851

John Henderson's second trial began in early February. But once again, the jury that heard the case could not agree on a verdict, and after deliberating for thirty hours, it deadlocked six to six. A second mistrial was declared on February 11. Three days later Quitman went to Judge McCaleb's courtroom and asked to be tried as soon as possible. But the federal judge said that Henderson's next trial took priority. Quitman would have to wait for his day in court.[61]

Henderson's third trial began on March 1. A week later, it, too, ended in a mistrial. This time the jury split eleven for acquittal, one for conviction. On March 7, the day the third mistrial was declared, Hunton rose and told the court that the prosecution now believed that no convictions were possible—not for Henderson or for any of the defendants. As Hunton prepared writs of nolle prosequi, ending all the prosecutions, Henderson and his supporters celebrated in Lafayette Square. They fired thirty-one cannon blasts, one for each state in the Union and one for Cuba. A headline in the next morning's *Delta* proclaimed,

> Finale of the Cuban Trials.
> THE MOUNTAIN BRINGING FORTH A MOUSE
> NOLLE PROSEQUIS IN ALL THE CASES.[62]

Hunton met some formidable courtroom forensics on the way to the government's rout. To at least one observer, however, Henderson's victory turned as much on the jury selection process as on trial oratory. Special Agent God-dard had left New Orleans after Henderson's first trial, already convinced that no conviction was possible. Once back in Washington, in a letter to Interior Secretary Stuart, Goddard explained that his pessimism was "not founded upon any belief that the great mass of respectable citizens of New Orleans are in favour of violations of the laws of the United States; but on the contrary my own experience enables me to know that a very large proportion are directly the reverse."

Whereas the state might have lost the first trial on the merits of its case, Goddard believed that the voir dire by judge and lawyers that preceded the second and third trials had guaranteed hung juries. What defeated the prose-cution in those trials, Goddard believed, was jury stacking by the defense— and López's popularity among the class that the court "had to go down into" to impanel a jury. Goddard claimed that the voir dire that impaneled the first jury excused "about twenty" prospective jurors for every one taken for the twelve-man panel. For the second trial the court drew the jury from a pool of "upwards of seven hundred." Further diminishing chances for a conviction, the jury for the second trial also included "two of the friends of the expedition who had sworn themselves on, for the purpose of hanging the jury." After the second trial, Goddard believed, the pool of jurors from Orleans parish stood so thoroughly winnowed of "respectable citizens" that the defense had no need to fix any jury. As the state prepared for a third trial, Goddard wrote, "that class of citizens which ought to set as jurors, had been gone through with, and in summoning a large number of others, the Marshal would be compelled to go down into a class of persons who care very little either for law or facts in deciding the most important cases. Therefore no proper verdict was likely to be had."[63]

✤ ✤ ✤ ✤ ✤ ✤ ✤ ✤ ✤ ✤ ✤ ✤ ✤ ✤ ✤

7   A Desperate Set of Men

✤ ✤ ✤ ✤ ✤ ✤ ✤ ✤ ✤ ✤ ✤ ✤ ✤ ✤ ✤

New York, April 14–26, 1851

On Monday, April 14, 1851, only four weeks after New Orleans's U.S. Attorney Logan Hunton dropped his case against the filibusters, John O'Sullivan, in New York, finalized his purchase of the *Cleopatra*, an aging steamer that had formerly plied Long Island Sound. O'Sullivan paid $413,000 for the boat and another $19,000 refitting it for ocean sailing. Though the ship's better days were long past—the New York *Herald* later remarked that "no person, with a particle of sense or intelligence, would risk his life by going ten miles beyond Sandy Hook in her"—its purchase nonetheless capped months of intrigue and fund-raising. Even as they stood indicted in New Orleans on Neutrality Act charges, Narciso López and his agents had been busy organizing another expedition against Cuba.[1]

The day before he purchased the *Cleopatra*, O'Sullivan had recruited Henry Burtnett, a young businessman of Spanish descent, well known in Manhattan from the drugstore he ran at the corner of St. Marks Place and Third Avenue. Weeks later a newspaper would describe him as "a young man about 26 or 28 years of age, tall in stature, long features, wearing his whiskers full, and rather animated in appearance." While professing fealty to the filibuster's cause, the energetic young man was in reality a self-appointed spy, determined to sabotage López's conspiracy. As Burtnett recalled in a later memoir, meeting O'Sullivan marked a signal moment in a long effort: "I had now a fair field, and feeling the necessity of great caution, I proceeded carefully to spread my nets in such a manner that they should all fall into them with as little effort as possible."[2]

Burtnett had been weaving those nets for at least five months before he met O'Sullivan. In October 1850—more than a month before former Mississippi senator John Henderson, in New Orleans, asked to be tried first and separately from his comrades—New York City was already abuzz with gossip of a new filibuster conspiracy. On certain evenings, in a house on Lower Manhattan's Cedar Street, Burtnett had heard, approximately eighty men were practicing military drills, preparing for an invasion of Cuba. His curiosity piqued, he visited the house and discovered the rumor was true. "I at once determined to watch those men, and if possible defeat an object so base in itself, and so fraught with evil consequences not only to *my own country*, but one with whom we were then at peace."

As Burtnett insinuated himself among the Cedar Street conspirators, returning for more visits, he jealously guarded what he learned, sharing it with neither Spanish nor U.S. officials. But Spain's minister to the United States, Angel Calderón de la Barca, had his own sources. As early as July 26, 1850, even as the diplomat was urging López's prosecution for the Cárdenas landing, he was also warning Secretary of State Daniel Webster that a new expedition was afoot. In September, Juan Laborde, Spain's consul in New Orleans, began supplying Calderón de la Barca with details of the renewed effort. The new conspiracy, he wrote on October 2, was under the leadership of John Quitman, "with the traitor Narciso Lopez, as second in command." The filibusters, Laborde reported, were in New Orleans waiting for a steamer chartered in New York and planned to sail for Cuba in November. Calderón de la Barca quickly relayed Laborde's letter to Webster.[3]

All the while he lingered in New Orleans under indictment, López had been busy organizing yet another expedition. Even as the government's case against him unraveled, López was trying to ensure that future operations escaped the purview of the Neutrality Act. Paper trails, he resolved, must be better hidden; logistical arrangements and military maneuvers more discreet.[4]

On June 25, 1850, a mere five days after the Neutrality Act indictments against López and his allies had been unsealed, O'Sullivan had met with fellow defendant John Quitman to try to persuade him to become supreme commander of a new conspiracy. The next day O'Sullivan wrote the governor seeking to allay his concerns about indigenous support for rebellion in Cuba and his personal fears of a second Neutrality Act indictment. Quitman could lead an army to Cuba of "say 2000 as an auxiliary force distinct & apart from that commanded by L." If indigenous support for the revolt seemed wanting, Quitman's army could take a "quiet and neutral course" and leave Cuba before any shots were fired. If, however, to Quitman's mind the island did seem ripe for revolution, "the General [López] would then agree to transfer to you the supreme command after you should have decided, in the island itself, to take part in support of the people against the military oppression of their tyrants." By deciding "in the island itself" to assist the rebellion, Quitman could avoid charges that might later arise of having "begun or set on foot" a military expedition from within the United States. Highlighting the conspiracy's newfound regard for secrecy, O'Sullivan stressed that should Quitman accept the invitation, "only the few who furnish the money shall know it—& that not till after they are . . . fully committed with pledge of secrecy." O'Sullivan asked Quitman to wire him in New York with his answer. "In order that the telegraph gentry may not make their own conjectures," Quitman's name should not appear on the telegram; "any friend of yours may sign it, and I will direct my reply to the same name." To further muffle their exchange, O'Sullivan asked that the telegram be addressed to his father-in-law, Dr. Kearny Rodgers of New York City.[5]

Though Quitman, contrary to Consul Laborde's information, had declined O'Sullivan's offer, a new conspiracy was well under way by June 1850, with López at its head. The latest effort envisioned departures from ports along both the Atlantic and Gulf coasts. As O'Sullivan supervised the New York operations, López and Gonzales left New Orleans in mid-July 1850 for an extended round of travels to shore up the conspiracy's national organization and find new allies. They arrived in Savannah on July 21, where they stayed at the Pulaski House hotel, spent the next day in Charleston, and reached Washington on the twenty-fifth. In late July López returned to Savannah, where on August 1 he applied for membership in the local Masonic chapter, and was back in New York a week later. On August 25, at Manhattan's Barnum Hotel, he was the honored guest at a banquet sponsored by Cuban exiles from New York, Philadelphia, and Boston. During the affair a group of Cuban women presented López with a sword and a Cuban flag. A week later, as Gonzales remained in New York, López, this time with O'Sullivan, headed south once again, to Charleston and Savannah. On September 9 Savannah's Masons welcomed López into their chapter. In turn, two of López's new Masonic brothers—Richard Wayne, Savannah's mayor, and John Lamar, a local importer—were promptly ushered into the conspiracy.[6]

By early August, López was back in New Orleans, at the home of *Delta* editor Laurent Sigur. Though his travels had generated political support for another Cuban expedition, finances remained a problem. Even ardent supporters wondered how the next operation would be funded. John Henderson alone had contributed $40,000 to the Cárdenas expedition through purchases of Cuban bonds. But in November Henderson stressed to Quitman that he could no longer afford such largesse. Personal financial constraints, the former U.S. senator wrote, now outweighed his admiration for López: "I need not tell you how much I desire to see him move again, and it is more useless to tell you also how wholly unable I am to assist him to make this move. With my limited means, I am under the *extremest* burdens from my endeavors on the former occasion. Indeed, I find my cash advances for the first experiment was *over half* of all the cash advanced to the enterprise, and all my present means and energies are exhausted in bringing up arrearages." The conspiracy's immediate task, Henderson suggested, was to acquire $25,000 for the purchase of a steamer to transport filibusters recruited in the Gulf coast states. He estimated that "about *half*" that amount was "within reach" in New Orleans, "but the other half delays the departure."[7]

Moreover, the filibusters could no longer depend upon many of their other, former supporters in Louisiana and Mississippi. Governor Quitman, for instance—caught up in his own growing political troubles—kept his distance from the new conspiracy. The filibusters, however, soon discovered other, untapped resources in Georgia and Cuba. Indeed, Ambrosio Gonzales later claimed that most of the new expedition's funds came from Cuba, "whose patriotic daughters of Havana and Puerto Principe, without distinction of class or station, generously added the offering of their jewels to the contributions of their brothers and husbands."[8]

López briefly entertained hopes of making Charleston a key part of his new plans, in the final weeks of 1850 ordering Juan Macías and Miguel Tolón to move there and organize a new cell of the conspiracy. On January 7, 1851, López asked Macías about the new cell's progress. "I would like to get," López wrote, "a report from you telling me that I can depend on fifteen to twenty young men with their horses and weapons."[9]

But as hopes for Charleston faded, Savannah emerged as the filibuster's south Atlantic center, under Ambrosio Gonzales's supervision. Gonzales met many Georgians eager to abet the conspiracy and later claimed that his stay in Georgia had "been successful in all departments." Georgia governor George W. Towns told Gonzales that even in the state's sleepy capital of Milledgeville, "there would be 10 or 12 who would go, if with you." More significantly, British diplomatic sources later claimed, Towns's "connivance" faciliated the shipment of weapons from Georgia's state arsenal to the filibusters. Gonzales claimed to have made arrangements to "collect one thousand men and from 200 to 300 horses." Beyond that, "several companies in the State both of cavalry & infantry have promised me their armaments." Gonzales raised an additional $12,000 in Georgia through the sale of Cuba bonds, funds that eventually defrayed most of the costs of that April's purchase of the *Cleopatra*.[10]

The new plan, whose details still remain murky, called for an expeditionary army with two wings. The eastern wing, with headquarters in New York and Savannah, would sail from New York on a single steamer, stopping at points below Savannah to pick up additional soldiers and weapons before landing in Cuba. The other wing, with headquarters in New Orleans, would sail from somewhere along the Gulf coast. A press report later claimed that the two wings planned to rendezvous on one of the islands "in the neighborhood of Key West." From there, the two wings would sail in separate ships to Cuba and make separate landings at two different points on Cuba's north coast. At the same time supporters inside Cuba would make false reports of filibuster landings on the southern coast, thereby drawing enemy forces away from the north coast and buying time for López to rally his Cuban supporters before the actual fighting began. López estimated that he could depend on some fourteen thousand Creoles to join his invading army.[11]

Because the *Cleopatra*, sailing from New York, would be stopping at points below Savannah to pick up soldiers and supplies, the filibusters transferred a cache of armaments collected for the previous year's expedition to Georgia, hiding them in the vicinity of Burnt Fork, a small community on the Satilla River, just north of the Florida border. According to a correspondent for the Newark, New Jersey, *Advertiser*, the *Cleopatra*'s crew also planned a stop at the mouth of Florida's St. Johns River. The reporter claimed to have personally seen men and horses gathered for the expedition in Jacksonville and to have visited a warehouse filled with filibuster provisions—up to four hundred bushels of oats, cannon, rifles, muskets, and ammunition, as well as "large quantities" of wood and resin to fuel the *Cleopatra*. "I have never seen so many implements of war, except in an arsenal."[12]

Though John O'Sullivan remained nominally in charge of recruiting efforts in New York, most of those duties soon fell to Major Louis A. Schlesinger. A former aide to the Hungarian patriot Louis Kossuth, Schlesinger had met O'Sullivan after fleeing to the United States in the wake of the failed Hungarian uprising of the late 1840s. Drawing on his refugee ties in New York, Schlesinger soon recruited scores of other young European exiles, especially Germans and Hungarians, into the conspiracy.[13]

Schlesinger's enlistment of foreigners into the filibuster, which accorded with López's wishes, marked a departure for the conspiracy—and from the nativism of that day. A popular reaction against the immigrants, mostly Irish and Germans, then streaming into the nation's cities, nativism by 1850 had become a sort of counterpoint to the era's expansionism into foreign climes. As Manifest Destiny gloried in the exotic and the new, so nativism reveled in the familiar and the traditional—the native. The trend achieved its most visible manifestation in the era's so-called Know-Nothing party. It even touched soldiers in López's army; as Richardson Hardy recalled the 1850 expedition's Kentucky regiment, "The qualifications of those who joined this company were, that they should be the best quality of robust, active, brave, and adventurous young *Americans*." Another López organizer of that year demanded: "I hope your men are of the right stripe. We want the best quality of young, adventurous *Americans*. No Dutch or foreigners of any kind."[14]

The presence of U.S. citizens in the Cárdenas expedition, of course, supported the propaganda likening the filibusters to heroes of earlier U.S. wars, and López in 1851 certainly assumed that any new expedition would include volunteers from the United States. But aware that many of the U.S. volunteers in the 1850 army had shown scant regard for military discipline, he also had resolved that the next expedition must include more professional—and foreign—soldiers. To López the veterans of the Hungarian and Polish uprisings more than met that new standard. As Schlesinger recalled, the refugee soldiers gave the expedition "a good body of experienced military men, accustomed to discipline and subordination." Beyond that, the foreigners "would also tend to relieve his expedition from the character of being an American annexation scheme." In accord with O'Sullivan's instructions, officers in the new army were promised commissions in the Cuban army and financial bonuses if the expedition proved successful. As before, to avoid Neutrality Act prosecution, recruits were not told to where they would be sailing. This time, however, the filibusters' leaders claimed Texas, not Chagres, as their expedition's destination.[15]

In the wake of López's May 1850 landing at Cárdenas, Spanish officials had vowed to exercise increased vigilance against filibustering. José de la Concha, Cuba's new captain general, who arrived on the island in November 1850, personified that new determination. The appointment of Concha, a former commander of Spain's cavalry, was prompted by Madrid's belief that former captain general Federico Roncali had shown too much laxity in countering López.[16]

Emboldening Madrid's resolve was a new spirit of cooperation between Washington and the Spanish government. Though Spain kept the two filibuster ships it had confiscated in April 1850, by November it had released all but 3 of the 42 prisoners taken on Contoy. In exchange, Washington displayed a new vigor in enforcing the Neutrality Act, and a new solicitousness toward Spanish intelligence on filibustering. Calderón de la Barca, for instance, ended an October 10, 1850, letter to Secretary of State Webster about a new filibustering expedition by expressing absolute confidence in Washington's goodwill, having "no doubt but that he will adopt such measures as may appear to him expedient, for ascertaining the facts mentioned by the Consul."[17]

Four days later Calderón de la Barca again wrote Webster, this time to report that the filibusters had made "a small village . . . recently designated Gainesville," on Mississippi's saltwater inlet Lake Borgne their new point of rendezvous. "From 600, to 700 men," the diplomat reported, had already been recruited in Mississippi and were awaiting the arrival of two chartered steamers to transport them to Cuba. Another dispatch, on November 28, included an unsigned note from a New York informer warning that López had just left New York for New Orleans and that the filibusters planned to sail for Cuba "between the 1st and 8th of December." The informer closed by asserting— mistakenly—that the filibusters planned to rendezvous on a key off the island of Bahama before sailing for Cuba.[18]

When 1851 arrived and no new expedition had sailed from the Gulf coast, Calderón de la Barca's suspicions drifted back to New York. On January 17 he forwarded to Webster a letter from Spain's New York consul, Francisco

Stoughton, warning that the steamer *Fanny*, which was to have been used in the Round Island expedition, had been in port for six months and that weapons and other supplies had been loaded aboard it for a new Cuban expedition set to sail on January 18.[19]

Webster within the week notified federal officials in New Orleans of the *Fanny*'s imminent arrival and ordered "a constant watch" placed on the steamer. The *Fanny* reached New Orleans on January 31 and stayed in port for several weeks, but two weeks of federal surveillance "by special officers on duty, day & night" yielded no evidence to support the Spanish minister's allegations.[20]

By January's end Calderón de la Barca had to concede that the *Fanny* had no filibuster ties, but he remained sure that López was preparing another invasion. By March he was convinced that López planned not one but two new expeditions. On March 12 he warned Webster that the first invasion would seek to supply the island's "colored population" with arms and to ignite rebellion among them. That assault would be followed by a "piratical attack . . . similar to that of Cardenas."

On April 14, 1851—the same day that O'Sullivan purchased the *Cleopatra*—Calderón de la Barca dispatched yet another letter to Webster with more filibuster accusations. The "same marauders who invaded Cardenas" were now training at Pascagoula, Mississippi. In Arkansas, Cálderon de la Barca claimed, the filibusters had set up a "school of Military tactics." By formally constituting themselves as a school, he wrote, the Arkansans hoped to avoid Neutrality Act charges. The filibusters in the Mississippi Valley, he added, were apparently working in tandem with Ambrosio Gonzales in Savannah. As Spain's sprawling U.S. intelligence network continued to produce new leads, Captain General Concha on April 20 sent a circular letter warning military district leaders across the island to prepare for an invasion.[21]

Henry Burtnett, meanwhile, since October 1850, had been conducting his own quiet surveillance in New York without breaching the conspiracy's inner sanctum. By early April 1851, he began seeking introductions to "the leading spirits of the band." In particular, Burtnett sought out Captain Frederick Freeman, a Cuban émigré prominent in local filibustering circles. When the two met, Burtnett learned that Freeman had left Cuba "one or two years" earlier and that his estate near the town of Trinidad de Cuba, on the island's southern coast, was now "unjustly held" from him by a U.S. citizen living on the island. Freeman told

Burtnett that he wanted to prosecute a claim against the interloper but "in the present state of excitement in the island he did not wish to expose himself there, and wanted an active business man" in Cuba who could "prosecute his claim." If that did not work, Freeman added, he need only await the imminent installation of a new regime in Cuba, "in which event there would be no trouble about getting back his estate, as the new government would give it back to him."

Freeman's casual reference to the impending creation of a new government in Cuba departed from the purposeful vagueness of the other filibusters Burtnett had met. "I saw at a glance," he recalled, "that this man must be used for my purposes, and accordingly cultivated his acquaintance." As their rapport grew, Freeman's political sympathies were "called out," and he spoke openly of his profilibuster political loyalties. The self-appointed spy, finally, seemed to have won his long-sought entrée into the conspiracy's inner circle. As Burtnett recalled in his memoir, Freeman, "at once admitted to me that an expedition was preparing to sail in a few days and that I could materially assist it by my counsel, being a practical man, and [by] my means."

On April 13 Freeman introduced Burtnett to two other leaders of the conspiracy, O'Sullivan and José María Sánchez Iznaga. "So confident had Capt. Freeman become of my co-operation that he imparted to the others a degree of confidence in me that was really astonishing." To Burtnett, O'Sullivan and Iznaga spoke openly of the landing at Cárdenas, their hopes for the second invasion, and their planned purchase, the next day, of the *Cleopatra*. The following day, the fourteenth, at another filibuster meeting, at the home of Sánchez Iznaga, Burtnett met other members of the conspiracy, including Louis Schlesinger and Armstrong Irvine Lewis, who had been the *Creole*'s captain.

Burtnett learned that the *Cleopatra* was to meet two ships at Sandy Hook, in Lower New York harbor. One from New York City, the other from New Jersey, both ships would be filled with filibusters. Burtnett, in exchange for $750 and, if all went well, $2,500 in Cuba bonds, was assigned to command the vessel from New York. A steamer, it would be cleared for Baltimore to pick up a load of coal. After anchoring at Sandy Hook long enough to transfer about four hundred filibusters to the *Cleopatra*, it would sail to Baltimore, load the coal, and return to New York City.[22]

In his memoir Burtnett made no effort to conceal his disdain for the conspirators. Of his initial meeting with O'Sullivan, Schlesinger, and the other filibusters, he declared that "a more desperate set of men were never congregated—

having neither character nor money to loose—they were prepared to commit *murder, piracy, anything* to better their degraded condition." Schlesinger later returned the compliment. In his own filibustering memoir, published in the *United States Magazine and Democratic Review*, the Hungarian recalled "a vile scoundrel who acted as their spy and informer in the matter, with whose name, already sufficiently familiar to the public, I will not soil the fair surface of this page."[23]

After O'Sullivan on April 14 ordered him to be ready to sail in thirty-six hours, Burtnett, after a night's sleep, decided that the moment had come to betray the filibusters to the proper government officials. But what government officials could he trust? Even in New York Burtnett wondered what confidence he could place in Uncle Sam's minions. He could wire his warning directly to Washington, but he knew that the filibusters had bribed "certain operators" within the telegraph system "to have any communications that might be sent by Government relative to their affairs, should they be discovered[,] immediately communicated to them." Burtnett eventually met with two friends—officials, respectively, of the U.S. and Spanish governments—and both advised him to convey all he knew to Spain's New York consul Francisco Stoughton. Meanwhile, Burtnett's U.S. friend James Ridgway, avoiding the telegraph system, traveled to Washington, where he personally informed President Fillmore of the planned expedition.[24]

The president, as it turned out, was already acting on reports of filibuster activity. From Atlanta on April 10, Fillmore had received a telegram from J. Reneas, editor of the Savannah *Republican*, reporting that "our rail-roads are crowded with an army of adventurers destined for Cuba—by way of Savannah beyond all doubt." Two days later the USS *Decatur* was ordered to sail for Havana, and port officials on both the Atlantic and Gulf coasts were asked to watch for any unusual activity.

With their plans thoroughly betrayed, on April 24 the conspirators' two adjunct vessels—in New York and South Amboy, New Jersey—were seized by federal agents while still at anchor. Federal agents had some unexpected help in stopping the *Cleopatra*'s departure when it was obstructed by a drunken crew that insisted on being paid before leaving New York. Heaping scorn, the New York *Herald* dismissed the filibusters as "foreigners, who cannot speak English, and know nothing of the laws they have violated. . . . Many of these characters are refugees from the recent revolutions in Europe, and are accustomed to arms, and would be very glad to engage in any expedition, no matter how wild or absurd." The next day President Fillmore issued a proclamation against fili-bustering. Though similar to President Taylor's dispatch of two years earlier, it focused on the foreigners in the conspiracy, suggesting that they deserved the condemnation of the entire "civilized world."[25]

Georgia, April 25–26, 1850

The conspiracy in the South unraveled just as quickly. Late in April, as the fitting out in Georgia neared its completion, Gonzales wired López, suggesting they meet in Macon, then travel together by rail to Savannah. Their rendezvous occurred on April 25; López and Gonzales, joined by about four hundred volunteers from throughout Georgia, organized into filibuster companies, converged on Macon's rail station. However, just before boarding the Savannah-bound train, Gonzales received a telegram from Savannah warning that the local U.S. marshal and customs collector were waiting to arrest them. Gonzales wired back asking that a stagecoach be sent to a rail station ten miles inland from Savannah on the same Georgia Central line.[26]

The filibusters left Macon later that afternoon. Disembarking at a station twenty miles outside of Savannah, they began a southward march along Georgia's coast—through Chatham, McIntosh, Glynn, and Camden counties—toward Burnt Fork and their hidden stash of weapons. López and Gonzales remained on the train and, ten miles down the line, met their awaiting stagecoach.[27]

That night, as federal officials waited in vain at the city's train depot, Gonzales and López entered Savannah via a lonesome country road. At midnight a local sympathizer took the two to the town of Thunderbolt, five miles from Savannah. From there, they rowed down St. Augustine Creek, a small tidal stream, to nearby Wilmington Island, where they spent the night at the plantation home of Ellas Barstow. Gonzales later claimed that Barstow's act had more to do with southern hospitality than politics. "I am a Whig," Barstow had said, "and opposed to the expedition; but as my guests you are welcome, and my house is yours."

When a dispatch from O'Sullivan arrived the next morning, April 26, informing them that their ships in New York had been seized, López left immediately for New Orleans. Gonzales, however, determined to inspect the weapons hidden at Burnt Fork, stayed behind. He never reached the weapons, instead spending the next two months dodging federal agents, hiding at various Georgia and South Carolina plantations. After succumbing to "a severe bilious fever," Gonzales retreated to a resort in White Sulphur Springs, in western Virginia, to recuperate.[28]

At the conspiracy's other gathering points in the South, meanwhile, the setbacks in New York and Savannah obviated any need for federal intervention. As word of the conspiracy's collapse in those two cities spread, filibusters mustered elsewhere in Georgia, in Florida, and along the Gulf coast simply abandoned their posts "slightly disgusted with the bad management of affairs on the Atlantic coast." The May 2 New Orleans *Delta* reported that "most of the officers and men who had assembled here have returned to their homes in the West. Several of the leading spirits and officers of the last expedition have left here within a few days past, on different up-river boats." A week later the Savannah *Morning News* reported a similar dispersal of forces from Burnt Fork on the Satilla River, where volunteers "were making arrangements to return to the interior." Likewise, "the men who had rendezvoused at Jacksonville had nearly all returned to their homes."

Acting on Burtnett's testimony, a federal grand jury in New York eventually returned Neutrality Act indictments against O'Sullivan, Schlesinger, and several others. After a mistrial in 1852, all of the charges were dropped. Gonzales, too, was later arrested, but he was never prosecuted.

For the filibusters the spring 1851 episode did offer one small consolation. The weapons stashed in Georgia and Florida escaped confiscation; government officials reached the Burnt Fork camp too late to seize any armaments. A hunt by federal officials aboard the steamer *Welaka* along the Georgia and Florida coasts for the filibusters and their weapons evolved into what the *Picayune* called "a wild-goose chase," and by early May the *Welaka* had returned to Savannah empty-handed.[29]

For Burtnett, the filibusters' naïveté left the strongest impression. At every step, he recalled, that naïveté mocked the grandiosity of their ambitions. "It seemed singular that those men who claimed calibre sufficient to control and destroy the power of a great nation with thousands of troops to sustain them should allow a single humble individual without power to control and entrap them." For his help Burtnett received about $8,000 from the Spanish government.[30]

✛ ✛ ✛ ✛ ✛ ✛ ✛ ✛ ✛ ✛ ✛ ✛ ✛ ✛ ✛

8 *Glorious News from Cuba*

✛ ✛ ✛ ✛ ✛ ✛ ✛ ✛ ✛ ✛ ✛ ✛ ✛ ✛ ✛

New Orleans, July 1851

In the weeks after the Fourth of July, 1851, reports of widespread revolts across Cuba began appearing in U.S. newspapers. Laurent Sigur's New Orleans *Delta* proclaimed:

GLORIOUS NEWS FROM CUBA.

THE REVOLUTION COMMENCED.

FIRST BATTLE ON THE FOURTH OF JULY!

THE PATRIOTS TRIUMPHANT! . . .

THE GOVERNMENT PANIC STRICKEN! [1]

Similarly, the New York *Herald* declared, "The revolution having begun, it cannot go backward; and it is more than probable that the days of Spain's rule here, are at least to be much embarrassed." Describing the "Insurrection at Puerto Principe" as "her Lexington," the *Herald* reported that Cuban rebels in that city had repulsed a dragoon of Spanish regulars, with the royalist army suffering some twenty to sixty casualties. In the wake of the battle, according to the *Herald*, the rebels had fled into the mountains to gather more arms and recruits. The paper's Cuban correspondent put the Spanish army's numbers at fourteen thousand, though "the troops are deserting in squads to the insurgents." But even with those numbers the Spanish army still faced grave tactical problems. "The Spanish troops are scattered all over the island, and cannot with facility be now concentrated. If, therefore, the [rebel] movement becomes at all general, they [the Spanish army] will probably fall or pass to the other side—a thing that is not at all improbable."

Predicting widespread *pronunciamentos*—republican uprisings within the Spanish army—the *Herald*'s correspondent found ample precedents for rebel optimism in Spain's own recent Carlist civil wars. "The civil war in Spain has so accustomed the army to change sides, that there is hardly a regiment that has not fought once or more for each." For the *Herald* correspondent, then, only one question remained: "Whether the struggle be a long or a short one, will depend upon the 'aid and comfort' the Cubans receive from the United States in the shape of guns, pistols, powder, ball, and men that can teach them to organize and manoeuvre."[2]

After four failed efforts to rid Cuba of Spanish rule—one from inside Cuba, three from the United States—Narciso López had resolved that any future filibuster led by him would have to await signs of a genuine indigenous uprising on the island. Cuba's Creoles must strike the first blow for their freedom. An alliance with indigenous rebels would, of course, increase the filibusters' odds for victory. It also would shield them from accusations that their rhetoric of republican freedom was simply a cover for avaricious plunder of a foreign nation.[3]

Ironically, as it turned out, the *Cleopatra* debacle seemed to have struck the tocsin that López had been waiting so long to hear. Early in 1851 Joaquín Agüero, a lawyer in the central Cuban city of Puerto Príncipe, had been corresponding with members of López's organization, eagerly awaiting their arrival aboard the *Cleopatra*. Agüero's own Sociedad Libertadora had even distributed broadsides across the island calling on Creoles to revolt against the Spanish upon López's arrival. Though Puerto Príncipe was a prosperous city, Creole discontent there had been stirred by Captain General José de la Concha's recent abolition of the city's *ayuntamiento*, its municipal council. He took the action after learning of support in Puerto Príncipe for López and of how local women had sold their jewelry to help defray the purchase of the *Cleopatra*.[4]

After the *Cleopatra* debacle Agüero had decided to proceed without López and organize his own revolt. Working with a small band of conspirators, he set July 4 as the day for their uprising. Agüero would lead an insurrection at Puerto Príncipe; Isidoro Armenteros, another friend of López's, would lead a second revolt at Trinidad, on Cuba's southern coast. Hoping that their efforts would spark widespread revolt, the rebels distributed flags, broadsides, and proclamations throughout the rest of the island.[5]

When late July brought more reports of uprisings, it seemed that revolution had finally come to Cuba. Arriving in New Orleans on July 28, Louis Schlesinger recalled, "I found all in a blaze of sympathizing excitement about Cuba and for Cuba. The mere traversing of the streets revealed in a few minutes to the stranger the public sentiment by which the community was strongly moved. The Cuban flag . . . was to be seen in almost every direction, displayed in ample folds from buildings, or in miniature form in windows. Placards on the walls invited to public meetings, and Cuba, Cuba, Cuba, was the topic of the newspapers, the Exchange, the street corners, and the barrooms. It even ascended into the pulpits."[6]

Also arriving in New Orleans during those heady July days, young Tennesseean Tom Bryan, soon to be a filibuster—and determined not to miss any of the "funn"—found no shortage of venues in which to express his pro-López sympathies. "I went on down to whear they were fyring cannon and there I got full of Patriotism to the top and hollered untill I was hoarse," he wrote in his diary, describing a profilibuster rally. On another evening Bryan attended a rally at Bank's Arcade at which Felix Huston, a former general in the Texas republic's army, was the main speaker. "Houston," Bryan recalled, "was a fine speaker and made everything look plausible and after the speaking was over we fired cannon and hooped things up all knight." At another rally in Bank's Arcade, López himself—with *Delta* editor Laurent Sigur interpreting—was the main speaker. Recalled Bryan, "We run all knight as before."[7]

When the Hungarian filibuster Louis Schlesinger got to New Orleans, he went to Laurent Sigur's home on Customhouse Street, where López was once again living. "I found the old chief in a state of eager impatience for his departure, chafing at the delay like an imprisoned lion," he recalled. Indeed, López was now so confident that Cuba's liberation was at hand that he convinced himself that even with a small filibuster army he could finish the job.

The federal government eventually had returned the *Cleopatra* and its provisions to the conspirators. The filibusters, in turn, had sold both ships, using revenues from the sales as seed money for a brand-new expedition. Besides resolving that any new mission to Cuba would have to be coordinated with a revolt on the island, the filibusters also had decided that the next expedition required a much larger army, composed of two divisions: one division would depart from New Orleans; the other, with "1500 to 2000 men" to be raised by Ambrosio Gonzales, would leave from Savannah.[8]

In July, as the reports of rebel victories in Cuba drifted back to New Orleans, López decided that his own expedition needed to get under way. By his reasoning, the urgency of providing immediate support for a rebellion already in progress outweighed whatever advantage might be gained by waiting to organize a larger army. His army at that moment remained far below the troop-strength requirements he had set after the *Cleopatra* fiasco. Ambrosio Gonzales was in Virginia, recuperating from ailments caused by "the incessant labor and anxious solicitude of the preceding months," and had not yet begun to organize his promised Georgia regiment.⁹ Even so, encouraged by the reports from the island, López was convinced that with only a fast boat and "a few of his Cuban friends," he could now grasp victory. He fixed his attention on the *Pampero*, an old steamer once used in the New Orleans-to-Galveston trade that the conspiracy had purchased that month and whose arrival they were now awaiting.

En Route: New Orleans to El Morrillo, Cuba, August 4–11, 1851

On Saturday, August 2, when the *Pampero* finally arrived in New Orleans, the filibusters discovered that the ship needed substantial mechanical repairs. That same day they also learned that federal agents, alerted to the ship's presence by the Spanish consul, planned to seize it the following Monday. The government's plans had been leaked to the filibusters by Kentuckian William L. Crittenden, a López conspirator who worked at the U.S. customshouse. The son of President Fillmore's attorney general, John J. Crittenden, the younger Crittenden—a West Point graduate who had served as a regular U.S. Army officer in the Mexican War—enjoyed wide associations throughout the federal government.¹⁰

Upon learning, that Saturday, of the government's plans to seize the *Pampero*, López made plans to sail the next night. Repairs would be made somewhere downriver before they reached the Gulf. As before, arms and munitions would be transported on the towboat that would pull the *Pampero* from New Orleans and transferred to the filibusters' ship just before it reached the Gulf.¹¹

López arrived at Lafayette, the New Orleans suburb where the *Pampero* was docked on St. Mary's Street, at one o'clock in the morning on Monday, August

4. As Schlesinger later recalled, López was "in fine spirits, but with his accustomed calmness, and quiet energy. He went at once on board, greeted with wild hurrahs both from the officers and men already collected on board, and from the thousands of citizens who were assembled to witness the departure."[12]

Just hours before sunrise that morning, the *Pampero*, unmolested by federal officials and pulled by the towboat *Union*, finally slipped away from its berth. The ship's presence and its mission had been widely known for days, but why had no federal action been taken? Crittenden's warning certainly played a role, but at least one other federal official also helped López. Though Spain's consul alerted customs collector William Fretet of the *Pampero*'s destination the Friday before its departure, the federal agent took no action. A week later President Fillmore fired Fretet, in all likelihood a López confederate.[13]

Below New Orleans the *Pampero* picked up two contingents of reinforcements, bringing the army's ranks to about five hundred. The ship dropped anchor again, at about 5:00 P.M., at Balize, where, at the wide river's brackish mouth, the steamer sat for two days as repairs were made and weapons were transferred from the towboat. Amid the bustle López noticed that the *Pampero* seemed overcrowded and ordered about a hundred men, against their protests, to disembark and return to New Orleans with the towboat. The army of just over four hundred—Tom Bryan put the figure at 435—that eventually set out to sea on Wednesday, August 6, consisted of three regiments. López was the army's commander in chief. Since Gonzales remained in Virginia, recuperating, López's second in command and chief of staff was John Pragay—along with Schlesinger, one of several Hungarian officers in the expedition. Armstrong Irvine Lewis, who had been the *Creole*'s captain, also commanded the *Pampero*. Of the three regiments, one—under Captain Urdaneta Oberto, a Cuban—included 49 Cubans, 9 Hungarians, and 9 Germans. U.S. citizens apparently rounded out the ranks of the other two regiments, both of which were commanded by Mexican War veterans: Colonel Crittenden led a regiment of 114 men, and the final regiment, under Colonel R. L. Downman, had 219 soldiers. The three regiments were divided into nine companies. Once again López, ever the optimist, expected recruits in Cuba to fill out each of the companies' ranks.[14]

As before, once at sea, insubordination proved a problem, and crowded conditions strained nerves, producing irritable behavior. During the ship's hurried departure from New Orleans, there had been little time to properly stow away baggage and other materials; "barrels, boxes, trunks, bags, knapsacks, &c. &c., were piled in heaps or littered about." Making matters worse, López spoke only Spanish, but the crew included speakers of English, Spanish, Hungarian, and German; and English was the closest thing they had to a shared language. "It was an unfortunate circumstance," Schlesinger lamented, "that the General could not speak English, so as to have had facility for direct communication and intelligence with the whole of his little force in which it was so important that there should exist that unity of spirit of which the chief is the centre and the representative, but of which a community of language at least, if not of nationality, is perhaps a necessary condition."

López's original plans called for the *Pampero* to sail to Key West, then northward up Florida's Atlantic coast to the mouth of the St. Johns River, where reinforcements—and cannons shipped from Savannah—would be brought aboard. Before leaving New Orleans, López had been assured that the steamer carried enough coal for fifteen days of sailing. However, on August 10, six days out of port, the expedition's officers discovered that the *Pampero* had coal for only three more days of travel—and it had yet to round the tip of the Florida peninsula. Causing more worries, the old *Pampero*, which normally made fifteen knots without difficulty, was averaging only eight or nine. The repairs at Balize had not been as sound as they had assumed.

That same evening of the tenth, however, during a brief stopover at Key West, the filibusters' sagging spirits got a lift when several friends—including Stephen Mallory, soon to be a U.S. senator—came aboard and related "glowing accounts of the reported progress of the insurrection in the island." According to the reports, the Cuban revolution was still gathering force, and "the Cubans generally were anxiously awaiting our arrival."

López and his officers had not mentioned the coal shortage to the volunteers. Now, with fresh reports of uprisings, the officers could make a virtue of abandoning the St. Johns River leg of the voyage. As Schlesinger recalled, "Such was the inspiriting effect produced on the men by the accounts reported at Key West, that without knowing the General's own already formed change of plan, nor the cause which had necessitated it, the men themselves were now impatient to strike straight across for the nearest part of the Island, and unwilling to go round first to the St. John's." Some officers even ordered champagne brought aboard the *Pampero*. "There was a genial flow both of the sparkling fluid and of patriotic sentiments among them and their Key West friends." López, however, abstained; "the General himself, as was well known to his friends, never drank wine, excepting coloring a glass of water with a light claret at dinner. He was always . . . simple and abstemious at the table."

In recasting his plans, López assumed that Spanish troops had been dispatched from Havana into Cuba's east to put down uprisings at Puerto Príncipe. So he decided to land near the town of Bahia Honda, fifty miles west of Havana. The *Pampero* could then return to Florida and pick up the reinforcements assumed to be waiting at the mouth of northeastern Florida's St. Johns River.

The *Pampero* stopover at Key West on the evening of August 10 lasted only a few hours. They sailed for Bahia Honda that same night, but an overnight navigational error left them at ten o'clock the next morning, the eleventh, gazing on an unexpected sight—Havana harbor. "There was the Morro, the lighthouse, the signal flag-staff, and by the time we fairly recognized where we were, and had put about, the sentinels could even be distinguished on the walls, and men at work on the shore!" The *Pampero*'s master, Armstrong Irvine Lewis steamed northwesterly, back to sea. The encounter had been close, but, López concluded, they seemed to have escaped the notice of Spanish officials in Havana.

After several hours at sea with no Spanish ships in sight, López decided to return to the coast. As the *Pampero* steamed toward Cuba's coast, "we saw at some distance what the General was anxiously looking out for, a little coasting schooner, from which he wanted to take a pilot." The crew of the challenged Spanish merchant ship, seeing that the filibusters were heavily armed, complied with López's demand that they give up their pilot, and minutes later the boat's hapless navigator was aboard the *Pampero*.

López, by then, had decided to land at the Bay of Cabanas, twenty miles east of Bahia Honda, but when a Spanish frigate gave chase at Cabanas, he once again made Bahia Honda their destination. With their landing now imminent, uniforms, weapons, and ammunition were distributed. For this expedition the uniforms consisted of blue shirts and gray pants. Each soldier also received a rubber knapsack, a pouch for cartridges, a slung water flask, a blanket, a pistol, and from eighty to one hundred cartridges. Although many, if not most, of the filibusters had muskets, no more than ten rifles existed within the entire army.

As the filibusters steamed toward Bahia Honda, to break tensions aboard the ship, López circulated among the soldiers, amusing them with an old hobby—phrenology, the discernment of character traits through feeling the shape of an individual's skull. As Schlesinger recalled, "He was habitually observant of men in this point of view, and as the troops pressed upon him for his inspection of their heads he very freely gave his judgment, which was often received with much applause. To many he spoke in flattering terms, to others somewhat otherwise. It was rather a novel kind of military review, but every one was anxious to pass under it. It had its good effects upon the spirit of the men, and upon the individual relations thus opened between them and their chief; as the General meant that it should."

When the *Pampero* reached Bahia Honda's narrow entrance just before nightfall on August 11, the ship's impressed Cuban pilot balked at entering the bay until certain of its depth. To allay his concerns, the pilot, Captain Fayssoux, and several others climbed into a small boat and rowed into the bay for a sounding. But when the scouting party spotted the lights of a small Spanish fort, they returned to the *Pampero*, which once again retreated to the sea.

At ten o'clock that night, with the *Pampero* steaming on a westerly course, the filibusters spotted another possible landing site: about ten miles west of Bahia Honda bay lay the tiny village of El Morrillo, inside a small cove ringed by gently rolling mountains. At 11:30 P.M., as the filibusters sailed in for a closer look, moonlight revealed a lonesome beach with several piers and two small boats loaded with wood; they could spot no one along the shore. As they steamed toward the coast, however, the *Pampero*, repeating the *Creole's* bad luck, ran aground on a sandbar. Though they were still a mile from the shore, López decided that he could no longer delay their landing; their position was too vulnerable. So, carrying provisions and weapons, the filibusters climbed into rowboats and in successive waves paddled to the beach. The remaining crew—those assigned to stay on the *Pampero* and sail to Florida for the reinforcements—would have to wait for a rising tide to lift them off the shoal.[15]

López, as it turned out, had erred in assuming that Spanish authorities had failed to notice the *Pampero* when it sailed within view of Havana on the morning of August 11. Even before the filibusters realized their navigational error, Captain General Concha was informed that a suspicious warship from the United States had been spotted near the harbor's mouth. That same morning, he got yet another warning: hours earlier, a Spanish frigate, the *Esperanza*, had put in at Mariel, a fort just west of Havana, to report that its crew had spotted a suspicious steamer heading west. The commander of the unknown vessel had seemed to want to avoid the Spanish frigate. Concha assumed that the elusive ship was López's, for he had been expecting an invasion. Over the past few months, intercepted letters between the filibusters and their allies in Cuba had convinced the captain general that another invasion could come any day.[16]

Further compromising the filibusters' position, the Cuban schooner pilot impressed aboard the *Pampero*, upon being released at El Morrillo, went directly to Havana and reported López's landing to Concha. Havana, the pilot assured the captain general, was the filibusters' ultimate destination, because López believed that Havana was about to erupt in indigenous rebellions. He also reported that López thought the captain general, expecting an uprising at Puerto Príncipe, had dispatched the Spanish army into Cuba's east and thus "stripped" Havana of its garrison. In fact, Concha had assumed that the filibusters were headed toward remote Mantua, near Cuba's far *western* coast. López a year earlier had tried unsuccessfully to persuade the filibusters aboard the *Creole* to sail toward Mantua after their retreat from Cárdenas. Mantua, Concha reasoned, would make an ideal filibuster staging base: it was close to New Orleans, it had no army garrison, and that part of the island had no good roads, making the town virtually unapproachable except by sea. Concha had been so confident that the filibusters were bound for Mantua that upon hearing the first reports of the invaders, he ordered the frigate *Pizarro* readied to sail for the west.[17]

Armed now with accurate reports of the filibusters' position, Concha recast his counterstrategy. Thus, even as López and his men in the predawn hours of August 12 were unloading the *Pampero* at El Morrillo, the captain general was acting to surround and choke them. General Manuel Enna and 750 soldiers left Havana for Bahia Honda at 7:30 that morning aboard the frigate *Pizarro*. Colonel Joaquin de Rada Morales, meanwhile, left Havana by rail for Guanajay, an inland town forty miles southeast of Bahia Honda, where he gathered a force of four hundred men and 120 horses. Another division, under Colonel Angel Elizalde, began marching toward López from the town of Pinar del Río, in the southwest. As Elizalde attacked from the south, Morales could block any eastward filibuster movement toward Havana. Enna's forces could thwart any retreat to sea from the north coast, and the *Pizarro* could interdict the arrival of any reinforcements by sea.[18]

Cuba, August 12–16, 1851

The filibusters began slipping across El Morrillo's moonlit bay in their rowboats at midnight. By 4:00 A.M. on Tuesday, August 12, the entire army and its provisions were ashore. Though the first filibusters ashore heard some errant musket shots from a handful of fleeing customs and postal officials, they seemed to have the beach all to themselves. For López the return to Cuba was a moment to savor: as his rowboat cut through the foamy breakers fringing the beach, he was resplendent in a white jacket and pantaloons, with a red sash around his waist. He carried no arms, only a spyglass in a leather case over his shoulder. Schlesinger recalled that "on reaching the shore, the first thing that the General did was to kneel and kiss the soil of his '*querida Cuba*,' 'beloved Cuba.'"

With the army ashore and the tide rising, López ordered the *Pampero* to lift anchor and sail for Florida and the reinforcements waiting at the mouth of the St. Johns River. His latest strategy called for the reinforcements to attack at a point east of Havana, where López believed insurrections were already in progress. As for the 400 filibusters already ashore, one regiment of about 120 men under Crittenden would remain at El Morrillo to guard the army's supplies until oxen and carts could be procured to move the provisions inland. The other regiment of about 280 filibusters, under López's direct command, would march inland into the mountains.

The filibusters stood together on the beach and watched as the *Pampero*, freed now from the cove's bottom by the rising tide, returned to the sea, bound for Florida. As the steamer disappeared into the marine dawn, "it seemed that there would be no end to the shouts of delight with which she was greeted from our ranks, as she began to move off with a freshening breeze, signaling to us her farewell. She was carrying home the news of our landing and our letters; we hoped that she would bring back more friends, especially our howitzers, field-pieces, rifles and more cartridges."[19]

Sometime after nine o'clock that morning, López's division turned onto a sandy road that led out of El Morrillo into Cuba's mountainous interior. Their destination was Las Pozas, a highland village ten miles inland, where López planned to establish a base from which to rally local supporters. After marching only a short distance, the filibusters came upon what they took to be a good omen for finding such indigenous allies: waiting for them were four horses equipped with saddlery and ready to ride. "It was evident that they had been left by some friendly hands. The General and his principal staff officers were thus at once mounted." However, even with officers on horseback now leading the way, the marching filibusters evoked no image of martial élan. The same insubordination that had dogged the Cárdenas expedition now followed them into Cuba's highland interior. "The men would straggle along in a disorderly fashion, and the advance guard had frequently to halt to enable the rear to close up," Schlesinger recalled. Tom Bryan remembered, "We didnot have any rear guard to keep them up and they scattered along the road most any way." At one point General Pragay and a filibuster came close to shooting at one another after Pragay caught the soldier trying to loot a country store along the road.

August's tropical heat exacerbated discipline problems. "Two or three" of the filibusters "actually threw away their muskets to lighten their march under the oppressive heat." Still later, two others dropped out to rest, promising that they would catch up that evening; they were never seen again. Insects proved another nuisance. "Of the mosquitoes that accompanied the filibusters on the march to Las Pozas," Schlesinger recalled, "[do] not think I exaggerate when I assure you that they would darken any part of the body left exposed to their access. Handkerchief over the head and face, and gloves on the hands, afforded but imperfect protection from them. I have brushed them off with one hand from the other, so that fifty or sixty would fall to the ground at a stroke. They drew the first blood of the campaign and plenty of it. They were certainly Catalan not *Creole* musquitoes."

Reaching the top of a ridge at about two o'clock that afternoon, August 12, the filibusters gazed across a broad valley to another rise. Las Pozas, which sprawled over the next ridge, appeared to be "a poor little village of perhaps fifty houses"; upon reaching it, the filibusters discovered that most of those houses were deserted. "Besides whatever fear any might have felt, the inhabitants had been ordered off by the local authorities." To allay fears among those who had not fled, López posted proclamations announcing that the filibusters had come as their "friends and auxiliaries against their oppressors." He then ordered the procurement of oxen and carts to be sent to Crittenden, "paying" the peasants from whom the livestock and wagons were confiscated with filibuster-issued scrip. By four o'clock that afternoon, eight filibusters had left Las Pozas with the carts and oxen to join Crittenden.

Fifteen minutes after their departure, however, López heard unsettling news from a peasant who had just returned from the north coast. That afternoon, the peasant said, the *Pizarro* had landed a regiment of Spanish soldiers at Bahia Honda. In fact, the entire disembarkation that the peasant described—that of

General Enna's army—was completed by eleven o'clock that evening. Once ashore, the general divided his army into two divisions: one, under Enna himself, left for Las Pozas; the other, under Commander Juan Antonio Villaoz, headed for El Morrillo.

López had hoped to linger at Las Pozas long enough to recruit the indigenous Cuban forces—both volunteers and deserters from the Spanish army—that he assumed awaited his arrival. He also wanted time to shape his ragtag collection of mercenaries into a cohesive army. As Schlesinger recalled, "General Lopez had no intention of bringing his men into action until he should have had a little more time to discipline them." But with Spanish soldiers already at Bahia Honda, just twelve miles from Las Pozas, López realized that he and the men would have to go elsewhere for their drills and recruiting—to another village, deeper in the mountains. In recasting his plans, a new concern suddenly weighed on López. Leaving Las Pozas so quickly risked being permanently cut off from the 120 men of Crittenden's division. As Schlesinger recounted, "To lose Crittenden and his force now, nearly a third of the Expedition, would be a dreadful blow, both from the weakening of our actual number, and still more from the bad moral influence such a calamity would have on the country!" With that new fear now burdening him, López, upon hearing of the *Pizarro*'s landing, sent a messenger to Crittenden with orders to abandon the oxcarts and all the heavy provisions and to rush to Las Pozas.[20]

Crittenden and his unit were encamped by a *tienda*, a general store, in the village of Tabla de Agua, about halfway between El Morrillo and Las Pozas, when López's new orders reached them. But Crittenden, questioning the wisdom of abandoning the provisions, balked at complying. Since they were already encamped for the night, he saw no urgent need to rush to Las Pozas. They would march the next day.[21]

The following morning, Wednesday, August 13, Crittenden's regiment was preparing breakfast when a small company from Enna's army launched a surprise attack. The filibusters fought well in the ensuing battle, eventually driving Enna's forces back into the forest. Flushed now with a foretaste of victory, Crittenden and about eighty of his men disappeared into the forest in pursuit of the fleeing enemy. Captain J. A. Kelly and the approximately forty other filibusters of Crittenden's regiment, meanwhile, stayed behind at Tabla de Agua to guard the provisions.

Crittenden's bravado in giving chase soon proved a costly error. Ten minutes later Enna attacked with a much larger force, driving a permanent wedge between Crittenden's and Kelly's divisions. Kelly and his men, like Crittenden's unit, disappeared into the forest and that night found their way to Las Pozas and rejoined López. Crittenden and his men also tried to reach Las Pozas, but on every route they tried, enemy soldiers stood between them and López's division.[22]

As Crittenden's regiment battled at Tabla de Agua on the morning of August 13, López's battalion at Las Pozas was facing an even larger Spanish attack. At about eight o'clock the filibusters had just killed some cows for breakfast when musket fire erupted from a house on the edge of the village. Enemy soldiers apparently had sneaked into the house that morning after, unbeknownst to López, the filibuster sentries guarding approaches to the village had decided "for themselves that they had been on guard long enough." Bayonet-wielding filibusters drove the Spanish riflemen from the house. But a much larger column of Spanish soldiers—"over 800," according to Schlesinger—soon arrived via the road from El Morrillo.

The filibusters formed into companies and rushed into the fight. "There was pretty prompt hurrying to our arms and into position, with great alacrity and spirit on the part of our men," Schlesinger recalled. After two hours of pitched fighting, the attacking Spanish column was dispersed. The battle cost the filibusters three of their most experienced officers, including infantry commander Colonel Robert L. Downman, a Mexican War veteran. Captain Urdaneta Oberto, leader of the Cuban regiment, and the Hungarian general John Pragay, López's second-in-command, both suffered nonmortal wounds; immobilized and with no desire to be a burden to the filibusters or a prisoner to the Spaniards, each soon committed suicide. By Schlesinger's account, their predicament was a Hobson's choice: in the battle's aftermath "the same care was taken of the wounded of the enemy as of our own. This humanity, shown on our side, was afterwards repaid by the *massacre and mutilation* of our wounded, who fell into the enemy's hands."

According to Schlesinger, "Our loss was from 30 to 35 in killed and wounded; not including eight or ten so slightly wounded as to be still able to march with us. Of the enemy we counted in and immediately near the road one hundred and eighty dead bodies." Nevertheless, the manner in which the filibusters had fought gave Schlesinger pause. By his lights, they still failed to meet the standards of "discipline and subordination" that López had hoped to instill. The filibusters had fought more as individuals than as a cohesive army. "In this battle each man was fighting as it were on his own hook, and in his own way. The officers could do nothing more than get their men on the ground, and then cheer them with their presence and example, fighting and firing meanwhile themselves among them, pretty much on terms of equality. There was not much of giving or obeying of orders." Though López had recruited more professional soldiers with experience for this expedition, the military culture of filibustering—with all its quirky habits and ragged discipline—still prevailed.[23]

Before and after the battle of Las Pozas, López dispatched patrols to search for Crittenden's unit. But by late afternoon on the thirteenth, with Crittenden's regiment still missing, the general decided that the growing presence of enemy troops in the area argued against the filibusters' remaining at Las Pozas. They would have to leave without their missing comrades. That night at 2:00 A.M.—the morning of August 14—López and his men left Las Pozas, marching until daybreak, when they stopped at nine o'clock at a small farm, a *vega*, for breakfast. To recompense the farm's owner, López once again left behind his filibuster scrip.

The filibusters left at three o'clock that afternoon, again marching through the night and stopping the next morning, the fifteenth, at another farm, a *cafetal*, about four miles from the town of Bahia Honda. The filibusters began killing cattle, building fires, and preparing for a feast, but their work came to an abrupt halt just past noon when a local man passed by with more details of the Spanish army's landing at nearby Bahia Honda. The man, a filibuster sympathizer, reported that about twelve hundred infantrymen and two hundred cavalry, backed by artillery, were gathered at the port, and that they knew that the filibusters were at the *cafetal*. Making matters worse, he added, the Spanish soldiers were, certainly by then, already marching toward the filibusters. The enemy troops planned to occupy the juncture where the road to the *cafetal* diverged from the road into the mountains. By the Spaniards' strategy, if the filibusters' retreat into the mountains could be blocked, they would make easy prey for a direct assault later that evening.

Before leaving the *cafetal* at about one o'clock, López took a moment to try to reinvigorate sagging spirits. "He told them that he looked to each of them to set an example to the men in the cheerful endurance of fatigue and hardship.

He believed it would not be long before they would unite with insurgent parties of the Cubans, and acquire such force as to be able to take up positions in which all their wants would be supplied. Before long, too, he expected . . . that reenforcements would also come from the United States; and that they would be enabled to assume the offensive, instead of having now to avoid present engagements with superior forces of the enemy."

López and his soldiers reached the main road and ascended into the mountains ahead of their Spanish pursuers. But his brave words had only underscored the increasingly bleak predicament of the hungry, fatigued filibusters. On their forced march into the rain-soaked mountains that night, the steep footpath they trod soon gave way to flooded ravines and gullies. At 11:00 P.M. on August 15 they stopped at a small farmhouse at the top of a mountain, where they met two young men. López sympathizers from Havana, the two had ventured into the highlands in hopes of joining the filibusters. But whatever good cheer the appearance of the two recruits brought was blunted by the news they imparted: there had been uprisings at Puerto Príncipe and Trinidad, but both had been quickly suppressed by the Spanish army, even before López left the United States. After hearing their latest bad news, the filibusters posted a few sentries and stole a few hours of sleep.

Early the next morning, the sixteenth of August, López and his men resumed their march, "getting deeper into the mountains, marching up and down steep ascents and descents, over ground extremely rough, tangled, and fatiguing." By eleven o'clock they had stopped at another plantation to rest and eat. "A couple of cattle were killed, plantains and corn were gathered (a receipt being given for them by the General, as before)." Soon after the filibusters left the plantation, at four o'clock that afternoon, they met a peasant along the road who had still more rebel news: while confirming that there had been a failed revolt at Pinar del Río, he also said that another uprising was about to erupt, in the town of San Cristóbal, on the southern side of the mountains.

For the wearied filibusters the possibility of a revolt at San Cristóbal was intriguing news. Outnumbered and outgunned, they had been in a debilitating stalling action ever since fleeing Las Pozas, hoping only to elude their pursuers long enough to find reinforcements from the United States or local uprisings. As Schlesinger recalled, "Constant motion was the present policy of our situation, so as to baffle the efforts of the troops to attack us with their superior forces, until we should be strengthened." By Schlesinger's count, a week after leaving Las Pozas, López's regiment stood at "about 260" men, a loss of from 20 to 30 filibusters in less than a week. The most recent attrition had come not from combat—they had seen none since leaving Las Pozas—but "from their dropping behind or straying from the places at which we had stopped." Beyond that, "we had lost *from 60 to 70 muskets.*" Most of the guns had simply been tossed aside by men weary of carrying them.[24]

The loss of the provisions abandoned as Crittenden's regiment fled from Tabla de Agua haunted the army: without the "perfect and minute" topographic maps left behind, their sense of direction was crippled. The loss of most of their ammunition also dogged them; at Las Pozas the filibusters had been reduced to scavenging the bodies of fallen Spanish soldiers for ammunition—according to Schlesinger, recovering "over 12,000" cartridges. Since the filibusters carried U.S. muskets of smaller bore than the enemy's English rifles, as Schlesinger recalled, "we had to beat down the bullets somewhat in the cartridges to reduce their circumference." During the battle of Las Pozas, Tom Bryan recovered some Spanish cartridges but despite his best efforts with his ramrod could only push the bullet "about two-thirds" of the way down his rifle. Nonetheless, he took aim at a Spanish soldier and fired. "When I came to myself I was lying on my back. I felt of my right shoulder to see if there was a bullet hole in it but there was none. My clothes was bloody but I found that blood was coming from my nose. I looked for my gunn and it was lying several feet behind me with about two inches of dirt in the muzzle. The gunn had kicked the sences out of me. The Spanish bullet was too large for my gun was the trouble. I then got the Spanish gunn and I was all right."[25]

Cuba, August 17–31, 1851

The report of an imminent anti-Spanish uprising boosted the filibusters' spirits, and López turned all his energies toward reaching its reputed center, the city of San Cristóbal, on the southern slope of Cuba's interior mountains. Pushing southward, at noon on August 17, they stopped at Cafetal de Frías, a plantation once owned by López's in-laws, to look for food. Only two hours later their lunch was interrupted by a surprise attack by General Enna's army of about six hundred infantry soldiers and some three hundred lancers.[26] Fortunately for the 260 filibusters, they had selected a mango grove on a ridge above and away from the plantation's main buildings for their afternoon bivouac, and so they missed the brunt of the Spanish attack. Indeed, it was Enna's soldiers who made themselves vulnerable—totally exposed to filibuster muskets—by charging into the open field that spread between the mango ridge and the plantation's main buildings. What could have been the filibusters' last stand turned out to be a nominal victory. As Schlesinger recalled, once the smoke cleared, "horses and men strewed the ground before and below us." Though most of the Spanish forces had escaped in a mass retreat from the *cafetal*, General Enna himself numbered among the battle's casualties. As for the filibusters, "we sustained no other loss than *three wounded*, and, of those three, one was wounded only through the carelessness of a comrade."

To Schlesinger, however, the engagement seemed more like another missed opportunity than a victory. "Oh, that we had but fifty horses, and willing riders, to pursue them with! Oh that, without horses, our own men could but have been made to pursue!" López, exposed to enemy fire, rode out in front of his soldiers and tried to rally them to pursue the escaping Spaniards, but few followed. The failure to pursue the Spaniards not only cost the filibusters a decisive victory; it also meant the loss of additional weapons and recruits." We had but to rush down upon them, and the abandoned howitzers were ours! Who knows how many of the enemy would have laid down their arms, then to have assuredly joined us! Pursuit would have consummated a victory which would have been perhaps decisive, if it had been possible to follow it up, at a moment when *moral effect* was everything."

By then, the filibusters harbored no illusions about their deteriorating situation. Vastly outnumbered, their position now known to the enemy, it was only a matter of time before they faced an even larger Spanish attack. In the end, then, the victory at Cafetal de Frías only increased their eagerness to reach San Cristóbal. As Schlesinger recounted, "We thus made ourselves a precipitate retreat from the field of our own victory, before the smoke of the musketry by which we had won it had well cleared off. From a field of triumph, in which a handful of men had scattered to the right and left an army with artillery, in utter panic rout and flight, General Lopez thus retired with a deeper gloom in his heart than he had known at any former hour of our adventures."

Over the next week López tried to maintain "a cheerful and cheering countenance," even as he and his men expended their dwindling energies trying to elude their Spanish pursuers long enough to reach San Cristóbal. On the

evening of August 17, four days of tropical rains began pounding the filibusters. At a muster on the nineteenth, they discovered that only 90 of the 160
men still had muskets, and many of those had been damaged by the rains. Two
days later, when a small company of Spanish soldiers surprised the filibusters
at a *cafetal* where they had stopped, the once defiant "liberators" were reduced
to fleeing into the forests. "Resistance," Schlesinger recalled, "under those circumstances, with our trifling number of effective muskets, was out of the
question."

Fleeing deep into the mountain forests, away from roads and paths, the filibusters tried to improvise a cross-country passage to San Cristóbal. "Our position was now a dreadful one indeed," Schlesinger remembered. "The mountain where we were was indeed inaccessible to any enemy, but it proved to be
utterly destitute for sustenance. The storm kept on till it became fairly a hurri-
cane." On the twenty-first López killed his horse to supply a meal for troops
who had not eaten in four days. The next day several officers demanded that
López abandon the expedition, find a small ship, and return them to the
United States. In refusing their request López, blaming their plight on those
who had deserted the expedition, tried to assure the mutineers that reinforcements and indigenous uprisings would yet save them. After the filibusters exhausted their supply of horse meat, they survived on the sweet pulpy interior
of palm trees. "The young palm trees, or *palmitas*, were now for several days
almost our sole dependence for sustenance, as they were likewise to most of
our scattered comrades, wandering like ourselves forlorn fugitives over these
weary mountains."

On August 23, hungry, tired, and wet, their clothes tattered, the filibusters
had about forty muskets left, only about ten of which worked. More than a few
of the men no longer had shoes; "many a foot was not only shoeless, but
bruised and swollen." As they descended from the mountains to the gently
sloping plain near San Cristóbal, the exposed attack the filibusters had eluded
for so long finally came. Upon hearing musket fire, the ragged soldiers scattered from the banks of the road in all directions. Those, including López, not
immediately shot or taken prisoner hid in the woods for several days until
they were captured. In all, fifteen were shot in the ambush; others were executed on the spot after their capture.[27]

On August 26 General Concha issued an order, an *indulto*, that those filibusters who surrendered would be spared execution. López, who assumed

that the *indulto* would not apply to him, eluded capture until August 28. In his by then tattered white linen uniform, López was walking along a country road with a handful of other filibuster refugees when a peasant spotted them and alerted Spanish troops. The peasant, José Antonio Castañeda, later received ten thousand pesos for his services. According to Schlesinger, even at the end the general remained unbowed: "When they [the filibusters] came in sight of the armed party [the Spanish soldiers], the latter called out to them to throw themselves faced on the ground, *vientre á tierra*, all obeyed, except the General, who stood erect; and the horsemen charged down roughly upon and into the midst of them as they lay. The General at once told them that he was General Lopez, and he called all to witness [as] he claimed for his companions, who surrendered voluntarily, the benefit of the *indulto*, the period of which had not expired."[28]

At the moment of his own capture, López was unaware of the fate accorded Crittenden and his men two weeks earlier. Once split off from Captain Kelly's division, Crittenden's unit had tried and failed to reach López at Las Pozas. Crittenden thus decided that his unit's only remaining option was to attempt an escape from Cuba. He and the fifty remaining members of his division returned to El Morrillo and on August 14 took to sea in four small boats, in hopes of reaching Key West. On their second day out, they were captured by the frigate *Habanero* and taken to Havana.

On August 16, at three o'clock in the morning, Captain General Concha learned of the arrival of Crittenden and his men in Havana. Having already decided that they should face a firing squad, the captain general set their execution for seven o'clock the next morning. A quick dispatch of the sentences, he reasoned, would preempt any legal efforts to free the prisoners. The government lawyers would have four hours to interview the filibusters and obtain confessions, a precaution against any legal questions that might arise after their death.

Once in Havana, the prisoners were transferred to another frigate, the *Esperanza*, where the Spanish lawyers conducted their grim depositions. Two lawyers did the initial interviews that morning; since they conversed with the condemned men through translators, the work went slowly. When seven o'clock arrived, and only ten prisoners had been interviewed, extra attorneys and translators came aboard. Once the interrogations were over, Crittenden and his men were taken to Castle Atares, not far from Havana harbor. They died on a slope just outside the castle at eleven o' clock on the morning of August 16.[29]

Whereas others in the regiment faced the firing squad in groups of six or twelve, Crittenden was executed first and alone. According to a soon widespread legend, Crittenden refused to be blindfolded or to prostrate himself before his executioners. Seconds before his death he reputedly declared, "A Kentuckian kneels to none except his God, and always dies facing his enemy." Even after it had become obvious to López that his own capture was inevitable, he had taken heart in believing that the *Pampero* would return to claim victory in Cuba's east. Crittenden, however, died well weaned from any such optimism. Minutes before his death he wrote to his uncle, U.S. Attorney General John J. Crittenden:

> Dear Uncle:
>
> In a few minutes some fifty of us will be shot. We came here with Lopez. You will do me the justice to believe that my motives were good. I was deceived by Lopez. He, as well as the public press, assured me that the island was in a state of prosperous revolution. I am commanded to finish writing at once. I will die like a man.[30]

Havana, September 1, 1851

Between the wide Gulf sky and the waters of Havana harbor, the Gothic Morro Castle's high tabby walls gleamed in the Sunday morning light on September 1, 1851. Though it was barely seven o'clock, a noisy crowd of four thousand already had gathered in a public plaza just across the harbor from the Morro. The plaza spread below the walls of the Punta, a small citadel guarding the western side of Havana's finger-shaped harbor. At the center of the crowd's attention on the cloudless dawn was a ten-foot high wooden scaffold that rose from the plaza. At its top was a garrote, an iron chair with a pair of clasps on its back. The mechanics of this grim machine were simple: just below its clasps, designed to grip the condemned man's head, was a metal collar for his throat. With a turn of a screw on the garrote's back, the collar tightens, strangling the prisoner.

Narciso López had hoped that his captor's memories of another day might spare him, if not death, then at least this means of execution. As a soldier and former general in the Spanish army, he preferred death by firing squad. But two decades yawned between this new morning and the days when Captain

General Concha served under López, then a young officer in the Spanish army. Since those days López had tried five times in three years to vanquish Spain's dominion over its most valued remaining New World colony. Even before organizing his filibustering armies in the United States, López already faced the death sentence rendered in absentia in 1848 for his aborted uprising at Cienfuegos.

López was brought out at seven o'clock. At age fifty-four, with his mustache, white hair, and dark piercing eyes, he remained a handsome man. Accompanied by a line of Spanish soldiers, he wore a long white gown and a white cap. His wrists were tied in front. Another rope, binding his elbows, was knotted from behind, its strands held by guards. With two friends who had been allowed to join him, López climbed the steps of the wooden tower. At the top he knelt in prayer for a moment, then rose and faced the crowd. "Countrymen," he said in a steady voice that observers would recall as one of remarkable composure, "I most solemnly, in this last awful moment of my life, ask your pardon for any injury I have caused you. It was not my wish to injure anyone, my object was your freedom and happiness." When an officer interrupted, López quickly concluded, "My intention was good, and my hope is in God."

He bowed, took his seat in the iron chair, and eased his head back. The executioner, a black man, placed the iron clamps around López's throat. His feet were then tied to bolts on the sides of the chair. He exchanged a few words with his friends and kissed a small cross. Then, with a turn of a screw, Narciso López's three-year campaign to vanquish Spain's dominion over Cuba came to an end.[31]

Conclusion

Two weeks after Narciso López's death, federal officials seized the *Pampero* in Dun's Lake, near the town of Palatka, Florida, south of Jacksonville along the St. Johns River. Its crew had abandoned the ship after their futile return to Florida for more weapons. Published accounts, meanwhile, of the executions in Havana and reports, probably false, of mutilations of the bodies of Crittenden and his men sparked demonstrations across the United States. In New Orleans rioters sacked the Spanish consulate. The conspiracy's ties to New Orleans—and efforts by southern nationalists to exploit resentments stirred by Washington's antifilibuster actions—gave López's army a public identification with the South. But, as the breadth of the demonstrations prompted by López's death made clear, his support was hardly confined to the South. In the weeks before and after the filibuster's defeat, the New York *Herald* reported demonstrations in New Orleans, Philadelphia, Jersey City, Baltimore, Cincinnati, Nashville, Savannah, and New York. On August 26 one of several demonstrations in lower Manhattan drew "a multitude [that] could not have been under 8,000 persons."[1]

Outrage deepened when news arrived that 135 of López's men had been shipped to a Spanish prison at Ceuta, on Africa's northern coast. Among them was David Q. Rousseau, later reputed to be the one prisoner from Crittenden's company who escaped the firing squad. According to one account, when Spanish officers ordered the condemned men of Crittenden's regiment to write last letters to their loved ones, Rousseau—certain that his captors would inspect the letters—composed a missive, brimming with familial felicities, to Secretary of State Daniel Webster, a man whom Rousseau did not even know. "Dan, my dear old boy," it began, "little did you think when we parted at the close of that last agreeable visit of a week which I lately paid you, that within a month I would be 'cabined, cribbed, and confined' in the

durance vile from which I write this." Upon reading the letter, Spanish officials, sensitive to diplomatic concerns, allegedly decided to spare the venerable
Webster's "dear" friend and sent him to Ceuta.[2]

The prisoners at Ceuta were released in 1852 after negotiations between
Washington and Madrid produced pardons from Queen Isabella. To gain their
release, the United States eventually paid $25,000 in compensation for damage
done by pro-López rioters in New Orleans to Madrid's consulate and other
properties owned by Spanish nationals.

In the U.S. press López's demise provoked the expected partisan choruses.
In the *Journal and Messenger* of Macon, Georgia, a local poet found in López's
death the end of all hopes for Cuba's liberation: "The hero has perished and
deep in his grave / Lies buried the hopes of the true and the brave." The *United
States Magazine and Democratic Review* praised López as a fallen patriot in the
traditions of "Kosciusko, Pulaski, Steuben, DeKalb and La Fayette. . . . If the
people of the United States hope to preserve their freedom, they must refrain
from trampling on the ashes of its martyrs; and if those of Cuba ever become
free, or deserving of freedom, they will erect statues to Narcisso Lopez." With
similar indignation the Charleston *Courier* dismissed a correspondent who
had questioned the morality of López's expedition. "Has he reflected that setting aside that great purifier in the eyes of the world, *success*, that Lopez occupied much the same position toward Cuba that Washington occupied towards
this country?"[3]

In more Whiggish quarters such claims to republican pedigree were obviated by the financial and political support López drew from southern and
Cuban planters and the conspiracy's obvious intention to retain Cuba's slave
economy. While James Gordon Bennett's New York *Herald*—switching sides
one last time—compared the failed invaders of Cuba to the feckless heroes of
the European uprisings of 1848, Horace Greeley's New York *Tribune* found no
Cincinnatus in López's profile. "The 'revolutions' in Europe which The *Tribune* has favored all looked to the Enfranchisement and Elevation of the Laboring Class—the Cultivators of the Soil—as their chief end," the *Tribune* inveighed. "The 'revolution in Cuba' proposes to leave the cultivators of *her* soil
in the position of beasts or chattels, subject to be flogged, starved, sold or tortured as the caprice or fancied interest of the landlord caste shall decide. He
who does not perceive a very wide difference between these two kinds of

'revolution' is welcome to his own optics: we must continue to see through ours."[4] *Harper's Monthly* also detected a bogus republicanism:

> The failure of López cooled the ardor of that class of our population whose opinions of the morality and legality of any action, depend upon its success or failure; while the slightest reflection was sufficient to show the great mass of our people, that without a declaration of war against Spain by our Government, we had no right to invade her colonies. If a revolution had existed there, our people, as in the case of Texas, could have emigrated thither, and after becoming Cubans and abandoning all claims to American citizenship, have taken such part as they might see fit in the affairs of the island. But no such revolution existed.[5]

What about the revolution that López, in August 1851, had rushed to Cuba to save? Where were the revolts supposedly erupting throughout the island? There had, in fact, been no mass uprisings. The revolution that led López to rush his departure for Cuba had been a political mirage. Headlines of rebel victories notwithstanding, Joaquín Agüero's revolt had foundered quickly and badly. When the date of his planned uprising, July 4, arrived, his forces numbered but forty-four men. Beyond that, his plot had been revealed by a priest, his wife's confessor, to Captain General José de la Concha. Sixteen leaders of Agüero's Puerto Príncipe group were quickly arrested. Following a brief battle in the mountains, Agüero, too, was captured. Government troops also put down a similarly ill-organized uprising in the town of Trinidad.

But how to explain the brazenly erroneous press reports of rebel victories? In the weeks after López's death, critics of the press's sensationalism attacked the papers that had so loudly trumpeted those alleged victories. The press, however, had assumed a major role in Narciso López's career long before his death. True to the jingoistic tradition it had nurtured during the Texas Independence and Mexican wars, the nation's popular press had led the way in fanning the flames of his ambitions and his popularity. And no papers, as the *Southern Press* of Washington, D.C., angrily noted, fanned harder harder than those of New Orleans:

> New Orleans papers, there is your work! There is the result of your diragrations, of your iniquitous falsehoods, of your placards with large black letters, and your detestable extras. There we have that scattered blood, and that will be scattered in future. There you have it, smoking in accusation against you, perverse instigators

against you, who have murdered those deluded men, whom you have sent to death—for you knew well that they certainly would be killed. This blood must flow, drop by drop, upon your heads—this blood will torment you in your sleep, for they have lost their lives when you were in security in your houses.[6]

For all its bloody-shirt hyperbole, the Southern Press had offered the filibusters and their buffalo hunt an apt epitaph. Once in the United States, López developed a perilous reliance on newspapers; his need for publicity undermined the secrecy he also needed. But without newspapers, as López instinctively understood, he risked fading from the popular imagination—the wellspring of his political strength. President Millard Fillmore, on September 2, 1851, revealed a keen grasp of López's dilemma in a letter to Secretary of State Daniel Webster. "He cannot remain in status quo," wrote the president, contemplating López's increasingly erratic behavior. "He must advance or fail." Unbeknownst to Fillmore, López had been executed one day earlier.[7]

López's troubles were exacerbated by the errors that riddled press coverage of his activities—errors that by exaggerating the filibusters' chances of success lured them into strategically hopeless situations. Coverage of Cuba and López became so erroneous that an exasperated Philadelphia Public Ledger as early as August 1849 prefaced a filibuster story from New Orleans with the warning that it "looks very much like a hoax." Similarly, the Richmond Whig in August 1851 introduced a story depicting a purported López victory with the headline, "THE LATEST FABRICATION OF INTELLIGENCE FROM CUBA." If that disclaimer was not enough, the Whig added another caveat before the actual story: "From the despatches of the Charleston papers we gather the following very doubtful intelligence."[8]

Whence the source of such "doubtful" reporting? Whence the "GLORIOUS NEWS FROM CUBA"? In a memoir of his filibustering years, Ambrosio Gonzales speculated that exaggerated reports of uprisings at Puerto Príncipe and elsewhere arose from what a later age would call "disinformation." López's adjutant general charged that the New York Tribune and other Whig papers deliberately published "false or exaggerated accounts from the Island, which contributed, with the perfidious statements of Spanish emissaries, to precipitate the departure of the too confiding Lopez, and caused him to land where he could be most speedily annihilated."[9]

Louis Schlesinger—who, unlike Gonzales, accompanied López on that final expedition—suspected a deliberate Spanish effort to propagate misleading information—not to the filibusters, but to potential supporters in Cuba. Among the baggage abandoned by William Crittenden's division at Tabla de Agua, Schlesinger recalled, were "all the printed proclamations which the General had brought with him, addressed to the people of the Island, to the Spaniards, and to his old soldiers of the army." Such propaganda, he noted, might have proved "useful" in bringing native reinforcements into López's army. Instead, with the papers in enemy hands, "the authorities had full swing to spread the most lying accounts of our purposes and actions, representing us as a lawlesss, practical banditti, marking our way with blood, rapine, and every manner of outrage."[10]

While Schlesinger's suspicion of Spanish rumormongering is plausible, Gonzales's charge that Whig editors deliberately published falsehoods seems doubtful. The U.S. press coverage of López was too vast, too contradictory, to be the handiwork of any single partisanship. If nothing else, the sheer volume of the filibusters' own manipulation of the press undermines Gonzales's theory. The filibusters' habit of talking—of boasting—to journalists nurtured an inability to protect secrets. Department of Interior agent Malcolm Mearis, for instance, observed in 1849 that the New York *Herald* teemed with reports about secret expeditions, secret soldiers, and even the "secret signs, by which he knows his fellows." He noted that according to their instructions, "they are to divulge nothing." But, then again, Mearis wondered, if the operation was such a secret, "How then, does the correspondent know so much about it?"[11]

A likelier explanation for the erroneous reports lamented by Gonzales lay in the manner by which the pennies gathered their news. Penny editors in general—and profilibuster penny editors in particular—often relied on hearsay. Operating with catch-as-catch-can sources, they felt no compulsion to reconcile contradictory reports or await verified information. Freely indulging whims, the pennies' editors published stories that accommodated their politics or just their sense of what readers wanted to read. In that climate they often took a sanguine view of filibuster activity, exaggerating the fortunes of personages whose appeal to readers, after all, rested on their purported sagacity in overcoming adversity.

Perils for the Cuba filibusters were increased by López's general impatience—his preference for action over tactical discretion—and magnified by his inability to rein in, or even recognize, that shortcoming. In an aside stunning in its introspective blindness, López in 1850 claimed to Cirilo Villaverde that "God in his endless mercy has favored me with such patience that I myself admire."[12]

In the end, then, any search among journalists for the authors of López's death yields many suspects—some Whigs, some Democrats—as well as López himself. As for the false reports of uprisings in Puerto Príncipe, exclude one editor from the lineup; as López, lured by false accounts of revolution, rushed his departure from New Orleans in 1851, Laurent Sigur was no longer editing the New Orleans *Delta*. He had sold his share of the paper that June for $75,000, money he used to buy the *Pampero*.[13]

In 1856 López's widow, Dolores Frías y Jacott, married Creole historian and polemicist José Antonio Saco, who had opposed López's filibuster.[14] John Quitman, Ambrosio Gonzales, and others continued sporadic anti-Spanish intrigues after López's death, but their efforts proved even less effective than those of their fallen leader. By 1856 the domestic political alignments in the United States that had nurtured filibustering had fallen victim to more vital forces. Free-soilism's steadily gaining strength, culminating in the creation of the Republican party in 1854 and the election of Abraham Lincoln as president in 1860 doomed the Jeffersonian-Jacksonian politics of old. Manifest Destiny was finished, and by 1863—as free-soilism's qualified polemic against slavery gave way to Lincoln's resolve to ban the institution—so too was slavery.

With slavery's abolition in the United States in 1865, wealthy Cubans still determined to preserve the island's own economy of human chattel could no longer look northward for help. Cuba's slavery died a slow death, finally collapsing in 1886. Spain's dominion over the island, however, staggered on for another twelve years. In 1898 the destruction of the U.S. battleship *Maine*, blown up in Havana harbor, furnished the United States a casus belli against Spain that López's tiny, over-crowded *Pampero* could never have delivered. Cuban rebels led by José Martí and assisted by U.S. Army soldiers finally vanquished Spain's four-hundred-year dominion over the island. Though the Cuban rebels of that year embraced a different credo than that of their filibuster predecessors of 1850 and 1851, the flag they carried had a familiar look. It was the Lone Star flag of Narciso López, the same banner that today, as the official flag of the Republic of Cuba, flies over Morro Castle—and, across the harbor, over the plaza where Narciso López on September 1, 1851, met his death.

Notes

Introduction

1. According to the same 1841 figures, whites numbered 418,000 on the island, free people of color 153,000. See Knight, *Slave Society in Cuba*, 22.

2. *New York Daily Tribune*, April 28, 1851.

3. Caldwell, *Lopez Expeditions*, 44–46.

4. Portell Vilá argued in *Narciso López y Su Época* that López deftly united two groups of Cubans who, for different reasons, pined to see their island joined to the United States."Annexationists" of "patriotic motives" sought to join Cuba to the United States for idealistic reasons—a desire for liberal freedoms denied by a tyranni-cal Spain. Annexationists of "economic motives" favored the linkage as a means of protecting the institution of slavery and the wealth of Creoles, the fortunes amassed by whites born in Cuba. Many economic annexationists, Portell Vilá argued, feared Spain might soon abolish slavery. The United States, they believed, would offer the institu-tion better protection from abolitionist pressures. For discussion of motives of Cuban annexationists, see ibid., 1:190–216. According to Portell Vilá, López's other remarkable feat lay in the sagacity by which he enlisted annexationists in both Cuba and the United States—unwittingly on the part of the latter—to advance the cause of Cuban independence. By this interpretation, if López had been victorious, he would have es-tablished an independent republic, thus dashing the hopes of the various annexation-ists. To support his view, Portell Vilá quoted from a now lost diary, as well as an 1891 letter, both by López's longtime ally Cirilo Villaverde. In the letter, Villaverde asserted that he and López always favored Cuba's independence and opposed annexation to the United States. Even if Portell Vilá had marshaled more compelling evidence to support this view, its plausibility would remain low. Most obviously, an abundance of other primary source documents from within the filibuster suggests that the campaign sought annexation. And, even if López had privately nursed dreams of an indepen-dent Cuba, if he had been victorious, it still seems unlikely that he would have been

able to arrest the trajectory of the movement away from annexation. Too many men, and too much political and monetary capital, had already been invested in preparing the ground for annexation. Finally—and perhaps most significantly—whatever private visions López might have indulged, his defeat consigned them to irrelevancy. His campaign lived and died as an annexationist movement. About how it might have governed, we can only speculate. See ibid., 190–203.

5. Bemis, *Diplomatic History of the United States*, 315; Nevins, *Fruits*, 556; Franklin, *Militant South*, 98; Merk, *Manifest Destiny*, 202–14.

6. Genovese, *Political Economy of Slavery*, 248.

7. McCardell, *Idea of a Southern Nation*, 235–36; Brown, *Agents of Manifest Destiny*, 41.

8. For Davis's and Mallory's attitude toward López, see Ley, "Expansionists All?" 214–16. For Towns, see Ambrosio Gonzales to Mirabeau Lamar, March 14, 1851, in Gulick, *Papers of Lamar* 4, pt. 1:282–84; unsigned letter from informer in Savannah to Henry Lytton Bulwer, April 12, 1851, in Manning, *Diplomatic Correspondence: Inter-American Affairs* 7:433 n.

9. For O'Hara and Wheat, see Ranck, *Bivouac of the Dead and Its Author*; Dufour, *Gentle Tiger*; Hamilton, *Taylor*, 368.

10. Scroggs, *Filibusters and Financiers*, 8, 67; Stout, *Liberators*, 185.

11. Likewise, during this same period, historians have also come to view nineteenth-century expansionism in general in similar terms. See Graebner, *Empire on the Pacific*; Hietala, *Manifest Design*.

12. Freehling, *Reintegration of American History*, 168–69; Rauch, *American Interest in Cuba*, 208; Van Alstyne, *Rising American Empire*, 152–54; Goetzmann, *When the Eagle Screamed*, 77.

13. May, *Southern Dream*, 22–45; May, "Young American Males and Filibustering," 859–63.

14. Morgan, *American Slavery, American Freedom*, 381.

15. Quoted in Lamask, *Aaron Burr, 1805–1836*, xv.

16. John L. O'Sullivan to Jefferson Davis, Sept. 5, 1863, Davis Papers, Perkins Lib., Duke Univ., Durham, N.C.

17. Potter, *The South and the Sectional Conflict*, 88.

18. See New York *Herald*, March 21, 1850.

19. Other figures identified with Young America included steamship magnate George Sanders; J. Knox Walker, a Washington lobbyist and former private secretary to President Polk; and Cincinnati newspaper editor William M. Corry. See Curti, "Young America," 34–55; Johannsen, *Douglas*, 339–73.

20. Johannsen, *Douglas*, 347.

21. Ward, *Jackson*, 133–49; May, *Southern Dream*, 18.

22. According to May, to most southern radicals of the antebellum years, Caribbean expansion "represented an alternative to secession." May, "Epilogue to the Missouri Compromise," 209.

23. See May, *Southern Dream*, 11, 12; Gonzales, article in New Orleans *Times-Democrat*, March 30, 1884; McCardell, *Idea of a Southern Nation*, 235–36.

Chapter 1

1. Strode, *Pageant of Cuba*, 98 and pl. 9; Rauch, *American Interest in Cuba*, 39; Suchlicki, *Historical Dictionary of Cuba*, 11.

2. See Paquette, *Sugar Is Made with Blood*.

3. Poyo, *"With All, and for the Good of All,"* 5–8.

4. See Harris, "O'Sullivan"; Pratt, "O'Sullivan and Manifest Destiny," 225; O'Sullivan, "Annexation," 5–10.

5. Rauch, *American Interest in Cuba*, 51; Harris, "O' Sullivan," 275.

6. Harris, "O'Sullivan," 262, 263; Poyo, "Cuban Separatist Thought," 485–91; Rauch, *American Interest in Cuba*, 51–55.

7. See O'Brien, *Story of the Sun*, 89–120; Nelson, *Secret Agents*, 72–95; Rauch, *American Interest in Cuba*, 58, 60, 62 (Rauch misidentifies "Cora Montgomery" as Beach's daughter); Reilly, "Jane McManus Storms," 21–39; Harris, "O'Sullivan," 274–93; James B. Buchanan to Moses Y. Beach, Nov. 21, 1846, in Moore, *Works of Buchanan* 7:119–20.

8. The relationship sparked a scandal that ended Burr's brief marriage to the wealthy New York heiress Madame Eliza Jumel. On Burr's advice she and her brother went to Texas in 1822 and embarked on an unsuccessful venture to found a colony with German immigrants. She later participated in the Texas independence movement and during the 1840s became a journalist and fervent advocate of Manifest Destiny. Her marriage in 1850 to Texas politician William Cazneau only deepened her political activism. For the next three decades, the couple remained immersed in U.S. diplomacy and West Indian political intrigue. See Lamask, *Aaron Burr, 1805–1836*, 393–403; W. E. Bard, "McManus, Jane," in Webb, *Handbook of Texas* 2:122; May, "Lobbyists for Commercial Empire," 383–412; W. E. Bard, "Cazneau, William Leslie," in *Handbook of Texas* 1:318.

9. Harris, "O'Sullivan," 276.

10. John O'Sulllivan to James Buchanan, July 6, 1847, Buchanan Papers, Historical Soc. of Pa.; Rauch, *American Interest in Cuba*, 55; Harris, "O'Sullivan," 40–57, 154–213, 276–79.

11. Paquette, *Sugar Is Made with Blood*, 29–35.

12. Murray, *Letters*, 243; Dana, *To Cuba and Back*, 68; see also Pérez, *Travel Accounts of Cuba*.

13. Worcester and Schaeffer, *Growth and Culture of Latin America* 1:123; Pérez, *Cuba between Reform and Revolution*, 34–38; McNeill, *Atlantic Empires*, 85–92.

14. Pérez, *Cuba between Reform and Revolution*, 36–38; McNeill, *Atlantic Empires*, 85–92, 132, 133.

15. Rauch, *American Interest in Cuba*, 11; Langley, *Struggle for the American Mediterranean*, 42, 43; Pérez, *Cuba between Reform and Revolution*, 57, 58.

16. Rauch, *American Interest in Cuba*, 13–16; for background on sugar trade, see Ely, "Old Cuba Trade," 457, 458 n. See also Paquette, *Sugar Is Made with Blood*, 187; Foner, *History of Cuba* 2:15.

17. Pérez, *Cuba and the United States*, 18–22; Foner, *History of Cuba* 2:12.

18. Pérez, *Cuba and the United States*, 15–22; Langley, *Struggle for the American Mediterranean*, 26, 27.

19. Langley, *Struggle for the American Mediterranean*, 1, 2; Paquette, *Sugar Is Made with Blood*, 183, 184.

20. Langley, *Struggle for the American Mediterranean*, 28, 32, 37, 40, 41.

21. Van Alstyne, *Rising American Empire*, 98; Williams, *Tragedy of American Diplomacy*, 21; Merk, *The Monroe Doctrine and American Expansionism*, vii.

22. Rauch, *American Interest in Cuba*, 22; see also Langley, "The Whigs and the Lopez Expeditions."

23. Quoted in Hietala, *Manifest Design*, 67.

24. Langley, *Struggle for the American Mediterranean*, 60–65, 82–92.

25. Paquette, *Sugar Is Made with Blood*, 55, 56, 132; Knight, *Slave Society in Cuba*, 23, 28, 50; Aimes, *Slavery in Cuba*, 83.

26. Paquette, *Sugar Is Made with Blood*, 98; Gonzales, *Manifesto*, 6.

27. John O'Sullivan to James Buchanan, July 6, 1847, Buchanan Papers, Historical Soc. of Pa. See also Bergeron, *Polk* , 97, 98.

28. New York *Sun*, July 23, 1847, quoted in Rauch, *American Interest in Cuba*, 59.

29. John O'Sullivan to James Buchanan, July 31, 1847, Society Collection, Historical Soc. of Pa.

30. Rauch, *American Interest in Cuba*, 61, 62.

31. *Congressional Globe*, Senate, 29th Cong, 1st sess. (Dec. 22, 1845), 92; ibid. (Dec. 27, 1845), 96; Rauch, *American Interest in Cuba*, 45. In December 1845 the senator from Florida had yet to change his surname from Levy to Yulee.

32. *Appendix to the Congressional Globe*, Senate, 30th Cong., 1st sess. (May 10, 1848), 613–20.

33. Rauch, *American Interest in Cuba*, 71; Harris, "O'Sullivan," 284.

34. In addition to his steamship lines, Law controlled New York's Dry Dock Bank, the Eighth Avenue Railroad, and the Staten Island Ferry. See Leard, "Bonds of Destiny," 149; Rauch, *American Interest in Cuba*, 192–95.

35. During the late 1840s two steamboat lines dominated U.S. shipping in the Gulf of Mexico and Pacific, and each enjoyed monopolies on U.S. mail deliveries in their respective zones. Despite those monopolies, however, the two lines competed vigorously in both Gulf and Pacific waters until 1851, when they agreed to not compete with one another. George Law's United States Mail Steamship Company delivered the post from New York via New Orleans and Havana to Chagre on Panama's eastern coast. The federal government then transported the mail across the narrow, 47–mile isthmus to Panama City on the western coast. From there, the Pacific Mail Steamship Company assumed responsibility for the post's delivery to California and Oregon. Rauch, *American Interest in Cuba*, 191, 194; Leard, "Bonds of Destiny," 149–50.

36. See Johannsen, *Douglas*, 316, 323, 348, 349; Kemble, *Panama Route*, 1–57, 180; Rauch, *American Interest in Cuba*, 193–95.

37. Quaife, *Diary of Polk* 3:446.

38. Bergeron, *Polk*, 4, 5, 9–12.

39. Hietala, *Manifest Design*, 56, 114.

40. See Marx, *Machine in the Garden*.

41. Merk, *Manifest Destiny*, 95, 96.

42. Graebner, *Empire on the Pacific*, 5–8.

43. Merk, *Manifest Destiny*, 216, 217.

44. Hietala, *Manifest Design*, 80; Calhoun speech of May 15, 1848, in Crallé, *Works of Calhoun* 4:454–78; Graebner, *Empire on the Pacific*, 6–9, 47–51.

45. Merk, *Manifest Destiny*, 66.

46. Quaife, *Diary of Polk* 3:348.

47. New York *Tribune*, Aug. 30, 1849.

48. See Weinberg, *Manifest Destiny*.

49. Whitman, *Leaves of Grass*, 158.

50. Philadelphia *Public Ledger*, Oct. 8, 1847.

51. Ibid., Nov. 17, 1847.

52. Quaife, *Diary of Polk* 3:446.

53. Robert B. Campbell to Buchanan, May 18, 1848, in Manning, *Diplomatic Correspondence* 11:439–40.

54. Knight, *Slave Society in Cuba*, 3, 4, 30–46; Perez, *Cuba between Reform and Revolution*, 70.

55. Knight, *Slave Society in Cuba*, 17, 22, 32, 33, 75–82; Pérez, *Cuba between Reform and Revolution*, 58–61, 70–74; Aimes, *Slavery in Cuba*, 158, 159.

56. Rauch, *American Interest in Cuba*, 2–14; Langley, *Struggle for the American Mediterranean*, 1–5, 39.

57. Paquette, *Sugar Is Made with Blood*, 71, 72, 92, 93; Knight, *Slave Society in Cuba*, 86.

58. Paquette, *Sugar Is Made with Blood*, 82–84, 91, 92; Cornelius P. Van Ness to John Forsyth, Dec. 10, 1836, in Manning, *Diplomatic Correspondence: Inter-American Affairs* 11:303; Daniel Webster to Millard Fillmore, Aug. 5, 1851, in Webster, *Diplomatic Papers* 2:367–68.

59. See Joel Roberts Poinsett to Martin Van Buren, Aug. 9, 22, Sept. 2, 22, Oct. 2, 1829, George Prager to Van Buren, Aug. 10, 1829, José María de Bocanegra to Poinsett, Sept. 22, 1829, in Manning, *Diplomatic Correspondence: Independence* 3:1697–1705. See also Langley, "The Whigs and the Lopez Expeditions," 10; Rauch, *American Interest in Cuba*, 25–30; Langley, *Struggle for the American Mediterranean*, 40, 45–50.

60. Gonzales, *Manifesto*, 6; Paquette, *Sugar Is Made with Blood*, 47–49, 103.

61. Foner, *History of Cuba* 2:9, 10; Ben Green to John Clayton, July 7, 1849, Clayton Papers, Lib. Cong.

62. Rauch, *American Interest in Cuba*, 70–72.

63. Quaife, *Diary of Polk* 3:469.

64. Ibid., 476–78, 485–88.

65. Since the White House meeting took place before the Club de la Habana joined López's Cienfuegos conspiracy—before he agreed to postpone his June 4 uprising—the club's members had no reason to fear reprisal if Polk relayed their information to Spanish authorities. However, since the three Cubans conveyed a letter to the president, detailing plans for the uprising, from López lieutenant José Maria Sánchez Iznaga (nephew of José Aniceto Iznaga), Polk would have had ample opportunity to pass the information along to Spanish authorities. See Rauch, *American Interest in Cuba*, 78.

66. Polk, *Diary of James K. Polk* 3:498–500.

67. Ibid., 485–88.

68. Portell Vilá, *López* 1:279–82; Morales y Morales, *Iniciadores* 2:19–21; New Orleans *Picayne*, Aug. 8, 1848; Caldwell, *Lopez Expeditions*, 46. See also the report prepared by Bruno Gayosa for the captain general, March 4, 1849, Asuntos Politos, legajo no. 122, sig. 8, Archivo Nacional, Havana.

69. Portell Vilá, *López* 1:13, 14 and n. 7.

70. "General Lopez, the Cuban Patriot," *United States Magazine and Democratic Review* 26 (Feb. 1850): 99.

71. Portell Vilá, *López* 1:77, 78.

72. Caldwell, *Lopez Expeditions*, 43–45; Portell Vilá, *López* 1:59, 81; Wilson, *Authentic Narrative*, 4.

73. Portell Vilá, *López* 1:161, 162; José María Sánchez Iznaga to José Aniceto Iznaga, May 25, 1848, ibid., 221, 222; Caldwell, *Lopez Expeditions*, 45.

74. "General Lopez, the Cuban Patriot," *United States Magazine and Democratic Review* 26 (Feb. 1850): 104–5; Portell Vilá, *López* 1:241, 242; Caldwell, *Lopez Expeditions*, 45–46.

75. Wallace, *Worth*, 185; Portell Vilá, *López* 1:235.

76. Wallace, *Worth*; William A. Ganoe, "Worth, William Jenkins," *DAB*; Charles H. Brown, *Agents of Manifest Destiny*, 45, 46. See also Bauer, *Mexican War*, 87–101, 371–74; Rauch, *American Interest in Cuba*, 75–76; Portell Vilá, *López* 1:241, 242.

77. Quaife, *Diary of Polk* 3:475–79. Rauch asserted (*American Interest in Cuba*, 76) that O'Sullivan at the time of these meetings with Polk "apparently did not know" of the Havana club's arrangements with López and Worth. By betraying the conspiracy to the president, Rauch suggests, O'Sullivan sought to warn against anti-Spanish mischief that might scuttle talks for Cuba's purchase. Worth, in fact, had died two weeks earlier—a fact of which O'Sullivan, then based in Washington, was likely aware. As for O'Sullivan's motivation, judging by Polk's reaction to the exchange as recorded in his diary, the disclosure seems more likely to have been an implicit request for U.S. assistance to the filibuster. Given O'Sullivan's bent as an inveterate intriguer, it seems unlikely that he would be in the president's office to counsel otherwise.

78. J. G. deR. Hamilton, "Saunders, Romulus," *DAB*. By orchestrating the passage of a convention rule changing the nominating threshold from a mere majority to a two-thirds majority, Saunders sank former president Martin Van Buren's candidacy and cleared the way for Polk's nomination.

79. James Buchanan to Romulus M. Saunders, June 17, 1848, in Manning, *Diplomatic Correspondence: Inter-American Affairs* 11:54–64.

80. Saunders to Buchanan, July 29, 1848, ibid., 445.

81. Saunders to Buchanan, Aug. 18, 1848, ibid., 449–50.

82. Campbell to Buchanan, Oct. 23, 1848, quoted in ibid., 451, 452; Rauch, *American Interest in Cuba*, 81–100, 112; New York *Herald*, Oct. 20, 1848. See also Caldwell, *Lopez Expeditions*, 35, 36.

Chapter 2

1. See Andrews, *Concise Dictionary*, 356–57; Craigie, *Dictionary of American English.* 2:970, 971; Mencken, *American Language*, 180.

2. New Orleans *Times-Democrat*, March 30, 1884; Gonzales, *Manifesto*, 6, 7; Wallace, *Worth*, 185.

3. New Orleans *Times-Democrat*, March 30, 1884; Gonzales, *Manifesto*, 6, 7.

4. New Orleans *Times-Democrat*, March 30, 1884; Gonzales, *Manifesto*, 6, 7; Morales y Morales, *Inciadores* 2:188, 193; Wallace, *Worth*, 186, 187.

5. Morales y Morales, *Iniciadores* 2:194–195.

6. John O'Sullivan to Calhoun, Aug. 24, 1849, quoted in *Annual Report of the American Historical Association, 1899* 2:1202–3; Gonzales, letter to the editor, Charleston *Mercury*, Aug. 25, 1851. Basil Rauch identifies the four senators but offers no source reference

(*American Interest in Cuba*, 112). Although Quitman's biographer J. F. H. Claiborne is often the best source on the López-Calhoun connection, he identifies the four congressmen to whom Calhoun introduced López only as "four distinguished senators" (*Quitman*, 2:53, 55 n.). See also Gonzales article in New Orleans *Times-Democrat*, April 6, 1884.

7. Davis, *Memoir by His Wife* 1:412–13. Mrs. Davis sets this interview with López in the early summer of 1848, but Gonzales, who seems to have been the translator, did not arrive in the United States until August; for that and other reasons it seems more likely that the year was 1849. For Gonzales, see de la Cova, "Gonzales"; Latimer, *Story of the State*, 367–72.

8. Davis, *A Memoir by His Wife* 1: 412–13.

9. General Taylor had watched as his former son-in-law, Jefferson Davis, leading a regiment of Mississippians, boldly repulsed a Mexican cavalry charge. Davis had married Taylor's daughter Sarah in June 1835; she died, of either yellow fever or malaria, the following September. See Davis, *Davis*, 70–75, 153–60.

10. Davis, *Memoir by His Wife* 1:412–13.

11. Jefferson Davis quoted in Caldwell, *Lopez Expeditions*, 49. See also Davis, *Memoir by His Wife* 1:413.

12. Belden, *New-York*, 44, 60–71, 85, 133; Spann, *New Metropolis*, 430.

13. Belden, *New-York*, 61

14. Albion, *New York Port*, 165.

15. Ibid., 182.

16. Ibid., Rauch, *American Interest in Cuba*, 191–93.

17. Albion, *New York Port*, 182; Rauch, *American Interest in Cuba*, 64, 191; Pérez, *Cuba and the United States*, 8; Williams, *Sketches*, 38.

18. Worcester and Schaeffer, *Growth and Culture of Latin America* 1:427–28; Albion, *New York Port*, 167, 168.

19. Herskowitz, "'Land of Promise."

20. Harris, "O'Sullivan," 30.

21. Ibid., 1–30.

22. O'Sullivan "Annexation," 5.

23. Harris, "O'Sullivan," 250.

24. This assumption rests on information gleaned by historian Basil Rauch. In 1855, Laurent Sigur, editor of the New Orleans *Delta*, suddenly decided to oppose James Buchanan's upcoming presidential campaign. According to a letter from Louisiana's U.S. Senator John Slidell to Buchanan, Sigur made his decision after learning, from former Cuban consul Robert B. Campbell, that Buchanan had betrayed López in 1848. If, as Rauch reports, this was news to Sigur in 1855, it is reasonable to assume that Sigur's intimate friend—and, in 1850, housemate—López was also unaware of both

O'Sullivan's and Buchanan's damaging revelations to Polk in 1848. Beyond that, it is unlikely that López, had he been aware of O'Sullivan's actions, would have allied himself so closely with the New York editor. See Rauch, *American Interest in Cuba*, 78.

25. See Donovan, *Barnburners*, 32, 33; New York *Morning News*, July 13, 15, 1846, paraphrased in Mushkat, *Tammany*, 229, 232.

26. Harris, "O'Sullivan," 54.

27. Foner, *Free Soil*, 15; Hershkowitz, "Loco-Foco Party," 325–28.

28. Hietala, *Manifest Design*, 152; Hershkowitz, "Loco-Foco Party," 326–28.

29. Hershkowitz, "Loco-Foco Party," 316–21.

30. Foner, *Free Soil*, 59–61, 116, 266, 267; Albany *Evening Journal*, Nov. 10, 1847.

31. Harris, "O'Sullivan," 53, 137; Mushkat, *Tammany*, 232.

32. Havemeyer numbered among the lawyers and other prominent New Yorkers listed by the New York *Herald* of Aug. 27, 1851, as "officers" of an Aug. 26, 1851, pro-López demonstration in lower Manhattan. For background on Havemeyer, see "Havemeyer, William Frederick," *National Cyclopedia of American Biography* 17:28. See also Rauch, *American Interest in Cuba*, 192–94; Mushkat, *Tammany*, 224; Nevins and Thomas, *Diary of Strong* 2:65; Ernst, "Mike Walsh," 58–59.

33. Nichols, *Forty Years* 2:158–64.

34. New Yorkers had accepted mobs as part of the city's life even before the American Revolution. During the eighteenth century mobs often engaged in limited, usually nonviolent, protests against violations of the "moral economy," a shared sense of economic fair play assumed to regulate public conduct. Causes of protest ranged from rises in the price of bread to changes in specie exchange rates. While some New Yorkers viewed such lawless actions with alarm, most apparently accepted mobs as a sort of insurance against statist abuses—against "tyranny." As the eighteenth century waned, however, rapid growth rendered the city a discordant assemblage of noisily competing interests, classes, ethnicities, religions, and parties. In that milieu gangs no longer seemed to represent shared concerns. Often violent, they came to be viewed as more a threat than a boon to civil liberties. In the years after the American Revolution, popular distaste for the memory of occupying British redcoats had remained so strong that New York and other American cities had refused to establish municipal police forces. New Yorkers had abandoned that prejudice by 1845, when they established a city police force. Gangs, however, continued to thrive. Gilje, *Road to Mobocracy*, 7–14, 260–64.

35. New York *Herald*, Aug. 24, 1851; Richmond *Whig*, Aug. 26, 1851; both papers quote Rynders among the speakers at a pro-López rally in New York's City Hall Park. For background on Rynders's Empire Club and involvement in radical politics, see Mushkat, *Tammany*, 4, 208, 253.

36. Moody, *Astor Place Riot*, 111, 189–92; Nichols, *Forty Years* 2:160–61; Harris, "O'Sullivan, 190–213.

37. Spann, *New Metropolis*, 350–52; Stott, *Workers*, 205–9, 287; see also Gorn, *Manly Art*; New York *Tribune*, Sept. 1, 1849.

38. *New York Tribune*, Aug. 30, 1849; New York *Herald*, Aug. 28, 1851. For list of prisoners, see Quisenberry, *Lopez's Expeditions*, 126–29. See also New York *Tribune*, Sept. 1, 1849; May, "Young American Males and Filibustering," 857–86.

39. Bryan, "Memoirs," 7, 11, 12, Tenn. State Lib. and Archives, Nashville; Hardy, *History and Adventures*, 4.

40. New York *Tribune*, Aug. 30, Sept. 8, 1849; New York *Herald*, Aug. 28, 1851.

41. New York *Herald*, Aug. 13, 1849; New York *Tribune*, Aug. 15, 1849.

42. Figure is for 1851; post office employees numbered 21,391. Bureau of the Census, *Historical Statistics* 2:1103.

43. Weber, *Mexican Frontier*, 43–68.

44. Bauer, *Taylor*, 239–42.

45. Summers, *Plundering Generation*, 27; Nevins, *Fruits* , 174.

46. Bauer, *Taylor*, 293–94.

47. Nevins, *Fruits*, 241; Jackson *Mississippian*, May 18, 1849.

48. Taylor to John J. Crittenden, April 18, 1849, quoted in Nevins, *Fruits*, 239.

49. Bauer, *Taylor*, 268; Hamilton, *Taylor*, 219–28.

50. New York *Tribune*, Aug. 15, 1849; for the full text of the presidential message, see Richardson, *Messages and Papers of the Presidents* 4:2545, 2546.

51. New York *Herald*, Aug. 16, 1849.

52. Cincinnati *Enquirer*, Aug. 18, 1849; Detroit *Free Press*, Aug. 16, 1849.

53. Macon *Georgia Journal and Messenger*, April 4, 11, 1849.

54. New York *Herald*, Aug. 8, 1849; Baltimore *Patriot* quoted in New York *Tribune*, Aug. 30, 1849.

55. New York *Herald*, Sept. 5, 8, 1849; New York *Tribune*, Sept. 1, 1849.

56. New York *Herald*, Aug. 15, Sept. 5, 1849.

57. John Clayton to Malcolm Mearis, July 31, 1849, to James E. Harvey, Aug. 19, 1849, to Leonidas McIntosh, Aug. 27, 1849, to J. Prescott Hall, Sept. 6, 1849, entry 37, vol. 19, Records of Special Agents, RG 59, National Archives (hereafter NA).

58. A. Delmas to John Clayton, Aug. 1, 1849, D. E. Twiggs to George Crawford, July 31, 1849, *Senate Executive Documents*, 31st Cong., 1st sess., doc. no. 57, 4, 68; see also Feipel, "Navy and Filibustering."

59. New York *Herald*, Sept. 8, 1849; Thomas Gibbes Morgan to Logan Hunton, Aug. 5, 1849, Hunton to John Clayton, Aug. 8, 1849, deposition of filibuster Henry Wilson, Sept. 24, 1849, *Senate Executive Documents*, 31st Cong., 1st sess., doc. no. 57, 5–7, 107–8; William Ballard Preston to Foxhall A. Parker, Aug. 9, 1849, quoted in Feipel, "Navy and Filibustering," 770, 771.

60. Logan Hunton to John Clayton, Aug. 7, 1849, Clayton Papers, Lib. Cong.; Angel Calderón de la Barca to John Clayton, Aug. 13, 1849, in Manning, *Diplomatic Correspondence* 11:470.

61. V. M. Randolph to William Preston, Aug. 23, 28 (two letters), 1849, "Summons" of Commander Randolph, "To the Persons Encamped on Round Island, near Pascagoula," Aug. 28, 1849, Randolph to Capt. J. Thomas Newton, Aug. 29, 1849, *Senate Executive Documents*, 31st Cong., 1st sess., doc. no. 57, 76–80.

62. Remini, *Jackson*, 352–68; Reed, *Caste War*, 85, 86; Bergeron, *Polk*, 106–8, 110; May, *Southern Dream*, 40–76.

63. Bauer, *Taylor*, 293–95; Nevins, *Fruits*, 327–31.

64. Background on neutrality legislation from Leopold, *American Foreign Policy*, 36–37; "The Late Cuba State Trials," *United States Magazine and Democratic Review* 30 (April 1852): 310.

65. Bauer, *Taylor*, 244, 245, 274, 275; Clayton to Mearis, July 31, 1849, Records of Special Agents, RG 59, NA.

66. Clayton to Mearis, July 31, 1849, Records of Special Agents, RG 59, NA.

67. New York *Tribune*, Sept. 8, 1849.

68. Randolph to Preston, Sept. 5, 1849, to Lt. Commandant E. Farrand, Sept. 2, 1849, to Capt. John Thomas Newton, Sept. 4, 1849, and depositions taken from some of Round Island volunteers, *Senate Executive Documents*, 31st Cong., 1st sess., doc. no. 57, 90–94, 107–16; Portell Vilá, *López* 2:176–77; see also Feipel, "Navy and Filibustering," 776–80.

69. New York *Tribune*, Sept. 8, 1849; Clayton to Hall, telegram, Sept. 7, 1949, Records of Special Agents, RG 59, NA.

70. New York *Herald*, Aug. 22, 1849; Hardy, *History and Adventures*, 3; New Orleans *Times-Democrat*, March 30, 1884.

Chapter 3

1. New York *Herald*, Sept. 19, 1849; New Orleans *Commercial Bulletin*, Aug. 25, 1849.

2. "General Lopez, the Cuban Patriot," *United States Magazine and Democratic Review* 26 (Feb. 1850): 112; New Orleans *Delta*, Sept. 3, 1849.

3. Morales y Morales, *Iniciadores* 2:194–95.

4. Ibid., 194–95.

5. Ibid., 194–95, 151–52; Caldwell, *Lopez Expeditions*, 49; Rauch, *American Interest in Cuba*, 121.

6. O'Sullivan to Pedro de Agüero, Dec. 21, 1849, Portell Vilá, *Lopez* 2:450–51; López to Juan Manuel Macías, Dec. 3, 1849, Colección Manuscritos, Annexíon Documentos, 51, Biblioteca Nacional "José Martí," Havana; Gonzales, *Manifesto*, 8.

7. Text of Dec. 5, 1849, junta announcement, New Orleans *Delta*, Dec. 9, 1849.

8. Portell Vilá, *Narciso López* 1:243–44.

9. Hobsbawm, *Age of Revolution*, 114–16. Though popularized by the French Revolution, "liberty caps" had a history that went back to the sixteenth-century Dutch revolt and, beyond that, to ancient Rome; see Harris, "Red Cap of Liberty"; Schama, *Citizens*, 603.

10. Failed revolts in Cuba in 1810 and 1823 against the Spanish regime had Masonic roots, and many of López's comrades—in both the United States and Cuba—were active Masons. See de la Cova, "Gonzales," chaps. 2–7.

11. Wood, *Creation of the American Republic*, 319–28; Hobsbawm, *Age of Revolution*, 114–16; Gonzales, *Manifesto*, 8. See also Gilje, *Road to Mobocracy*, 7–14, 260–64.

12. Philadelphia *Public Ledger*, May 20, 1850; New Orleans *Delta*, May 26, 1850.

13. See de la Cova, "Gonzales"; Latimer, *Story of the State*, 367–72; Jones, "Gonzales"; see also Woodward, *Mary Chesnut's Civil War*, 143, 149.

14. De la Cova, "Gonzales," 44.

15. Nicholas P. Trist to Isaac E. Holmes, Dec. 6, 1848, Jane McManus Storm to Daniel Dickinson, Jan. 4, 1849, Ambrosio Gonzales to James K. Polk, March 4, 1848, Polk Papers, Lib. Cong.; de la Cova, "Gonzales," chaps. 2, 3; Ambrosio Gonzales to Mirabeau Lamar, March 14, 1851, in Gulick et al., *Papers of Lamar* 4, pt. 1:282–84.

16. Gonzales, New Orleans *Times-Democrat*, March 30, 1884; Gonzales to López, Dec. 23, 1849, quoted in Portell Vilá, *López* 2:97.

17. O'Hara later served in William Walker's filibuster and, still later, became best known as the author of "The Bivouac of the Dead," an elegiac poem now inscribed on the gateway to Arlington National Cemetery. O'Hara was also, oddly enough, the son of Kane Taylor, an Irish immigrant to the United States who, in Kentucky years earlier, had served as schoolmaster to a youthful Zachary Taylor. See Ranck, *Bivouac of the Dead and Its Author*; Hamilton, *Zachary Taylor*, 368.

18. Gonzales, New Orleans *Times-Democrat*, March 30, 1884; Portell Vilá, *López* 2:97; Hardy, *History and Adventures*, 21, 22.

19. Gonzales, New Orleans *Times-Democrat*, March 30, 1884; Hardy, *History and Adventures*, 3.

20. López to unnamed correspondent, Jan. 21, 1850, Colección Manuscritos, Annexíon Documentos, no. 47, Biblioteca Nacional "José Martí," Havana.

21. New Orleans *Times-Democrat*, March 30, 1884; Harris, "O'Sullivan," 294–95.

22. Gonzales, New Orleans *Times-Democrat*, March 3, 1884; Hardy, *History and Adventures*, 3.

23. New Orleans *Delta*, Jan. 14, 1851, as quoted in Urban, "New Orleans and the Cuban Question," 1122; Gonzales, New Orleans *Times-Democrat*, March 30, 1884.

24. See May, *Quitman*.

25. Ibid., 87.

26. Holcomb, "Mississippi Governor's Mansion"; Claiborne, *Quitman* 2:55–57; May, *Quitman*, 236–39; May, *Southern Dream*, 261–62; May, *Quitman*, 236–39.

27. John O'Sullivan to John C. Calhoun, Aug. 24, 1849, *Annual Report of the American Historical Association, 1899* 2 (1900): 1202–3; May, *Quitman*, 31, 32.

28. Richmond *Enquirer*, June 26, 1850.

29. See New Orleans *Times-Democrat*, March 30, 1884; Schlesinger, "Personal Narrative," 218;

30. See Caldwell, *Lopez Expeditions*, 78 n., 79 n.

31. In May 1850, for instance, when reports surfaced that President Taylor had dispatched navy ships toward Cuba to hunt for López, Florida's outspoken Cuban annexationist David Yulee rose in the Senate and merely questioned whether such actions met the due process demands of the U.S. Constitution. Except for the vague charge that the administration had "of late appeared to lean rather to the side of despotism than to liberal progress," Yulee expressed no direct support for López; see *Congressional Globe*, Senate, 31st Cong., 1st sess. (May 21, 1850), 1032, 1034, and ibid. (May 23, 1850), 1055. For an astute discussion of the reluctance of southern Democrats in the U.S. Senate to openly support López, see Ley, "Expansionists All?" 207–24.

32. Among the southern papers which opposed López were the Washington, D.C., *Southern Press*, the Charleston *Mercury*, the New Orleans *Commercial Bulletin*, the Macon *Georgia Journal and Messenger*, the Savannah *Republican*, the Baton Rouge *Gazette*, and the Richmond *Whig*.

33. Washington, D.C., *Southern Press*, April 30, 1851.

34. Mirabeau Lamar to Narciso López [April 1851?], in Gulick et al., *Papers of Lamar* 6:316.

35. New Orleans *Crescent*, Aug. 27, 1849.

36. Howard, *Political Tendencies in Louisiana*, 23.

37. Undated editorial from Richmond *Whig* quoted in the Philadelphia *Public Ledger*, Sept. 4, 1851.

38. Philadelphia *Public Ledger*, Sept. 4, 1851, Aug. 22, 1849.

39. Hobsbawm, *The Age of Revolution*, 114–16; New Orleans *Delta*, Sept. 2, 1849.

40. Goode, *Outdoor Sculpture of Washington*, 60.

41. See Paquette, *Sugar Is Made with Blood*, 131–205.

42. *Congressional Globe*, Senate, 30th Cong., 1st sess. (March 28, 1848), 549; ibid. (March 30, 1848), 567–70; ibid. (April 3, 1848), 580–81; ibid. (April 6, 1848), 590–92; Ley, "Expansionists All?," 193–97; *Appendix to the Congressional Globe*, Senate, 31st Cong., 1st sess. (Jan. 31, 1850), 85.

43. Washington, D.C., *Southern Press*, Aug. 7, April 30, 1851.

44. Philadelphia *Public Ledger*, Sept. 4, 1851.

45. Twain, *Life on the Mississippi*, 243.

46. Cable, *Lost New Orleans*, 47–50, 170–71.

47. De Bow, *Statistical View* (1850 federal census), 4:248–49.

48. Mott, *American Journalism*, 248–50.

49. Asbury, *French Quarter*, 155–78.

50. *Cohen's New Orleans Directory*, 175; Rauch, *American Interest in Cuba*, 125, 126; Asbury, *French Quarter*, 172–80; Cable, *Lost New Orleans*, 156, 157; Schott, *Norman's New Orleans*, 156–57. The latter work remains an indispensable guide to the architecture and physical layout of mid-nineteenth century New Orleans.

51. Urban, "New Orleans and the Cuban Question," 1122–24.

52. Morales y Morales, *Iniciadores*, 19–21, 190–91, 196; Gonzales, *Manifesto*, 11.

53. Gonzales, *Manifesto*, 11.

54. John Clayton to Logan Hunton, Jan. 22, 1850, introduced as evidence against López by New Orleans's U.S. Attorney Logan Hunton, in entry 21, case 6685, General Case Files, U.S. District Court, Eastern District of Louisiana, New Orleans, RG 21, NA, SW Region, Fort Worth, Texas.

55. Patriotic junta for the promotion of the political interests of Cuba, promissory note for $2,000 and Cuban lands, given in return for aid to Cuban expedition of 1850 (New Orleans, 1850), in Bancroft Lib., Univ. of California, Berkeley; see also Brown, *Agents of Manifest*, 56.

56. Johannsen, *To the Halls*, 66; Davis, *History of the Late Expedition*, 3, 4.

57. Hardy, *History and Adventures*, 18.

58. Schott, *Norman's New Orleans*, 201.

59. Tansey, "Southern Expansionism," 230.

60. Sinclair, *New Orleans*, 175–76.

61. Tansey, "Southern Expansionism," 229, 230.

62. New York *Herald*, Aug. 19, 1848; see also Schlesinger, *Almanac of American History*, 255.

63. Tansey, "Southern Expansionism," 229–32; see also New Orleans *Delta*, Sept. 17, 1849.

64. Charleston *Daily Courier*, May 29, 1850; Thomas R. Hietala, *Manifest Design*, 71–83; "Free Trade," *Democratic Review* 14 (March 1844): 301.

65. Hietala, *Manifest Design*, 71–73.

66. *Appendix to the Congressional Globe*, Senate, 31st Cong., 1st sess. (March 13, 14, 1850), 365.

67. Tansey, "Southern Expansionism," 233; New Orleans *Crescent*, May 24, 1850; Goetzmann, *When the Eagle Screamed*, 76, 77.

68. *De Bow's Review* 12 (Jan.1852): 84.

69. Partially, Cuba's high ranking among U.S. export customers arose from the fact that Louisiana could supply only about one-third of the nation's sugar demand. It also may be attributed to the fact that, at midcentury, the U.S. still had few substantial trad-

ing partners. In the Caribbean and the Pacific, the British and French still maintained formidable barriers to keep U.S. commerce out of their far-flung colonies. See Ely, "Old Cuba Trade," 457–58.

70. Urban, "New Orleans and the Cuban Question," 1101, 1102.

71. Washington, D.C., *Southern Press*, Aug. 11, 1851; Jackson *Mississippian*, May 10, 1850.

72. Tansey, "Southern Expansionism," 249.

73. Ibid., 239.

74. Ibid., 238–40. New Orleans *Delta*, June 9, 1850. In his biography of Jefferson Davis, the poet Allen Tate called Prentiss "the most famous orator of the south before the rise of William Lowndes Yancey." While, according to a contemporary source, Prentiss "condemn[ed]" filibustering, he also admired López and considered him "sincere and a patriot." Dickey, *Prentiss*, 223 n., 399, 400; Prentiss, *Prentiss* 2:554–55 n.

75. Hardy, *History and Adventures*, 3–5.

76. Ibid., 4; Taylor, "Diary," 80

77. Cincinnati *Enquirer*, April 6, 1850.

78. Ibid., April 6, 1840; Hardy, *History and Adventures*, 6.

79. Hardy, *History and Adventures*, 8, 9.

80. Ibid., 8–11.

81. Ibid., 8, 10, 11; Taylor, "*Diary*," 80.

82. Hardy, *History and Adventures*, 10, 11.

83. Taylor, "Diary," 80, 81.

84. Juan Y. Laborde to Captain General José de la Concha, March 25, 1851, in Asuntos Politicos, legato 44, sig. 32, Archivo Nacional, Havana; de la Cova, "Gonzales," 26; Hardy, *History and Adventures*, 11, 12.

85. James Robb to Zachary Taylor, May 6, 1850, *Senate Executive Documents*, 31st Cong, 1st sess., doc. no. 57, 49, 50.

86. Cable, *Lost New Orleans*, 109–11.

87. Hardy, *History and Adventures*, 11–12.

88. Undated Baltimore *Sun* story quoted in Cincinnati *Enquirer*, April 6, 1850; New York *Herald*, April 15, 1850; Rauch, *American Interest in Cuba*, 64; New Orleans *Delta*, May 14, 1850.

Chapter 4

1. Hardy, *History and Adventures*, 16.

2. Ibid., 6, 12, 16; Caldwell, *Lopez Expeditions*; Hardy, *History and Adventures*, 6, 16.

3. Hardy, *History and Adventures*, 6, 16; Taylor, "Diary," 81; Benson identified and *Georgiana* described in *Ship Registers of New Orleans, Louisiana* 4:114, 115.

4. Hardy, *History and Adventures*, 16; Taylor, "Diary," 81.

5. Hardy, *History and Adventures*, 18.

6. Sinclair, *New Orleans*, 3, 267.

7. Hardy, *History and Adventures*, 18–20.

8. Ibid., 19–20; Taylor, "Diary," 81.

9. Hardy, *History and Adventures*, 20, 23; Taylor, "Diary," 81; *Ship Registers of New Orleans* 4:114, 115.

10. Sources differ on the date of the Contoy landing: Hardy, May 7; Taylor, May 6 (Hardy, *History and Adventures*, 23, Taylor, "Diary," 82). Since Hardy's is the more exacting account, the text defers to his chronology.

11. Hardy, *History and Adventures*, 24, Taylor, "Diary," 82; Stephens, *Incidents of Travel in Yucatan* 2:357.

12. Hardy, *History and Adventures*, 23–25; Taylor, "Diary," 82.

13. See Johannsen, *To the Halls*, 30, 38, 40–44; McCaffrey, *Army of Manifest Destiny*, 129–46.

14. Hobsbawm, *Age of Revolution*, 114–16; New Orleans *Delta*, May 26, 1850; Taylor, "Diary," 84; Deposition of Round Island filibuster Charles Wilson, *Senate Executive Documents*, 31st Cong., 1st sess., doc. no. 57, 110–12; Davis, *History of the Late Expedition*, 39.

15. Jackson *Mississippian*, May 10, 1850; Hardy, *History and Adventures*, 17; López quoted in filibuster broadside in entry 21, case 6685, General Case Files, U.S. District Court, Eastern District of Louisiana, New Orleans, RG 21, NA, SW Region, Fort Worth, Texas.

16. New Orleans *Delta*, May 17, 1850; Hardy, *History and Adventures*, 5; Bauer, *Mexican War*, 397. See also New Orleans *Delta*, May 23, 1850.

17. See Royster, *Revolutionary People at War*; Martin and Lender, *Respectable Army*.

18. McCaffrey, *Army of Manifest Destiny*, 117; Johannsen, *To the Halls*, 64; Hardy, *History and Adventures*, 9, 32.

19. Johannsen, *To the Halls*, 40, 41; Hardy, *History and Adventures*, 6; "W.H.B." (apparently Lt. Col. W. H. Bell of the Louisiana regiment; see ibid., 70–71), undated letter, quoted in Davis, *History of the Late Expedition*, 45, 46.

20. Hardy, *History and Adventures*, 25–29.

21. Johannsen, *To the Halls*, 27, 28; Hardy, *History and Adventures*, 9, 32. Passing, anecdotal references to individuals in primary sources suggests that López's filibusters were exclusively white and male—and most were young. Beyond that, they constituted a socially and geographically broad sampling of the population. No roster, however, of any of López's armies has been located. A list of 135 filibusters captured by the Spanish in 1851 and sent to hard labor does provide an illuminating—if random and incomplete—glimpse into the demography of López's last expeditionary army. The docu-

ment contains both the ages and occupations of those listed. Unlike the spring 1850 expedition, which seemed to be composed exclusively of men from the United States, the fall 1851 army contained numerous foreigners: those from the United States numbered 89, foreigners 53. Ages ranged from 16 to 40. The average age of all men listed was 24.6—that of those from the United States was 24.1, that of the foreigners 25.7. Among those from the United States, "clerks" comprised the largest occupational group, with 24. "Boatmen" ran second, with 9. The occupational status of the rest of the listed soldiers—both U.S. and foreign—ranged across a broad array of skilled and unskilled vocations. Most, however, listed themselves as members of skilled occupations—including farmers, bricklayers, engineers, butchers, and merchants. See Quisenberry, *Lopez's Expeditions* , 126–29.

22. Hardy, *History and Adventures*, 23, 25; Davis, *History of the Late Expedition*, 18, 19; McCaffrey, *Army of Manifest Destiny*, 16, 17; Boggess, *Veteran of Four Wars*, 10.

23. Weigley, 110–11; Bauer, *Mexican War*, 33, 34; Johannsen, *To the Halls*, 42; Hardy, *History and Adventures*, 5, 23; Davis, *History of the Late Expedition*, 18, 19, 39; Taylor, "Diary," 85.

24. McCaffrey, *Army of Manifest Destiny*, 106–10; Hardy, *History and Adventures*, 28.

25. Davis, *History of the Late Expedition*, 20.

26. Hardy, *History and Adventures*, 27, 36, 31, 32.

27. Boggess, *Veteran of Four Wars*, 10.

28. Hardy, *History and Adventures*, 28, 29.

29. Ibid., 29; date of ceremoney from Taylor, "Diary," 84.

30. Davis, *History of the Late Expedition*, 4–6, 21.

31. Dufour, *Gentle Tiger*.

32. Hardy, *History and Adventures*, 9, 31; Rauch, *American Interest in Cuba*,126; Davis, *History of the Late Expedition*, 21.

33. Davis, *History of the Late Expedition*, 17.

34. Ibid., 17; Rauch, *American Interest in Cuba*, 62; Cirilo Villaverde, "Nuestra Bandera," Feb. 12, 1873 (letter to editor of *La Revolución de Cuba* newspaper in New York), in Morales y Morales, *Iniciadores* 2:167–71.

35. Angel Calderón de la Barca to John Calhoun, May 16, 1850, in Manning, *Diplomatic Correspondence: Inter-American Affairs* 11:479–80; Urban, "New Orleans and the Cuban Question," 1123; Hardy, *History and Adventures*, 5, 32; Davis, *History of the Late Expedition*, 24; sales receipt for *Creole*, in entry 21, case 6685, General Case Files, U.S. District Court, Eastern District of Louisiana, New Orleans, RG 21, NA, SW Region, Fort Worth, Texas.

36. Davis, *History of the Late Expedition*, 22–24; John M. Clayton to Calderón de la Barca, May 18, 1850, *Senate Executive Documents*, 31st Cong., 1st sess., doc. no. 57, 29–31.

37. Davis, *History of the Late Expedition*, 23, 24.

38. Deposition by Simeon Pendleton, master mariner from Boston, June 3, 1850, *House Executive Documents,* 32d Cong., 1st sess., doc. no. 83, 154–56; Davis, *History of the Late Expedition,* 24, 25; Hardy, *History and Adventures,* 31.

39. Davis, *History of the Late Expedition,* 24, 25, 30, 31.

40. Hardy, *History and Adventures,* 32.

41. Ibid., 23, 32; Davis, *History of the Late Expedition,* 32.

42. Hardy, *History and Adventures,* 33, 34; broadside, in entry 21, case 6685, General Case Files, U.S. District Court, Eastern District of Louisiana, New Orleans, RG 21, NA, SW Region, Fort Worth, Texas.

43. Davis, *History of the Late Expedition,* 33.

44. Ibid., 30–33; Hardy, *History and Adventures,* 34.

45. Davis, *History of the Late Expedition,* 33.

46. McCaffrey, *Army of Manifest Destiny,* 129; Johannsen, *To the Halls,* 89, 155–57, 161, 171.

47. Johannsen, *To the Halls,* 165, 166, 281.

48. Davis, *History of the Late Expedition,* 40, 42; New Orleans *Delta,* June 15, 1850.

49. Davis, *History of the Late Expedition,* 9, 10.

50. Ibid., 10. See Merk, *Manifest Destiny,* 160, 161, 223. As to why Cuba's Creoles did not rise up on their own against the Spanish but, instead, required outside liberators to effect their revolution, the New Orleans *Delta,* on June 14, 1850, provided an equally convenient answer to that question: "They live on an island which can be surrounded and blockaded by a naval force and against which the powers of foreign nations can be concentrated. A navy cannot be created by an unorganized people, however unanimous for change and revolution. The Creoles have no widespread country to retreat and operate in, as the patriots of this country, of Mexico, and South America had. Despite these great disadvantages, however, they are ready and willing for the effort. They only ask a little sympathy, encouragement, and aide, from a people who they have learned to regard as invincible." New Orleans *Delta,* June 14, 1850.

51. Davis, *History of the Late Expedition,* 34, 35, 37–39.

52. Ibid., 38–39; Johannsen, *To the Halls,* 30–39.

53. Davis, *History of the Late Expedition,* 39.

54. Ibid., 43–44.

55. Hardy, *History and Adventures,* 35; Taylor, "Diary," 84; Davis, *History of the Late Expedition,* 44.

56. Theodore O'Hara, report of events, June 26, 1850, in Hardy, *History and Adventures,* 65, 66; ibid., 35.

57. Davis, *History of the Late Expedition,* 50; the *Creole,* ship's master, Armstrong Irvine Lewis, and owner, William H. White, listed in *Ship Registers of New Orleans* 4:65.

58. Hardy, *History and Adventures*, 35–36.

59. Ibid.; Theodore O'Hara, report of events, June 26, 1850, ibid., 65, 66; Davis, *History of the Late Expedition*, 58.

60. Hardy, *History and Adventures*, 36.

61. Ibid., 36–37.

62. Ibid., 37; Taylor, "Diary," 85.

63. Hardy, *History and Adventures*, 38; Pérez, *Cuba and the United States:*, 20; interview with Ana Gloria Mesa, researcher at Museo "Oscar Maria de Rojas," Cárdenas, Cuba, Jan. 28, 1995; War Department, *Military Notes on Cuba*, 309.

64. Hardy, *History and Adventures*, 38, 39.

65. Ibid.; War Department, *Military Notes on Cuba*, 308–10; Davis, *History of the Late Expedition*, 65.

66. Davis, *History of the Late Expedition*, 65; Brown, *Agents of Manifest Destiny*, 62, 63. Hardy, *History and Adventures*, 38–39, gives a slightly different account of the landing at Cárdenas, stating that the *Creole*'s captain, A. J. Lewis, swam ashore with the rope; on this particular incident, however, Davis's account comports with, among other sources, Gonzales's memoir in New Orleans *Times-Democrat*, March 30, 1884.

67. Hardy, *History and Adventures*, 38–39; Quisenberry, *Lopez's Expeditions*, 54, 55.

68. Hardy, *History and Adventures*, 39–40.

69. Taylor, "Diary," 85; Hardy, *History and Adventures*, 40.

70. Hardy, *History and Adventures*, 41.

71. Ibid., 40–41; Davis, *History of the Late Expedition*, 70–71.

72. Hardy, *History and Adventures*, 41–42; Davis, *History of the Late Expedition*, 71.

73. Davis, *History of the Late Expedition*, 50; Hardy, *History and Adventures*, 42.

74. Hardy, *History and Adventures*, 41–42.

75. Davis, *History of the Late Expedition*, 65–66; Quisenberry, *Lopez's Expeditions*, 57; William S. Pickett, report of events, June 26, 1850, in Hardy, *History and Adventures*, 68.

76. William S. Pickett, report of events, June 26, 1850, in Hardy, *History and Adventures*, 68; W. H. Bell, report of events, June 26, 1850, ibid., 71.

77. Davis, *History of the Late Expedition*, 72; W. H. Bell, report of events, June 26, 1850, Hardy, *History and Adventures*, 71; Portell Vilá, *López* 2:346–49; John Bagley to unknown correspondent ["My dearest"], May 20, 1850, in Despatches from U.S. Consuls in Matanzas, 1820–99, vol. 4, NA.

78. Davis, *History of the Late Expedition*, 72, 73; Caldwell, *Lopez Expeditions*, 69, 70.

79. Davis, *History of the Late Expedition*, 73; Hardy, *History and Adventures*, 42, 43.

80. Hardy, *History and Adventures*, 44, 45; W. R. Hackley to John Clayton, May 22, 1850, *Senate Executive Documents*, 31st Cong., 1st sess., doc. no. 57, 47–48.

81. Hardy, *History and Adventures*, 45.

82. Ibid., 45; Davis, *History of the Late Expedition*, 77. While Hardy suggests that 200 filibusters were evacuated to the island, Davis's assertion of 90 seems, in the context of his more detailed account of this episode, the more plausible figure.

83. Hardy, *History and Adventures*, 46,-47; Davis, *History of the Late Expedition*, 77.

84. Hardy, *History and Adventures*, 46–47; Davis, *History of the Late Expedition*, 79–82.

85. Hardy, *History and Adventures*, 47; Davis, *History of the Late Expedition*, 79–82.

86. Hardy *History and Adventures*, 47.

87. [Federal] Writers' Program, WPA, Florida, *Guide to Key West*, 21, 55; Hardy, *History and Adventures*, 47, 48; Browne, *Key West*, 112–14, 162–66; De Bow, *Seventh Census* 1:401.

88. Hardy, *History and Adventures*, 47, 48, Davis, *History of the Late Expedition*, 79–82; Browne, *Key West*, 12, 78, 79, 116; Francisco Avenero to John Clayton, May [22], 1850, Francisco Avenero to "the Spanish consul at Key West," May 22, 1850, *House Executive Documents*, 32d Cong., 1st sess., doc. no. 83, 44–46.

89. Boggess, *Veteran of Four Wars*, 24; Hackley to Clayton, May 22, 1850, *Senate Executive Documents*, 31st Cong., 1st sess., doc. no. 57, 47–48; Hardy, *History and Adventures*, 49.

90. Hardy, *History and Adventures*, 49–51.

91. Ibid., 50–51; New Orleans *Times-Democrat*, March 30, 1884.

92. New York *Tribune*, June 11, 1850; Hardy, *History and Adventures*, 51–54; Taylor, "Diary," 87–89.

Chapter 5

1. Savannah *Georgian*, May 27, 1850; New York *Tribune*, May 31, 1850; Savannah *Morning News*, March 17, 1935; Northern, *Men of Mark in Georgia* 2:295–97; Mott, *American Magazines*, 606–7.

2. Savannah *Republican*, May 28, 1850; Savannah *Daily Morning News*, May 27, 1850; Bell, "City Hotel," 552–55; Henry Williams to John Clayton, May 27, 1850, Correspondence on the Lopez Expedition, RG 59, NA.

3. J. Prentiss Hall to John Clayton, May 28, 1850, Correspondence on the Lopez Expedition, RG 59, NA.

4. Clayton to Paul Hamilton telegram alluded to in Hamilton to Clayton, May 31, 1850, ibid.

5. "The Land of the Cherokee," *United States Magazine and Democratic Review* 28 (April 1851): 321.

6. New York *Evening Post*, May 25, 1850.

7. New Orleans *Delta*, May 26, 1850; Baltimore *Sun*, June 7, 1850.

8. New Orleans *Picayune*, June 6, 1850; Cincinnati *Enquirer*, Aug. 30,1851.

9. Gonzales, New Orleans *Times-Democrat*, March 30, 1884.

10. See Crouthamel, *Bennett's New York* Herald, 43–45; Emery, *The Press and America*, 160, 161, 166, 169, 192, 195, 201–2; Mott, *American Journalism*, 312–16.

11. Merk, *Manifest Destiny*, 56; Johannsen, *To the Halls*, 129.

12. Philadelphia *Public Ledger*, Sept. 4, 1851; Jackson *Mississippian*, May 10, 1850.

13. Boston *Daily Times*, Aug. 26, 1851; Memphis Daily *Appeal*, July 28, 1851.

14. Hardy, *History and Adventures*, 7, 20, 21, 46; Ranck, *Bivouac of the Dead*, 33.

15. Portell Vilá, *López* 2:364.

16. U.S. diplomacy secured Thrasher's release in 1852, but he continued to mix journalism and political activism. In the spring of 1863, with headquarters in Atlanta, he became superintendent of the Press Association of the Confederate States of America, a news service for newspapers of the fledgling southern nation. See Webster, *Diplomatic Papers* 2:341–49; Allen Ferdinand Owen to Daniel Webster, Dec. 2, 1851, John S. Thrasher to U.S. Government, Nov. 21, 1852, ibid., 408–11; also Rauch, *American Interest in Cuba*, 54, 172; Eaton, *Southern Confederacy*, 220, 221.

17. Durkin, *Mallory*, 32.

18. Nerone, "Mythology of the Penny Press."

19. Emery, *Press and America*, 160; Mott, *American Journalism*, 203, 216, 237; De Bow, *Statistical View*, 155, 156.

20. Mott, *American Journalism*, 232, 294, 295; Crouthamel, *Bennett's New York* Herald, 19–42.

21. Mott, *American Journalism*, 244, 245, 248–50; see also Winston, "New Orleans Newspapers and the Texas Question," and "Attitude of the Newspapers," 161.

22. Barker, "United States and Mexico," 8; Winston, "Attitude of the Newspapers," 160–65, 174; Summers, *Plundering Generation*, 37–41.

23. Leonard, *Power of the Press*, 63–96.

24. Nevins, *Fruits*, 7–8.

25. Mott, *American Journalism*, 256, 257.

26. Bauer, *Taylor*, 215–16, 239. *Savannah Republican*, April 15, 1847; Baton Rouge *Gazette*, May 4, 1850, paraphrasing an item from the Feliciana, La., *Whig*.

27. New York *Herald*, Aug. 31, 1835; Emery, *The Press and America*, 169–71; Crouthamel, *Bennett's New York* Herald, 64–65; Van Deusen, *Horace Greeley*, 371–72, 388, 391, 392, 404–6.

28. New Orleans *Delta*, March 20, 1850; Youngman, "Historic Sketches," 14, 29, New Orleans Public Lib.

29. New Orleans *Delta*, Sept. 1, 1849.

30. Nevins, *Fruits*, 355; Tremenheere, *Notes*, 133.

31. Horace Greeley to Schuyler Colfax, Sept. 15, 1848, quoted in Nevins, *Fruits*, 209; New York *Sun*, Dec. 11, 1847, quoted in Merk, *Manifest Destiny*, 138.

32. Merk, *Manifest Destiny*, 123, 154; New York *Herald*, Aug. 16, 23, Dec. 6, 1849, Jan. 6, 1851; Crouthamel, *Bennett's New York* Herald, 62, 63.

33. New York *Tribune*, Aug. 28, 1851; New Orleans *Delta*, Feb. 14, 1850; Gonzales, *Manifesto*, 11.

34. Quaife, *Diary of Polk* 2:483.

35. Thomas Ewing, Sr., to Logan Hunton, June 10, 1850, RG 48, NA; New York *Herald*, Oct. 6, 1849.

36. Kaplan, *Walt Whitman*, 128–30; Rubin, *Historic Whitman*, 144, 145; Whitman, *Gathering of Forces* 1:240–42; Tremenheere, *Notes*, 135, 136.

37. New York *Sun*, May 24, 1850, as reprinted in the New York *Herald*, May 25, 1850. Extant issues of the *Sun* from his period, both originals and microfilmed copies, are rare; and the author was unable to locate this issue quoted in the *Herald*.

38. New York *Herald*, May 25, 1850.

39. Emery, *The Press and America*, 169; New York *Herald*, March 26, 1851.

40. Looking back on his own career—and no doubt overstating the impact of his own wire service—Daniel H. Craig, a manager of the New York Associated Press before the Civil War, in 1873 reflected, "Previous to this organization, in 1850, there was no regular or systematized arrangement for gathering the general domestic news of the country by telegraph." And when wire dispatches were received, newspaper editors showed no reverence toward any imagined empirical integrity. As Craig recalled, once "a few words" did reach their intended newspaper, in-house writers were called upon "to draw upon their imaginations for [the story's] details" and to write up and sell to "the editors nearly as many paragraphs as there had been words telegraphed." Baltimore *Sun*, Sept. 14, 1849; New York *Herald*, Aug. 15, 1849; Craig quoted in Schiller, *Objectivity and the News*, 4, 5.

41. New Orleans *Delta*, Aug. 18, Sept. 2, 1849.

42. Ibid., June 1, 1850.

43. Indeed, the depth of self-consciousness about reporting processes among editors, and presumably readers, recalls art historian Neil Harris's notion of an "operational aesthetic" in nineteenth-century American culture; in their appreciation of both the "high" and the popular arts of their day, Harris argues, nineteenth-century Americans reveled in an "instinctive pleasure in uncovering process." They focused as much on the internal workings—the mechanics—of artifice as much as on the finished product. Harris, *Humbug*, 82.

44. Baltimore *Sun*, May 27, 1850.

45. Savannah *Republican*, May 31, 28, 1850.

Chapter 6

1. Paul Hamilton to John Clayton, May 30, 31, 1850, Correspondence on the Lopez Expedition, RG 59, NA.

2. See Clayton to Logan Hunton, Jan. 22, 1850, in Manning, *Diplomatic Correspondence: Inter-American Affairs* 11:74.

3. Text of López's letter and account of arrest in New Orleans *Delta*, June 8, 1850.

4. Ibid; Schott, *Norman's New Orleans*, 127–29.

5. Hunton to Clayton, June 7, 1850, Clayton to Hunton, June 10, 1850, Correspondence on the Lopez Expedition, RG 59, NA; obituary of Hunton, New Orleans *Times Picayune*, June 30, 1880.

6. Clayton to Hunton, June 9, 1850, Correspondence on the Lopez Expedition, RG 59, NA; Manning, *Diplomatic Correspondence: Inter-American Affairs* 11:83 n.

7. Benjamin first appeared in court for the prosecution on June 12. New Orleans *Delta*, June 13, 1850.

8. As the hearing progressed, three other lawyers joined the defense team: John C. Larue to replace an ill Prentiss on June. 10; after Larue, a state court judge, was called away on judicial proceedings, "Col. Field," Randall Hunt, and "Mr. Moise" on June 13 joined the team. Ibid., June 11, 14, 1850.

9. Thomas Ewing, Sr., to Logan Hunton, June 17, 1850, Records concerning the Cuban Expedition, RG 48, NA; Hunton to Clayton, June 22, 1850, Clayton Papers, Lib. Cong.; New Orleans *Delta*, June 8, 1850.

10. New Orleans *Delta*, June 8, 1850; New Orleans *Picayune*, June 7, 1850.

11. New Orleans *Delta*, June 8, 1850.

12. Ibid.

13. Ibid., June 9, 1850; Urban, "New Orleans and the Cuban Question," 1133.

14. New Orleans *Delta*, June 12, 18, 1850; *Cohen's New Orleans Directory*, 174; obituary of Sigur in New Orleans *Commercial Bulletin*, Sept. 21, 1858.

15. New Orleans *Delta*, June 9, 11, 12, 14, 1850; New Orleans *Picayune*, June 9, 1850; Urban, "New Orleans and the Cuban Question," 1133–34.

16. New Orleans *Delta*, June 16, 18, 1850; New Orleans *True Delta*, June 15, 16, 18, 1850; Urban, "New Orleans and the Cuban Question," 1133.

17. The others indicted were N. J. Bunce, Peter Smith, R. Hayden, Thomas T. Hawkins, and W. H. Bell; see Caldwell, *Lopez Expeditions*, 78 n., 79 n.

18. Bauer, *Taylor*, 314–15.

19. Ibid., 315.

20. Webster, *Writings and Speeches* 16:423.

21. Bauer, *Taylor*, 273, 278, 283–88.

22. For the full text of Taylor's message, see Richardson, *Messages and Papers of the Presidents* 6:2547–62.

23. Bauer, *Taylor*, 297.

24. William H. Seward to Thurlow Weed, Dec. 3, 1849, quoted in Bauer, *Taylor*, 298. See also ibid., 289–313; Nevins, *Fruits*, 251–52.

25. Grayson, *Fillmore*, 11–38; Nevins, *Fruits*, 335–45.

26. Bauer, *Taylor*, 310; Nevins, *Fruits*, 335–45.

27. Calderón de la Barca to Daniel Webster, Aug. 2, 1850, in Webster, *Diplomatic Papers* 2:349–58.

28. Logan Hunton to Webster, Oct. 2, 1850, Records concerning the Cuban Expedition, RG 48, NA.

29. See *House Executive Documents* 83, 32d Cong., 1st sess., doc. no. 83, 1–179.

30. Logan Hunton to Webster, Oct. 2, 1850, in Records concerning the Cuban Expedition, RG 48, NA. With the exception of a four-year period (1854–58), Goddard served as Washington police chief from 1842 to 1861. Bryan, *National Capital* 2:274, 403 n., 462.

31. John Goddard to Thomas Ewing, Sr., June 15, 17, July 8, 1850, Goddard to Alexander Stuart, Nov. 15, 23, Dec. 12, 1850, and [March 1851], Records concerning the Cuban Expedition, RG 48, NA.

32. Miller, *Spying for America*, 79, 130; see also Nelson, *Secret Agents*, 72–95.

33. Burtnett, "Lopez's Expeditions," 351.

34. Bureau of the Census, *Historical Statistics* 2:1103; De Bow, *Statistical View* 4:31; W. C. Maloney to unknown, May 21, 1850, William R. Hackley to Zachary Taylor, June 6, 1850, Records concerning the Cuban Expedition, RG 48, NA.

35. As North-South sectional tensions increased immediately before the Civil War, political representatives of both regions, already contemplating possible war, were wary of preserving a large standing army. Thus, the sectional crisis and other, traditional republican concerns about regular armies kept the U.S. regular army relatively small until the war's actual commencement. Total troop strength for the U.S. regular army in 1860 stood at 16,000; a year later, it had risen to 187,000. Weigley, *United States Army*, 567.

36. Schlesinger, *Age of Jackson*, 518.

37. Nevins, *Fruits*, 163; Bauer, *Taylor*, 273.

38. The Judiciary Act of 1789 called for the appointment of a person "learned in the law" to represent the United States in the Supreme Court and, when called upon, to provide legal advice to the president and department heads. Revelations about expenditures by other departments for outside legal advice during the Civil War led, in 1870, to the expansion of the attorney general's office and its elevation to a cabinet-level executive department. Short, *National Administrative Organization*, 101, 102.

39. Nevins, *Fruits*, 227, 228; Interior Department budget and description of duties, *House Executive Documents*, 31st Cong., 2d sess., doc. no. 1, 25–246.

40. John Clayton to Logan Hunton, June 9, 1850, Correspondence on the Lopez Expedition, RG 59, NA; Thomas Ewing, Sr., to Logan Hunton, June 10, 1850, Records concerning the Cuban Expedition, RG 48, NA.

41. Nevins, *Fruits*, 159–63, 227, 228.

42. Ibid., 227, 228; Hyman and Wiecek, *Equal Justice*, 199, 200.

43. James E. Harvey to Clayton, Aug. 13, 1849, Records of Special Agents, RG 59, NA.

44. Hardy, 51; V. M. Randolph to William Ballard Preston, *Senate Executive Documents* 31st Cong., 1st sess., doc. no. 57, 87–89.

45. Goddard to Stuart [circa March 1851], Records concerning the Cuban Expedition, RG 48, NA.

46. Hunton to Clayton, May 23, 1850, Correspondence on the Lopez Expedition, RG 59, NA.

47. Paul Hamilton to Clayton, May 30, 1850, ibid.

48. Miller, *Spying for America*, 129 n.

49. Goddard to Stuart, Nov. 23, 1850, Records concerning the Cuban Expedition, RG 48, NA; Millard Fillmore to Daniel Webster, Sept. 2, 1851, in Webster, *Diplomatic Papers* 2:372–74; Burtnett, "Lopez's Expeditions," 351.

50. "Bonds of Destiny," 151, 152; Goddard to Stuart, June 15, 1850, Records concerning the Cuban Expedition, RG 48, NA; Angel Calderón de la Barca to Clayton, June 22, 1850, in Manning, *Diplomatic Correspondence: Inter-American Affairs* 11:509–10.

51. Angel Calderón de la Barca to Clayton, June 22, 1850, in Manning, *Diplomatic Correspondence: Inter-American Affairs* 11:509, 510; Lt. H. J. Hartstene to John Quitman, May 26, 1850, Quitman Papers, Miss. State Dept. of Archives and History.

52. See O'Sullivan, "Late Cuba State Trials," 307, 307 n., 308, 310.

53. New Orleans *Delta*, Jan. 7, 1851.

54. Ibid.; O'Sullivan, "Late Cuba State Trials," 310.

55. New Orleans *Delta*, Jan. 7, 1851.

56. Urban, "New Orleans and the Cuban Question," 1136–37.

57. May, *Quitman*, 242, 243, 248; Hunton to Samuel J. Gholson, July 26, 1850, Harris to Fillmore, Nov. 10, 1850, Records concerning the Cuban Expedition, RG 48, NA.

58. May, *Quitman*, 249; New Orleans *Delta*, March 14, 1851.

59. New Orleans *Picayune*, quoted in the New Orleans *Delta*, Feb. 11, 1851; and *Delta* editorial from same issue.

60. May, *Quitman*, 251.

61. New Orleans *Delta*, Feb. 14, 1851; Urban, "New Orleans and the Cuban Question," 1136–37.

62. New Orleans *Delta*, March 8, 1851; Urban, "New Orleans and the Cuban Question," 1137.

63. Goddard to Stuart [circa March 1851], in Records concerning the Cuban Expedition, RG 48, NA.

Chapter 7

1. New Orleans *Times-Democrat*, April 6, 1884; Harris, "O'Sullivan," 306, 307; New York *Herald*, April 28, 1851; Gonzales, *Manifesto*, 10.

2. New Orleans *Delta*, May 8, 1851; New York *Herald*, April 28, 1851; Burtnett, "Lopez's Expeditions."

3. Angel Calderón de la Barca to Daniel Webster, July 26, 1850, alluded to in Webster to Calderón de la Barca, Sept. 3, 1850, in Webster, *Diplomatic Papers* 2:358, 359; see also Juan Y. Laborde to Calderón de la Barca, Oct. 2, 1850, Calderón de la Barca to Webster, Oct. 10, 1850, in Manning, *Diplomatic Correspondence: Inter-American Affairs* 11:574 and n., 575.

4. Schlesinger, "Personal Narrative," 211.

5. John O'Sullivan to John Quitman, June 26, 1850, Quitman Papers, Miss. State Dept. of Archives and History.

6. Portell Vilá, *López* 2:436; see also de la Cova, "Gonzales," 137–40, 169–70.

7. John Henderson to John Quitman, Nov. 6, 1850, in Claiborne, *Quitman* 2:69–71.

8. Gonzales, *Manifesto*,10; New Orleans *Times-Democrat*, April 6, 1884; Portell Vilá, *López* 3:90.

9. John O'Sullivan to John Quitman, June 26, 1850, Quitman Papers, Miss. Dept. of Archives and History; Narciso López to Juan Macías, Jan. 7, 1851, Miscellaneous MSS Collection, Lib. Cong.; see also Portell Vilá, *Narciso López* 3:90.

10. Ambrosio Gonzales to Mirabeau Lamar, March 14, 1851, in Gulick, *Papers of Lamar*, 4, pt. 1:282–84; unsigned letter from informer in Savannah to Henry Lytton Bulwer, April 12, 1851, in Manning, *Diplomatic Correspondence: Inter-American Affairs* 7:433 n.; Gonzales, *Manifesto*; New Orleans *Times-Democrat*, April 6, 1884.

11. New Orleans *Picayune*, May 6, 1851; Burtnett, "Lopez's Expeditions," 352–53; Caldwell, *Lopez Expedition*, 83–85; Harris, "O'Sullivan," 306–8.

12. Gonzales, *Manifesto*, 10; interview with John Christian, director of Bryan-Lang Historical Library, Woodbine, Ga., Feb. 6, 1996; Newark *Advertiser* dispatch dated April 25, 1851, reprinted in New York *Tribune*, May 2, 1851.

13. Schlesinger, "Personal Narrative," 211.

14. Hardy, *History and Adventures*, 4, 5.

15. Schlesinger, "Personal Narrative," 211; Harris, "O'Sullivan," 303, 306, 307; Gonzales, *Manifesto*, 10.

16. Concha, *Memorias*, 134, 136, 174, 201.

17. Caldwell, *Lopez Expeditions*, 79–81; Calderón de la Barca to Webster, Oct. 10, 1850, in Manning, *Diplomatic Correspondence: Inter-American Affairs* 11:574, 575.

18. Calderón de la Barca to Webster, Oct.14, Nov. 28, 1850, and unsigned note from informer in New York to Calderón de la Barca, Nov. 27, 1850, in Manning, *Diplomatic Correspondence: Inter-American Affairs* 11:575–76, 574, 580–81 and nn. The anticipated arrival of the two steamers at New Orleans is alluded to in Laborde to Calderón de la Barca, Oct. 2, 1850, ibid., 574.

19. Calderón de la Barca to Webster, Jan. 17, April 14, 1851, Francisco Stoughton to Calderón de la Barca, Jan. 16, 1851, ibid., 582–83 and n., 587–88.

20. Webster to Calderón de la Barca, Jan. 22, 1851, to the U.S. Collector at New Orleans [William Fretet], Jan. 21, 1851, ibid., 98 and n.; Webster to Hunton, Jan. 28, 1851, Fretet to Webster, Feb. 1, 8 1851, Hunton to Webster, Feb. 8, 1851, Correspondence on the Lopez Expedition, RG 59, NA.

21. Calderón de la Barca to Webster, Jan. 24, 1851, March 12, April 14, in Manning, *Diplomatic Correspondence: Inter-American Affairs* 11: 583–88; de la Cova, "Gonzales," 176.

22. Burtnett, "Lopez's Expeditions," 347–51.

23. Ibid.: 350–51; Schlesinger, "Personal Narrative," 211.

24. Burtnett, "Lopez's Expeditions,": 351–53.

25. J. Reneas to Millard Fillmore, April 10, 1851, William A. Graham to Hiram Roberts, April 11, 1851, to Commodore F. A. Parker, April 12, 1851, in Manning, *Diplomatic Correspondence: Inter-American Affairs* 11:103n.; New York *Herald*, April 28, 1851; Fillmore's April 25, 1851, proclamation against filibusters, in Richardson, *Messages and Papers of the Presidents* 4: 2647–48.

26. New Orleans *Times-Democrat*, April 6, 1884.

27. Ibid.; New Orleans *Picayune*, May 18, 1851.

28. New Orleans *Times-Democrat*, April 6, 1884.

29. New Orleans *Picayune*, May 2, 7, 1851; Savannah *Morning News*, May 10, 1851, as quoted in New Orleans *Picayune*, May 18, 1851; Burtnett, "Lopez's Expeditions," 346, 359; Harris, "O'Sullivan," 313–21; Gonzales, *Manifesto*, 10.

30. Burtnett, "Lopez's Expeditions," 346, 354, 355.

Chapter 8

1. New Orleans *Delta*, July 28, 1851.

2. New York *Herald*, July 22, 1851.

3. Leard, "Bonds of Destiny," 86–87.

4. Foner, *History of Cuba* 2:57, 58; Concha, *Memorias*, 204, 205.

5. Concha, *Memorias*, 204; Foner, *History of Cuba* 2:57, 58.

6. Schlesinger, "Personal Narrative," 212.

7. Bryan, "Memoirs," 11, Tenn. State Lib. and Archives; "Huston, Felix," *National Cyclopaedia of American Biography* 12:278.

8. Gonzales, *Manifesto*, 10, 11.

9. Ibid., 10.

10. Quisenberry, *Lopez's Expeditions*, 74; Schlesinger, "Personal Narrative," 212, 213. Schlesinger stated that López received the warning from Crittenden on "Saturday, the first of August," but that Saturday fell on Aug. 2. I have assumed that Schlesinger remembered the day of the week accurately and the calendar date inaccurately and have made adjustments accordingly.

11. Schlesinger, "Personal Narrative," 213.

12. Ibid., 212–14; see also Bryan, "Memoirs."

13. "Relación de un expedicionario," *Boletín de los Archivos de la República de Cuba* 1 (Jan.–Feb. 1904): 13; Angel Calderón de la Barca to William S. Derrick, Aug. 25, 1851, Juan Ygnacio Laborde y Rueda to Angel Calderón de la Barca, Aug. 6, 1851, Millard Fillmore to Daniel Webster, Sept. 2, 1851, Webster, *Diplomatic Papers* 2:369–74

14. Relación de un expedicionario," *Boletín de los Archivos* 1 (Jan.–Feb. 1904): 13; Bryan, "Memoirs," Tenn. State Lib. and Archives, 13; Schlesinger, "Personal Narrative," 215, 216; New York *Herald*, Sept. 5, 1851; Caldwell, *Lopez Expeditions*, 92.

15. Schlesinger, "Personal Narrative," 214–24, 559.

16. Concha, *Memorias*, 204–6, 209, 210.

17. Ibid., 210, 211; Schlesinger, "Personal Narrative," 354, 355.

18. Concha, *Memorias*, 211, 212.

19. Schlesinger, "Personal Narrative," 222–24.

20. Ibid., 352–56.

21. Ibid., 355 and n. Schlesinger, confusing Tabla de Agua with another village in the region, mistakenly asserted that the filibusters stopped at San Miguel, which is not located on the road from El Morrillo to Las Pozas, as I discovered on my visit to the area on Jan. 29, 1995, and confirmed with a map published one year after the landing at Morillo by the Spanish government, Carles y Casadevall, *Plano*.

22. See "Narrative of Major J. A. Kelly, One of the American Prisoners in Havana," New Orleans *Picayune*, Sept. 13, 1851. Schlesinger, "Personal Narrative," 363. The *Picayune* account, based on an interview with Kelly by a *Picayune* correspondent, contains numerous chronological and other errors; it, for instance, gives Kelly's troop strength as eight hundred, double its actual size. But while not as reliable as Schlesinger's account of the expedition, the Kelly narrative, in its depiction of the main events, comports with other primary sources.

23. Schlesinger, "Personal Narrative," 356–62.

24. Ibid., 553–59.

25. Schlesinger, "Personal Narrative," 358, 555; Bryan, "Memoirs," 15, Tenn. State Lib. and Archives.

26. Estimate of enemy troops from Quisenberry, *Lopez's Expeditions*, 99. Schlesinger gives different, seemingly inflated, figures of 1,200 infantry and 120 cavalry in Schlesinger, "Personal Narrative," 560.

27. Schlesinger, "Personal Narrative," 560–71.

28. Ibid., 566, 575; Asuntos Politicos, Legajo no. 51, sig. 3, Archivo Nacional de Cuba, Havana.

29. Quisenberry, *Lopez's Expeditions*, 84, 85.

30. Ibid., 90; Schlesinger, "Personal Narrative," 575.

31. Humboldt, *Cuba*, 104–6; Howe, *Cuba*, 79–80; Schlesinger, "Personal Narrative," 692–93; "A Filibustiero," *Lopez*, 27; Quisenberry, *Lopez's Expeditions*, 107–9. *Harper's Monthly* 3 (1851): 692–93.

Conclusion

1. Macon, Ga., *Journal and Messenger*, Sept. 17, 1851; New York *Herald*, Aug. 24, 25, 26, 27, 1851.

2. Quisenberry, *Lopez's Expeditions*, 135–37.

3. Macon, Ga., *Journal and Messenger*, Oct. 8, 1851; "Narcisso Lopez and His Companions," *United States Magazine and Democratic Review* 29 (1851): 293, 301; Charleston *Courier*, Sept. 10, 1851.

4. New York Daily *Tribune*, Aug. 28, 1851, answering a New York *Herald* jibe against the *Tribune*. A fragment of the offending (undated) *Herald* editorial appears at the beginning of the *Tribune* response: "The Tribune, in favor of revolutions in Europe, is opposed to the revolution in Cuba."

5. "Monthly Record of Current Events," *Harper's Monthly* 3 (1851): 693.

6. Washington, D.C., Southern *Press*, Aug. 25, 1851.

7. Millard Fillmore to Daniel Webster, Sept. 2, 1851, in Webster, *Diplomatic Papers* 2: 372–74.

8. Philadelphia *Public Ledger*, Aug. 15, 1849; Richmond *Whig*, Aug. 26, 1851.

9. Gonzales, *Manifesto*, 12.

10. Schlesinger, "Personal Narrative," 563.

11. Malcolm Mearis to John Clayton, Aug. 11, 1849, Records of Special Agents, RG 59, NA.

12. López to Cirilo Villaverde, Nov. 9, 1850, Narciso López, folio no. 1, Biblioteca Nacional "José Marti," Havana.

13. Quisenberry, *Lopez's Expeditions*, 74; Youngman, "Sketches," 17. The latter source differs with, and is less precise about, the cost of Sigur's investment in the *Pampero*: "his interest in the DELTA was invested in the Pampero, a ship whose value exceeded $40,000." Since Quisenberry is generally a reliable chronicler of the expedition, his figure appears in the narrative.

14. Portell Vilá, *López* 1:81.

Bibliography

Primary Sources

MANUSCRIPT COLLECTIONS

Archivo Nacional de Cuba, Havana: Asunto Politicos.

Biblioteca Nacional "José Martí," Havana: Colección Manuscritos, Annexíon Documentos.

Duke University, William R. Perkins Library, Durham, N.C.: Jefferson Davis Papers.

Harvard University, Houghton Library, Cambridge, Mass.: John Quitman Papers.

Historical Society of Pennsylvania, Philadelphia: James Buchanan Papers; Society Collection.

Library of Congress, Washington, D.C.: John Clayton, Thomas Ewing, Sr., James K. Polk, Zachary Taylor papers, and Miscellaneous Manuscripts Collection.

Mississippi State Department of Archives and History: John A. Quitman Papers.

New Orleans Public Library, Louisiana Division, New Orleans, Charles F. Youngman, "Historic Sketches of the *Daily Delta* and New Orleans *Daily Delta* and the *Era* and the New Orleans *Daily Independent*, from Oct. 12, 1845, to Jan. 19, 1865." Typescript. 1939.

New York Public Library, Manuscripts and Archives Division: James Gordon Bennett Papers.

Tennessee State Library and Archives, Nashville: Tom Bryan Memoir (typescript of MS journal).

Tulane University, Howard-Tilton Memorial Library, New Orleans: Callender I. Fayssoux Collection, in William Walker Papers; and Latin American Library.

University of California, Bancroft Library, Berkeley: Documents for the Study of Cuban Relations with the United States, 1492–1910, and "Patriotic junta for the promotion of the political interests of Cuba," New Orleans, 1850, promissory note for $2,000 and Cuban lands, given in return for aid to Cuban expedition of 1850.

University of North Carolina, Southern Historical Collection, Chapel Hill: Daniel Moreau Barringer Papers; Elliott and Gonzales Family Papers; Nicholas Philip Trist Papers.

U.S. GOVERNMENT DOCUMENTS AND PUBLICATIONS

U.S. Congress. *Congressional Globe*, 29th Cong., 1st sess., to 32d Cong., 1st sess., Dec. 2, 1845, to Aug. 31, 1852.
——. *House Executive Documents*, 31st Cong., 2d sess, 1850–51, doc. no. 1, and 32d Cong., 1st sess., 1852–53, doc. no. 83.
——. *Senate Executive Documents*. 31st Cong., 1st sess., 1849–50, doc. no. 57.
U.S. Department of Commerce. Bureau of the Census. *Historical Statistics of the United States from Colonial Times to 1970*. 2 vols. Washington, D.C., 1975.
U.S. Department of Interior. J. D. B. De Bow. *The Seventh Census of the United States: 1850*. 4 vols. Washington, D.C., 1853.
——.——. *Statistical View of the United States . . . .* Washington, D.C., 1854.
——. Entry 142, box 1, Records concerning the Cuban Expedition, 1850–51, Records of the Office of the Secretary of the Interior, Record Group 48, National Archives, Washington, D.C.
U.S. Department of Justice. Entry 21, case 6685, General Case Files, U.S. District Court, Eastern District of Louisiana, New Orleans, Record Group 21, National Archives, SW Region, Fort Worth, Texas.
U.S. Department of State. Entry 119, box 1, Correspondence on the Lopez Expedition to Cuba, 1849–51, Records of the Department of State, Record Group 59, National Archives, Washington, D.C.
——. Despatches from United States Consuls in Matanzas, 1820–99, vol. 4, Jan. 1, 1844–Dec. 7, 1850, National Archives, Washington, D.C.
U.S. Department of War. Adjutant General's Office, War Department. Doc. no. 85. *Military Notes on Cuba*. Washington, D.C., 1898.

ACCOUNTS, LETTERS, AND OTHERS

Ballou, Maturin. *Due South, or Cuba Past and Present*. 1885. Rept. New York, 1969.
——. *History of Cuba: Notes of a Traveler in the Tropics, Being a Political, Historical, and Statistical Account of the Island from Its First Discovery to the Present Time*. Boston, 1854.
Belden, E. Porter. *New-York: Past, Present, and Future, Comprising a History of the City of New-York, a Description of Its Present Condition, and an Estimate of Its Future Increase*. 4th ed. New York, 1851.

Betancourt, Gaspar, and J. S. Thrasher. *Addresses Delivered at the Celebration of the Third Anniversary of the Martyrs for Cuban Freedom.* New Orleans, 1854.

[Boggess, F. C. M.] *A Veteran of Four Wars: The Autobiography of F. C. M. Boggess, a Record of Pioneer Life and Adventure and Heretofore Unwritten History of the Florida Seminole Indian War.* Arcadia, Fla., 1900.

Breen, Matthew P. *Thirty Years of New York Politics.* 1899. Rept. New York, 1974.

Buchanan, James. *The Works of James Buchanan, Comprising His Speeches, State Papers, and Private Correspondence.* Vols. 7, *1846–1848,* and 8, *1848–1853.* Ed. John Bassett Moore. Philadelphia, 1909.

Burtnett, Henry. "Lopez's Expeditions to Cuba, 1850–1851: Betrayal of the Cleopatra, 1851." Ed. L. M. Perez. *Publications of the Southern History Association* 10 (1906): 345–62.

Calhoun, John C. "Correspondence of John C. Calhoun." Ed. J. Franklin Jameson. *Annual Report of the American Historical Association, 1899* 2 (1900): 1–1218.

———. *The Works of John C. Calhoun.* 6 vols. Ed. Richard K. Crallé. New York, 1883.

Carles y Casadevall, Mariano. *Plano topografico historico militar de la invasion y derrota de Narciso López.* Havana, 1852.

Chesnut, Mary. *Mary Chestnut's Civil War.* Ed. C. Vann Woodward. New Haven, 1981.

Claiborne, J. F. H. *Life and Correspondence of John A. Quitman, Major General, U.S.A.; and Governor of the State of Mississippi.* 2 vols. New York, 1860.

Cohen's New Orleans and Lafayette Directory for 1851. . . . New Orleans, 1851.

Concha, José de la. *Memorias sobre el estado politico, gobierno, y administracion de la isla de Cuba.* Madrid, 1853.

Dana, Richard Henry, Jr. *To Cuba and Back: A Vacation Voyage.* Boston, 1859.

[Davis, Varina.] *Jefferson Davis, Ex-President of the Confederate States of America: A Memoir by His Wife.* 2 vols. New York, 1890.

A Filibustiero. *Life of General Lopez Together with a Detailed History of the Attempted Revolution of Cuba from Its First Invasion at Cárdenas Down to the Death of Lopez at Havana.* New York, n.d.

G. W. W. [George W. Williams]. *Sketches of Travel in the Old and New World.* Charleston, S.C., 1871.

Gonzales, Ambrosio José. *Manifesto on Cuban Affairs Addressed to the People of the United States, by Ambrosio José Gonzales, September 1st, 1852.* New Orleans, 1853.

Hardy, Lieutenant [Richardson], of the Kentucky Battalion. *The History and Adventures of the Cuban Expedition, from the First Movements Down to the Dispersion of the Army at Key West, and the Arrest of General Lopez. Also, an Account of the Ten Deserters at Isla de Mugeres.* Cincinnati, 1850.

Hone, Philip. *The Diary of Philip Hone, 1828–1851.* 2 vols. Ed. Bayard Tuckerman. New York, 1889.

Howe, Julia Ward. *A Trip to Cuba.* Boston, 1860.

Hudson, Frederic. *Journalism in the United States, from 1690 to 1872.* New York, 1873.

Humboldt, Alexander. *The Island of Cuba.* Trans. J. S. Thrasher. New York, 1856.

Lamar, Mirabeau Buonaparte. *The Papers of Mirabeau Buonaparte Lamar.* 6 vols. Ed. Charles Adams Gulick et al. Austin, Tex., 1921–27.

Manning, William R., ed. *Diplomatic Correspondence of the United States: Inter-American Affairs, 1831–1860.* Vol. 7, *Great Britain,* Washington, D.C., 1936. Vol. 11, *Spain.* Washington, D.C., 1939.

——, ed. *Diplomatic Correspondence of the United States concerning the Independence of the Latin-American Nations.* Vol. 3. New York, 1925.

Morales y Morales, Vidal. *Iniciadores y primeros mártires de la Revolucíon Cubana,* 1901. Rept. 2 vols. Havana, 1963.

Murray, Amelia M. *Letters from the United States, Cuba, and Canada.* New York, 1856.

Nichols, Thomas L. *Forty Years of American Life.* 2 vols. London, 1864.

Norman, Benjamin Moore. *Norman's New Orleans and Environs: Containing a Brief Historical Sketch of the Territory and State of Louisiana, and the City of New Orleans . . . With a Correct and Improved Plan of the City, Pictorial Illustrations of Public Buildings, Etc.* 1845. Rept. Ed. Matthew J. Schott. Baton Rouge, La., 1976.

"Nuevos documentos sobre las expediciones de Narciso López, Cuba." *Contemporánea* 12 (1916): 105–22.

O. D. D. O. [J. C. Davis]. *The History of the Late Expedition to Cuba, By O. D. D. O., One of the Participants, with an Appendix Containing the Last Speech of the Celebrated Orator, S. S. Prentiss, in Defence of Gen. Lopez.* New Orleans, 1850.

[O'Sullivan, John L.] "Annexation." *United States Magazine and Democratic Review* 17 (1845): 5–10.

[——.] "The Late Cuba State Trials." *United States Magazine and Democratic Review* 30 (1852): 307–19.

Polk, James K. *The Diary of James K. Polk during His Presidency, 1845–1849.* 4 vols. Ed. Milo Milton Quaife. Chicago, 1910.

[Pray, Isaac.] *Memoirs of James Gordon Bennett and His Times.* New York, 1855.

[Prentiss, George Lewis.] *A Memoir of S. S. Prentiss.* 2 vols. 1855. Rept. New York, 1899.

"Relación de un expedicionario." *Boletín de los Archivos de la República de Cuba* 1 (Jan.–Feb. 1904): 13–19.

Richardson, James D., ed. *A Compilation of the Message and Papers of the Presidents.* 11 vols. New York, 1897–1914.

Schlesinger, Louis. "Personal Narrative of Louis Schlesinger in Cuba and Ceuta." *United States Magazine and Democratic Review* 31 (1852): 210–24, 352–68, 553–92.

Stephens, John L. *Incidents of Travel in Yucatan.* Vol. 2. New York, 1858.

Strong, George Templeton. *Diary of George Templeton Strong.* 4 vols. Ed. Allan Nevins and Milton Halsey Thomas. New York, 1952.

Taylor, Marion C. "Col. M. C. Taylor's Diary in Lopez Cardenas Expedition, 1850." Introduction by A. C. Quisenberry. *Register of the Kentucky Historical Society* 19 (1921): 79–89.

Tremenheere, Hugh. *Notes on Public Subjects, Made during a Tour in the United States and in Canada.* London, 1852.

Turnbull, David. *Travels in the West. Cuba; with Notices of Porto Rico and the Slave Trade.* London, 1840.

Twain, Mark. *Life on the Mississippi.* 1883. Rep. New York, 1944.

Walker, William. *The War in Nicaragua.* Mobile, Ala., 1860.

Webster, Daniel. *The Papers of Daniel Webster. Correspondence.* Vol. 7, *1850–1852.* Ed. Charles M. Wiltse and Michael J. Birkner. Hanover, N.H., 1986.

——. *The Papers of Daniel Webster. Diplomatic Papers.* Vol. 2, *1850–1852.* Ed. Kenneth Shewmaker and Kenneth R. Stevens. Hanover, N.H., 1987.

——. *The Writings and Speeches of Daniel Webster Hitherto Uncollected.* Vol. 16. Boston, 1903.

Whitman, Walt. *The Gathering of the Forces.* 2 vols. Ed. Cleveland Rodgers and John Black. New York, 1920.

——. *Leaves of Grass, 1855.* New ed. Ed. Harold W. Blodgett and Sculley Bradley. New York, 1965.

Wilson, Thomas W. *An Authentic Narrative of the Piratical Descents upon Cuba Made by Hordes from the United States by Narciso Lopez, a Native of South America; To Which Are Added Some Interesting Letters and Declarations from the Prisoners, with a List of Their Names &c.* Havana, 1851.

Work Projects Administration. *Survey of Federal Archives in Louisiana Service Division, Ship Registers and Enrollments of New Orleans, Louisiana.* Vol. 4, *1841–1850,* and vol. 5, *1851–1860.* Baton Rouge, La., 1942.

NEWSPAPERS

Albany, N.Y., *Argus*
Albany, N.Y., *Evening Journal*
Baltimore *Morning Sun*
Baton Rouge, La., *Gazette*
Boston *Daily Times*
Charleston *Daily Courier*
Charleston *Mercury*
Cincinnati *Enquirer*
Columbus, Ga., *Enquirer*
Columbus, Ga., *Times*
Detroit *Free Press*

Illustrated London News
Jackson *Mississippian*
Memphis *Daily Appeal*
New Orleans *Bee*
New Orleans *Commercial Bulletin*
New Orleans *Crescent*
New Orleans *Daily Delta*
New Orleans *Picayune*
New Orleans *Times-Democrat*
New Orleans *True Delta*
New York *Courier and Enquirer*
New York *Daily Times*
New York *Evening Post*
New York *Herald*
New York *Sun*
New York *Tribune*
Philadelphia *Public Ledger*
Richmond *Whig*
Savannah *Daily Morning News*
Savannah *Republican*
La Verdad (New York)
Washington, D.C., *Daily Union*
Washington, D.C., *National Intelligencer*
Washington, D.C., *Southern Press*

Secondary Sources

Aimes, Hubert H. S. *A History of Slavery in Cuba, 1511 to 1868*. New York, 1907.
Albion, Robert Greenhalgh, with Jennie Barnes Pope. *The Rise of New York Port, 1815–1860*. New York, 1939.
Alexander, DeAlva Stanwood. *A Political History of the State of New York*. 3 vols. 1909. Rept. Port Washington, N.Y., 1966.
Asbury, Herbert. *The French Quarter: An Informal History of the New Orleans Underworld*. New York, 1936.
Barker, Eugene C. "The United States and Mexico, 1835–1837." *Mississippi Valley Historical Review* 1 (1914): 3–30.
Barre, W. L. *The Life and Public Services of Millard Fillmore*. Buffalo, 1856.
Bauer, K. Jack. *A Maritime History of the United States: The Role of America's Seas and Waterways*. Columbia, S.C., 1988.
——. *The Mexican War, 1846–1848*. New York, 1974.

——. Zachary Taylor: *Soldier, Planter, Statesman of the Old Southwest*. Southern Biography Series. Baton Rouge, La., 1985.

Bell, Malcolm, Jr. "Ease and Elegance, Madeira and Murder: The Social Life of Savannah's City Hotel." *Georgia Historical Review* 86 (1992): 551–76.

Bemis, Samuel Flagg. *A Diplomatic History of the United States*. 2d ed. New York, 1942.

Bergeron, Paul H. *The Presidency of James K. Polk*. Lawrence, Kans., 1987.

Berthoff, Rowland. *An Unsettled People: Social Order and Disorder in American History*. New York, 1971.

Bethell, Leslie, ed. *The Cambridge History of Latin America*. Vol. 1, *Colonial Latin America*. Vol. 2, *Colonial Latin America*. Vol. 3. *From Independence to c. 1870*. Cambridge, 1984–85.

Bleyer, Willard Grosvenor. *Main Currents in the History of American Journalism*. Boston, 1927.

Blondheim, Menahem. *News over the Wires: The Telegraph and the Flow of Public Information in America, 1844–1897*. Cambridge, Mass., 1994.

Brown, Charles H. *Agents of Manifest Destiny: The Lives and Times of the Filibusters*. Chapel Hill, N.C., 1980.

Browne, Jefferson B. *Key West, the Old and the New*. 1912. Rept. Gainesville, Fla., 1973.

Bryan, Wilhelmus Bogart. *A History of the National Capital*. 2 vols. New York, 1914–16.

Cable, Mary. *Lost New Orleans*. New York, 1980.

Caldwell, Robert Granville. *The Lopez Expeditions to Cuba, 1848–1851*. Princeton, N.J., 1915.

Callahan, James Morton. *Cuba and International Relations: A Historical Study in American Diplomacy*. Baltimore, 1899.

Carr, Albert Z. *The World and William Walker*. Westport, Conn., 1963.

Carr, Raymond. *Spain, 1808–1975*. 2d ed. Oxford, 1982.

Chaffin, Tom. "'Sons of Washington': Narciso López, Filibustering, and U.S. Nationalism: 1848–1851." *Journal of the Early Republic* 14 (1995): 79–106.

Cole, Donald B. *Martin Van Buren and the American Political System*. Princeton, N.J., 1984.

Corbitt, D. C. "The Junta de Fomento of Havana and the López Expeditions." *Hispanic American Historical Review* 17 (1937): 339–46.

Cortada, James W. *Two Nations over Time: Spain and the United States, 1776–1977*. Contributions in American History series, no. 74. Westport, Conn., 1978.

Crouthamel, James L. *Bennett's New York Herald and the Rise of the Popular Press*. Syracuse, N.Y., 1989.

——. *James Watson Webb, a Biography*. Middletown, Conn., 1969.

Cunliffe, Marcus. *Soldiers and Civilians: The Martial Spirit in America, 1775–1865*. Boston, 1968.

Curti, Merle E. "Young America." *American Historical Review* 32 (1926): 34–55.

Davis, David Brion. *The Problem of Slavery in the Age of Revolution, 1770–1823*. Ithaca, N.Y., 1975.

Dawson, Joseph G., III, ed. *The Louisiana Governors, from Iberville to Edwards*. Baton Rouge, La., 1990.

De la Cova, Antonio Rafael, "Ambrosio Jose Gonzales: A Cuban Confederate Colonel." Ph.D. diss., West Virginia University, 1994.

Dicken-Garcia, Hazel. *Journalistic Standards in Nineteenth-Century America*. Madison, Wis., 1989.

Dickey, Dallas C. *Seargent S. Prentiss, Whig Orator of the Old South*. Southern Biography series. Baton Rouge, La., 1945.

Donovan, Herbert D. A. *The Barnburners: A Study of the Internal Movements in the Political History of New York State and of the Resulting Changes in Political Affiliation, 1830–1852*. New York, 1925.

Dufour, Charles L. *Gentle Tiger: The Gallant Life of Roberdeau Wheat*. Baton Rouge, La., 1957.

Durkin, Joseph T. *Stephen Mallory: Confederate Navy Chief*. Chapel Hill, N.C., 1954.

Eaton, Clement. *A History of the Southern Confederacy*. New York, 1954.

Ely, Ronald T. "The Old Cuba Trade: Highlights and Case Studies of Cuban American Interdependence during the Nineteenth Century." *Business History Review* 38 (1964): 456–78.

Emery, Edwin. *The Press and America: An Interpretative History of the Mass Media*. 3d ed. Englewood Cliffs, N.J., 1972.

Ernst, Robert. "The One and Only Mike Walsh." *New-York Historical Society Quarterly* 36 (1952): 42–65.

Fairlie, John A. *The National Administration of the United States*. New York, 1922.

[Federal] Writers' Program of the Works Projects Administration in the State of Florida. *A Guide to Key West*. New York, 1941.

Federal Writers' Program of the Works Projects Administration for the City of New Orleans. *New Orleans City Guide*. American Guide Series. Boston, 1938.

Feipel, Louis N. "The Navy and Filibustering in the Fifties." *United States Naval Institute Proceedings* 44 (1918): 769–80.

Foner, Eric. *Free Soil, Free Labor, Free Men: The Ideology of the Republican Party before the Civil War*. New York, 1970.

——. *Nothing But Freedom: Emancipation and Its Legacy*. Baton Rouge, La., 1983.

Foner, Philip S. *A History of Cuba and Its Relations with the United States*. 2 vols. New York, 1962–63.

Fox, Dixon Ryan. *The Decline of Aristocracy in the Politics of New York*. New York, 1919.

Franklin, John Hope. *The Militant South, 1800–1861*. Cambridge, Mass., 1956.

Freehling, William W. *The Reintegration of American History: Slavery and the Civil War.* New York, 1994.

———. *The Road to Reunion: Secessionists at Bay, 1776–1854.* New York, 1990.

Genovese, Eugene D. *The Political Economy of Slavery: Studies in the Economy and Society of the Slave South.* New York, 1965.

Gilje, Paul A. *The Road to Mobocracy: Popular Disorder in New York City, 1763–1834.* Chapel Hill, N.C., 1987.

Goetzmann, William H. *When the Eagle Screamed: The Romantic Horizon in American Diplomacy, 1800–1860.* New York, 1966.

Goode, James M. *The Outdoor Sculpture of Washington, D.C.: A Comprehensive Guide.* Washington, D.C., 1974.

Gorn, Elliot J. *The Manly Art: Bare-Knuckle Prize Fighting in America.* Ithaca, N.Y., 1986.

Graebner, Norman A. *Empire on the Pacific: A Study in American Continental Expansion.* New York, 1955.

Grayson, Benson Lee. *The Unknown President: The Administration of President Millard Fillmore.* Washington, D.C., 1981.

Greene, Laurence. *The Filibuster: The Career of William Walker.* Indianapolis, 1937.

Hamilton, Holman. *Zachary Taylor: Soldier in the White House.* New York, 1951.

Harris, Jennifer. "The Red Cap of Liberty: A Study of Dress Worn by French Revolutionary Partisans, 1789–94." *Eighteenth-Century Studies* 14 (1981): 283–312.

Harris, Neil. *Humbug: The Art of P. T. Barnum.* Boston, 1973.

Harris, Sheldon Howard. "The Public Career of John Louis O'Sullivan." Ph.D. diss., Columbia University, 1958.

Hershkowitz, Leo. "'The Land of Promise': Samuel Swartwout and Land Speculation in Texas, 1830–1845." *New York Historical Society Quarterly* 48 (1964): 307–25.

———. "The Loco-Foco Party of New York: Its Origins and Career, 1835–1837." *New-York Historical Society Quarterly* 46 (1962): 305–29.

———. *Tweed's New York: Another Look.* Garden City, N.J., 1977.

Hietala, Thomas R. *Manifest Design: Anxious Aggrandizement in Late Jacksonian America.* Ithaca, N.Y., 1985.

Hobsbawm, E. J. *The Age of Revolution: Europe, 1789–1848.* London, 1962.

Holcomb, Gene. "The Mississippi Governor's Mansion." *Journal of Mississippi History* 2 (1940): 3–21.

Howard, Perry H. *Political Tendencies in Louisiana.* Rev. and expanded ed. Baton Rouge, La., 1971.

Howe, Daniel Walker. *The Political Culture of the American Whigs.* Chicago, 1979.

Hyman, Harold M., and William M. Wiecek. *Equal Justice under Law: Constitutional Development, 1835–1875.* New York, 1982.

James, Marquis. *Andrew Jackson, Portrait of a President.* Indianapolis, 1927.

Jennings, Thelma. *The Nashville Convention: Southern Movement for Unity, 1848–1851.* Memphis, 1980.

Johannsen, Robert W. *Stephen A. Douglas.* New York, 1973.

———. *To the Halls of the Montezumas: The Mexican War in the American Imagination.* New York, 1985.

Johnson, Willis Fletcher. *The History of Cuba.* Vol. 5. New York, 1920.

Jones, Lewis Pinckney. "Ambrosio José Gonzales, a Cuban Patriot in Carolina." *South Carolina Historical Magazine* 56 (1955): 67–76.

Kaplan, Justin. *Walt Whitman: A Life.* New York, 1980.

Kemble, John Haskell. *The Panama Route, 1848–1869.* Berkeley, Calif., 1943.

Klein, Herbert S. *African Slavery in Latin America and the Caribbean.* New York, 1986.

———. *Slavery in the Americas: A Comparative Study of Virginia and Cuba.* Chicago, 1967.

Knight, Franklin W. *Slave Society in Cuba during the Nineteenth century.* Madison, Wis., 1970.

Lamask, Milton. *Aaron Burr: The Conspiracy and Years of Exile, 1805–1836.* New York, 1982.

———. *Aaron Burr: The Years from Princeton to Vice President, 1756–1805.* New York, 1979.

Langley, Lester D. *The Cuban Policy of the United States: A Brief History.* New York, 1968.

———. *Struggle for the American Mediterranean: United States–European Rivalry in the Gulf-Caribbean, 1776–1904.* Athens, Ga., 1976.

———. "The Whigs and the Lopez Expeditions to Cuba, 1849–1851: A Chapter in Frustrating Diplomacy." *Revista de Historia de América,* no. 71 (April–June 1971): 9–22.

Latimer, S. L., Jr. *The Story of the State, 1891 [to] 1969 and the Gonzales Brothers.* Columbia, S.C., 1970.

Leard, Robert Benson. "Bonds of Destiny: The United States and Cuba, 1848–1861." Ph.D. diss., University of California at Berkeley, 1953.

Leonard, Thomas C. *The Power of the Press: The Birth of American Political Reporting.* New York, 1986.

Leopold, Richard W. *The Growth of American Foreign Policy: A History.* New York, 1962.

Levine, Robert M. *Cuba in the 1850s, through the Lens of Charles DeForest Fredricks.* Tampa, Fla. 1990.

Ley, Douglas Arthur Ley. "Expansionists All? Southern Senators and American Foreign Policy, 1841–1860." Ph.D. diss., University of Wisconsin, 1990.

McCaffrey, James M. *Army of Manifest Destiny: The American Soldier in the Mexican War, 1846–1848.* New York, 1992.

McCardell, John. *The Idea of a Southern Nation: Southern Nationalists and Southern Nationalism, 1830–1860.* New York, 1979.

McGuire, James K., ed. *The Democratic Party of the State of New York: A History of the Origin, Growth, and Achievements of the Democratic Party of the State of New York, Including a History of Tammany Hall in Its Relation to State Politics.* Vol. 1. New York, 1905.

McNeill, John Robert. *Atlantic Empires of France and Spain: Louisbourg and Havana, 1700–1763.* Chapel Hill, N.C., 1985.

McPherson, James. *Battle Cry of Freedom: The Civil War Era.* New York, 1988.

Martin, James Kirby, and Mark Edward Lender. *A Respectable Army: The Military Origins of the Republic, 1763–1789.* Arlington Heights, Ill., 1982.

Martínez-Fernández, Luis. *Torn between Empires: Economy, Society, and Patterns of Political Thought in the Hispanic Caribbean, 1840–1878.* Athens, Ga., 1994.

Marx, Leo. *The Machine in the Garden: Technology and the Pastoral Ideal in America.* New York, 1964.

May, Robert E. "Epilogue to the Missouri Compromise: The South, the Balance of Power, and the Tropics in the 1850s." *Plantation Society in the Americas* 1 (1979): 201–25.

———. *John Quitman, Old South Crusader.* Baton Rouge, La., 1985.

———. "Lobbyists for Commercial Empire: Jane Cazneau, William Cazneau, and U.S. Caribbean Policy, 1846–1878." *Pacific Historical Review* 48 (1979): 383–412.

———. *The Southern Dream of a Caribbean Empire, 1854–1861.* 1973. Rept. Athens, Ga., 1989.

———. "Young American Males and Filibustering in the Age of Manifest Destiny: The United States Army as a Cultural Mirror." *Journal of American History* 78 (1991): 857–86.

Meade, Robert Douthat. *Judah P. Benjamin, Confederate Statesman.* New York, 1943.

Merk, Frederick, with Lois Bannister Merk. *Manifest Destiny and Mission in American History: A Reinterpretation.* New York, 1963.

———. *The Monroe Doctrine and American Expansion, 1843–1849.* 1966.

Meyers, Martin. *The Jacksonian Persuasion: Politics and Belief.* Stanford, Calif., 1957.

Miller, Nathan. *Spying for America: The Hidden History of U.S. Intelligence.* New York, 1989.

Millett, Allan R., and Peter Maslowski. *For the Common Defense, A Military History of the United States of America.* New York, 1984.

Millis, Walter. *Arms and Men: A Study in American Military History.* New York, 1956.

Mintz, Sidney W. *Sweetness and Power: The Place of Sugar in Modern History.* New York, 1986.

Moody, Richard. *The Astor Place Riot.* Bloomington, Ind., 1958.

Morgan, Edmund. *American Slavery, American Freedom: The Ordeal of Colonial Virginia.* New York, 1975.

Mott, Frank Luther. *American Journalism: A History, 1690–1960.* 3d. New York, 1962.

——. *A History of American Magazines, 1741–1850.* New York, 1930.

Mushkat, Jerome. *Tammany: The Evolution of a Political Machine, 1789–1865.* Syracuse, N.Y., 1971.

Nelson, Anna Kasten. *Secret Agents: President Polk and the Search for Peace with Mexico.* New York, 1988.

Nerone, John C. "The Mythology of the Penny Press." *Critical Studies in Mass Communications* 4 (1987): 376–404.

Nevins, Allan. *Ordeal of the Union.* Vol. 1, *Fruits of Manifest Destiny, 1847–1852.* New York, 1947.

Niven, John. *Martin Van Buren: The Romantic Age of American Politics.* New York, 1983.

Northern, William J. *Men of Mark in Georgia.* Vol. 2. Atlanta, 1907.

O'Brien, Frank M.. *The Story of the Sun, New York: 1833–1928.* Rev. ed. New York, 1928.

Osterweis, Rollin G. *Romanticism and Nationalism in the Old South.* New Haven, 1949.

Pacquette, Robert L. *Sugar Is Made with Blood: The Conspiracy of La Escalera and the Conflict between Empires over Slavery in Cuba.* Middletown, Conn., 1988.

Parry, J. H. *The Spanish Seaborne Empire.* New York, 1966.

Pedroso, Antonio Alvarez. *Miguel de Aldama.* Havana, 1948.

Pérez, Louis A. Jr. *Cuba and the United States: Ties of Singular Intimacy.* Athens, Ga., 1990.

——. *Cuba between Reform and Revolution.* New York, 1988.

——, ed. *Slaves, Sugar, and Colonial Society: Travel Accounts of Cuba, 1801–1899.* Wilmington, Del., 1992.

Pletcher, David M. *The Diplomacy of Annexation: Texas, Oregon, and the Mexican War.* Columbia, Mo., 1973.

Portell Vilá, Hermino. *Narciso López y su Epoca.* 3 vols. Havana, 1930–58.

Potter, David M. *The Impending Crisis, 1848–1861.* Comp. and ed. Don E. Fehrenbacher. New York, 1976.

——. *The South and the Sectional Conflict.* Baton Rouge, La., 1968.

Poyo, Gerald E. "Evolution of Cuban Separatist Thought in the Emigré Communities of the United States, 1848–1895." *Hispanic American Historical Review* 66 (1986): 485–507.

——. "*With All, and for the Good of All*": The Emergence of Popular Nationalism in the Cuban Communities of the United States, 1848–1898.* Durham, N.C., 1989.

Pratt, Julius W. "John O'Sullivan and Manifest Destiny." *New York History* 14 (1933): 213–34.

Quisenberry, Anderson C. *Lopez's Expeditions to Cuba, 1850–1851.* Louisville, Ky., 1906.

Ranck, George W. *The Bivouac of the Dead and Its Author.* Cincinnati, 1898.

Rauch, Basil. *American Interest in Cuba, 1848–1855.* New York, 1948.

Rayback, Joseph G. *Free Soil: The Election of 1848.* Lexington, Ky., 1970.

Reed, Nelson. *The Caste War of Yucatán*. Stanford, Calif., 1964.

Reilly, Tom. "Jane McManus Storms: Letters from the Mexican War, 1846–1848." *Southwestern Historical Quarterly* 85 (1981): 21–44.

Remini, Robert V. *Andrew Jackson and the Course of American Democracy, 1833–1845.* New York, 1984.

Rosewater, Victor. *History of Coöperative News-Gathering in the United States.* New York, 1930.

Royster, Charles. *A Revolutionary People at War: The Continental Army and American Character, 1775–1783.* Chapel Hill, N.C., 1979.

Rubin, Joseph Jay. *The Historic Whitman*. University Park, Pa., 1973.

Schama, Simon. *Citizens: A Chronicle of the French Revolution.* New York, 1989.

Schiller, Dan. *Objectivity and the News: The Public and the Rise of Commercial Journalism.* Philadelphia, 1981.

Schlesinger, Arthur M., Jr. *The Age of Jackson.* Boston, 1945.

Schudson, Michael. *Discovering the News: A Social History of American Newspapers.* New York, 1978.

Scroggs, William O. *Filibusters and Financiers: The Story of William Walker and His Associates.* New York, 1916.

Sears, Louis Martin. *John Slidell.* Durham, N.C., 1925.

Sellers, Charles. *James K. Polk: Continentalist, 1843–1846.* Princeton, N.J., 1966.

Short, Lloyd Milton. *The Development of National Administrative Organization in the United States.* Baltimore, 1923.

Sinclair, Harold. *The Port of New Orleans.* Garden City, N.J., 1942.

Skipper, Ottis Clark. *J. D. B. De Bow, Magazinist of the Old South.* Athens, Ga., 1958.

Slotkin, Richard. *The Fatal Environment: The Myth of the Frontier in the Age of Industrialization, 1800–1890.* New York, 1985.

Smith, Culver H. *The Press, Politics, and Patronage: The American Government's Use of Newspapers, 1789–1875.* Athens, Ga., 1977.

Soulé, Leon Cyprian. *The Know Nothing Party in New Orleans: A Reappraisal.* Baton Rouge, La., 1961.

Spann, Edward K. *The New Metropolis: New York City, 1840–1857.* New York, 1981.

Stott, Richard B. *Workers in the Metropolis: Class, Ethnicity, and Youth in Antebellum New York City.* Ithaca, N.Y., 1990.

Stout, Joseph Allen. *The Liberators: Filibustering Expeditions into Mexico, 1848–1862, and the Last Thrust of Manifest Destiny.* Los Angeles, 1973.

Strode, Hudson. *The Pageant of Cuba.* New York, 1934.

Summers, Mark W. *The Plundering Generation: Corruption and the Crisis of the Union, 1849–1861.* New York, 1987.

Tansey, Richard. "Southern Expansionism: Urban Interests in the Cuban Filibusters." *Plantation Society in the Americas* 1 (1979) 227–51.

Tindall, George Brown. *America: A Narrative History*. 3d ed., with David E. Shi. New York, 1992.

Urban, Chester Stanley. "New Orleans and the Cuban Question during the Lopez Expeditions of 1849–1851: A Local Study in 'Manifest Destiny.'" *Louisiana Historical Quarterly* 22 (1939): 1095–1167.

Van Alstyne, R. W. *The Rising American Empire*. New York, 1960.

Van Deusen, Glyndon G. *Horace Greeley, Nineteenth-Century Crusader*. Philadelphia, 1953.

———. *Thurlow Weed, Wizard of the Lobby*. Boston, 1947.

Vidal, Gore. *Burr*. New York, 1973.

Wallace, Edward C. *General William Jenkins Worth, Monterey's Forgotten Hero*. Dallas, 1953.

Walther, Eric H. *The Fire-Eaters*. Baton Rouge, La., 1992.

Ward, John William. *Andrew Jackson, Symbol for an Age*. New York, 1955.

Weber, David J. *The Mexican Frontier: The American Southwest under Mexico*. Albuquerque, N. Mex., 1982.

Weigley, Russell F. *History of the United States Army*. New York, 1967.

Weinberg, Albert K. *Manifest Destiny: A Study of Nationalist Expansionism in American History*. Baltimore, 1935.

Werner, M. R. *Tammany Hall*. New York, 1928.

Wilentz, Sean. *Chants Democratic: New York City and the Rise of the American Working Class, 1788–1850*. New York, 1984.

Williams, William Appleman. *The Roots of the Modern American Empire: A Study of the Growth and Shaping of Social Consciousness in a Marketplace Society*. New York, 1969.

———. *The Tragedy of American Diplomacy*. Cleveland, 1959.

Wilson, Major L. *Space, Time, and Freedom: The Quest for Nationality and the Irrepressible Conflict, 1815–1861*. Westport, Conn., 1974.

Winston, James E. "The Attitudes of the Newspapers of the United States toward Texan Independence." *Proceedings of the Mississippi Valley Historical Association* 8 (1916): 160–75.

———. "New Orleans Newspapers and the Texas Question." *Southwestern Historical Quarterly* 36 (1932): 109–29.

Wood, Gordon. *The Creation of the American Republic, 1776–1787*. Chapel Hill, N.C., 1969.

Woodford, Frank B. *Lewis Cass: The Last Jeffersonian*. New Brunswick, N.J., 1950.

Worcester, Donald E., and Wendell G. Schaeffer. *The Growth and Culture of Latin America*. 2 vols. 2d ed. New York, 1971.

REFERENCE AND BIBLIOGRAPHIC AIDS

Andrews, Wayne, ed. *Concise Dictionary of American History.* New York, 1962.

Biographical Encylopedia of Kentucky of the Dead and Living Men of the Nineteenth Century. Cincinnati, 1878.

Craigie, Sir William A. *Dictionary of American English on Historical Principles.* 2 vols. Chicago, 1940.

Instituto Cubano de Geodesia y Cartografía. *Nuevo atlas nacional de Cuba.* Havana, 1989.

Louisiana Historical Records Survey, Division of Community Service Programs, Work Projects Administration. *Louisiana Newspapers, 1794–1940: A Union List of Louisiana Newspaper Files Available in Offices of Publishers, Libraries, and Private Collections in Louisiana.* Baton Rouge, La., 1941.

Mencken, H. L. *The American Language: An Inquiry into the Development of English in the United States.* One-vol. abridgment of 4th ed., with annotations and new material by Reven I. McDavid, Jr. New York, 1967.

Morris, Richard B. *Encyclopedia of American History.* Rev. and expanded ed. New York, 1961.

National Cyclopedia of American Biography. 63 vols. Clifton, N.J., 1893–1984.

Pérez, Louis A. *Cuba, an Annotated Bibliography.* New York, 1988.

——. *A Guide to Cuban Collections in the United States.* New York, 1991.

Schlesinger, Arthur M., Jr., ed. *The Almanac of American History.* New York, 1983.

Suchlicki, Jaime, ed. *Historical Dictionary of Cuba.* Metuchen, N.J., 1988.

Webb, Walter Prescott. *Handbook of Texas.* 3 vols. Austin, Tex., 1952–76.

Index